THE OXFORD SHAKESPEARE

General Editor · Stanley Wells

The Oxford Shakespeare offers new and authoritative editions of Shakespeare's plays in which the early printings have been scrupulously re-examined and interpreted. An introductory essay provides all relevant background information together with an appraisal of critical views and of the play's effects in performance. The detailed commentaries pay particular attention to language and staging. Reprints of sources, music for songs, genealogical tables, maps, etc. are included where necessary; many of the volumes are illustrated, and all contain an index.

MICHAEL NEILL, the editor of *Anthony and Cleopatra* in the Oxford Shakespeare, is Professor of English, University of Auckland.

THE OXFORD SHAKESPEARE

Currently available in paperback

The rest of the plays and poems are forthcoming

OXFORD WORLD'S CLASSICS

WILLIAM SHAKESPEARE

The Tragedy of Anthony and Cleopatra

Edited by
MICHAEL NEILL

OXFORD
UNIVERSITY PRESS

OXFORD

UNIVERSITY PRESS

Great Clarendon Street, Oxford OX2 6DP

Oxford University Press is a department of the University of Oxford.
It furthers the University's objective of excellence in research, scholarship,
and education by publishing worldwide in

Oxford New York

Auckland Bangkok Buenos Aires Cape Town Chennai
Dar es Salaam Delhi Hong Kong Istanbul Karachi Kolkata
Kuala Lumpur Madrid Melbourne Mexico City Mumbai Nairobi
São Paulo Shanghai Singapore Taipei Tokyo Toronto

with an associated company in Berlin

Oxford is a registered trade mark of Oxford University Press
in the UK and in certain other countries

Published in the United States
by Oxford University Press Inc., New York

First published by the Clarendon Press 1994
First published as a World's Classics paperback 1994
Reissued as an Oxford World's Classics paperback 2000

British Library Cataloguing in Publication Data

Data available

Library of Congress Cataloging in Publication Data
Shakespeare, William, 1564–1616.
Anthony and Cleopatra / edited by Michael Neill
(Oxford world's classics)
1. Cleopatra, Queen of Egypt, d. 30 B.C.—Drama. 2. Antonius,
Marcus, 83?–30 B.C.—Drama. 3. Generals—Rome—Drama. 4. Queens—
Egypt—Drama. I. Neill, Michael. II. Title. III. Series.
[PR2802.A2N454 1994b] 822.3'3—dc20 94–9777
ISBN 0–19–812909–2 (hbk.)
ISBN 0–19–283425–8 (pbk.)

3 5 7 9 10 8 6 4

Printed in Spain by Book Print S.L., Barcelona

ACKNOWLEDGEMENTS

Like most editions this one consists largely of other people's work. Every editor balances more or less insecurely on the shoulders of his predecessors, but I am bound to acknowledge several more particular obligations. I am grateful to Cyrus Hoy, who generously handed over his draft text and collations when he withdrew his own editorship. He bears no responsibility for anything printed here, but it would be difficult to overestimate the value of being able at every point to measure my own textual decisions against his. I am also indebted to David Bevington, who courteously arranged to supply me with an early copy of his valuable New Cambridge edition. I owe much to the staff of Oxford University Press, especially to Frances Whistler, to my desk editor, Robert Ritter, and tirelessly good-humoured copy-editor, Edwin Pritchard. But I owe the largest debt to the General Editor of this series, Stanley Wells, whose own text of the play for the Oxford *Complete Works* constantly challenged my own preconceptions and conclusions, and without whose patient encouragement and thoughtful interventions I could never have brought this project to a successful conclusion. I must also express my extraordinary gratitude to the Folger Shakespeare Library whose award of the Hanson Lee Dulin Fellowship enabled me to complete the greater part of the textual work and commentary, whilst bringing me in contact with a number of scholars whose advice and assistance were of incalculable value: I wish particularly to mention the generous friendship of Albert Braunmuller, Barbara Mowat, Gail Kern Paster, and Linda Levy Peck. The staff of the Folger Library were unfailingly courteous and helpful—as were those of the British Library, the Senate House Library at the University of London, the Shakespeare Centre at Stratford-upon-Avon, and the University of Auckland Library. I am indebted to the University of Auckland for a grant of sabbatical leave in 1988 which allowed me to carry out much of the essential groundwork for the edition, and to the University of Auckland Research Committee for helping to fund my research. Jan Kelly, cartographer at the Auckland University

Geography Department, worked with unstinting enthusiasm to produce the elegant map on p. xii; and my colleagues Don Smith and Mac Jackson, whose distinguished bibliographic and editorial skills I have never scrupled to exploit, spent time they could ill afford reading and commenting on the manuscript. Through it all, in presence and absence alike, my family somehow put up with me.

MICHAEL NEILL

CONTENTS

LIST OF ILLUSTRATIONS

CHRONOLOGY OF HISTORICAL EVENTS (BC)

82   Birth of Marcus Antonius.

69   Birth of Cleopatra.

48   Battle of Pharsalus—defeat of Pompey the Great by Julius Caesar.

48–47   Cleopatra's liaison with Julius Caesar; birth of his reputed son Ptolemy Caesar, known as Caesarion.

44   Assassination of Julius Caesar.

43   Civil war between the rival claimants to Caesar's mantle, Marcus Antonius and Octavius Caesar. Defeat of Antonius at Mutina (Modena). Antonius retreats across the Alps and forms an alliance with Lepidus. Reconciliation of Antonius and Octavius; formation of three-man junta ('the Triumvirate') with Lepidus.

42   Battle of Philippi—defeat of Caesar's assassins, Brutus and Cassius by Antonius and Octavius.

41   Meeting of Antonius and Cleopatra at Cydnus. Civil war in Italy: campaigns by Lucius and Fulvia (Antonius's brother and wife) against Octavius.

40   Death of Fulvia.
            Tensions between Antonius and Octavius patched up in Treaty of Brundisium; sealed by Antonius's marriage to Octavia. Birth of Cleopatra's twin children by Antonius.

39   Meeting of Pompey and the Triumvirs at Misenum.

37   Antonius leaves Rome; separates from Octavia in Corfu; reunited with Cleopatra.

36–34   Antonius's campaigns against the Parthians and Armenians.

34   Donations of Alexandria: Antonius enthrones Cleopatra as 'Queen of Kings' and Caesarion as 'King of Kings', and distributes middle eastern kingdoms among their own children.

33   Preparations for war between Caesar and Antonius.

32   Antonius divorces Octavia.

31   Battle of Actium.

30   Battle of Alexandria. Suicides of Antonius and Cleopatra.

Historical note. The events of the play belong to a long period of intermittent civil war which brought about the end of the Roman Republic and the institution of the Empire under Octavius Caesar (the Emperor Augustus). The final defeat of the aristocratic faction of Gnaeus Pompeius ('Pompey the Great') by the army of Julius Caesar at Pharsalus was followed by a gathering republican reaction against Caesar's autocratic rule. His assassination led to a fresh outbreak of civil war, culminating in the defeat and death of the principal conspirators, Marcus Brutus and Caius Cassius, at Philippi—events which Shakespeare dealt with in his earlier tragedy, *Julius Caesar*. The Roman world was parcelled out between the victors of Philippi, the so-called 'triumvirate' of Octavius Caesar (Julius Caesar's grandnephew and adoptive son), Marcus Antonius, and Aemilius Lepidus. The eastern part was allotted to Antonius, and it was in Cilicia in Asia Minor that he first encountered the Egyptian queen, Cleopatra, and fell under her influence. Meanwhile fresh hostilities broke out between the factions of Caesar and Antonius. The action of the play covers events from the death of Marcus Antonius's wife, Fulvia, and his subsequent reconciliation with Octavius through to Antonius's defeat at the battles of Actium and Alexandria and the suicides of both Antonius and Cleopatra.

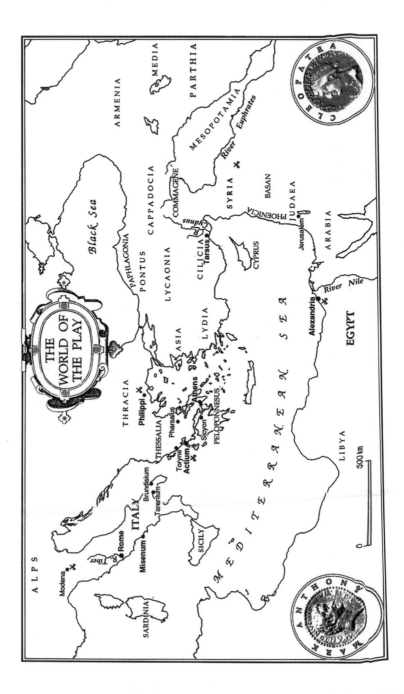

THE WORLD OF THE PLAY

ALPS

SARDINIA

SICILY

ITALY

Modena
Rome R. Tiber
Misenum
Tarentum
Brundisium

THRACIA

Black Sea

PAPHLAGONIA

PONTUS

CAPPADOCIA

ARMENIA

MEDIA

PARTHIA

MESOPOTAMIA

River Euphrates

COMMAGENE

Cydnus

SYRIA

BASAN

JUDAEA

PHOENICIA

Jerusalem

ARABIA

River Nile

EGYPT

Alexandria

CYPRUS

CILICIA
Tarsus

LYCAONIA

LYDIA

ASIA

Athens

PELOPONNESUS

Sicyon

Pharsalus

Toryne

Actium

THESSALIA

Philippi

MEDITERRANEAN SEA

LIBYA

0   500 km

CLEOPATRA

MARK ANTHONY

INTRODUCTION

Reception

In the judgement of G. Wilson Knight, *Anthony and Cleopatra* was 'probably the subtlest and greatest play in Shakespeare'; and it says much about the tragedy that it should have moved this notoriously magniloquent critic to some of his most visionary flights of enthusiasm:

This is the high metaphysic of love which melts life and death into a final oneness; which reality indeed is no pulseless abstraction, but rather blends its single design and petalled excellence from all life and death, all imperial splendour and sensuous delight, all strange and ethereal forms, all elements and heavenly stars; all that is natural, human, and divine; all brilliance and all glory.[1]

By any standards *Anthony and Cleopatra* is indeed an extraordinary feat. Arguably the most ambitious of all Shakespeare's designs, it was written near the end of the extraordinary burst of creativity that produced five major tragedies in as many years (*Othello*, c.1604; *King Lear*, 1605; *Macbeth*, 1606; *Anthony and Cleopatra*, 1606–7; *Coriolanus*, 1607–8), and is recognizably the work of a dramatist at the confident height of his powers—an artist who feels he can do *anything*. The historical and geographical sweep of the action is unmatched in any other play—even by the temporal and spatial permissiveness of Shakespeare's late romances. *Anthony and Cleopatra* traverses the ancient world in its imperious survey of a twelve-year history that determined the fate of two empires and innumerable petty kingdoms—a history that sealed the demise of Roman republicanism, and decisively shifted the balance of Mediterranean power from East to West, so preparing the way (as Renaissance providential historiography saw it) for the Universal Empire of Christendom, 'the time of universal peace' foreshadowed by Octavius Caesar (4.6.4). On this vast political stage is played out one of literature's great love stories, a saga of erotic compulsion, whose sublime

[1] Wilson Knight, 'The Transcendental Humanism of *Antony and Cleopatra*', in *The Imperial Theme* (London, 1961), pp. 199–262 (pp. 199, 262).

I

poetry puts the world of politics to the question, even as the realities of power threaten to expose it as the empty hyperbole of mere sexual infatuation.

To cope with this unwieldy mass of material Shakespeare devised a dramaturgy of extraordinary cinematic boldness, cutting with unusual freedom and rapidity from one location to another, especially in the complicated and fast-moving action of Acts 3 and 4, and alternating his clusters of short scenes with longer, more meditative sequences, like the marvellously orchestrated 5.2 which occupies nearly a whole act. His staging is equally various: reaching at unexpected moments for the most extravagant spectacular effects that his theatre could contrive (like the Roman 'triumph' that opens Act 3), at other times (as in the battle scenes) he confounds expectation by withholding spectacular display, or consigning it to the audience's imagination by the use of reportage. This is a play in which Shakespeare seems more than usually willing to break or challenge the rules of dramatic construction—not merely the Aristotelian unities of time, place, and action (with which he was habitually cavalier), but the most well-tried popular conventions and his own established practice—even to the point of staging the hero's death when the tragedy has a full act to run.

The style of the play has all the breathtaking variety that Enobarbus ascribes to Cleopatra herself—ranging from the lyric intensity and rhetorical extravagance of the lovers, through the clipped consonantal accents of Octavius (who habitually speaks, in Anthony's phrase, 'from his teeth', 3.4.10) and the hard-headed satirical prose of Enobarbus, to the frivolous chatter of Charmian, Iras, and Alexas. Not even Shakespeare's own English history plays offer greater contrasts of mood and effect than the forty-three scenes of *Anthony and Cleopatra*, which switch from courtly trifling to the nuanced menace of diplomatic skirmishing and machiavellian intrigue, and from episodes of drunken debauch to the drama of great battles and moments of high pathos.

But, for all this, the degree and nature of the play's success have long been a matter of dispute. Coleridge, who was amongst the first to restore its reputation, after nearly two centuries of neglect, rated *Anthony and Cleopatra* 'by far the most wonderful' of 'Shakespeare's historical plays', praising the fidelity of its historical representation, the 'happy valiancy' of its style, and the 'fiery force' of its composition. Yet even Coleridge stopped short of certainty that its 'giant power' made it a true rival of *Hamlet*, *Othello*, *King Lear*, and *Macbeth*;[1] while A. C. Bradley was to scold him for even making such a suggestion.[2] The fact that Coleridge should have identified *Anthony* with the history plays, rather than the tragedies with which the Folio grouped it, is significant; for the play has presented problems of classification, even to some of its most fervent admirers—to the point where Ernest Schanzer was prepared to nominate it as 'by far the greatest, as well as the most quintessential, of Shakespeare's *problem plays*'.[3] In the search for suitable ways of defining its obvious differences from the four great psychological tragedies which preceded it, perhaps the most satisfactory recourse has been to pair it with its immediate successor, *Coriolanus*, as an early example of the epic genre whose practice Davenant and Dryden were to codify more than half a century later— 'heroic tragedy'.[4] Certainly Shakespeare's play comes closer to realizing the aspirations of that form than any of its more conscious practitioners were able to achieve. With its deliberate echoes of Virgil's *Aeneid*, *Anthony* is an outstanding example of the Renaissance art of *paragone*, that mode of emulous imitation which sought to match or outstrip its

[1] S. T. Coleridge, *Shakespearean Criticism*, ed. T. M. Raysor, 2 vols. (London, 1960), i, 77. Hazlitt, while praising *Anthony* as 'a noble play' over which 'Shakespeare's genius has spread . . . a richness like the overflowing of the Nile', was more downright, judging it 'not in the first class of Shakespeare's productions'—even if it stood 'next to them' as 'the finest of his historical plays'. *Characters of Shakespeare's Plays* (1817; repr. London, 1955), pp. 74, 79.

[2] A. C. Bradley, *Oxford Lectures on Poetry* (Oxford, 1909), p. 282.

[3] Ernest Schanzer, *The Problem Plays of Shakespeare* (London, 1963), p. 183 (emphasis added). E. A. J. Honigmann, *Shakespeare: Seven Tragedies: The Dramatist's Manipulation of Response* (London, 1976), observing that the play can be read as either heroic or comical tragedy, writes that 'our uneasiness in defining the response to Antony mirrors our difficulty in describing the play's genre and tones. . . . the heroic Antony and the perpetual loser coexist in the same play' (pp. 150, 155).

[4] See, for example, Eugene M. Waith, *The Herculean Hero* (London, 1962), pp. 112–21, and *Ideas of Greatness* (London, 1971), pp. 107–11; and J. L. Simmons, '*Antony and Cleopatra* and *Coriolanus*, Shakespeare's Heroic Tragedies: A Jacobean Adjustment,' *SSu* 26 (1977), pp. 95–101.

original:[1] its epic ambitions are apparent in the scope and variety of its action; in its almost profligate range of characters; and in the colossal scale on which its protagonists are often imagined. Anthony is Mars and Bacchus in one, a new Hercules, the 'triple pillar of the world' whose 'legs bestrid the ocean'; Cleopatra an avatar of Isis, and a mortal Venus whose image, like his, outworks nature itself. Yet there are aspects of the work which are so resistant to a heroic reading that other critics have been tempted to link it with satiric tragedies like *Troilus and Cressida* and *Timon of Athens*, at one extreme, or with late romances like *Cymbeline* and *The Winter's Tale* at another.[2]

A number of factors may help to account for this generic uncertainty. In the first place, the question of genre is difficult to separate from the play's handling of its sources. An epic treatment of the story was certainly invited by the well-known historical connections between Caesar's defeat of Antonius and the composition of the greatest of Latin epics, Virgil's *Aeneid*. Yet the very familiarity and historicity of the source-material put constraints on such a treatment, making the plot vulnerable to some of the seeming shapelessness of the 'chronicle history' form. At the same time, while Shakespeare was certainly aware of earlier treatments of the story as a love tragedy, his interest in the political dimension of the sources tended to limit the amount of attention that could be given to his twin protagonists—thus inhibiting a full psychological treatment in the manner of his other mature tragedies. Moreover, given the profoundly equivocal nature of early modern

---

[1] Anthony himself is made to emphasize the parallels between the two texts when, in a homage to Virgil's account of Aeneas's visit to the underworld in *Aeneid* 6, he envisages his love for Cleopatra as paragoning the Trojan hero's famous liaison with the North African Queen Dido of Carthage (4.15.51–4).

[2] Bradley, oddly enough, supplied the cue for both positions: he found resemblances between the world of *Anthony* and that of *Troilus* with its 'cold and disenchanting light'; yet saw the ecstatic ending of the play as producing a mood of 'triumph, which is more than reconciliation'—albeit mingled with something like 'the sadness of disenchantment . . . we are saddened by the very fact that the catastrophe saddens us so little' (*Oxford Lectures*, pp. 291, 304). Schanzer (*Problem Plays*, p. 182) is prominent among those who find in the ending 'a sense of wonder, of exultation, and delight' which anticipates the late plays. The most unequivocal treatment of *Anthony* as a tragical satire is Daniel Stempel, 'The Transmigration of the Crocodile,' *SQ* 7 (1956), pp. 59–72.

attitudes to love (which was consigned to the realm of madness and disease as often as to that of transcendental revelation), 'love tragedy' was always something of a formal oxymoron. Love, as Francis Bacon observed, ' is ever matter of comedies' and only 'now and then of tragedies'.[1] Even the most lyrical and profound of love tragedies, as *Romeo and Juliet* and *Othello* can witness, have to cope with satirical reservations of a kind that would be quite out of place in *Macbeth* or *Lear*; and in *Troilus and Cressida* Shakespeare himself had shown how the genre might disintegrate under its own contradictions. Again and again *Anthony and Cleopatra* flirts with the possibility of such satiric collapse, only to defy its reductive logic. Constantly pushing, like its own protagonists, at the limits of kind, it emerges as a species of 'poem unlimited' (*Hamlet* 2.2.400), bafflingly resistant to satisfactory generic definition.

Sources

The question of how to define 'sources' is inevitably controversial, especially in the wake of a theoretical revolution whose emphasis on the cultural production of literary texts has rendered the business of fixing the proper boundaries of 'sources', 'influences', 'analogues', and 'context' extremely problematic. Thus David Bevington's New Cambridge edition follows Janet Adelman's *The Common Liar* in including under the rubric of 'sources' a wide variety of texts which in the past would have been regarded only as analogues, possible influences, or suggestive contextual material:[2] they include the story of Dido from Virgil's *Aeneid* ('a palpable influence, whether directly or as embodied in Renaissance drama and poetry'), various classical and Renaissance treatments of the stories of Mars and Venus, Venus and Bacchus, and Hercules and Omphale (which 'Shakespeare may well have . . . in mind' in his treatment of the lovers), mythographic accounts of the Egyptian deities Isis and Osiris (which 'serve collectively to enhance the mythic potency of Antony and Cleopatra'), the temptations of Acrasia from Book 2 of Spenser's *Faerie Queene*

[1] Francis Bacon, *Essays* (London, 1906), Essay X, 'Of Love', p. 29.
[2] See Janet Adelman's chapter on 'Tradition as Source' in *The Common Liar: An Essay on 'Antony and Cleopatra'* (New Haven, Conn., 1973), pp. 53–101.

(a possible 'model' for the enchantments of Cleopatra), and various conjectural 'models' for Enobarbus in the Elizabethan '[dramatic] convention of the protesting soldier'.[1]

In restricting myself here to a more traditional definition of a 'source' as material which the dramatist can be shown with fair probability to have consulted in the course of composing a particular work, I am not committing myself to any simple intentionalist position; nor do I wish to underestimate the suggestiveness of the material Bevington adduces—some of which, indeed, is cited in the commentary to the present edition. Barbara Bono's meticulous work has amply demonstrated the part played by such con-texts as the *Aeneid* in the creation of *Anthony and Cleopatra*. She reads Shakespeare's play as contributing to a prolonged cultural debate, initiated by Virgil's poem, that sets imperial Roman against 'barbaric' values—equating the opposition of East and West with the dualisms of female and male, the passionate and the rational: '*Antony and Cleopatra* elicits the full cultural context of the *Aeneid* in order to transmute it to romantic apotheosis'.[2] Since Virgil had himself designed his epic as a tribute to the triumphant Octavius/Augustus, in which Aeneas's stern rejection of one seductive North African queen was meant to criticize Antonius's supine capitulation to another, any subsequent treatment of the Cleopatra story necessarily participated in a dialectic with Virgil's fable of Roman virtue triumphant. But the difficulty about accommodating such contextual material amongst the play's 'sources' is that, this side of a complete reconstruction of the cultural matrix to which the play belongs, there is, in principle, no limit to it.[3] Moreover, it

[1] David Bevington (ed.), *Antony and Cleopatra*, The New Cambridge Shakespeare (Cambridge, 1990), pp. 7–12.

[2] Barbara J. Bono, *Literary Transvaluation: from Vergilian Epic to Shakespearean Tragicomedy* (Berkeley, Calif., 1984), p. 87. For a particularly ingenious contextualization of Acrasia and the Bower of Bliss, with obvious relevance for the kind of reading that Bono practises on *Anthony and Cleopatra*, see Patricia Parker, 'Suspended Instruments: Lyric and Power in the Bower of Bliss', in *Literary Fat Ladies: Rhetoric, Gender, Property* (London and New York, 1987), pp. 54–66.

[3] Thus, for example, one might argue that, since to Renaissance audiences the stories of Eve and Delilah must have provided irresistible analogues for Cleopatra, the whole long tradition of theological anti-feminism should be accounted a 'source'.

obscures the point that, for those interested in the craft of playwriting, there are things to be learned from a dramatist's selection, manipulation, and reshaping of deliberately borrowed material that are of a different order from the more speculative readings produced by cultural contextualization.

Anthony and Cleopatra is closely dependent on a work which Shakespeare exploited several times in his career: Sir Thomas North's translation of Plutarch's *Lives of the Noble Grecians and Romans.* The dramatist seems to have been busy with the *Lives* throughout the years 1606–8, when he was working on *Coriolanus* (1607–8) and *Timon of Athens* (1607–8) as well as *Anthony*; but he had already made substantial use of North for his tragedy of *Julius Caesar* (1599), which draws material not only from the Lives of Julius Caesar and Marcus Brutus, but also from that of Marcus Antonius—the text out of which *Anthony and Cleopatra* itself was principally to be quarried. Indeed since *Anthony* constitutes a kind of sequel to it, there is a sense in which *Julius Caesar* might claim to be the primary 'source' for the later tragedy.

Together the two plays form a study of that critical period of the Roman civil wars which saw the final collapse of the Republic and the establishment of the Empire under Julius Caesar's great-nephew and adoptive son, Octavius Caesar (the Emperor Augustus). With *Coriolanus*, they can be read as belonging to a loose trilogy in which Shakespeare ponders certain great issues of classical historiography[1]—the rival merits of republican and monarchical forms of government, the competing justifications of aristocratic and democratic politics, and the role of the great individual in the destiny of the state. Each of the plays probes the ideas of 'Rome' and of Roman 'virtue' (*virtus*) by which the characters measure their public lives; each investigates from a different angle the paradoxical relationship between name and identity, and the problematic ideal of heroic selfhood. *Anthony and Cleopatra* even seems to advertise its relationship with *Julius Caesar* by

[1] See e.g. Paul A. Cantor, *Shakespeare's Rome: Republic and Empire* (Ithaca, NY, 1976), for whom the plays form 'a kind of historical trilogy' (p. 16); and Robert S. Miola, *Shakespeare's Rome* (Cambridge, 1983), who sees Rome as the plays' 'central protagonist', rather as Tillyard made England the protagonist of Shakespeare's English history plays.

several times remembering that play's climactic actions—notably in Anthony's repeated invocations of his heroic role at Philippi, and Pompey's nostalgic portrait of the conspirators, 'all-honoured, honest, Roman Brutus, | With the armed rest, courtiers of beauteous freedom' (2.6.16–17). Above all, *Anthony* reintroduces three significant figures from *Julius Caesar*—the victorious avengers of Caesar's death, Octavius, Lepidus, and Anthony himself. Lepidus is identifiably the same 'slight unmeritable man' scorned by Anthony in the earlier play, 'A barren spirited fellow; one that feeds | On objects, arts, and imitations, | Which, out of use and staled by other men, | Begin his fashion . . . a property' (*Caesar* 4.1.12, 36–40); while Octavius, though much enlarged, is of a piece with the cool and ruthless young politician sketched in the last two acts of *Julius Caesar*.

However, the links between these two Roman histories are finally much less extensive than those between the various parts of Shakespeare's English history cycles; and there are also significant changes of focus and direction. Perhaps because the subject-matter became politically sensitive in the last three years of Elizabeth's reign,[1] seven years elapsed between the staging of *Julius Caesar* and its nominal sequel; and in the interim Shakespeare's approach to the material underwent considerable modification.

Most strikingly, the hero of the new play is a long way from either the frivolous playboy glimpsed in the early scenes of *Julius Caesar* or the ruthless machiavel who emerges following his patron's assassination. Although Plutarch offered good grounds for a continued emphasis on Anthony's ruthlessness (notably in his assassination of Pompey see 3.5.17–18 n.), Shakespeare suppressed this aspect of the historical character in order to heighten the dramatic contrast between the

---

[1] Bullough, for example, argues (pp. 215–16) that, in this story of a great soldier betrayed to his death by a queen, there were uncomfortable parallels with the story of Queen Elizabeth and her disgraced favourite, Essex, executed in 1601. Though the parallels may seem strained to us, they were enough to alarm Fulke Greville into burning his closet tragedy of Antony and Cleopatra, because he thought it ' "apt enough to be construed, or strained to a personating of vices in the present Governors, and government . . . seeing the like instance not poetically, but really fashioned in the Earl of Essex then falling" ' (p. 216).

magnanimity and extravagance of Anthony and the undeviating political calculation of his triumphant antagonist.

At the same time the play largely surrenders *Julius Caesar's* interest in popular politics and class conflict—though this was to return as a central theme in *Coriolanus*. In the early scenes of *Anthony and Cleopatra* we are several times reminded of the giddy factionalism of Roman political life, as Anthony and Caesar in turn reflect on the fickle enthusiasms of their 'slippery people' (1.2.184–8; 1.4.44–7); but the closest we get to the life of 'this common body' is the brief scene in Act 4 where a company of soldiers assigned to the night watch hear the mysterious music that announces Anthony's abandonment by the god Hercules—a scene as far removed from the political as any in the play. *Anthony and Cleopatra* remains a conspicuously public drama—but its public life is effectively confined to the princely and aristocratic realms of the court, diplomacy, and the military high command.

Finally, and most importantly of all, the play complicates its drama of public events by combining it with the love tragedy announced by its title—one that elevates a pair of protagonists to the heroic centre of the stage, and in the process significantly feminizes the masculine ethos of the other Roman plays. Such a transformation was perhaps prompted by the source material which the dramatist had chosen—but it was by no means an inevitable consequence of it.

The story of Antonius and Cleopatra was familiar to Shakespeare's contemporaries from a variety of texts, both ancient and modern. The Roman account of Cleopatra, substantially by the literary propagandists of Octavius Caesar, was overwhelmingly hostile.[1] In Virgil's *Aeneid*, written in direct response to Octavius's conquest of Antonius, Cleopatra's insidious menace is figured in the story of Dido and Aeneas, in which the seductive appeal of the African queen so nearly succeeds in luring Rome's heroic progenitor from the path of destiny. In Lucan's epic of the civil wars, *Pharsalia*, Cleopatra appears as a new Helen threatening destruction to the Roman Troy:

---

[1] For a lively account of how Roman propaganda shaped subsequent constructions of Cleopatra's story, see Lucy Hughes-Hallett, *Cleopatra: Histories, Dreams, Distortions* (London, 1990), chs. 1–3.

> The stain of Egypt, Rome's pernicious
> Fury, unchaste to Italy's disgrace;
> As much as Helena's bewitching face
> Fatal to Troy and her own Greeks did prove,
> As much Rome's broils did Cleopatra move . . .
> With Egypt's base effeminate rout prepared
> To seize Rome's eagles.[1]

For such Roman historians as Suetonius, L. Annaeus Florus, Dio Cassius, and Appian, Cleopatra was a wicked and scheming enchantress who had diverted two great soldiers, Julius Caesar and Antonius, from the course of duty. Antonius himself they portray as a doting fool, enslaved and emasculated by unworthy passion.[2] In all these accounts what was essentially a Roman civil war between rival political strongmen is presented as a contest between oriental barbarism and Roman civilization; and the crucial nature of this struggle is emphasized by the threat it apparently poses to the most fundamental of all the distinctions by which the world is ordered—that between male and female. Thus Dio Cassius's Octavius, who fights to ensure that 'no woman [will] make herself equal to a man', scorns the Egyptians as 'slaves to a woman and not to a man', and measures Antonius's falling away from Rome by the fact that he too has become 'the Egyptian woman's slave'; worn out by lust Antonius himself 'plays the woman' in a pantomime of disgraced manhood.[3]

Because it remained substantially unchallenged in the classical era, this propagandist version of the story inevitably coloured nearly all medieval and Renaissance versions, which however tend to simplify it into a straightforward moral parable, exhibiting the fatal consequences of reason overwhelmed

---

[1] Lucan, *Pharsalia*, trans. Thomas May (1627), Bk. 10, ll. 70–7, in Bullough, p. 326.

[2] The fullest account of the play's antecedents are in F. M. Dickey, *Not Wisely But Too Well: Shakespeare's Love Tragedies* (San Marino, Calif., 1957), chs. 10–11; and Marilyn L. Williamson, *Infinite Variety: 'Antony and Cleopatra' in Renaissance Drama and Earlier Tradition* (Mystic, Conn., 1974). See also Bullough's useful Introduction to his section on *Anthony and Cleopatra* (pp. 215–53); and Vivian Thomas, *Shakespeare's Roman Worlds* (London, 1989), ch. 3.

[3] Book 46, ch. 27, Book 48, ch. 24, Book 50, ch. 24, Book 50, ch. 28; cited in Hughes-Hallett, *Cleopatra*, pp. 40–1, 49, 57.

by passion. Writers as diverse as Dante and Montaigne concur in seeing the lovers as the justly confounded victims of their own desire—Dante placing Cleopatra in the second circle of Hell among those whose 'reason by lust is swayed' (*Inferno* 5.63), and Montaigne citing Antonius as one of those men 'whom pleasure hath made to forget the conduct of their own affairs' (*Essays* 2.33, p. 462). On the other hand, Chaucer's chivalric romanticization of the lovers in *The Legend of Good Women*—where Cleopatra is somewhat surprisingly given pride of place at the head of a procession of erotic 'martyrs' that includes Thisbe, Dido, and the heroic suicide, Lucrece—is testimony to the persistence of an alternative, less rigidly censorious tradition which may incorporate non-Roman perspectives.

For the Renaissance the most important mediator of this alternative tradition was undoubtedly the Greek essayist and biographer Plutarch. Of all the classical accounts of Antonius and Cleopatra, Plutarch's is the most complex and ambiguous in its treatment of the protagonists. This is partly an effect of the dialectical method of his Parallel Lives, in which the virtues and vices of one subject are repeatedly balanced against the vices and virtues of another; but it also reflects a fascination with the contradictions of human personality and a delight in paradox that can make his characterizations appear surprisingly 'modern'. Even in the standard Roman accounts, the denigration of Cleopatra was complicated by a number of factors. The need to present a civil war as a contest between civilization and barbarism required that a disproportionate prominence be given to Cleopatra's role; while an emphasis on her beauty, dangerous glamour, and seductive arts at once helped to account for the supposed subjugation of Antonius's martial valour, and served to present him as the de-Romanized plaything of a foreign queen. At the same time the formal pressures of this essentially tragic narrative often led (as in Horace's *Epode* 9) to expressions of admiration for the 'masculine' courage of Cleopatra's death: even a bad queen may be allowed a good end.

Plutarch often reproduces the standard Roman prejudices; but as a Greek, less rigidly committed to the ideological position which they serve, and no doubt aware of other versions of this history, he can allow fuller play to its incongruities and inconsistencies. It was Plutarch's willingness to entertain conflicting viewpoints, Lucy Hughes-Hallett argues, that effectively produced the idea of Cleopatra's changeful and capricious nature, the 'infinite variety' which Enobarbus so famously admires. But equally it was Plutarch who helped to create the image of Antonius as a man devoured by inner contradictions, warring against himself. Above all, it was the rediscovery of the *Lives*, with their resolutely dialectical stance, which made possible the Renaissance reinvention of the story as a tragedy of fatal infatuation in which the rival claims of public duty and private passion could be seriously weighed for the first time.

Of the several attempts to dramatize Plutarch's tragic narrative, it is Shakespeare's which comes closest in spirit and detail to the original. Nearly every scene in *Anthony and Cleopatra* has its counterpart in Plutarch, and numbers of close verbal parallels make it plain that the playwright must have worked with a copy of North beside him, occasionally supplementing *The Life of Marcus Antonius* with material from *The Comparison of Demetrius with Antonius* and from Simon Goulart's *The Life of Octavius Caesar* (added to the 1603 edition of North). Because the dependence on *The Life of Marcus Antonius* is so extensive, substantial excerpts have been reproduced here by way of an appendix. But Shakespeare's borrowing was necessarily highly selective. He had, after all, to condense an historical narrative encompassing more than ten years of intensive military and diplomatic activity. As a result, some episodes were radically compressed, others excised altogether. The effect was not merely to streamline the narrative, but also to bring into sharper relief, or significantly to alter, certain aspects of the central characters. For example, the haste with which Anthony first agrees to the political alliance with Octavia, and then casts her aside to return to Egypt, makes him seem at once more impulsive, more callous, and more helplessly in thrall to Cleopatra than Plutarch's Antonius, whose marriage lasts for eight years and produces several children; while the excision of Antonius's prolonged campaigns against the Parthians not only makes the process of his decline appear more rapid and ineluctable, but accords with a portrait in which the hero's martial prowess belongs essentially to the domain of nostalgic recollection. In the case of Cleopatra, as John Bayley has demonstrated, a host of small omissions and changes in emphasis serve to diminish the political seriousness of a queen whom Plutarch shows as Antonius's colleague in government, reducing her to an archetype of feminine frivolity and wilfulness, the perfect antithesis to Caesar and his single-minded obsession with power.[1]

Perhaps Shakespeare's single most striking alteration to Plutarch's narrative in *Anthony and Cleopatra*, however, lies in the promotion of Enobarbus to a major role in the action. In Plutarch he is barely even a name; in Shakespeare he becomes the most prominent of Anthony's followers, confidant of both lovers, and a quasi-choric presence, constantly manipulating the audience's reactions—like Kent and the Fool (in *King Lear*) rolled into one. But if the double-sidedness of Enobarbus's sensibility contributes more than anything else to the play of contradictory perspectives which is so characteristic of Shakespeare's treatment, there is a sense in which he merely magnifies tendencies that are already apparent in Plutarch. For much of the zest of Plutarch's *Life* comes from his sense of the paradoxical natures of both Antonius and Cleopatra.

As we have seen, the *Life of Antonius* generally concurs with the Roman view of the destructive effect of the affair with Cleopatra upon Antonius's character and career: 'the love of Cleopatra [was to be accounted] the last and extremest mischief of all other [for she] did waken and stir up many vices yet hidden in him . . .; and if any spark of goodness or hope of rising were left in him, Cleopatra quenched it straight and made it worse than before' (see Appendix A). Plutarch adopts a distinctly Roman perspective upon the 'childish sports . . . and idle pastimes' of Cleopatra's court, blaming Antonius for squandering 'the most precious thing a man can spend . . . and that is, time'. Yet, as he seeks to account for the Queen's extraordinary hold over her Roman lover, the historian develops a portrait of such power that Cleopatra acquires a

---

[1] See John Bayley, *Shakespeare and Tragedy* (London, 1981), ch. 5, 'Determined Things: The Case of the Caesars'.

sympathetic life of her own. Where other commentators were content to repeat predictable clichés about the Queen's physical beauty, Plutarch prefers to emphasize her mastery of the courtier's graces of 'company and conversation';[1] and his Cleopatra is as much an artist of public occasion as of private civility. It was in Plutarch that Shakespeare found the description of the magnificently theatrical water-pageant at Cydnus that became the rhetorical centrepiece of his tragedy (2.2.197–225); just as it was in Plutarch's description of 'Cleopatra stark dead, laid upon a bed of gold, attired and arrayed in her royal robes' that he found the clue for the equally histrionic self-display of his final scene. But it was also in the *Life* that he discovered many of those unexpected touches of spontaneity, like the fondness for disguising and practical jokes which humanize his portrait of the grand courtesan and contribute so much to the impression of her 'infinite variety' (1.1.55–6 and 2.5.15–17). It is part of Plutarch's attractiveness as a writer that he can convey the charm of episodes like these even as he is criticizing the destructive self-indulgence of 'fond and childish pastimes'.

If Plutarch's portrait of Cleopatra is brought alive by his sense of the astonishing variousness of her personality, and by his ability to entertain completely contradictory views of it, his portrait of Antonius is equally paradoxical: he makes us admire the leader's magnanimity even as he blames the lover's extravagance, setting episodes of extraordinary personal gallantry against the cowardly failure of nerve at Actium, and finding even in the man's vices the kind of magnificence that so dazzles Shakespeare's Lepidus (1.4.10–15). Jesting, boasting, and carousing with his troops, profligacy and promiscuity, 'things that seem intolerable in other men', only made Antonius the more loved, Plutarch observes; yet all the 'great credit' earned by his largeness of spirit 'himself did overthrow by a thousand other faults he had'.[2]

It was precisely this emphasis on the fatal contradictions of their characters that made the story of Antonius and Cleopatra seem a fit subject for tragedy to Renaissance neo-classicists like Giraldi Cinthio, whose *Cleopatra* (1542) was the earliest

---

[1] See Appendix A.   [2] See Appendix A.

attempt to dramatize Plutarch's *Life*.[1] In Giraldi the paradoxes
of Plutarch's psychology contribute to the structural tensions
of a play that alternately offers itself as 'a didactic tragedy of
shameful passion' and 'a tragedy of fate in which ... love
somehow emerges [as] a transcendent virtue'.[2] It is unlikely
that Shakespeare had any immediate acquaintance with this
play, or any of its three major continental successors, Cesare
de' Cesari's *Cleopatra* (1552), Estienne's Jodelle's *Cléopatra
Captive* (1552), and Robert Garnier's *Marc Antoine* (1578)—
though Giraldi's tragedy contains an interesting anticipation
of Caesar's 'she looks like sleep' (5.2.344) in the Priest's description of the dying Cleopatra:

> Then as by gentle sleep
> Borne down, without another word or breath
> She lay still on the couch like one just dead.[3]

However, while this is scarcely enough to establish any
direct line of descent, it seems probable that Shakespeare will
have known the European tradition at second hand through
the Countess of Pembroke's translation of Garnier, *The Tragedy
of Antony* (1590; printed 1592, 1595), in which Bullough
notes a number of small verbal parallels. Perhaps the most
striking of these is in the Countess's 'Argument' to the play,
where it is said that Antony 'for knitting a straighter bond
of amity between them, had taken to wife Octavia'[4]—a
description of his motives that is plainly echoed in Agrippa's

> To hold you in perpetual amity,
> To make you brothers, and to knit your hearts
> With an unslipping knot, take Anthony
> Octavia to his wife ...

> *Anthony*, 2.2.131–4

---

[1] Giraldi thought the story particularly suited to producing the required
catharsis of pity and horror because it fulfilled Aristotle's prescription for tragic
protagonists 'Who are not either wholly good or bad', G. B. Giraldi Cinthio,
Cleopatra Tragedia, Prologue l. 17 (in Bullough, p. 357).

[2] Bono, *Literary Transvaluation*, p. 97.

[3] Act 5, scene 6 (Bullough, p. 343).

[4] Mary Herbert (Sidney), *The Tragedy of Antony*, 'The Argument' (in Bullough,
p. 358); for further significant parallels see Commentary, notes to 2.7.16–23,
4.6.3.

Following Plutarch in his treatment of Antony as a man torn between love and duty, Garnier discovers a logic of self-annihilation which anticipates Shakespeare's portrait of Anthony as a man haunted by self-loss:

> Nay, as the fatted swine in filthy mire
> With glutted heart I wallowed in delights,
> All thoughts of honour trodden under foot,
> So I me lost . . . .
>
> *Tragedy of Antony*, 3.1155–8[1]

Although the two protagonists are never seen together in the course of this stiffly neo-classical drama, Antony's feelings for the Queen undergo the same violent oscillations between rage and doting remorse as those which torment Shakespeare's hero after the débâcle of Actium (*Anthony* 3.11, 3.13). Now raging at Cleopatra as 'cruel, traitress, woman most unkind!', the triumphant author of his humiliating servility, in the next breath Antony proclaims his glad submission: 'None else henceforth, but thou, my dearest Queen, | Shall glory in commanding Antony' (*Tragedy of Antony* 1.37–38).

Garnier's tragedy is also remarkable for its sympathetic treatment of Cleopatra, climaxing in a highly romanticized version of her suicide, whose erotic language is echoed in Shakespeare's death-scene.[2] Elsewhere, Cleopatra's speech at the beginning of Act 2, defending herself against the charge of betraying Antony, seems to provide a model both for the Queen's equivalent speech in Shakespeare's play (3.13.159–68) and for her protestations to Proculeius in 5.2 ('Rather a ditch in Egypt | Be gentle grave unto me! Rather on Nilus' mud | Lay me stark naked . . .', ll. 57–9): 'Rather sharp lightning lighten on my head; | . . . or rather let our Nilus send, | To swallow me quick, some weeping crocodile' (*Tragedy of Antony*, 2.393–8)

Generally acknowledged as a more significant influence is *The Tragedy of Cleopatra*, a closet drama written by the

---

[1] Compare also Charmian's pleas to Cleopatra, 'persist not still | To lose yourself . . . Ill done to lose yourself' (*Tragedy of Antony* 2.531–2, 549).

[2] Compare, for example, the quibbling on 'spend' in the Countess of Pembroke's translation ('I spent in tears, not able more to spend, | But kiss him now', *Tragedy of Antony* 5.2.1991–2) with Shakespeare's 'Spend that kiss | Which is my heaven to have' (*Anthony* 5.2.301–2; and see commentary).

Countess of Pembroke's protégé, Samuel Daniel, in 1594, and published in revised editions in 1599 and 1607. The marks of Daniel's influence are several times visible in the verbal detail of Shakespeare's play. When his Cleopatra protests, in the face of Seleucus's revelations about the wealth she has kept back from her account to Caesar, 'That I some lady trifles have reserved, | Immoment toys' (5.2.165–6), she seems to echo Daniel's Cleopatra, who admits to having 'reserved some certain women's toys' for Livia and Octavia (3.2.679); Cleopatra's wry acknowledgements of age (1.5.28–9, 73–4) surely owe something to the soliloquy which opens Daniel's tragedy, where the Queen, in an apostrophe to Antony, speaks of the 'Autumn of my beauty' and 'wrinkles of declining | Wrought with the hand of years' (1.1.181, 172–3); and the Queen's resolve in 4.16, 'My resolution and my hands I'll trust' (l. 51), paraphrases Daniel's 'I have both hands, and will and I can die' from that same soliloquy (1.54).[1]

But perhaps the most striking parallels between the two plays are to be found in their handling of Plutarch's story. Daniel's play is, for example, the first to make significant dramatic capital out of the episode involving Seleucus, where Cleopatra's parade of outrage at her treasurer's betrayal deceives Caesar into supposing that she intends to live. It is Daniel too who provides the model for Shakespeare's Dolabella, by developing Plutarch's thinly sketched character (one that 'did bear no evil will unto Cleopatra') into a courtly admirer whose sudden infatuation with the Queen becomes a testimony to her continued power to beglamour her enemies. The larger resemblances in the two dramatists' treatment of their material are less immediately obvious, partly because Daniel's play is even more resolutely obedient than its predecessors to the rules of neo-classical composition—governed as it is by an inflexibly rhetorical dramaturgy that consigns even Cleopatra's death to the report of a messenger, and by a strict observation of the unities which confines its action to the brief interim between Antony's death and Cleopatra's own suicide. But in its treatment of the perplexing contradictions of Plutarch's Octavius Caesar and, above all, of Cleopatra herself,

---

[1] 'But what have I save these bare hands to do it? . . . For who can stay a mind resolved to die' (*Cleopatra* 1162, 1171).

there are interesting anticipations of Shakespeare. Daniel absorbs and sharpens Garnier's interpretation of Caesar as both a bloody tyrant and an agent of historical necessity—the restorer of peace to a divided Rome; and combines it with a much more complex understanding of Cleopatra. Where Garnier's queen is all passionate sincerity, Daniel's (like Shakespeare's) is a self-consciously theatrical performer. To begin with, her histrionism registers simply as a kind of hypocrisy: in the first scene, for example, she confesses that, until his death, her love for Antony had been a deceitful pretence (*Cleopatra* 1.1.150–4). But this moralized portrait of the penitent hypocrite is significantly complicated by her heroic deception of Caesar; and in the final scene, where the *Nuntius* figures her suicide as a performance of 'that part | That hath so great a part of glory won' (ll. 1593–4), her acting is transformed into a mode of magnificent self-assertion:

> Well, now this work is done (saith she); here ends
> This act of life, that part the Fates assigned....
>
> And now O earth, the Theater where I
> Have acted this, witness I die unforced;
> Witness my soul parts free to Antony,
> And now, proud tyrant Caesar, do thy worst.
>
> *Cleopatra* 5.2.1603–9

Such troping of the encounter with death as a theatrical performance is conventional;[1] but what gives Daniel's version its special life is his paradoxical vision of Cleopatra's theatre of dying as at once an assertion of stoic self-mastery and an act of sensual self-indulgence—a vision epitomized in the presentation of her suicide as a conscious re-enactment of the water pageant at Cydnus in which she first won Antony's heart:

> Even as she was when on thy crystal streams,
> Clear Cydnos, she did show what earth could show,
> When Asia all amazed in wonder, deems

[1] The figure is at least as old as Seneca: 'It fareth with our life as with a stage-play: it skilleth not how long, but how well it hath been acted. It importeth nothing in what place thou makest an end of life—die where thou wilt, think only to make a good conclusion' (Epistle 77); cited from L. A. Seneca, *The Works of L. A. Seneca both Morall and Naturall*, trans. Thomas Lodge (London, 1620), 323.

> Venus from heaven was come on earth below.
> Even as she went at first to meet her love,
> So goes she now at last again to find him.
>
> *Cleopatra,* 5.2.1460–5

Having no equivalent of Enobarbus's intoxicated description of that erotic apotheosis on which to build, Daniel cannot manage the marvellously evocative brevity of 'I am again for Cydnus, | To meet Mark Anthony' (5.2.228–9); but Shakespeare's coup is wholly dependent on his conceit.

Equally, although Daniel's solemnly imagined spectacle, with its procession of reflective monologues, has nothing of Shakespeare's bold combination of high and low styles, its extraordinary juxtapositions of eldritch humour and impassioned lyricism, his vision of the dead Queen, illuminated by a 'grace that graceth death', prepares the way for the sharper oxymoronic wit of Shakespeare's 'strong toil of grace' (5.2.346), and for the later Cleopatra's mocking defiance of Death and Caesar (*Anthony* 5.2.2–4, 305–7):

> And in that cheer th' impression of a smile,
> Did seem to show she scorned Death and Caesar,
> As glorying that she could them both beguile,
> And telling Death how much her death did please her.
>
> *Cleopatra* 5.2.1626–9

Finally, in the closing words of his last chorus, Daniel articulated an idea of the innate self-destructiveness of the heroic individual which was to become one of the ruling themes of Shakespeare's last two tragedies:

> Is greatness of this sort
> That greatness greatness mars
> And wracks itself, self-driven
> On rocks of her own might?
> Doth Order order so
> Disorder's overthrow?
>
> *Cleopatra* 5.2.1748–53

In fact these paradoxes seem less than fully appropriate to Daniel's portrait of Cleopatra, but they perfectly anticipate Anthony's weary acknowledgement of the logic of self-cancellation enacted in his own suicide ('Now all labour | Mars what it does; yea, very force entangles | Itself with strength', *Anthony* 4.15.47–9), or Aufidius's perplexed assessment of his rival, Coriolanus ('One fire drives out one fire, one nail, one nail; | Rights by rights falter, strengths by strengths do fail', *Coriolanus* 4.7.54–5).

Date and Publication

On 20 May 1608 the publisher Edward Blount placed on the Stationers' Register two texts which are plausibly assumed, because of Blount's close links with the King's Men, to have been Shakespeare's plays: '*The booke of* PERICLES *prynce of Tyre*' and '*A booke Called.* ANTHONY. *and* CLEOPATRA.' Since no publication ensued under Blount's imprint (though *Pericles* was issued by a rival publisher in the following year) it is often supposed that these were so-called 'blocking entries', designed to protect the company's investment in valuable pieces of dramatic property. The entry indicates with fair certainty that *Anthony and Cleopatra* was written no later than early 1608. Other evidence suggests that the play was enjoying a certain vogue in 1606–7. Barnabe Barnes's tragedy, *The Devil's Charter*, written for Shakespeare's own company, the King's Men, and probably first staged in late 1606,[1] appears to make ironic capital from the last scene of *Anthony and Cleopatra* (bizarrely combining it with the murder of the young princes in *Richard III*). Near the end of Barnes's play, the villain, Alexander, comes to poison two young princes with the aid of a box of 'aspics'. Addressing the snakes as 'Cleopatra's birds', he applies them to the breasts of the sleeping princes, who become 'competitors with Cleopatra' as the asps 'Take [their] repast upon these princely paps' (ll. 2768–86).[2]

---

[1] Entered in the Stationers' Register on 16 Oct. 1607, the play had enjoyed a court performance on 2 Feb. 1607, which makes a public debut late in the previous year seem probable.

[2] Cited (in modernized form) from the edition by Jim C. Pogue (New York, 1980). Unfortunately the court performance of *The Devil's Charter* does not fix the date of Barnes's allusion as precisely as one might hope, since it remains possible that this passage was among the additions to the text, which was published late in 1607 and advertised as 'revised, corrected, and augmented'—though E. K. Chambers argued otherwise (*William Shakespeare: A Study of Facts and Problems*, 2 vols. (Oxford, 1930), pp. 476–8). The argument of Wells and Taylor (*Textual Companion*, p. 129) that Barnes is more

While scholars have noted other possible sources for Barnes's suckling asps (see 5.2.302 n.), it seems unlikely that he would have elaborated his conceit at such length unless he had been able to assume the audience's familiarity with specifically *theatrical* representations of Cleopatra's death; and significantly Shakespeare's seems to have been the only play to follow the non-classical iconographic tradition in which Cleopatra applies the asp to her breast, rather than (as in Plutarch) to the arm. Moreover there are specific verbal details that suggest Barnes's conscious dependency on Shakespeare's text: 'Fed fat . . . with proud Egyptian *slime* . . . of Nilus' recalls Shakespeare's repeated references to 'Nilus' slime' and its generative and nurturing properties; while Barnes's 'proud worms' seems to catch up Cleopatra's 'make death proud to take us' (4.16.89), together with the Clown's mocking encomium on his own 'odd worm'.

The likelihood that Barnes was capitalizing on Shakespeare's play is increased by the alterations which Samuel Daniel seems to have made to his *Tragedy of Cleopatra* (1594) at about the same time.[1] In 1607 he published a 'newly altered' text, which, as if impressed by the greater theatricality of his popular rival, markedly increased the amount of dialogue in his rather static Senecan closet drama, with its extensive reliance on reflective monologue. The revision expands the parts of certain characters who have greater prominence in *Anthony and Cleopatra*; and it adds new characters, including Dircetus, Diomedes, and Gallus, all of whom figure in Shakespeare's play, making use of Dircetus as a *nuntius* to announce Anthony's (off-stage) death, when he presents the hero's sword to Caesar. It has been suggested that these details might derive from a rereading of Plutarch, or simply reflect the influence of Daniel's patron, the Countess of

likely to be indebted to a similar episode in George Peele's *Edward 1* (1593) introduces a needless complication since the Peele passage does not specifically invoke Cleopatra. It seems more likely that Peele's influence on Barnes (if any) comes via Shakespeare.

[1] The complex question of *Anthony*'s relationship to Daniel's and Barnes's plays is investigated in a still contentious essay by J. Leeds Barroll, 'The Chronology of Shakespeare's Jacobean Plays and the Dating of *Antony and Cleopatra*', in Gordon R. Smith (ed.), *Essays on Shakespeare* (University Park, Pa., 1965), pp. 115–62.

Pembroke, whose translation of Garnier's *Tragedy of Antony*
was completed some four years before his own play;[1] but it
is not easy to explain why Daniel should suddenly have
undertaken this kind of revision after thirteen years and five
editions, unless he had been stimulated by Shakespeare's
recent example. Taken together, these considerations suggest
a probable date of late 1606 or early 1607 for the first
performance of *Anthony and Cleopatra*—that is to say, just a
little later than *Macbeth* (*c*.1606) and about a year after *King
Lear* (*c*.1605).[2]

The nature of Daniel's response to *Anthony*, together with
Barnes's reworking of the death scene, make it seem likely
that both men had seen the play on the stage. But the Folio
text, though evidently prepared from copy close to Shakespeare's own manuscript,[3] shows no trace of a theatrical
history. The proliferation of minor characters (though it could
easily be dealt with by the standard Elizabethan practice of
doubling),[4] is unnecessarily exaggerated by the appearance
of 'ghost' characters who appear at the beginning of scenes
only to play no part in the action (see 1.2, 1.6, 3.2, 4.2, 4.6,
5.2). Such slips, like the occasional mistaken speech-prefixes,
and anomalous stage directions (e.g. the direction that Alexas
enters '*from Caesar*' at 1.5.34, when he really comes from
Anthony) are typically authorial, and would almost invariably
have been tidied up in a prompt-book. Similarly one would
expect that any text adapted for use in the playhouse would
have expanded manifestly inadequate stage directions—for
example those which describe the action of the two monument
scenes, 4.16 and 5.2 (see Appendix B), which do not even
make it clear whether the upper stage or 'tarras' was required

---

[1] See e.g. Ernest Schanzer, 'Daniel's Revision of his *Cleopatra*', *RES* NS 8
(1957), pp. 375–81.

[2] Wells and Taylor note that all stylistic tests are 'resolutely consistent' in
placing *Anthony* after both *Lear* and *Macbeth*; although in the case of *Macbeth*
the issue is complicated by the possibility of revision by another hand (*Textual
Companion*, pp. 129–30).

[3] See 'Editorial Procedures', below, p. 131.

[4] The play contains more than forty speaking parts, including messengers,
soldiers etc.; but these could readily be distributed among the twenty or so
actors who made up the average London company—indeed with sensible
doubling twelve would be sufficient. See below, p. 90 n. 1 for a suggestion that
Enobarbus's part was doubled with that of the Clown.

to represent the monument; or the opening stage direction for 3.1 '*Enter Ventidius, as it were in triumph* . . .', which seems curiously sparse and offhand when compared with the frequently careful detailing of such pageantry in texts with a playhouse provenance.

These things are disquieting, given that the Folio was assembled by Heminges and Condell, members of Shakespeare's own company who would normally have had access to prompt-books. Indeed the absence of contemporary production records, when combined with the unsuitability of the Folio text for use in a Jacobean playhouse, makes it possible that the play was never actually performed in Shakespeare's lifetime. However, the case is not unique, and if the play were not often revived, the prompt-book might easily have been lost or destroyed. Generally it seems difficult to credit that the King's Men would have passed up the opportunity of staging so magnificently theatrical a work—even granted the difficulty of finding a boy actor gifted enough to rise to the unusually demanding role of Cleopatra.

The Play in Performance

For a play that is widely acknowledged to be amongst the greatest of Shakespeare's creations and perhaps the only fully successful heroic drama in the language, *Anthony and Cleopatra* has a surprisingly limited stage history. Paradoxically, however, this relative neglect may have more to do with the play's epic ambitions than with any perceived shortcomings. To modern critics *Anthony and Cleopatra* has often seemed to 'defy production',[1] to the point where, in the words of its historian Margaret Lamb, it is 'always in danger of becoming what *King Lear* was before the 1930s: a play too great to do perfectly, and so too often left on the shelf.'[2] The history of the various attempts made to overcome the difficulties presented by the sheer scale of the play and by the bafflingly contradictory character of its protagonists, especially Cleopatra, make this limited history an especially telling one. It

---

[1] Clifford Leech, reviewing Glen Byam Shaw's 1953 Stratford production in *SQ* 4 (1953), p. 464.
[2] Lamb, p. 179.

reveals a radically unstable drama of extremes whose proper theatrical balance is extremely difficult to get right.

Clearly the problematic nature of *Anthony and Cleopatra* is compounded by the lack of any contemporary comment or early production history of the sort which can sometimes give valuable clues as to how a work was interpreted in its own day. According to a note in the Lord Chamberlain's records for 1669, it had been 'formerly acted at the Blackfriars [play-house]'; and certain aspects of the dramaturgy make it seem probable that it was composed with an eye to this smaller and more exclusive indoor theatre, which Shakespeare's company were able to use as a winter venue from 1606. In particular, the scanting of the battle scenes (which partly accounts for the paradoxically 'domestic' feeling on which critics like Jan Kott have commented) accords with what we know of the taste of Blackfriars and other so-called 'private' playhouses, where such 'sword-and-buckler fights' were disdained as a comic barbarism.

In other circumstances the want of any contemporary performance record, and of any printed editions of the play before the First Folio (1623), might be taken as signs of theatrical failure. But theatrical records for the whole period are confusingly patchy; and the failure to publish, far from suggesting a lack of contemporary interest in the play, might just as well indicate that the King's Men regarded *Anthony* as too valuable a property to let out of their hands. The appearance of two new Cleopatra plays, Fletcher and Massinger's historical tragicomedy, *The False One* (1619–23), and Thomas May's neoclassical tragedy, *Cleopatra, Queen of Egypt* (1626), could suggest that Shakespeare's play was considered old-fashioned by the 1620s; but they might equally, in the light of their evident dependence on *Anthony and Cleopatra*, be seen as attempting to capitalize on its continuing popularity. Indeed *The False One*, written for Shakespeare's own company, and dramatizing Cleopatra's affair with Julius Caesar, might almost have been written as a belated first part to *Anthony*— rather as *The First Part of Hieronimo* seems to have been written as a 'prequel' to *The Spanish Tragedy*.

Whatever the fortunes of Shakespeare's play in the early seventeenth century, the swing of Restoration theatrical taste towards the rule-bound formalities of neo-classical composition ensured its virtual disappearance from the English stage for 150 years. *Anthony* does not seem to have been amongst the plays thought worthy of revival after the Interregnum; for, although Thomas Killigrew secured rights to it (along with twenty other plays) in 1669, there is no evidence of its being played before 1677, when it was effectually displaced by two rival versions of the story, Sedley's *Anthony and Cleopatra*, and Dryden's *All for Love*—the last of which continued to be preferred to Shakespeare's play until the early nineteenth century.

Although Dryden's play professes 'to imitate the divine Shakespeare' (Preface, ll. 329–30)[1] and contains a number of ill-judged homages to the master, including an elaborate two-part pastiche of Enobarbus's Cydnus speech (3.160–82, 4.238–47), it stands at a much greater distance from the original than most Restoration reworkings of Shakespeare, such as Dryden's *Troilus and Cressida*, the Dryden/Davenant *Tempest*, or the Tate *King Lear*. Reverting to the neo-classical convention favoured by Shakespeare's predecessors, it is structured around a series of debate scenes in which Antony's love for Cleopatra is tested against the rival demands of honour (Ventidius), friendship (Dolabella), and married love (Octavia). Cleopatra is a reduced and simplified character, little more than a sentimentalized version of that stock Restoration type, the cast mistress:

> my love's so true
> That I can neither hide it where it is,
> Nor show where it is not. Nature meant me
> A wife, a silly harmless, household dove,
> Fond without art, and kind without deceit;
> But Fortune, that has made a mistress of me,
> Has thrust me out to the wide world, unfurnished
> Of falsehood to be happy.

> 4.89–96

What results (as Dryden's subtitle, *The World Well Lost*, might suggest) is an essentially domestic drama, focusing almost exclusively on the moral crisis of the hero. Politics are

---

[1] Cited from David M. Vieth (ed.), *All for Love*, Regents Restoration Drama Series (London, 1972).

relegated to the margins of the action, where Octavius Caesar, a purely off-stage character, plays with 'This rattle of a globe ... This gewgaw world' (2.443–4). The diminished scale of Dryden's tragedy is perhaps best revealed by its way of representing Antony's oscillation between his Roman and Egyptian selves: in Shakespeare the varying tide of the hero's allegiance is embodied in the very structure of the play—its to-and-fro traversing the Mediterranean between Egypt and Rome; in Dryden it is reduced to the strangely 'disturbed motion' that characterizes Antony's physical presence on the stage: '*Goes to the door and comes back. . . .* Antony *goes again to the door and comes back. . . . Goes out and returns again*' (4.26.1; 30.1; 35.1). Nevertheless the 1991 revival of *All for Love* at the Almeida surprised most reviewers by showing it to be an eminently playable tragedy, the tightness of its construction provoking Michael Billington to compare its last act favourably with 'Shakespeare's interminably protracted conclusion' (*Guardian*, 2 June 1991). Something of the baroque feel of Dryden's version is preserved in the engraving of *Anthony*'s final scene commissioned for Rowe's 1709 edition of Shakespeare (Fig. 2), which clearly draws on Restoration staging traditions.

In the next century only one attempt was made to dislodge the preference for Dryden, when David Garrick mounted a revival of *Anthony and Cleopatra* in 1759. Despite the boldness of this departure, Garrick's production, in a text specially commissioned from Edward Capell, was very much influenced by *All for Love*. It reduced the scale of the tragedy by severely pruning its overplus of scenes and characters, and further emphasized its domestic qualities by maximizing the number of interior scenes—though, unlike Dryden, Garrick sought to simplify the audience's response to the protagonists by downplaying the part of Octavia, consequently eliminating the scenes of her departure from Rome and abandonment by Anthony (3.2 and 3.4). Garrick was closest to Dryden in minimizing the public dimension of the story, cutting much of the political intrigue or replacing it with episodes of pageantry—the keynote to the production's spectacular ambitions being set by the transposition of the Cydnus speech to the opening scene, where it was given to Thyreus. Despite its

2. Restoration scenic magnificence: the death of Cleopatra (5.2) from Rowe's edition (1709). The inclusion of Anthony's corpse suggests the influence of Dryden's *All for Love*; but a tradition of combining the two death scenes persisted into the present century (see Fig. 4).

emphasis on lavish display, the production was a failure, warranting only six performances. According to the prompter, Richard Cross 'This play, though all new dressed and had fine scenes, did not seem to give the audience any great pleasure, or draw any applause'.[1]

The principal reason for this indifferent response, according to Thomas Davies, who played Eros, was Garrick's own Anthony, since 'his person was not sufficiently important and commanding to represent the part'.[2] Nevertheless Garrick's débâcle evidently inhibited any further attempts to revive *Anthony and Cleopatra* until John Philip Kemble mounted it at Covent Garden in 1813. Kemble, who had played Dryden's Antony opposite Sarah Siddons in 1788, seems to have had a long-standing interest in Shakespeare's tragedy, apparently being deterred from staging it by the anxieties of Siddons who even in 1813 felt her reputation would be compromised by playing this scandalous Cleopatra 'as [she] ought to be played'.[3] Early in the century Kemble had prepared an acting version which, though almost certainly never performed, pointed the way for most nineteenth-century revivals.[4] It reduces the cast to a manageable twenty, and makes extensive cuts in order to accommodate some elaborately detailed archaeological spectacle. Episodes that are felt to compromise the work's exotic grandeur, like the Clown scene in 5.2, are ruthlessly excised; while the spectacular aspect of the play is highlighted in Garrick's fashion by transposing the Cydnus set-piece to the opening chorus (here spoken by Enobarbus and Thyreus). The note facing 1.1, citing 'Norden's Antiquities of Egypt, Montfaucon, [and] M. Knight's Antiques', gives some idea of the effect Kemble envisaged:

The Palace in Alexandria should be of the most magnificent orders of the purest Grecian architecture; yet the decoration and furniture of every apartment should remind one that the scene lies in Egypt.

[1] Cited in Lamb, pp. 44–5.   [2] Cited ibid., p. 45.
[3] See Hughes-Hallett, *Cleopatra* 182; Lamb, p. 54.
[4] The text exists as a manuscript in the Folger Shakespeare Library, prepared as if for a prompt-book with blank facing pages to accommodate stage-directions and other directorial material; these, however, have been left untouched, except for a few notes about scenery.

View of the Sea—ships etc
The Pharos
Pompey's Pillar
Cleopatra's Obelisk
Statues of Hercules—Alexander—Anubis.

The vast new Theatre Royal at Covent Garden, opened in 1808, was perfectly suited to the kind of production Kemble had in mind; and the version he produced for it was even more extensively revised to meet the needs of scenic theatre. Supposedly extraneous political episodes, like the Pompey scenes, together with such embarrassments as the Clown, were cut, to be replaced '*with alterations, and with additions from Dryden*'[1]—notably an extensive love and honour debate between Anthony and Ventidius at the beginning of Act 4, culled from *All for Love*. Act 3 was made the occasion for the spectacle of 'A Grand Sea Fight', while the two death scenes in Acts 4 and 5 were run together and extensively rewritten in a more public mode—so that Cleopatra's valedictory tribute to Anthony (5.2.76–92) was transposed to become Dolabella's funeral oration.[2] The whole action climaxed in 'A Grand Funeral Procession', accompanied by a funeral hymn from a choir of forty-five singers. '*Antony and Cleopatra*', the *Examiner* critic noted, 'is acted for the sake of the sea-fight and the funeral procession'.[3]

For all its splendours, Kemble's production received mixed notices and ran for a mere nine performances; but it was prophetic. Kemble's eagerness to capitalize on the play's spectacular potential was well attuned not merely to the requirements and technical possibilities of the palatial new theatres at Covent Garden and Drury Lane, but also to a gathering public fascination with the exotic and with romantic reconstructions of the past, fed by imperial ideology on the one hand and by the new science of archaeology on the other. Of

[1] Citations are from a copy of the 1813 edition with Kemble's prompt-book annotations, now held in the library of the Shakespeare Centre, Stratford-upon-Avon.

[2] This running together of the death scenes, adopted by a majority of nineteenth-century productions, is foreshadowed in the frontispiece to Rowe's edition (Fig. 2) where it probably reflects the illustrator's familiarity with Dryden's play.

[3] Cited in Lamb, p. 57.

course nineteenth-century archaeology, with its ruthlessly acquisitive drive, was itself a province of empire; and the archaeological treatment of *Anthony and Cleopatra* married happily with readings of the play as a drama of imperial conquest, in which the decadent and effeminate splendours of oriental barbarism were inevitably overwhelmed by the virile energies of Western civilization. So powerful did Kemble's approach prove that nearly two centuries later directors must still struggle to liberate themselves from the expectations it created—expectations which had their apotheosis in Joseph L. Mankiewicz's film *Cleopatra* (1962), with Elizabeth Taylor in the title role and Richard Burton as Antony, a cinematic extravaganza which owed little to Shakespeare beyond the aura of erotic glamour and extravagance which it ruthlessly exploited.

The modest financial success of Kemble's venture, however, helped to keep *Anthony and Cleopatra* off the stage for another twenty years, before it was somewhat reluctantly revived by William Macready in 1833. This revival employed a text which like Kemble's, was extensively cut and rearranged, with major speeches reassigned and even rewritten. Macready, too, excised the clown, pared away much of the political interest, and ran together the suicide scenes. The prompt-book directions reveal a similar emphasis on processions, marches, and display of all kinds; and the production again announced its spectacular intention in the opening dialogue by parcelling out the Cydnus speech between Philo, Eros, and Thyreus, thus providing a suggestive rhetorical frame for the lovers' first entry—a lavishly festive procession accompanied by the bacchic song transposed from the scene on Pompey's galley (2.7). Not surprisingly, perhaps, it was Clarkson Stanfield's magnificent painted scenes that drew the only critical acclaim in a production that stopped after three performances.

In the following decade, however, the play at last came into its own with a production very much in the Kemble-Macready tradition—Samuel Phelps's 1849 triumph at Sadler's Wells. Because productions at this theatre tended to be fairly modest by Victorian standards, Phelps was able to make use of a fuller and more authentically Shakespearian text than any of his predecessors, purging the relics of Dryden, and restoring such important cuts as the scene on Pompey's galley—which indeed became one of the theatrical high-points of the play. But despite this relative purism, Phelps placed considerable reliance on spectacle, making use of his large cast to create elaborate processional scenes; and the production was praised for its historical verisimilitude, the Egyptian scenes being 'exceedingly *vraisemblable*', in the opinion of the *Illustrated London News*.[1]

If the Victorian 'Turkish' look of Isabella Glyn's Cleopatra rather belied this enthusiasm, later productions were at pains to demonstrate their archaeological authenticity. When Glyn reappeared at the Princess's Theatre in 1867, the sets included a faithful representation of the Colosseum (ironically built sixty years after Cleopatra's death); while F. B. Chatterton's 1873 production of Shakespeare's 'Grand Historical Tragedy' at Drury Lane boasted that Mr E. C. Barnes's costumes were copied 'From the Splendid Collection of Roman and Egyptian Antiquities in the British Museum'. Textual authenticity was another matter—Victorian producers cheerfully hacking away large portions of Shakespeare's text (typically the scenes of political intrigue) in order to accommodate such spectacular additions as the 'Alexandrian Festival' with which in 1867 Isabella Glyn celebrated Anthony's return to Egypt. If this festival had at least the textual basis of Caesar's description of the Donations of Alexandria in 3.6, the same could hardly be said for Chatterton's rival display, the 'Grand Roman Festival in honour of Antony and Octavia', which formed the climax of his Act 2. In this hugely successful production, performed 'on a scale of unprecedented Splendour', according to the playbill, mere actors were 'felt to be but the stopgaps of the representation, the . . . vehicles of the scene painter and the costumier'.[2] Nowhere was this more evident than in Chatterton's decision to replace Enobarbus's great set-piece with 'The Gorgeous Spectacle of Cleopatra in her state barge . . . on the Cydnus', an elaborate animated tableau in which the arts of the perfumer were added to those

[1] Review in *Illustrated London News*, 27 Oct. 1849, cited from John Russell Brown, *Antony and Cleopatra: A Casebook* (London, 1968), p. 51.

[2] Lamb, p. 81.

3. Lily Langtry as Cleopatra, Princess's Theatre, 1890.

of the painter and costumier, 'here transferred to Egypt in
order that so magnificent a scene may not be lost'.

Such was the popularity of this opening spectacle that it
was imitated even in the version presented by Edmund
Tearle's company in the 1890s which began with Anthony
and Cleopatra crossing the stage in a lavishly appointed barge,
rowed by six slaves and fanned by garlanded women; and it
was repeated in the most opulent of all the Victorian and

Edwardian *Anthonys*—the 1890 Princess's production starring Lily Langtry (Fig. 3), and Herbert Beerbohm Tree's masterpiece of panoramic extravagance at His Majesty's in 1906 (Fig. 4). So unchallenged was the spectacular approach that even the normally restrained Frank Benson reverted to it at Stratford in 1898 and 1912; whilst Louis Calvert was careful to decorate his more austere Manchester version (1897) with elaborate stage effects when transferring it to London. But the Langtry and Tree productions turned out to mark the high-tide of scenic magnificence. Although the 'pictorial effects' at the Princess's were praised for their decadent reminiscences of Delacroix, Gautier, Gérôme, and Constant,[1] the performance, lasting for nearly four and a half hours, bored audience and critics alike. The general impression, according to the critic of *The Speaker*, was 'one of weakness eked out by noise and polychromatic pageantry'—though, like most others, he was inclined to divide the blame between Shakespeare's uneconomical dramaturgy (Pompey 'never would be missed')

4. Archaeological spectacle: the death of Cleopatra in Beerbohm Tree's lavish production (His Majesty's Theatre, 1906).

[1] A. B. W[alkley], in *The Speaker*, 22 Nov. 1890, p. 575.

and the pallid performance of the hapless Langtry.[1] *The Times*, however, complained that the excess of archaeological display had simply overwhelmed the action.

Tree's production generally had a better reception, being almost universally admired for the 'Magnificent Spectacle' hailed in the *Daily Telegraph*'s headline. Critics saw it as realizing the spirit of a play that 'is a panorama rather than a well-composed tragedy'.[2] Tree had responded to 'Shakespeare's instinct for picturing the luxury of the East' in staging 'this story of Eastern life with the glowing intensity that is characteristic of the Oriental mind';[3] and his use of 'weird, nerve-thrilling Oriental strains [of music]', together with a 'lavish display of Oriental ballets', expressing the 'strange pervasive influence of Oriental luxury and vice'[4] was seen as perfectly explaining 'why Antony's moral energy was so sapped'.[5] Dissenting voices were heard, however, especially after the play's tour to Berlin, where the German press was most unfavourable to Tree's extensive cuts and interpolated tableaux.[6]

If then, as A. B. W[alkley] had remarked in *The Speaker*, 'the stage history of *Antony and Cleopatra* [had] always been a history of scenic display',[7] and if scenic display was now in danger of killing the play, could it be that the tragedy was fundamentally unplayable? W. L. Courtney's preview of Tree in the *Telegraph*, though agreeing that 'scenic magnificence is the very essence of the story', seemed to imply just that. Reflecting on the relative scarcity of revivals, Courtney suggested that 'by the very nature of the subject, [*Anthony*] is too psychological to be a history play, and too historical to be a close and analytical study of temperament'.[8] The disappearance of the tragedy from the English stage for the next fifteen years suggests a real uncertainty about how it could be rescued from the blind alley of archaeological spectacle into

---

[1] A. B. W[alkley], p. 575, and cf. Lamb, p. 83.
[2] *Daily Telegraph*, 28 Dec. 1906.
[3] B. W. Findon in *The Play Pictorial*, 54/9 (1906).
[4] *The Times*, 4 Jan. 1997; *Daily Telegraph*, 28 Dec. 1906.
[5] Lamb, p. 94.
[6] *Daily Telegraph*, 16 Apr. 1907.
[7] *The Speaker*, 22 Nov. 1890, p. 575.
[8] *Daily Telegraph*, 26 Dec. 1906.

which Tree and his predecessors had driven it. The form in which *Anthony and Cleopatra* reappeared after the First World War was to be radically affected by the theories of William Poel and Harley Granville-Barker, with their advocacy of a return to the continuous staging employed in Elizabethan theatres. Although Granville-Barker's own ambitions for the play were frustrated by the war, many of his ideas were laid out in a remarkable *Preface* which has continued to exercise a shaping influence on productions as recently as those of Jonathan Miller (1981) and Peter Hall (1987).[1] His approach was first reflected in strikingly austere versions by W. Bridges-Adams at Stratford in 1921 and by Robert Atkins (using a simple neo-Elizabethan setting) at the Old Vic in 1922, which set the style for many inter-war *Anthonys*.

Turning his back on the spectacular tradition, Bridges-Adams spoke of the need to free the protagonists from the constraints of nineteenth-century didacticism: Anthony and Cleopatra he saw as 'our great irregulars' who were not to be coerced 'into more governed ways'.[2] The history of the most challenging productions since his Stratford experiment has been one of seeking a theatrical form adequate to this sense of vibrant irregularity—an irregularity as much characteristic of the play's whole design as of its protagonists' natures. Responding to Andrew Leigh's production for the Old Vic in 1925, *Punch* discovered 'a strange magnificent medley'—a play that, in its assault upon all the rules of playmaking, 'breaks them all triumphantly', and which, if it were a new play, would be berated for 'shamelessly borrowing the techniques of the cinematograph'.[3] To champions of the scenic theatre, like James Agate, Leigh's production seemed drab and underpopulated (a criticism he was to level again at Glen Byam Shaw's 1946 production at the Piccadilly): 'if ever a Shakespearean play called for music, processions and Tadema-like excesses in bathroom marble, *Antony and Cleopatra* is that play.'[4] When Shaw returned to the play at Stratford in 1953,

[1] Harley Granville-Barker, *Prefaces to Shakespeare: Antony and Cleopatra; Coriolanus* (1930; repr. London, 1963).

[2] Lamb, p. 113.

[3] *Punch*, 30 Dec. 1925, p. 720, reviewing the Edith Evans/Baliol Holloway *Anthony* at the Old Vic.

[4] Quoted in Lamb, p. 117.

however, it was to mount a production widely praised for its avoidance of spectacular clutter, whose 'magnificence,' according to the *Times*, 'consists in avoiding magnificence for the sake of allowing the 42 scenes to follow each other in rapid sequence'.[1] Most of the action was played against 'simple space' to emphasize the 'cosmic immensities' of the play, and the single set was varied only by the use of columns and drops behind a false inner proscenium, by the suggestive use of lighting—cold for Rome and warm, glowing effects for Egypt—and by the dominating display of a vast Roman eagle.[2]

Since the 1950s rapid continuous staging has become so much the rule that its demands have threatened the text with their own oppressiveness—as for example in Robin Phillips's production for the 1985 Chichester Festival which made cuts as extensive as many nineteenth-century versions, largely in the interests of pace. Although most productions have tended to offset the shift towards barer and more stylized settings with relatively lavish costuming, the detail of costume design has also been important in this process of liberating the play from the tyranny of archaeology. At the Old Vic in 1930 Harcourt Williams made the revolutionary move (followed next year by Bridges-Adams at Stratford) of adopting Renaissance dress to match Shakespeare's own relaxedly anachronistic practice. Williams styled his production after Veronese, the painter who was to provide significant inspiration for both Jonathan Miller's television version (BBC, 1981), and Peter Hall's National Theatre production (1987). The shock of defamiliarization revealed John Gielgud's Anthony as a figure 'more native to the London of Raleigh and of Essex, a Bankside gallant as flash with sonnets as valiant with the sword'.[3]

It is of course a testimony to the continuing power of the archaeological tradition that directors can still count on seventeenth-century costume to provide a slight jolt of the unexpected. At the Bankside Globe in 1973, however, Tony Richardson dispensed with period costume altogether, presenting Vanessa Redgrave's Cleopatra as 'a decadent imperialist

---

[1] *The Times*, 29 Apr. 1953.
[2] Lamb, p. 146.
[3] Ivor Brown, in the *Observer*, 30 Nov. 1930, cited in Lamb, p. 122.

in a red wig, orange sunglasses, and white pantsuit, [who] reeled drunkenly on three-inch heels, threw coke-bottles at flunkies, and shouted raucously at her drably dressed maids'. Julian Glover's Anthony was 'a dissipated officer in British Khaki', and David Schofield's psychopathic Caesar 'a fascist blackshirt'.[1] Only slightly less controversial was the bare costuming of Peter Brook's minimalist version for the Royal

5. 'Give me my robe . . .' Cleopatra (Glenda Jackson) prepares to die (Royal Shakespeare Theatre, 1978).

[1] John Barber, *Daily Telegraph*, 10 Aug. 1973; Lamb, p. 170.

Shakespeare Company in 1978, which made the Egyptian court resemble 'a small but respectable family of Galilean shepherds and shepherdesses.'[1] (Fig. 5).

Deliberately setting out to correct a number of 'misunderstandings . . . [especially the notion] that *Anthony and Cleopatra* is a spectacular play'[2]—Brook's 'analytic, clear but rather chilly' production announced its expository stance in an opening speech which Philo delivered directly to the audience.[3] Michael Billington praised the rapid pace and immaculate liaison of scenes which characterized Brook's handling of the uncut text, for 'giv[ing] us the play's architecture and none of its archaeology. . . . [showing] that this is a play of intimate scenes and invisible pageantry', whose 'spectacle lies not in noise, smoke and processions, but in rich global imagery'.[4] Crucial to this stripping away of theatrical accretions was Sally Jacobs's design. The centrepiece of her permanent setting, matching the director's 'spare, dry, cerebral' conception,[5] was a pavilion of frosted glass panels, furnished with enormous cushions, the private space of the lovers, around which surged the turmoil of public events. A battle could be represented here simply 'by silhouetting the watching Enobarbus on the far side of the glass' or by having soldiers throw clots of blood onto the outside of the panels; while Cleopatra's monument was merely a square of a symbolic red carpet.'[6]

Though to some critics it resembled 'a municipal bath house' or 'an overblown sauna',[7] Jacobs's design was appropriate to a reading that systematically subordinated the play's romantic rhetoric to its harsh political realities; and was clearly important in conveying Brook's conception of *Anthony and Cleopatra* as a tragedy of 'essentially public people trapped in a private play'.[8] Strongly influenced by Jan Kott's essay, 'Let Rome in Tiber Melt', with its disillusioned view of politics

---

[1] Benedict Nightingale, *What's on in London*, 13 July 1979.

[2] Brook, cited by Roger Warren, *SSu* 33 (1980), p. 177.

[3] Warren, p. 177; J. C. Trewin, *SQ* 30 (1979) p. 152.

[4] *Guardian*, 10 July 1979.

[5] Francis King, *Sunday Telegraph*, 15 July 1979.

[6] Michael Scott, *Antony and Cleopatra: Text and Performance* (London, 1983), p. 47; Roger Warren, *SSu* 33 (1980), p. 177.

[7] King, *Sunday Telegraph*; Nightingale, *What's on in London*.

[8] Nightingale, *What's on in London*.

and paradoxical insistence that in *Anthony and Cleopatra* 'the world is small', Brook had set out to stage what Kott announced as the theme of the play:

dignity and love cannot be reconciled with the struggle for power which forms the matter of history. . . . The heroes are restless, like big animals in a cage. The cage gets smaller and smaller, and they writhe more and more violently.[1]

To set the programmatic asceticism of Brook's production against the equally programmatic magnificence of Tree's Edwardian pageant is to be forcibly reminded that no production of a play can be ideologically innocent. Indeed from its very beginning the anti-spectacular reaction had involved an ideological agenda, in so far as it sought to liberate the play not merely from the tyranny of spurious archaeological authenticity, but also from the Victorian moral attitudes implicit in that style. For, as contemporary comments on Tree's production reveal, the spectacular approach was not only closely tied to the culture of imperialism, but derived part of its ideological power from the indulgence of certain characteristically Romantic fantasies of self-destructive sexuality. 'For nineteenth century Europeans, as for the Romans of Cleopatra's own era,' writes Lucy Hughes-Hallett, 'the rhetoric of imperialism and of heterosexuality [were] inextricably entwined'—so that a Roman love affair with an Oriental queen could be figured not merely as an act of sexual possession but as 'geographical exploration, and political conquest'.[2] The conquest of such a feminized Other, however, always carried with it the danger that the victor's masculinity might be engulfed in the very act of possession, and the conqueror 'go native'. Thus for Georg Brandes 'just as Antony's ruin results from his connection with Cleopatra, so does the fall of the Roman Republic result from the contact of the simple hardihood of the West, with the luxury of the East. Antony is Rome. Cleopatra is the Orient. When he perishes, a prey to the voluptuousness of the East, it seems as though Roman greatness and the

[1] Jan Kott, *Shakespeare our Contemporary*, trans. Boleslaw Taborski, preface by Peter Brook (London, 1964).
[2] Hughes-Hallett, *Cleopatra*, pp. 207, 205. Hughes-Hallett is drawing here on Edward Said's classic study, *Orientalism* (London, 1978).

Roman Republic expires with him.'[1] Spectacular Victorian productions of *Anthony and Cleopatra*, revelling in the sensuous extravagance of an Orient whose destruction they presented as both necessary and inevitable, reflected a profound ambiguity towards the exotic. In them Cleopatra became the very type of the Romantic *femme fatale*, the supreme object of forbidden desire whose achievement constitutes its own punishment. 'How unlike the home life of our own dear Queen!' a lady is said to have exclaimed, in tones of mingled satisfaction and reproof, after watching a late Victorian production in the Orientalist mode. On its public level the play was interpreted as a contest between Oriental decadence and the rational order of European empire, on the private level it was understood as the story of a martial hero's surrender to a sensuality so intense that its fulfilment could only mean death.[2] The triumph of Caesar over Anthony and Cleopatra thus embodied both a moral and a political imperative. As the French historian Michelet wrote of the historical Cleopatra, 'the asp which kills and delivers Cleopatra closes the long dominion of the eastern dragon. This sensual world, this world of the flesh, dies to rise again more pure in Christianity'[3]—a reading of events which the play's own streak of millenarian prophecy might seem to encourage.

Of course the Orientalist approach no more disappeared with Tree than did the attractions of spectacular staging. Indeed Orientalist prejudice remained part of the reviewer's armoury of standard responses until at least the 1950s, when Peggy Ashcroft's 'sleek and tigerish' Cleopatra was simultaneously criticized by some critics for falling short of the proper 'Oriental mood', and justified by others as its perfect embodiment:

[1] Georg Brandes, *William Shakespeare: A Critical Study*, trans. William Archer and Diana White (New York, 1963 [first published 1898]), cited in L. T. Fitz [Linda Woodbridge], 'Egyptian Queens and Male Reviewers: Sexist Attitudes in *Antony and Cleopatra* Criticism', *SQ* 28 (1977), pp. 297–316 (p. 307).

[2] Hughes-Hallett (*Cleopatra* p. 6) cites John Keats's telling reaction to an Anglo-Indian beauty he met at a Hampstead tea party in 1819: 'She is not a Cleopatra but she is at least a Charmian. She has a rich eastern look . . . she makes an impression the same as the beauty of a Leopardess. I should like her to ruin me.'

[3] Introduction to J. Michelet, *The History of the Roman Republic*, trans. William Hazlitt, cited in Hughes-Hallett, *Cleopatra*, p. 222.

'If Miss Ashcroft does not satisfy Occidental concepts of regality, it must be remembered that this is a corrupt and half-barbarous Oriental court'.[1] Ashcroft herself was to insist: 'I think of [Cleopatra] as a Greek, not as an Egyptian'; but she went on to reveal her own Orientalist assumptions: 'her wiles are not those of an Oriental. *As a Greek she possessed a mind that put her on the same level with Antony,* and gave her the power to destroy him'.[2] A revealing stage direction pencilled into Glen Byam Shaw's prompt-copy suggests that his production still incorporated a good deal of the old imperial attitude: 'As soon as they're off all wogs jabber'.[3] Even Peter Brook's revelation that he had modelled Glenda Jackson's Cleopatra on her playing of Madam Nhu, 'the Vietnamese lady with a taste for barbecued Buddhists' in *US*,[4] suggests a great deal about the unconscious persistence of the stereotypical *femme fatale* of nineteenth-century oriental fantasy.

Not surprisingly perhaps, the play's reviewers often reveal an equally persistent nostalgia for the lavish pageantry of Victorian productions;[5] and in the post-war era the spectacular *Anthony and Cleopatra* has made at least two striking reappearances—in 1951 with Michael Benthall's production at the St James', and again in 1972 when Trevor Nunn directed it with the other Roman tragedies in the RSC's epic tetralogy, *The Romans*. Pitched at the imperialist revivalism of Festival of Britain audiences, Benthall's romanticized version (which he alternated with Shaw's *Caesar and Cleopatra*) capitalized on the real-life glamour of his stars, Laurence Olivier and Vivien Leigh, rather as the Princess's Theatre exploited the notoriety of Lily Langtry, and as Joseph L. Mankiewicz's

---

[1] *Nottingham Guardian*, 30 Apr. 1953; *Coventry Evening Telegraph*, 19 Apr. 1953; *Scotsman*, 30 Apr. 1953.

[2] *Picture Post*, 7 Nov. 1953. Italics added.

[3] Note after the lovers' exit in 1.1; prompt-copy held in the library of the Shakespeare Centre, Stratford-upon-Avon.

[4] Peter Jenkins, *Guardian*, 21 Oct. 1978.

[5] See e.g. Kathy O'Shaughnessy's review of the 1986 Theatre Clwyd *Anthony*: 'Toby Robertson's production lacks spectacle. How are we to believe Enobarbus's famous description of Cleopatra's barge when we have the ascetic white-trousered Redgrave without a wig in front of us?', *Spectator*, 7 June 1986. Cf. also Irving Wardle's scathing review of Robin Phillips's Chichester production in the *Observer*, 17 May 1985; or Anthony Seymour's criticisms of Brook's 'anaemic' staging in the *Yorkshire Post*, 17 July 1979.

film capitalized on the much publicized off-screen liaison of Richard Burton and Elizabeth Taylor. Benthall reverted to nineteenth-century practice in cutting or playing down the elements of satire and political realism, and sought to combine theatrical splendour with fluid direction by means of an elaborate and innovative revolving stage—though even here the contrasts between Rome and Egypt were established in a relatively stylized fashion, Rome being represented by five heavy marble pillars, and Egypt by light Corinthian columns topped with a delicate cornice.

Two decades later, in a production that significantly coincided with the great Tutankhamun exhibition at the British Museum, Trevor Nunn's reasons for reverting to a form of pictorial staging—which even included a lavish tableau-procession to open the play—were ostensibly rather different. As in his *Julius Caesar* the tableau was designed to embody the social structures of the play-world, preparing the audience for a production that laid considerable stress on public themes.[1] For Nunn, the unifying preoccupation of the Roman plays was the idea of civilization embodied in the imperial destiny of Rome. His reading of *Anthony and Cleopatra* was thus emphatically political, playing down the love tragedy in order to emphasize the brutal factionalism of the Romans, and the mortal power struggle between Octavius's Rome and Cleopatra's Egypt.[2] Making use of a set with elaborate hydraulic machinery and a variety of acting levels, and costuming that recalled the most extravagant archaeological indulgences of the Victorian stage (Fig. 6),[3] Nunn strained all the

---

[1] Nunn's production subsequently became the basis for his television version, with Janet Suzman and Richard Johnson again in the title roles (BBC TV, 1975).

[2] Reviewers were, however, curiously divided about how well the director's intention was realized: Michael Billington (*Guardian*, 16 Aug. 1973) found 'both the politics and the poetry' in a production which to Derek Malcolm (*Listener*, 24 Aug. 1973) seemed to play up the love story to the exclusion of politics, and to John Elsom (*Observer*, 20 Aug. 1973) seemed weighed down by an 'over-deliberate [political] logic'.

[3] The RSC's exhibition 'Staging the Romans' at the Hayward Gallery insisted, for example, that 'Cleopatra's turquoise silks were historically authentic' (see Benedict Nightingale in the *New Statesman*, 12 Jan. 1973). The *Evening News* reviewer, who welcomed the spectacle but thought the text could have been cut with advantage, linked the play with the great Tutankhamun exhibition of 1972, remarking that 'the costumes . . . looked as though they had been borrowed

6. Cleopatra's Court (I.I), Royal Shakespeare Theatre, 1972.

technical resources of his theatre to establish the atmospheric contrast between Rome and Egypt. Bathed in rich, warm tones, his Egypt was 'a whirl of voluptuous opulence in which people move[d] drowsily under billowing Felliniesque canopies', 'all orange and gold and blue and purple . . . finely-wrought bird-masks and weird music, vast luxurious cushions and cringing servants', in which the black-clad Roman soldiery seemed a sinisterly intrusive presence; while Rome was 'a place of brazen trumpets, cold calculation and white knees', 'a coldly lit study in black and white, relieved only by the imperial purple, with a background of either a clear sky or a political map that filled the proscenium arch in austere board-room fashion' (Fig. 7).[1] Clearly this contrast preserved some of the

direct from the British Museum', *Evening News*, 16 Aug. 1972. Peter Thomson (*SSu* 26 (1973), pp. 142, 147) whilst admiring the spectacular effects saw them as signalling a dangerous retreat from Poellian values.

[1] Michael Billington, *Guardian*, 16 Aug. 1972; Thomson, n. 86 above, p. 147; Robert Speaight, *SQ* 23 (1972), p. 386; J. W. Lambert, *Sunday Times*, 20 Aug. 1972; Lamb, pp. 165–6.

7. Caesar (Corin Redgrave) is reconciled with Anthony (Richard Johnson), Royal Shakespeare Theatre, 1972.

superficial trappings of Orientalist staging, and Nunn's own programme note made it plain that what was at issue was nothing less than 'the ultimate contest for the whole known world, *between East and West*' (my emphasis); but the style of Janet Suzman's Cleopatra, witty, self-aware, and ruthlessly calculating, her voice ringing 'like a cash-register' on her opening line, 'If it be love indeed, tell me *how much*' (1.1.14),[1] was almost as far from the sensual eastern siren as the anti-Romantic Cleopatras of her principal rivals in the seventies, Vanessa Redgrave and Glenda Jackson.

Suzman's performance received mixed critical notices; praised for its intelligence, it was generally reckoned deficient in high

[1] *Plays and Players*, Oct. 1972, p. 42, cited in Lamb, p. 167.

passion and poetry, suggesting to one critic 'a canny and knowing precursor of Christabel Pankhurst'.[1] In this it was hardly exceptional, for if theatrical design has been one great bugbear of *Anthony and Cleopatra* in performance, casting has been another; and the two typically involve similar kinds of contradiction. If a production seeks to match the challenge made by Shakespeare's gorgeous rhetoric, the spectacle overwhelms the action, leading to complaints that the play is 'long-winded and . . . tedious';[2] if, on the other hand, a production attempts a more austere style, it is likely to be criticized as small-scale, domestic, and imaginatively impoverished. If actors are reckoned to cope well with one facet of either central role they are almost invariably deemed to have failed with another; whilst the few performances hailed as thoroughly successful by some reviewers are often denounced by others as abject failures or vulgar miscalculations. Though Anthony is usually acknowledged to be the less complex and demanding of the two central roles, actors from David Garrick to Anthony Hopkins have regularly been rebuked for falling short of the proper heroic stature on the one hand, or blamed for empty posturing on the other. As for Cleopatra, though it is perhaps the most coveted of women's roles in the Shakespearian repertory, it makes such demands on both the virtuosity and theatrical charisma of the performer that it has come to seem almost unplayable. By way of revealing contrast actors in the secondary roles of Caesar, Enobarbus, and Pompey can usually count on a measure of critical respect—precisely because their parts seem to allow for so *little* variety of approach: renditions of Enobarbus are routinely praised as 'bluff', 'blunt', and 'gruffly cynical', while Octaviuses are 'cold', 'steely', and 'calculating', like perfect embodiments of seventeenth-century Characters of a Soldier and a Machiavel.[3]

[1] Benedict Nightingale, *New Statesman*, 20 Oct. 1978.
[2] *Literary Review and Stage Manager*, 22 Nov. 1849, cited from Brown, *Casebook*, p. 49.
[3] The extreme of this tradition was represented in the Talawa Theatre Company production (Bloomsbury Theatre, London, 1991) in which Octavius was presented 'as not just a cold calculator but a murderous pragmatist' who had Pompey quietly strangled at the end of the galley scene, and later coolly supervised the detention of Lepidus (Michael Billington, *Guardian Weekly*, 2 June 1991).

If each of the two central parts is difficult to bring off successfully, a satisfactory pairing is almost unheard of. Samuel Phelps, for example, though persuasive in scenes of revelry and political intrigue was thought more 'familiar' than 'heroic'.[1] His partner, Isabella Glyn, by contrast, was among the few Cleopatras generally reckoned to have matched the 'infinite variety' of Shakespeare's conception, and was able to repeat her triumph in two subsequent productions (1855 and 1867):

She combined grace and dignity . . . she was, as it were, the impersonation at once of the sublime and the beautiful. . . . Gorgeous in person, in costume, and in her style of action, she moved, the Egyptian Venus, Minerva, Juno—now pleased, now angry—now eloquent, now silent—capricious and resolved, according to the situation and sentiment to be rendered. Withal she was classical, and her *poses* severely statuesque.[2]

Better than any other, she seems to have fulfilled the Orientalist fantasy of an all-consuming sensuality, and critics especially admired the 'joyous rapture' with which she met her death. But it is difficult now, looking at the rather stern-faced high-Victorian figure in its crinolines to imagine those 'Asiatic undulations of form' by which Glyn created the sense of 'a woman in whom the one thing ripe is animal desire'; and even amongst her contempraries there were those who thought 'the less said about Miss Glyn's Cleopatra the better'.[3]

By contrast with Glyn, Lily Langtry (Fig. 3) disappointed reviewers with her inability to translate her off-stage reputation into a convincingly sinuous portrait of a Nilotic courtesan. An extensive review in the *Speaker* praised 'the sculptural beauty of her picture of Cleopatra in death', but thought the performance ruined by 'her thin, inflexible voice'. Langtry was 'at her best in scenes of coquetry, but even that suggest[ed] the coquetry of modern Mayfair'—the critic observing cruelly of her 'Let's to billiards' (2.5.3): 'here was evidently a Cleopatra who had gone the round of the best country houses, and was doubtless an adept with the cue.'[4] Bernard Shaw found Janet Achurch's lapses in decorum even more unfortun-

[1] Lamb, p. 65.
[2] *Illustrated London News* review in Brown, *Casebook*, p. 51.
[3] Lamb, pp. 71, 74–6; Brown, *Casebook*, p. 50.
[4] *The Speaker*, 22 Nov. 1890.

ate: though praised by Clement Scott as 'a panther' and by James Agate as the best Cleopatra he had ever seen, she embarrassed Shaw by her awkward lapses from 'Egyptian warrior queen into a naughty English *petite bourgeoise*'; and though he admired her 'unforgettable statue-death',[1] the total effect reminded him of 'Brynhild-cum-Nora Helmer in an Ibsen-and-Wagner pie.'[2]

Achurch, like Langtry, harked back to *All for Love* by dying on a throne rather than the day-bed indicated by the text—one of those small production touches which indicate the beginning of a significant shift in theatrical interpretation. While the presentation of Cleopatra as a languorous Oriental temptress clearly did not die with the nineteenth century, the translation of her death from a profoundly eroticized stage-property (the day-bed), to one symbolic of transcendent royal authority (the throne), stressed the political and sacramental dignity of a scene that is as much coronation rite as *Liebestod*. It involved, of course, substantial changes to the ending of the play—notably the removal of the final funeral procession so as to allow Cleopatra rather than Caesar to dominate the closing moments—as most strikingly in the final tableau of Edmund Tearle's 1890s touring production where Caesar removed his helmet, knelt before the enthroned Cleopatra and kissed her royal robe.[3] Langtry's innovation occasioned a considerable critical furore at the time, but was followed, in an even more Drydenesque form, by the influential Beerbohm Tree in 1906. The dominance of Tree's Cleopatra, Constance Collier, was visibly represented by the contrast between her enthroned splendour on one side of the stage and the prostrate corpse of Anthony on the other (Fig. 4). By 1925, indeed, this style of ending had become so much the expected thing that Agate criticized Edith Evans' reversion to the day-bed for diminishing the grandeur of the tragic finale.[4] It was fol-

---

[1] Cited in Lamb, pp. 83–4.

[2] Cited by George Rylands in *SSu* 6 (1953), p. 140.

[3] Tearle's production was full of such sentimental touches: on the eve of the battle of Alexandria, for example, he showed Anthony and Cleopatra asleep in one another's arms as the curtain fell. The details are from a prompt-book in the Shakespeare Centre Library, Stratford-upon-Avon.

[4] So persistent is the image of the enthroned Cleopatra that Michael Scott (though he elsewhere discusses Edith Evans's return to the original day-bed

lowed at the Stratford Memorial Theatre in 1931 and 1935, as well as in Glen Byam Shaw's 1945 production; and retained for such influential performances as those of Peggy Ashcroft (1953—Fig. 8), Margaret Leighton (1969), Janet Suzman (1972), Glenda Jackson (1978), and Helen Mirren (1982).

Despite the interpretative shift represented by this staging convention, critics continued to judge Cleopatras by their ability to match some preconceived standard of oriental barbarism and sensuality—just as Anthonys tended to be measured against an ideal of heroic 'Romanness'. Constance Collier's Cleopatra impressed English critics as 'a beautiful savage thing', 'handsome, dark-skinned, barbaric',[1] but to the Germans 'had only the merit of tastefully chosen costume'; while Tree's own Anthony was alternatively regarded as 'a fine, masculine, resolute rendering of a hero ruined by love', or as ponderous, 'fatigued and monotonous'.[2] Edith Evans's 1925 performance, opposite Baliol Holloway, was 'seductive' and 'passionate', according to the *Punch* reviewer (who detected in it 'the effect of Oriental repose'), but struck others as 'too dry and cerebral'[3]—a criticism echoed in the response to her 1946 reappearance at the Piccadilly, where Evans was rated as intelligent and technically brilliant, but, like Godfrey Tearle's rather sober Anthony, essentially miscast. In the years between the two world wars, only Dorothy Green, Cleopatra for both Bridges-Adams in 1921 and Harcourt Williams in 1930, achieved almost unalloyed success in the part; and John Gielgud, her Anthony at the Old Vic, was almost equally praised for bringing out the 'extravagant romanticism' of a character 'valiant, melancholy, and yet marching as a Roman to his grave'.[4]

In the next four decades, perhaps only Laurence Olivier and Vivien Leigh came near to matching Green's and Gielgud's critical and popular success, in what was acclaimed at the time as a landmark production. Though Leigh was 'cold, smooth,

staging), writes of Shakespeare's ending as 'an epilogue in which . . . the dead Queen of Love sits "marble constant" *on her throne*' (my emphasis), *Antony and Cleopatra: Text and Performance* (London, 1983), p. 48.

[1] Her Charmian similarly 'presented a beautiful picture of Eastern womanhood', according to the *Daily Telegraph* (28 Dec. 1906).

[2] *Daily Telegraph*, 28 Dec. 1906, 16 Apr. 1907; Lamb, p. 92.

[3] *Punch*, 30 Dec. 1925; Lamb, p. 117.

[4] Ivor Brown, *Observer*, 30 Nov. 1930, cited in Lamb, p. 122.

pale, and dazzlingly beautiful' where Cleopatra is 'hot, bewrinkled, and black-complexioned', her intelligence, in Harold Hobson's estimate, became 'an adequate substitute for heat, duskiness, and even wrinkles'.[1] But the general enthusiasm for Leigh's beauty and for the polished precision of her acting was qualified by reservations about her lack of warmth and emotional range. Olivier, who deliberately scaled down his performance to match Leigh's, was hampered by difficulties of his own in coming to terms with the part. He complained of a 'lack of character drawing' in the early part of the play; and perhaps as a result his Anthony lacked any heights from which to fall.[2] To George Rylands, the domestic softening of the central characters, which necessitated 'sugar[ing] over' Cleopatra's 'great betrayal' with Thidias, and effacing the unflattering perspectives created by the Ventidius and Seleucus scenes (3.1 and 5.2.140–75), produced an effect almost indistinguishable from 'Dryden's nostalgia for heroism in a disillusioned age'.[3]

In retrospect it is the *Anthony and Cleopatra* of Peggy Ashcroft and Michael Redgrave (Fig. 8), mounted at Stratford two years later, which has come to seem the more important. Though he 'misse[d] the satirical edge injected into the role by Olivier', Redgrave triumphed over his own doubts about the part through sheer physical presence and the power of his poetic delivery.[4] His Anthony was 'huge, besotted, almost another Falstaff in debauchery'.[5] Nevertheless he seemed to at least one reviewer to lack 'the full recklessness and the final desperate shame' which the part required.[6] The *Spectator*, although thinking him 'extraordinarily fine', regretted that 'he fail[ed] to discover, as Mr Godfrey Tearle so memorably did, a streak of small-boyishness in the great commander'.[7]

---

[1] *Sunday Times*, 13 May 1951.

[2] Lamb, pp. 140–3.   [3] *SSu* 6 (1953), p. 141.

[4] Michael Conway, *Evening Standard*, 29 Apr. 1953; Lamb, p. 150. To Redgrave, Anthony seemed 'a very curious leading part because it has all the appearance of nobility and strength when in fact Anthony is a weak man, and except for what Enobarbus says about him, he's not a very noble man, at least you never see him do anything noble. You have to create, convincingly, the image of a man who held part of the world in thrall, and you have very little to do it with; all you have is his voluptuousness. And what's more he dies at the end of the fourth act' (quoted in Lamb, pp. 149–50).

[5] *Nottingham Guardian*, 30 Apr. 1953.

[6] Cecil Wilson, *Daily Mail*, 29 Apr. 1953.

[7] Peter Fleming, *Spectator*, 8 May 1953.

8. Cleopatra's death scene, Shakespeare Memorial Theatre (1953)
Peggy Ashcroft as Cleopatra.

If Redgrave lacked 'the power to freeze', his partner, Peggy Ashcroft, was criticized as 'a Cleopatra [who] makes the blood run not hot but cold', lacking 'not merely the Oriental mood, but also the sense of great passion'.[1] A majority of critics, however, agreed that her miniaturist performance was 'a triumph of technical resource over physical limitations'.[2] Although Ivor Brown complained that she lacked 'the full mischief of the part', most felt she succeeded in capturing the harlot more than the queen: 'pale-faced and red-haired, [she was] a ragingly selfish but irresistible nymphomaniac'.[3] Philip Hope-Wallace, on the other hand, was especially impressed by her more plangent moments, finding her stronger in the poetry of lament than in the scenes of raillery, so that she overcame the early danger of being 'the Marie Corelli of old Avon [to become] a noble and elegiac Cleopatra';[4] and, by the time the production had transferred to London, she had become 'more frankly sensual' and so full of 'imaginative fire [that] she really seemed to be turning into "fire and air" at the end'.[5] Nevertheless even for an admiring Richard Findlater the limitations of Ashcroft's performance—she was 'too intelligent for such exotically feminine stupidity; too English for so violent and public a love-life; too limited in voice for such a range of poetic richness'—seemed to demonstrate the ultimate unplayability of Shakespeare's creation.[6]

Typically, productions in the 1960s and 1970s attempted to sidestep the difficulties of casting by ironizing the central relationship in various ways—emphasizing the elements of

[1] J. C. Trewin, *Illustrated London News*, 16 May 1953; Harold Hobson, *Sunday Times*, 3 May 1953; *Coventry Evening Telegraph*, 29 Apr. 1953. Ivor Brown (*Observer*, 3 May 1953) similarly complained that Ashcroft's Cleopatra was 'without tincture of the East'.

[2] Cecil Wilson, *Daily Mail*, 29 Apr. 1953.

[3] Ivor Brown, *Observer*, 3 May 1953.

[4] *Guardian*, 30 Apr. 1953.

[5] *Punch*, 11 Nov. 1953; Philip Hope-Wallace, *Time and Tide*, 14 Nov. 1953.

[6] *Tribune*, 20 Nov. 1953. Benedict Nightingale's brief roll-call of the insults visited on some of the most distinguished twentieth-century Cleopatras might seem to confirm this bleak assessment. If Kenneth Tynan saw Edith Evans as 'Lady Bracknell cruelly starved of cucumber sandwiches', to another critic Ashcroft resembled 'a ravenous famine victim', while Margaret Leighton was 'a neurotic society hostess zonked out on tranquillizers and martinis'; Vanessa Redgrave recalled 'a half-cracked flapper', and Dorothy Tutin 'an inscrutable pedigree cat with an odd, out-of-breath purr' (*New Statesman*, 20 Oct. 1978).

self-conscious theatricality in Anthony's and Cleopatra's love-making, and setting the lovers' hyperbolic rhetoric against an increasingly disillusioned view of imperial power-politics. Related to these strategies was a tendency to place younger actors in the parts—a practice initiated by Robert Helpmann's casting of the 30-year-old Keith Michell and 23-year-old Margaret Whiting at the Old Vic in 1957, and followed by Michael Langham's 1967 Stratford, Ontario production with Christopher Plummer and Zoe Caldwell. Both Caldwell ('Witty, extremely passionate, shrewish and vulgar') and Plummer played down the sensuality of their relationship to emphasize its game-playing qualities in a version that emerged as 'a chilly Jacobean rejection' of classical *realpolitik*.[1]

In some ways Janet Suzman's consummately 'clear-headed' Cleopatra represented the culmination of this deliberate thinning out of the part. Playing sophisticatedly against the clichés, she was 'a clever girl tackling a dangerous game and revelling rather too much in her own skill'.[2] But, although Benedict Nightingale thought her the only Cleopatra who 'actually might "hop forty paces through the public street" ',[3] there was a hint of wilfulness in this portrait of 'a volatile, quick-tempered young shrew' which looked forward to the more extreme idiosyncrasies of Glenda Jackson and Vanessa Redgrave. This trait was perhaps exaggerated by contrast with the rather stolid Anthony of Richard Johnson. Johnson had a fine physical presence, grizzled and slightly flabby, a blustering 'old ruffian', with enough hints of the dying lion about him to seem a plausible personation of a man who had once been 'the greatest soldier of the world'; in Rome he 'stood straight, and spoke decisively, [whereas] in Egypt he was slightly stooped, self-consciously ageing' But a certain woodenness in his delivery perhaps accounted for the fact that Corin Redgrave's Caesar, a 'dainty-stepping, wry-smiling' psychopath, and Patrick Stewart's Enobarbus, 'dangerously steely . . . behind the heartiness', received more attention than is usual for these roles.[4]

[1] Lamb, p. 161.
[2] John Elsom, *Observer*, 20 Aug. 1972.
[3] *New Statesman*, 25 Aug. 1972.
[4] Jeremy Kingston, *Punch*, 24 Aug. 1972; J. W. Lambert, *Sunday Times*, 20 Aug. 1972; Peter Thomson, *SSu* 26 (1973), p. 147.

When Nunn's *Anthony and Cleopatra* transferred from Stratford to London in 1973 it had to compete with the most icono-
clastic of all twentieth-century productions, Tony Richardson's
modern dress version at the Bankside Globe. If Corin Redgrave's Caesar was disconcertingly cool, the 'ungovernable
rages' of David Schofield seemed frankly psychotic; standing
over Cleopatra's corpse, his trembling fingers clutching a
joint, he became a 'salivating necrophiliac', looking as if he
were 'likely to enter a psychiatric ward, not soon to be
released'.[1] Julian Glover reduced Anthony to a 'dandyish,
cigar-smoking subaltern', surviving on 'faded boyish charm',
while Vanessa Redgrave's Cleopatra was a red-haired, white-
uniformed Ruritanian queen 'who shouts like an alley-cat
and has the manners of a gangster's moll. . . . a tart unparalleled'.[2] Cleopatra's domineering relation with the taciturn
Charmian and Iras recalled Genet's *The Maids*, while her
'delight in physical violence' suggested that she was 'the
reigning welter-weight champion of Alexandria'.[3] In a production that seemed, even to its greatest admirer, Harold Hobson,
motivated by a contemptuous hatred of the protagonists, the
death scenes were played in a mood of vicious burlesque.
Anthony's 'I am dying Egypt, dying' became a comically peevish
interruption of her egotistical chatter, 'whilst her lamentation
over him [was] not a threnody but a screech'; Redgrave
showed a 'childish glee in painting her face and robing herself
for what [became] the cheap thrill of her suicide', in which
she bellowed the final speeches 'in a voice increasingly harsh
and strident'.[4] In Hobson's view these 'flamboyant and
acrid performances' gave the play 'what, in more reverential
presentations it always lacks: that is, life, provocation, and
excitement', but most reviewers seemed closer to Michael
Billington's baffled complaint that Richardson's 'trivial foot-
ling production' had made virtual 'nonsense' of 'a complex
masterpiece'.

[1] Harold Hobson, *Sunday Times*, 12 Aug. 1973; Lamb, pp. 170–1.
[2] Lamb, p. 170; John Barber, *Daily Telegraph*, 10 Aug. 1973.
[3] Irving Wardle, *The Times*, 10 Aug. 1973; Michael Billington, *Guardian*,
10 Aug. 1973.
[4] Hobson, *Sunday Times*, 12 Aug. 1973; Barber, *Daily Telegraph*, 10 Aug.
1973; Billington, *Guardian*, 10 Aug. 1973.

The iconoclasm of Peter Brook's 1978 production for the Royal Shakespeare Company (Fig. 5) was a much more carefully meditated affair—not least in its treatment of Cleopatra: 'instead of a lolling vamp [Glenda Jackson] created a crop-haired woman of mercurial, quicksilver energy who wants a match for her own restlessness'.[1] Capable of 'a breathtaking thunder-and-lightning transformation' in her confrontation with the messenger, and of 'a superb death-scene', which the exceptional coolness of the production made even more powerful, Jackson found at least some of Cleopatra's variety. Her performance was admired for 'wit and authority'—even if her lack of sensuality made one reviewer pine for Dorothy Tutin's 'richly seductive and calculating' Cleopatra in the previous year's Prospect production.[2] To Robert Cushman Jackson's playing was over-reminiscent of her recent television appearance as Elizabeth I, while for Benedict Nightingale her steely performance revealed 'a born Octavius Caesar'.[3] If Jackson was 'alive from the neck up', her partner, Alan Howard, appeared 'exhaustingly alive from the neck down'; his Anthony was a man who had never fully grown up—'an adolescent hothead peeps out of the tall frame'.[4] The lack of any strongly felt erotic bond between the two central characters made Cleopatra's tribute to the dead Anthony seem like an exercise in deliberate self-deception; and such curiously distanced treatment of the poetry made this more 'a kind of commentary' on the legendary love affair than an attempt to realize it. The distancing effect was enhanced by Brook's emphasis on the choric role of Patrick Stewart's Enobarbus, whose speeches tended to be delivered downstage and out-front, as if he were guiding the audience's response to the tragedy.[5] Apart from the eldritch humour of Richard Griffiths's red-nosed, harlequinesque clown, the acknowledged success of the production was Jonathan Pryce's Octavius, from behind

---

[1] Michael Billington, *Guardian*, 10 July 1979.

[2] Lamb, p. 176; *Country Life*, 13–25 Oct. 1978.

[3] Robert Cushman, *Observer*, 15 Oct. 1978; Benedict Nightingale, *New Statesman*, 20 Oct. 1978.

[4] *Country Life*, 13–25 Oct. 1978; John Barber, *Daily Telegraph*, 10 July 1979.

[5] Robert Cushman, *Observer*, 15 July 1979; John Elsom, *Scotsman* 19 Oct. 1978; Scott, *Text and Performance*, p. 72.

whose disconcerting stare emerged a character of surprising tenderness—a loving brother, a sensualist, and 'a man of strong passions always alert to his rivalry with Antony'.[1]

The small scale of Jonathan Miller's production in the BBC Shakespeare television series (1981) apparently had more to do with the exigencies of finance than with any particular sympathy for Brook's approach. Denied the use of a film studio Miller found that the BBC's production facilities imposed an unavoidably intimate style on his production, an effect that was probably enhanced by the over-naturalistic playing of Colin Blakely's scruffily anti-heroic Anthony and Jane Lapotaire's rather skittish Cleopatra. Brook's minimalism had a more appreciable influence on the RSC's next adventure with the play, Adrian Noble's chamber production for Stratford's Other Place and the Barbican Pit (1982–3), with its bare, black-carpeted arena. Noble's Cleopatra was Helen Mirren, returning to a part she had first attempted with limited success at the age of 20 for the National Youth Theatre (1966–7). Playing against a bluff, masculine, if rather external Anthony from Michael Gambon, Mirren's 'blond vamp of the Nile' was admired for her 'instantaneous and calculated transformations from tantrums to seductions and pique to command' (Fig. 9). Vivid, volatile, and 'hauntingly reminiscent of Peggy Ashcroft in appearance and delivery', this 'sensuous tigress' convinced her critics of her powers of seduction; but, 'except in her peremptory aggression', gave little sense of being a queen. In a production which threatened to reduce the struggle for empire to 'a domestic tiff on a blurred canvas', it was perhaps unsurprising that Jonathan Hyde's 'chilling' Octavius, bitterly puritanical yet half in love with Anthony, should strike some as melodramatically overplayed.[2] Neither the energy of the central performances, nor the acerbic intelligence of Bob Peck's Enobarbus ('a Thersites finally come to judgment') was sufficient to persuade most reviewers of the production's

---

[1] Lamb, p. 177; John Barber, *Daily Telegraph*, 10 July 1979; Michael Billington, *Guardian*, 10 July 1979.

[2] Ned Chaillet, *Wall Street Journal*; Giles Gordon, *Spectator*; Keith Nurse, *Daily Telegraph*; Rosalind Carne, *Guardian*; Michael Coveney, *Financial Times*; Rosemary Say, *Sunday Telegraph*—all reprinted in *London Theatre Record* 3, 8 (9–12 Apr. 1983), pp. 266–7; and see also Scott, *Text and Performance*, pp. 73–5.

9. Michael Gambon and Helen Mirren as Anthony and Cleopatra, The Other Place, Stratford-upon-Avon, 1982

superiority to its more orthodox rival directed by Keith Hack at the Young Vic. Although some reviewers were disconcerted by the 'strangely modern ... mannerisms' of Judy Parfitt's Cleopatra, 'a glamorous society belle' whose delivery of the verse sometimes suggested 'a disgruntled debutante rather than a seasoned woman of infinite variety',[1] there was general admiration for Keith Baxter's 'commanding' Anthony. In contrast to the externalized swagger of Gambon's grizzled warrior, Baxter's much more various performance, strongest in its rendering of anger and despair, discovered a genuine pathos in the hero's middle-aged decline; 'played with all the fervour and longing of a man who knows that this grand passion will be his last', this Anthony was especially moving in the suicide scene where his conviction of Cleopatra's betrayal brought the audience 'to the very heart of loss'. Hack's conception of the play as a tragedy of heroic decay was perfectly expressed in the 'gaudy grandeur' of Voytek's spectacular set,

[1] Rosalind Carne, *Guardian*; Charles Spencer, *Standard*—both repr. in *London Theatre Record* 3, 8 (9–12 Apr. 1983), pp. 197–8.

over which loomed 'a soaring, headless statue' whose flowing gold robes covered almost the entire acting area.[1]

If Nunn's strongly political emphasis and the anti-heroic minimalism of Richardson and Brook represented the dominant styles of the 1970s, Hack's was the first of a series of productions in the 1980s which sought to restore something of the play's heroic dimension—a development which it is possible to see as an oblique expression of the same post-imperial nostalgia that produced a small rash of films and television drama set in the twilight of the Anglo-Indian Raj. At the Chichester Festival Theatre in 1985, Robin Phillips conspicuously downplayed Shakespeare's *realpolitik* (to the point of omitting the scene on Pompey's galley completely), and radically cut the last two acts—including Cleopatra's fearful refusal to open her monument to the dying Anthony, and the entire Seleucus episode—so as to remove any doubts of the Queen's courage and fidelity to Anthony. Unfortunately Diana Rigg's 'well-mannered Englishwoman' (like Denis Quilley's heroically simplified Anthony) was not well calculated for this somewhat operatic conception of her role.[2]

An excessively 'English' queen of a different type was reckoned to be a fault of Toby Robertson's Theatre Clwyd production at the Haymarket in 1986. Nevertheless Vanessa Redgrave's performance clearly offered to make amends for her spiteful treatment of the part thirteen years earlier, and the Toby Robertson/Christopher Selbie production was greeted as 'a return to full-scale Victorian values'.[3] In a production styled on the paintings of Caravaggio, the 'vaulting, ruined arches' of the Roman *palazzo* in Simon Higlett's single set, though blurring the central distinction between Rome and Egypt, clearly signalled the production's theme of imperial decline;[4] while Timothy Dalton's Anthony, in his magnificent Turkish robes, brought plenty of charismatic swagger to

---

[1] Francis King, *Sunday Telegraph*; Charles Spencer, *Standard*—both repr. in *London Theatre Record* 3, 8 (9–12 Apr. 1983), pp. 197–8.

[2] Michael Ratcliffe, *Observer*, 19 May 1985, cited in Bevington, p. 69; Roger Warren, *SQ* 37 (1986), p. 119. Significantly, Rigg's style seems to have been much better suited to the performance of Dryden's Cleopatra at the Almeida (*Times Literary Supplement*, 10 May 1991).

[3] Sheridan Morley, *Punch*, 11 June 1986.

[4] Carole Woddis, *City Limits*, 12 June 1986; Francis Wheen, *Sunday Today*, 8 June 1986.

the part. Opinions were strangely divided as to the effective-
ness of the central pairing—one reviewer welcoming 'the best
sexual chemistry since Janet Suzman and Richard Johnson,
with an extra dollop of lissom carnality', another complaining
that 'at no point do you sense that this pleasant, rational
couple live through their senses'.[1] To many, Dalton's heroic
Anthony seemed altogether too young and vigorous—emotion-
ally effective in the mid-play scenes of disappointment, but
missing the taint of unconscious self-parody in Shakespeare's
'old ruffian', and falling short of the high pathos to which
he rises at the end.[2] Redgrave's Cleopatra drew even more
contradictory notices. Some reviewers were stirred to breathless excitement by this 'crop-haired, ginger tigress of Old Nile',
discovering both 'a volatile, witty sensualist with the cunning
of a wicked monkey', and 'a fecund, husky, flame-haired
temptress of real authority'.[3] But others found only a Fabian
acolyte of Gandhi, 'a twentieth-century *Guardian* reader', or
'an . . . eccentric bluestocking who would be more at home
in the gardens of Sissinghurst than on a barge'—'one can
understand how this fey harpy came to destroy Antony, but
not why he held her in thrall'.[4] If Redgrave's performance
seemed deficient in majesty and 'imperial pride', its self-conscious theatricality was generally admired: her Cleopatra was
'a consummate actress, trying on and discarding roles as
lesser women try on hats', yet capable of rising to 'a spectacle
worthy of her stupendous reputation' in the final scene. Here
the actress's 'dark, grief-laden voice' combined with the 'lucid,
lyrical intelligence' of her verse-speaking to produce an effect
that some reviewers found irresistibly moving, though for
others the display of feeling remained immature and over-
histrionic, lacking 'depth, size, integrity, power'.[5] Nicholas

[1] Michael Coveney, *Financial Times*, 27 May 1986; Mary Harron, *Observer*,
1 June 1986.

[2] John Barber, *Daily Telegraph*, 24 June 1986; Francis King, *Sunday Telegraph*,
1 June 1986.

[3] Michael Coveney, *Financial Times*, 27 May 1986; John Barber, *Daily
Telegraph*, 24 May 1986; Francis Wheen, *Sunday Today*, 8 June 1986.

[4] Michael Billington, *Guardian*, 28 May 1986; Kathy O'Shaughnessy,
Observer, 7 June 1986; Mary Harron, *Observer*, 1 June 1986; Francis King,
Sunday Telegraph, 1 June 1986.

[5] Michael Billington, *Guardian*, 28 May 1986; Jack Tinker, *Daily Mail*, 27
May 1986; John Barber, *Daily Telegraph*, 24 May 1986; Kathy O'Shaughnessy,
Observer, 7 June 1986.

Shrimpton thought that playing Cleopatra as 'an imperious older woman, more "grizzled" than her youthful Antony' produced a telling symmetry in which 'it seemed every bit as remarkable for Cleopatra to think the world well lost as it did for the soldier and statesman Antony'. Yet Benedict Nightingale concluded that Redgrave's view of Cleopatra 'seems to be that she's a big girl, a lanky girl, an ageing girl, but a girl none-theless. Something about her has never left the playroom.'[1]

Any maturity missing from Redgrave's conception was amply recovered in Judi Dench's Cleopatra a year later, per-haps the most complete realization of the role in recent years. Amplitude was in fact the keynote of Peter Hall's production, the first attempted by the National Theatre, which emphasized the epic dimensions of the tragedy by its generous orchestra-tion of an almost uncut text. Running for nearly four hours and played with scrupulous attention to both the meaning and the music of Shakespeare's verse, it struck some reviewers as slow-paced, 'ruminative, even plodding', but impressed most by its 'symphonic cohesion' and deliberate, monumental power.[2] Designed after the classical paintings of Mantegna, Titian, and Veronese (whose *Mars and Venus United by Love* (Fig. 11) adorned the posters and programme cover),[3] the production relied for its spectacular effects on the massing of sumptuously costumed extras and elaborately choreographed processions. Alison Chitty's rather cumbersome setting fea-tured a massive earth-red façade, with a large pedimented central doorway framed by crumbling masonry on one side and a single Corinthian column on the other; set against a maroon cyclorama and capable of various configurations, often sug-gesting broken or decayed arches, it represented Rome and Egypt impartially, the contrasting atmosphere of the two worlds

[1] Nicholas Shrimpton, *SSu* 40 (1988), p. 183; Benedict Nightingale, *New Statesman*, 28 May 1986.
[2] Ros Asquith, *City Limits*, 16 Apr. 1987; Jim Hiley, *Listener*, 23 May 1987; Francis King, *Sunday Telegraph*, 12 May 1987; Michael Billington, *Guardian*, 11 Apr. 1987; Michael Coveney, *Financial Times*, 10 Apr. 1987.
[3] The echoes of these painters were suggested by a remark in Harley Granville-Barker's *Preface* to the play (p. 49)—see Lowen, p. 10. Lowen's book, though it oscillates uneasily between hagiography and gossip, contains some invaluable details of how Hall's production and the actors' interpretation of their roles evolved in the course of performance. Also interesting in this respect is the BBC documentary *Jonathan Miller Directs Antony and Cleopatra* (1981).

being registered largely by changes in lighting and costume colour—red and gold for Egypt, blue and grey for Rome—until Cleopatra's death scene where her symbolic reconciliation of contraries was figured in a gown of brilliant blue, spangled with golden stars. Stephen Wentworth's lighting frequently picked out the protagonists in pools of brilliant illumination, amid a darkness that emphasized both their moral isolation and the sense of impending catastrophe.

Hall himself had a clearly formed notion of *Anthony and Cleopatra* as 'about two people who, despite the romantic mythology, were totally self-indulgent and egocentric, and Caesar, a monstrous opportunist who disgracefully used the precepts of ancient Rome for his own ends';[1] but the use of so full a text gave some critics the impression that they were watching a transparent production in which 'the play unfolds naturally at its own pace, [and] nothing is forced, [so that] one does not have to peer through the intellectual fog of directors' "interpretation" to discern Shakespeare's creation'.[2] However chimerical such directorial purity may be, this was certainly a production which allowed unusually full play to *Anthony and Cleopatra*'s bewildering shifts of perspective, its paradoxical fondness for juxtaposing contradictory attitudes and incompatible points of view. At the beginning of Act III, to take one small example, Hall restored and gave full theatrical weight to a brief scene—Ventidius's return from his victory over the Parthians—that is routinely cut from most productions of the play. The perplexing thing about this seemingly unimportant episode is that, in a work which repeatedly refuses to deliver on the lavish visual promise of its rhetoric, it asks to be staged with all the spectacular resources of the Elizabethan theatre as a full Roman triumph *all'antica*. Staging it in this fashion, however, as Hall triumphantly showed, not only creates a brilliant dramatic contrast with the preceding debauch on Pompey's galley, but ironically serves to demystify

[1] Quoted in Lowen, p. 112.

[2] Charles Osborne, *Daily Telegraph*, 11 Apr. 1987. By contrast Della Couling in the *Tablet* (2 May 1987) complained that the scale of the production made 'the two lovers almost recede in the background', while Sue Jameson (*London Broadcasting*, 10 Apr. 1987) thought that 'the play could have been cut to emphasize the relationship . . . between the lovers, for this is what it is about essentially'.

the spectacular magic of power as Enobarbus's Cydnus speech (for example) has created it; for even as the splendour of the triumphal procession appears to reinvest Anthony's cause with the heroic glamour appropriate to 'his name, that magical word of war', the effect is undercut by the contemptuous treatment of Pacorus's corpse, and by Ventidius's matter-of-fact emphasis on 'well-paid ranks' and the virtues of competent lieutenantry.[1]

Perhaps the most striking successes of Hall's production, however, were in the area of casting. David Schofield nicely realized Hall's conception of Pompey as a man. crazed by his own sense of virtue, 'John Knoxian, Paisleyan . . . an obsessed demi-god, bent on revenging his father and bringing in a new puritanism'.[2] Tim Pigott-Smith's frigid and disdainful Octavius was interestingly coloured by a surprisingly intense (perhaps even incestuous) affection for his sister which, together with a kind of disappointed hero-worship, became the principal motive for his vindictive hunting down of Anthony and Cleopatra.[3] Michael Bryant's hard-bitten, laconic, cockneyfied Enobarbus was full of striking individual touches, including a beautifully calculated reinvestigation of the Cydnus speech. The difficulty for any actor approaching a famous set-piece of this sort is to escape the sense of hackneyed quotation that a simple surrender to its sensual music is likely to produce. Bryant's solution was to play the first 28 lines precisely *as* quotation—a favourite piece of barrack-room soft porn—only for his cynicism to be overwhelmed by the sudden shock of personal recollection, poetry welling up when least anticipated as a kind of innocent astonishment: 'I saw her once | Hop forty paces through the public street . . .'.

---

[1] The Ventidius scene was cut from Trevor Nunn's production when it was first staged in Stratford (1972), but restored when the play transferred to the Aldwych in the following year. There, however, it was not played as a triumphal entry; Ventidius and Sillius entered after their troops, and Ventidius was given a new speech instructing Eros to carry news of his victory to Anthony. If this version seemed to diminish the complex ironies of the scene, they were exaggerated and simplified in Peter Brook's anti-heroic 1978 version beginning with a dumb-show of the brutal killing of Pacorus and stripped of all triumphal suggestions.

[2] Cited in Lowen, p. 101.

[3] Lowen, pp. 15, 54, 129, 157.

Perhaps only a Cleopatra as full of the unexpected as Judi Dench's could produce such a response. Like her Anthony, the strikingly unheroic Anthony Hopkins, Dench was cast against type. In physical appearance they made a conspicuously unglamorous couple, Dench 'somewhat bedraggled' and a little dumpy, Hopkins 'rather podgy' and gone to seed.[1] Yet they were capable of making the erotic poetry sing with a rapture and intensity unmatched by any couple since Peggy Ashcroft and Michael Redgrave. The effect, as Michael Billington noted, was to capitalize on the play's frequently uncomfortable tension between rhetoric and reality to reveal it as the tragedy of 'two chunkily real people living out some epic fantasy'.[2] The extraordinary vocal range which gave such power to Dench's verse speaking, also contributed significantly to the dazzling variety for which her performance was admired. Although the roles for which she was best known seemed to have established her among 'nature's Englishwomen', Dench's 'prowling, darting high-vitality creature' struck most reviewers as surprisingly sensuous, full of 'sexual abandon, feline cunning, passionate jealousy and unquenchable possessiveness'. Dench discovered Cleopatra's sexual magnetism 'not in any [*Playboy*] centrefold posturing but in emotional extremism'. By turns 'scornful and sassy, blessed with terrific energy, temper and wit', she was a 'volatile . . . mistress of all moods who in the course of a single scene can switch easily from breathy languor . . . to cutting humour . . . to a pensive melancholy'.[3] 'Recognising that the play is both sumptuous and satiric', this was a performance that paid full attention to Cleopatra's histrionic narcissism:

she does rich justice to the luscious speeches dripping with hyperbole, sensuous excess and gorgeous perversities of syntax and imagery, but also keeps you aware of Cleopatra's tawdriness—the peevish insecurity of the mistress behind the swagger of the Queen, the crafty calculation and occasional panic, the stagy luxuriating in her own performance.[4]

---

[1] Steve Grant, *Time Out*, 15 Apr. 1987.   [2] *Guardian*, 11 Apr. 1987.
[3] Milton Shulman, *Evening Standard*, 10 Apr. 1987; Peter Kemp, *Independent*, 11 Apr. 1989; Michael Billington, *Guardian* 11 Apr. 1987; Michael Ratcliffe, *Observer* 12 Apr. 1987.
[4] Peter Kemp, *Independent*, 11 Apr. 1987.

Yet this chameleon actress-queen could rise to a full-throated operatic magnificence that turned the last act into 'a riveting emotional journey from tragic self-pity to the ecstatic embrace of death in marmoreal splendour'.[1]

Anthony Hopkins's 'oak-like and massive' Anthony drew a more mixed response, perhaps because his performance itself was more variable—so that on one night he could seem 'boisterous' to the point of tedium, while on others reviewers were struck by the 'slack-limbed understatement' of a curiously 'inert' and 'somnambulistic' performance.[2] Yet at its best this was a 'memorable study of grizzled nobility gone to seed', and Hopkins's 'smouldering volcano of a man' was at least a match for Dench's 'spit-fire Cleopatra'. The *Punch* reviewer noticed 'a brooding restlessness . . . at the core of both interpretations, a physical unquiet born of frustration and despair'; and behind the superficial *bonhomie* and heroic posturing this was a dangerous Anthony in whom the heavy drinking and bouts of sensual indulgence emerged as the half-frenzied recourse of a man consumed with impotent anger at the effects of advancing age. For all its deceptive understatement, it was a performance of delicate shading: 'humorous, manipulative, an old fox among the cubs surrounding Caesar', Hopkins was 'an old, besotted dog' in the company of Cleopatra, yet 'an old lion' among his own troops; and his ability to suggest 'overpowering inward grief' beneath the forced gaiety of Anthony's farewell to his servants in Act 4, scene 2 was extraordinarily moving. Of course there was about even this scene a suggestion of suspect theatricality: in Hall's conception Anthony, in his own way, was almost as much of a self-conscious performer as Cleopatra: 'seeing themselves as great actors upon the world of the stage . . . They need to be "the great lovers", "the tragic hero", "the paramour," using extravagant gestures which are also slightly tacky.'[3] If Hopkins's underplaying of some earlier scenes could seem a touch

---

[1] Michael Coveney, *Financial Times*, 10 Apr. 1987.

[2] Michael Coveney, *Financial Times*, 10 Apr. 1987; Paul Anderson, *Tribune*, 24 Apr. 1987; Jim Hiley, *Listener*, 23 Apr. 1987; Charles Osborne, *Daily Telegraph*, 11 Apr. 1987; the odd suggestion of 'sleepwalking' in Hopkins's performance was also noted by Ros Asquith, *City Limits*, 16 Apr. 1987, as well as in the much more positive review of Michael Coveney.

[3] Lowen, p. 38

perverse, it had the inestimable advantage of allowing him plenty of space to rise, in a magnificent display of Welsh *hwyl*, to the elegiac challenge of Anthony's final scenes.[1] The distance between his first entrance—flagon in hand, sitting astride the shoulders of a roped and bull-masked Mardian, and towed by a mocking Cleopatra—and his last, where his own roped carcass is winched up to the monument by his distraught queen, became the measure of an exceptional achievement.

Yet for all the outstanding success of this production, there remained the uneasy feeling even amongst its most enthusiastic admirers that 'the range of this play always seems to escape production'.[2] Barbara Everett found the central couple 'too nice, too sympathetic', lacking the proper 'dangerous edge', and criticized the production's failure to realize Shakespeare's complex adjustments of 'humour and sadness and irony'. What resulted was 'a major rendering of something curiously like Dryden's ... *All for Love*'[3] Even the general chorus of praise for the 'consummate artistry' of Judi Dench's 'colossal performance' was tempered by a feeling that 'the ideal Cleopatra exists only in the imagination'; and among the few dissenters there were several who felt she lacked 'the sexual allure necessary for the role'.[4] Significantly, Dench's own anxieties about the part apparently centred on a fear of being 'too English' and 'the need to fight physical preconceptions'.[5] Three decades earlier Richard Findlater had confessed to similar reservations about the Englishness of Peggy Ashcroft, the other great Cleopatra of the post-war era, and a significant influence on Dench's conception of the part. Findlater concluded that 'no English player ... can act Cleopatra, and no actress of any other nation can speak it'.[6]

[1] Robin Ray, *Punch*, 22 Apr. 1987; Clive Hirschhorn, *Sunday Express*, 12 Apr. 1987; Milton Shulman, *Evening Standard*, 10 Apr. 1987; Michael Billington, *Guardian*, 11 Apr. 1987

[2] Michael Coveney, *Financial Times*, 10 Apr. 1987.

[3] Barbara Everett, *Times Literary Supplement*, 14 Apr. 1987, p. 439.

[4] Clive Hirschhorn, *Sunday Express*, 12 Apr. 1987; Francis King, *Sunday Telegraph* 12 Apr. 1987; Nick St George, BBC Radio London, 25 Apr. 1987; Val Jones Evans, *Today*, 10 Apr. 1987.

[5] In a similar fashion Hopkins worried about his ability to inhabit the heroic side of Anthony and to make his 'glamour and attractiveness' convincing (Lowen, p. 85).

[6] *Tribune*, 20 Nov. 1933; for Ashcroft's influence on Dench's performance, see Lowen, p. 80.

Oddly perhaps, given the persistence of Orientalist responses to the play, there have been remarkably few attempts to test the second half of this proposition; but the rare examples have tended to confirm it. Komisarjevsky's innovative but controversial production at the New Theatre in 1936 appears to have been so severely handicapped by Eugenie Leontovich's mangled English that it was easily dismissed as a foreign interloper's desecration of an English masterpiece.[1] There was a more sympathetic reception for the black American Franchelle Stuart Dorn at Washington's Shakespeare Theatre in 1988 (Fig. 10); but it perhaps had more to do with director Michael Kahn's bold decision to stress the African nature of Cleopatra's court by casting black actors in the Egyptian roles than with the quality of Dorn's own performance. Dorn's naturalistic approach worked engagingly with the 'riggish' side of Cleopatra and in more-or-less comic scenes like those with the messenger, but her technique was less well fitted to the poetry of the role, contrasting so awkwardly with the rather Edwardian orotundity of Kenneth Haigh's Anthony that the climactic struggle between Rome and Egypt often seemed reduced to an indecisive battle of acting styles. Whatever its weaknesses, however, the production's casting of Ms Dorn issued an important challenge to traditional theatrical practice. For it is a telling paradox of the play's stage history that, despite Shakespeare's clearly envisaging Cleopatra as a North African queen whose skin is either 'tawny' or 'black', there is no history of black Cleopatras as there has been, since the triumphs of Ira Aldridge in the mid-nineteenth century, a series of striking black Othellos. Instead the same Orientalism which laboured to transform Othello into a pale-skinned Arab of the highest caste[2] has been entirely successful in presenting Cleopatra as an eastern exotic, whose race (when it is even allowed to be an issue) is established by appeal to the historical 'facts' of her Greek ancestry.[3] Although the English theatre has recently nourished a whole generation of

---

[1] Lamb, pp. 128–9.

[2] For the orientalizing of *Othello*, see Julie Hankey (ed.), *Othello*, Plays in Performance (Bristol: Bristol Classical Press, 1987), pp. 56–113.

[3] The question of 'Cleopatra's Blackness' is addressed by Janet Adelman who links the play with Ben Jonson's *Masque of Blackness* (1605) and other contemporary representations of Moors and Ethiopes (*Common Liar*, Appendix C, pp. 184–8).

10. Franchelle Stuart Dorn as Cleopatra, Folger Shakespeare Theatre, 1988

classically trained black actors, no major company has been willing to capitalize on this development to explore the play's treatment of racial and cultural otherness.

The 1991 production of *Anthony and Cleopatra* at London's Bloomsbury Theatre by the Talawa Theatre Company (in conjunction with the Merseyside Everyman), though a courageous initiative, hardly disturbed this general picture since the use of an all-black cast, while it may have had a usefully defamiliarizing effect, continued to obscure the racial anxieties that contribute so materially to the ambivalent Roman construction of Egyptian difference. Far from restoring a missing African dimension, the production only served, in the judgement of Michael Billington, to prove once again 'that Shakespeare is universal property'. It would be a crass mistake, however, to suppose that restoration of an 'African' Cleopatra is likely to resolve the problems of casting the play. The greatest weakness of Yvonne Brewster's production, Billington thought, was 'the odd lack of sexual chemistry' and a 'studied decorum' in the love scenes that made it 'one of the most chaste productions on record' (*Guardian*, 2 June 1991). Whilst one might speculate a conscious effort by Talawa to resist the stereotyping implicit in routine complaints about the lack of sensuality in most 'English' Cleopatras, the effect of both Franchelle Dorn's and Dona Croll's performances was to confirm the seeming impossibility, suggested by the larger stage history, of a casting adequate to the 'infinite variety' of the play's own beglamoured imagination. But then it will be part of my argument in what follows that such disappointments, such tensions between imagination and realization are an inescapable consequence of the play's daring dramatic method, and an indispensable part of its effect: they are, in a profound sense, 'in the script'.

Interpretation[1]

THE PATTERN OF ANTICLIMAX

In his essay 'Of Love', Francis Bacon comments wryly on the 'strange ... excess of this passion, and how it braves the

---

[1] The section which follows does not pretend to offer a complete account of the wealth of critical approaches to *Anthony and Cleopatra*; a comprehensive

nature and value of things, by this, that the speaking in a perpetual hyperbole is comely in nothing but love'.[1] No love-tragedy is more excessive in its braving of 'the nature of things' than *Anthony and Cleopatra*; and in *The Common Liar* Janet Adelman has shown how hyperbole is stitched into the very fabric of its design. But the essence of hyperbole, as the Elizabethan rhetorician George Puttenham understood, is that it is an 'over reacher'[2]—a figure whose precarious splendour depends on its constant hazarding of bathos. Shakespeare's willingness to exploit the dangerous interplay of these two figures, the boldness with which he courts the perils of anti-climax, goes some way to account for the unstable brilliance of this tragedy. But it may also help to account for some of the uncertainties of its reception.

For if there is a linking theme to the stage history, it is surely to be found in the recurrent sense of unease at a perceived gap between expectation and performance. On the one hand there is a feeling that staging almost invariably fails to match the spectacular excitements suggested by the scope of the play's action and its intoxicating rhetoric; on the other repeated disappointment at the inability of successive performers to realize the stature of the central characters. Yet the most conscientious attempts to overcome these difficulties have only served to generate fresh problems. Thus the effect of the colossal archaeological spectacles favoured by nineteenth-century impresarios was to invite a grumbling dissatisfaction with Shakespeare's dramaturgy, which came to seem disconnected, pageant-like, and (despite the use of heavily cut texts) sprawlingly uneconomical. Yet the efforts of Poel's and Granville-Barker's disciples to approximate the

survey of the literature will be found in Marvin Spevack (ed.) *Antony and Cleopatra*, New Variorum Edition (New York, 1990), pp. 627–726; a more economical, but admirably efficient survey of the field is incorporated in David Bevington's introduction to his New Cambridge edition, pp. 13–44.

[1] 'Of Love', p. 29. Bacon's sceptical reflections on the inflated rhetoric of love—to whose destructive excesses he avers (citing Marcus Antonius as an example) that 'martial men' are exceptionally prone—might almost have been inspired by Shakespeare's play.

[2] George Puttenham, *The Arte of English Poesie*, ed. Gladys Doidge Willcock and Alice Walker (Cambridge, 1936), p. 154; cited in Adelman, *Common Liar*, p. 114.

fluid simplicities of Jacobean stage practice (like post-Kottian attempts to emphasize the domestic smallness of the play-world) have typically been criticized for a perverse refusal of spectacle.

The balance in performance values seems almost equally difficult to get right: attempts to honour Shakespeare's language with an acting style adapted to the tragedy's loftier rhetorical flights have often seemed wooden and two-dimensional; while productions stressing the play's satirically accented realism are blamed for reducing its poetry of transcendence to empty hyperbole. Realizations of the two central characters, in particular, are said either to fall short of the glamour and heroic splendour with which Shakespeare's poetry invests them, or to miss the complexity which the play's multitude of con-flicting perspectives seems to require. The perfect Cleopatra, above all, begins to emerge as a creature of the extra-dramatic imagination—the strange contradictions of her character, the 'infinite variety' that so dazzles Enobarbus, seeming to put the role beyond the reach of any single performer. Observing that 'no production . . . seems ever to have provided a cor-relative to the text's poetic power,' Stanley Wells, after view-ing Adrian Noble's 1982 production, was driven to wonder if *Anthony and Cleopatra* were not merely a magnificent closet drama: 'Is the fault Shakespeare's? Is this a play which can be fully realised only in the theatre of the mind?'[1]

In the judgement of Bernard Shaw there was no question that the fault was indeed the dramatist's, and the gap between expectation and performance a function of his deficient dra-maturgy. For Shaw the tension between realism and poetry resulted from an attempt to cheat the audience's feelings; and he contrasted the sentimental indulgence of Shakespeare's tragedy with the sterner practice of such 'resolute tragi-comedians' as Strindberg and himself:

The very name of Cleopatra suggests at once a tragedy of Circe, with the horrible difference that whereas the ancient myth rightly repres-ents Circe as turning men into hogs, the modern romantic conven-tion would represent her as turning hogs into heroes . . . After giving a faithful picture of the soldier broken down by debauchery, and the

[1] *Times Literary Supplement,* 29 Oct. 1982, 1191.

typical wanton in whose arms such men perish, Shakespeare finally strains all his huge command of rhetoric and pathos to give a theatrical sublimity to the wretched end of the business, and to persuade foolish spectators that the world was well lost by the twain. Such falsehood is not to be borne except by the real Cleopatras and Antonys (and they are to be found in every public house) who would no doubt be glad enough to be transfigured by some such poet as immortal lovers . . . such maudlin tricks may impose on tea-drunkards, not on me.[1]

It is significant, however, that, in evoking the play's supposed rhetorical deceptions, Shaw should have found himself echoing not Shakespeare's language but the subtitle of Dryden's *All for Love* ('The World Well Lost').[2] For it can be argued that no play is actually more resolutely tragi-comic in its approach than *Anthony and Cleopatra*, 'a tragic experience embedded in a comic structure', as Janet Adelman has described it, whose 'entire tragic vision is subjected to the comic perspective'.[3] Indeed, it is surely no accident that when

[1] Bernard Shaw, Preface to *Three Plays for Puritans*, 1901 (London, 1946), pp. 29–30. Bradley's observation that Cleopatra becomes a tragic character only in the fifth act (*Oxford Lectures*, p. 299) has some bearing on Shaw's indignation. For a more sophisticated version of Shaw's attack, see H. A. Mason's two-part article on the 'magnificent subterfuges' of the play, '*Antony and Cleopatra*: (i) Angelic strength—Organic weakness?' and (ii) 'Telling *versus* Shewing,' *Cambridge Quarterly* 1 (1966), 209–36; 330–54—subsequently incorporated in his *Shakespeare's Tragedies of Love* (London, 1970). Cf. also Robert Heilman's dismissive account of the play's ending as illustrating the perfection of male fantasy—'the soul of the promiscuous woman faithful, in the end, to oneself alone'; see Robert B. Heilman, 'From Mine Own Knowledge: A Theme in the Late Tragedies,' *Centennial Review* 8 (1964), pp. 17–38 (p. 28)

[2] Significantly, Shaw's attack resembles a colourful paraphrase of Dr Johnson's more sober strictures on Dryden's tragedy: 'it has one fault equal to many, though rather moral than critical, that by admitting the romantic omnipotence of Love, he has recommended as laudable and worthy of imitation that conduct which, through all ages, the good have censored as vicious, and the bad despised as foolish', 'The Life of Dryden', from *Lives of the Poets*, ed. Mrs Alexander Napier (London, 1890), p. 381.

[3] *Common Liar*, p. 52. Cf. also Anne Barton, ' "Nature's piece 'gainst fancy": The Divided Catastrophe in *Antony and Cleopatra*', Inaugural Lecture, Bedford College, University of London, 1972. Unlike Adelman, for whom the play's multiple perspectives mean that 'we are simply not permitted the luxury of the tragic vision' (p. 49), Barton describes a tragic ending which turns precisely upon Cleopatra's triumph over Comedy, 'personified by that ribald and garrulous countryman who brings her asps concealed in his basket of figs'. For Barton it is the very fact that Cleopatra 'has walked through the fire of ridicule' that authenticates her final tableau: 'comedy simply flowers into tragedy' (p. 18).

Shaw complained about the dramatist's unscrupulous use of 'the undertaker's handkerchief, duly onioned with some pathetic phrase', he should have paraphrased the language of the play's own satirical commentator, Enobarbus: 'the tears live in an onion that should water this sorrow' (1.2.168–9).

In fact the moment we admit Enobarbus's cynical perspective, the high pathos of the lovers' ebbed fortunes threatens to collapse into one of those reductive burlesques in which Cleopatra will imagine herself and Anthony travestied on the stages of Rome:

> The quick comedians
> Extemporally will stage us, and present
> Our Alexandrian revels—Anthony
> Shall be brought drunken forth, and I shall see
> Some squeaking Cleopatra boy my greatness
> I'th'posture of a whore.

> 5.2.216–21

The daring metatheatrical flourish of her 'squeaking Cleopatra'—anachronistically invoking Elizabethan rather than Roman theatrical practice—risks shattering the whole grand illusion of the Queen's carefully staged death in order to remind us that in Shakespeare's playhouse every performance of the role was, in the most literal sense, a 'travesty' performed by a boy-actor in woman's attire.[1] *Anthony and Cleopatra* openly courts ironic alienation in a fashion reminiscent of Shakespeare's comedies with their extensive use of transvestite disguise; and the extent to which it does so may help to account for the surprising fact that, in the modern theatre, it has typically been those actresses cast *against type*—Edith Evans, Peggy Ashcroft, and Judi Dench—whose Cleopatras have been most admired.[2]

---

[1] For some discussion of the effect of this convention on Shakespeare's characterization of Cleopatra, see Granville-Barker, pp. 81–4. By contrast with Granville-Barker, Phyllis Rackin stresses how the boy-Cleopatra becomes a sign of art's power to transcend nature *through its very limits*, 'Shakespeare's Boy Cleopatra, the Decorum of Nature, and the Golden World of Poetry,' *PMLA* 87 (1972), pp. 201–11.

[2] On Evans's success in a 'triumph of classical acting', see Anthony Cookman's review (*Tatler and Bystander*, 15 Jan. 1947), reprinted in Brown, *Casebook*, p. 55.

Far from seeking to disguise the gulf between the high rhetoric in which the lovers clothe themselves and the harsh reality of their decline, Shakespeare, as Adelman and others have shown, goes to unusual lengths to expose it.[1] From the straining paradoxes of Philo's dramatized prologue, with its simultaneous inflation and deflation of Anthony's temperamental excesses, to the half-sceptical reservation of Caesar's 'O noble weakness' (5.2.342), we are repeatedly made aware of the difficulty of taking these lovers either at their own or at others' valuation.

In an odd way, then, the aura of disappointment which hangs over its stage history seems to be anticipated by the play itself. *Anthony and Cleopatra* begins, after all, with a dramatized prologue whose function, like that of many prologues, is to arouse certain expectations about the central characters. Anthony, in Philo's imagination, is a 'triple pillar of the world', a demi-god reminiscent of his heroic ancestor, Hercules, whose eyes glow 'like plated Mars', and whose heart so swells with courage that it 'burst[s] | The buckles on his breast'. Yet the hyperbolic imagery and confidently ascending martial rhythms of Philo's exordium are three times punctured by deliberate bathos:

> those his goodly eyes,
> That o'er the files and musters of the war
> Have glowed like plated Mars, *now bend, now turn*
> *The office and devotion of their view*
> *Upon a tawny front*; his captain's heart,
> Which in the scuffles of great fights hath burst
> The buckles on his breast, *reneges all temper,*
> *And is become the bellows and the fan*
> *To cool a gypsy's lust.*
>
> Take but good note, and you shall see in him
> The triple pillar of the world *transformed*
> *Into a strumpet's fool.*
>
> 1.1.2–10, 11–13 (emphases added)

The bathos of a martial heart successively reduced to a blacksmith's bellows and a courtesan's fan is given a start-

---

[1] *Common Liar*, pp. 11–12, 103–6, 167–8 and *passim*.

lingly burlesque life in the carefully placed visual pun of the stage direction 'eunuchs *fanning* her', which implicitly reduces the superbly masculine hero to a mere instrument of the emasculated drones who surround the queen. The effect, when combined with the oxymoronic conjunction of herculean 'pillar' and 'strumpet's fool', is to set up precisely the kind of tragi-comic tension that Shaw found wanting in the play. No sooner does the scene insist that we acknowledge Anthony's heroic stature, than it invites us to dismiss his high language of erotic intoxication as no better than the mimic posturing of a licensed fool. If Anthony's apocalyptic boasting ('Then must thou needs find out new heaven, new earth'; 'Let Rome in Tiber melt, and the wide arch | Of the ranged empire fall', 1.1.17, 35–6) consistently strives to redeem the ensuing scene from comic collapse, it will be deflated in turn by the prosaic interruption of the messenger ('News, my good lord, from Rome'), and by Cleopatra's own playful mockery ('Excellent falsehood'—an oxymoron which contains its own ironic bathos).[1]

To find an equivalent in Shakespeare for such an unexpected opening we have to look back five or six years to that strange hybrid drama *Troilus and Cressida*—another love tragedy played out against an epic contest of empires. *Troilus* is an elaborate exercise in dramatic and verbal anticlimax, an exploration of the art of sinking in tragic poetry, whose style lurches wildly between straining erotic hyperbole and the most prosaic bawdy, and whose largest heroic gestures habitually collapse into burlesque.[2] As the lofty claims of love

---

[1] Like her 'excellent dissembling' in 1.3, Cleopatra's reaction to Anthony's hyperbole effectively paraphrases Puttenham's paradoxical description of the figure, which he called 'the loud liar', as a '*great dissimulation*, because I mean nothing less than what I speak'. Cited in Adelman, ibid., p. 114 (italics added).

[2] Jacqueline Pearson's essay 'Romans and Barbarians: The Structure of Irony in Shakespeare's Roman Tragedies', in Malcolm Bradbury and David Palmer (eds.), *Shakespearian Tragedy*, Stratford-upon-Avon Studies 20 (London, 1984), 159–82, identifies 'calculated anti-climax' as a characteristic of the Roman tragedies generally, linking it to their use of 'irony . . . shifting perspectives, [and] disturbing juxtapositions' (p. 160). In *Anthony and Cleopatra* the technique is closely related to the recurrent 'sense of surrender, the drop from achievement to indifference' which John Bayley sees as so important in the treatment of the central love-relationship: 'the whole effect is one of sexual rise and fall, endorsing and yet also ironically contradicting the admiration

and chivalry are reduced to the chaotic indistinction of 'wars and lechery', *Troilus* seems positively to delight in confounding the 'promised largeness' of its own epic ambitions—as if to illustrate Agamemnon's reflections on the ironic gap between all ideal constructions and their realization in the imperfect material world:

> The ample proposition that hope makes
> In all designs begun on earth below
> Fails in the promised largeness . . . .
> Sith every action that hath gone before
> Whereof we have record, trial did draw
> Bias and thwart, not answering the aim
> And that unbodied figure of the thought
> That gave't surmisèd shape.

Troilus 1.3.3–17

Though it resists the earlier play's comprehensively satiric vision, *Anthony and Cleopatra* shares this paradoxical tendency to hollow out and undermine its own most cherished values.[1] As in *Troilus*, the opening scene foreshadows the way in which the principle of anticlimax will shape a great deal of the dramatic structure. This is true not merely of the shaping of numerous individual episodes—even so celebrated a rhetorical climax as Enobarbus's Cydnus speech suddenly gives way, as H. A. Mason noticed with some frustration, to

---

of Cleopatra as making hungry where most she satisfies' (*Shakespeare and Tragedy*, p. 135).

[1] For a reading which seeks to demonstrate 'that in mood and theme *Antony and Cleopatra* is very similar to the ironic view expressed in *Troilus and Cressida* that fair is fool, [and] that neither heaven nor spectator should care very much about what happens to the characters in the play because the absence of value to be lost makes the losses meaningless and untragic', see Richard L. Nochimson, 'The End Crowns All: Shakespeare's Deflation of Tragic Possibility in *Antony and Cleopatra*', *English*, 26 (1977), pp. 99–132. For John Danby, similarly (though he does not specifically invoke *Troilus*), the play falls short of tragic grandeur because of its sense of 'ripe-rottenness and hopelessness': 'the fourth and fifth acts . . . are not epiphanies. They are the ends moved to by that process whereby things rot themselves with motion—unhappy and bedizened and sordid, streaked with the mean, the ignoble, the contemptible': see '*Antony and Cleopatra*: A Shakespearian Adjustment', in *Elizabethan and Jacobean Poets* [*Poets on Fortune's Hill*] (London, 1964), pp. 128–51 (pp. 148, 150). Janet Adelman, by contrast, interprets *Anthony* as a play that ultimately 'undoes *Troilus and Cressida*'—see Janet Adelman, *Suffocating Mothers* (New York, 1992), p. 342 n. 59.

a scene-ending that makes the scene appear 'abrupt, shapeless and anticlimactic'[1]—but of much larger components of the design. The play's entire action, after all, is to turn upon the violent disappointment of 'promised largeness' at Actium, the hopelessly mismanaged battle which Shakespeare's careful reshaping of Plutarch places at the very centre of his play. The audience's expectation of this decisive trial of strength is worked up through the curiously wavering movement of the first two and a half acts: like the 'vagabond flag' of popular politics in Rome, the action moves 'to and back', seeming 'to rot itself with motion', and producing an intense desire for climactic resolution, which the sudden tumble of events beginning at Act 3, scene 5 promises, and then (just as abruptly) refuses to gratify. The great sea-fight, which continues through several pages of Plutarch's narrative, continuing even after Antonius's sudden departure, is here shrunk to a brief off-stage encounter that seems over almost before the frustrated land-commanders on stage are aware it has begun. Anthony's much bruited 'absolute soldiership' is reduced to 'the noble ruin of [Cleopatra's] magic' (3.10.18) before we have so much as seen him draw his celebrated 'sword Philippan'.

It is not for nothing that at the point of utmost humiliation the hero is made to recall the battle which gave that sword its name (3.11.35–40); for to appreciate the effect of deliberate anticlimax here it is only necessary to think of the narrative weight and dignity that *Julius Caesar* allows to the defeat of Brutus and Cassius at Philippi. And if Philippi is now remembered as the defining moment of Anthony's heroic presence and fullness, then Actium is its anti-type—the point at which he seems most entirely emptied out and absent from himself. Enobarbus insists scornfully on his 'emptiness' (3.13.36), while to Anthony it seems as if his very self had deserted itself:[2]

---

[1] Mason, 'Angelic Strength', p. 231; for further discussion of scenes in which hyperbole collapses into bathos (especially in the latter half of the play), see Honigmann, *Shakespeare: Seven Tragedies*, pp. 150–69, and Bevington, 'Introduction', pp. 17–21.

[2] For some very acute (though stylistically clotted) discussion of 'leaving' as the 'organising idea of the play', see H. W. Fawkner, *Shakespeare's Hyperontology: 'Antony and Cleopatra'* (Rutherford, NJ, 1990), p. 93 and *passim*.

I have fled myself . . .

>   Let that be left
> Which leaves itself . . .
>
> Leave me, I pray, a little—pray you now—
> Nay, do so; for indeed I have lost command . . .
>
>   3.11.7, 19–20, 22–3

This self-absence has been figured theatrically by his absence from the stage at the moment of crisis. We are forced to witness his defeat at second hand, through the eyes of baffled and incredulous subordinates, for whom he becomes a type of radical self-violation (3.10.22–3), his self-betrayal rendering suddenly concrete Philo's initial paradox of an Anthony who 'is not Anthony' (1.1.59): 'Had our general | Been what he knew himself, it had gone well' (3.10.25–6).

The effect of striking anticlimax, once again associated with self-loss, is repeated in Act 4 when, after the fleeting success of the first battle of Alexandria, Anthony prepares to face his great competitor for the last time. Once again the audience hears the off-stage alarums 'as at a sea-fight', but this time Anthony's ships go over to the enemy before the battle is even joined. The detail here is substantially Plutarch's, but Shakespeare's disposition of the material gives the first skirmish far greater structural prominence than it has in Plutarch's narrative (the scenes of preparation, combat, and triumph occupying roughly as much playing-time as the entire Actium sequence), as if to emphasize the inexplicable let down of the second day's surrender. The impression of anticlimax is further enhanced through the painfully prolonged spectacle of Anthony's death. The hero's attempt to clothe his dying in the rhetoric of erotic transcendence (pointedly echoing his own 'The nobleness of life is to do thus' from the opening love scene) collapses into a shocking bathos:

>   But I will be
> A bridegroom in my death, and run into't
> As to a lover's bed. Come then—and Eros,
> Thy master dies thy scholar: *to do thus*
> I learned of thee.
>   *He falls on his sword*
>   How? Not dead? Not dead?
>
>   4.15.99–103 (emphasis added)

It is a moment which deliberately courts embarrassed laughter from the audience; and the humiliation of the botched suicide is mercilessly drawn out as Anthony, begging helplessly for the guard to finish him off, is exposed to the final degradation of Dercetus' theft of his sword.[1] Even the ensuing death scene, the celebrated *Liebestod* which on the page seems so fully controlled by Anthony's stoic self-control and Cleopatra's plangent music of lament, lurches in performance between high poetry and the grossest physical awkwardness, as Cleopatra and her women struggle to haul up Anthony's mutilated body into the monument.[2]

The anticlimax of the hero's unheroic end is completed by Caesar's tribute to his dead rival, which flouts epideictic convention to register the victor's sense of slightly disdainful disappointment:

> The breaking of so great a thing should make
> A greater crack. The round world
> Should have shook lions into civil streets,
> And citizens to their dens.

> 5.1.14–17

Octavius is remembering the death of his adoptive father, Julius Caesar, when thunder and lightning split the heavens and lions indeed prowled the streets of Rome (*Caesar* 1.3); but to announce Anthony's demise there has been only the faint sound of music 'under the earth' as 'the god Hercules, whom Anthony loved' stole away from him (4.3.11, 14).

Cleopatra's own death, staged as a pageant of royal self-assertion ('Show me, my women, like a queen . . .', 5.2.227), is free from such obvious bathos. But even here the self-consciously theatrical language of the scene ('act', 'play', 'performed') serves as a reminder that this is a pageant acted out against the play's own ruthless questioning of theatrical display—an essentially comic scepticism of which the asp-bearing Clown, emissary of Antic Death, with his talk of honest women 'somewhat given to lie', is the last and most irreverent spokesman.

---

[1] According to Stanley Wells, Olivier included a marvellous piece of stage-business at this point: his sword having somehow fallen out of reach, he tried desperately—but failed—to recover it.

[2] See Appendix B.

THE DISLOCATION OF IDENTITY

Shakespeare's handling of Cleopatra's death scene is representative in a way that can help us to understand the mixed reception of this tragedy. Hers is the most self-consciously *performed*, the most elaborately gestural dying in all Shakespearian tragedy. While the tone and direction of the performance are controlled by her unfamiliar need to fix an identity that has hitherto revelled in its own elusiveness, the histrionic self-consciousness of the Queen's dying is altogether characteristic. Even its most intimate emotions seem tuned to the presence of an audience:

> I *see* him rouse himself
> To *praise my noble act* . . .
>
> *Dost thou not see* my baby at my breast,
> That sucks the nurse asleep?
>
> 5.2.283–4, 308–9 (emphases added)

By comparison, even Othello's notoriously theatrical projection of his fate onto the screen of public memory ('When you shall these unlucky deeds relate') seems an oddly inward matter, full of private meanings that remain opaque to the uncomprehending Venetian bystanders.[1] From a technical point of view, too, the strikingly exterior treatment of the scene is absolutely consistent with the play's method of realizing its central characters. For *Anthony and Cleopatra* is a work which almost completely eschews the device by which Shakespearian tragedy had hitherto achieved its most powerful psychological successes—soliloquy.[2] At the same time it is a

---

[1] Even Leavis, in the best-known attack on Othello's 'self-dramatization', notices the essentially inward turn of the performance: 'contemplating the spectacle of himself, Othello is overcome with the pathos of it'. See F. R. Leavis, 'Diabolic Intellect and the Noble Hero', in *The Common Pursuit* (Harmondsworth, 1962), pp. 136–59 (p. 152).

[2] The difference in approach from what he calls 'the tragedies of consciousness' is well discussed in ch. 5 of John Bayley's *Shakespeare and Tragedy*: Shakespeare's ancient world, Bayley remarks, 'is as flat and bright as a painted board' (p. 122). Linda Bamber, *Comic Women, Tragic Men* (Stanford, Calif., 1982) argues that the play's fundamentally masculine ideology excludes 'an inside view of Cleopatra' (p. 55), so that she remains Other rather than Self; but it seems to me highly questionable whether such an 'inside view' is available even of Anthony.

love-tragedy whose lovers (as if in defiance of the conventionally private nature of the genre) are never seen alone together,
but are always required to act out their passion in public—to
the point where this parading of mutual desire is felt as itself
a source of sexual excitement.[1]

The effect of this psychological exteriority, combined with
the essentially public nature of the lovers' passion, is at once
to deny the audience the full emotional identification with the
protagonists on which traditional Bradleian 'catharsis' depends, and to make the whole question of 'sincerity', of what
Cleopatra (or Anthony) 'really' feels a matter of constantly
teasing conjecture. If this does much to account for the
shimmering, enigmatic quality often admired in the play, it
also contributes to the sense, voiced by a number of distinguished critics as well as by reviewers, and even some actors,
that it falls somehow short of tragic expectation. H. A. Mason,
for example, complains of the 'stinted feeling' produced by the
play: 'I try to enter into the action but I am kept at a distance,
forced to be merely a watcher, a reporter with an almost
empty notebook.'[2] The play's fascination with rhetorical
surfaces, combined with its discontinuous, moment-by-
moment psychology, means that it is difficult to speak of
anything 'beneath' or 'behind' its language. Not surprisingly,
then, the most effective criticism of *Anthony and Cleopatra* has
often been that which concentrated on its formal aspects—
Janet Adelman's analysis of its rhetorical patterns, or Anne
Barton's exploration of its unorthodox double ending.[3] Conventional explicatory criticism often founders in its attempt to
penetrate the marvellously painted surface: either it falls back
on the extravagant rhetorical redundancy with which Wilson
Knight sought to match the work's own transcendental
flights; or it resorts to the irritable reductivism that confuses

---

[1] I take it that the ostentatiously public nature of their affair is partly
what Jonathan Dollimore has in mind when he stresses the interpenetration
of sexuality and power in the play: 'if *Antony and Cleopatra* celebrates anything
it is not the love which transcends power but the sexual infatuation which
foregrounds it'; see Jonathan Dollimore, *Radical Tragedy: Religion, Ideology and
Power in the Drama of Shakespeare and his Contemporaries* (Brighton, 1984),
p. 217.

[2] 'Angelic Strength', p. 219.   [3] See above. p. 70 n. 3.

the complex play of surfaces with deliberate or unwitting superficiality.

To the distinguished nineteenth-century actress Ellen Terry, for example, the problem of satisfactorily interpreting the part of Cleopatra lay less in any actual psychological complexity than in the Queen's histrionic ability to create the illusion of deep feeling by putting 'all her emotions into words'. In spite of this eloquence, however, Terry found that 'she gives ... the impression sometimes of saying more than she feels'. The dramatist had clearly conceived the Queen 'as a woman with a shallow nature', she concluded, 'and·I should like to see her played as such':

> If she were not idealized in the theatre, it would be clear to us that Shakespeare has done what no other writer, novelist, dramatist or poet has done—told the truth about the wanton. Yes, Cleopatra is that, and if she is represented as a great woman with a great and sincere passion for Antony, the part does not hang together.[1]

Yet if Cleopatra is played as Terry recommended, the play is already more than half-way to becoming the melodrama of middle-aged infatuation that her friend Bernard Shaw insisted it was—a kind of seventeenth-century *Blue Angel*. Her approach, however, was grounded in a psychological naturalism which we can now see as inappropriate to the play: indeed it may well be that the part was never meant to 'hang together' with the self-consistency that the nineteenth century regarded as 'natural'. For, as recent feminist criticism has insisted, the psychology of female characters in Renaissance drama can never be wholly detached from the notion of women as biologically 'governed by the moon', and thus so passionately given to change as to be virtually incapable of unified subjectivity.[2] The two Cleopatras of Enobarbus's great set-piece in Act 2, scene 2—the mortal Venus at Cydnus and the child-queen hopping forty paces through the streets

[1] Ellen Terry (c. 1911) in John Russell Brown (ed.), *Shakespeare: 'Antony and Cleopatra', A Casebook* (London, 1968), p. 54.

[2] For variously accented feminist interpretations of the literary consequences of this belief, see Bamber, *Comic Women, Tragic Men*; Catherine Belsey, *The Subject of Tragedy* (London, 1985); Kathleen McLuskie, *Renaissance Dramatists* (Atlantic Highlands, NJ, 1989); and Dympna Callaghan, *Woman and Gender in Renaissance Tragedy* (Atlantic Highlands, NJ, 1989).

of Alexandria—no more 'hang together' than the harridan who abuses the messenger in 2.5 'hangs together' with the supremely self-confident courtesan who flirts with Thidias in 3.13, or this conniving and treacherous 'boggler' with the lyrical elegiast and regal suicide of Act 5. But to seventeenth-century audiences the seemingly 'infinite variety' of her performances may not have appeared quite as exceptional as it does to us; for, however extravagant the admiration or indignation it invites from those who are exposed to it, Cleopatra's power of metamorphosis arguably amounts to nothing more than an extreme and self-delighting version of quintessential female changeability—a changeability which contemporary prejudice habitually associated with the deceitful proteanism of theatrical performance.[1] Indeed Cleopatra's own self-consciously 'masculine' resolve to die 'after the high Roman fashion' seems to account for her own mutability in just this way, as she turns her back at once on her own female nature ('I have nothing | Of woman in me,' 5.2.238-9), and upon the moon-goddess, Isis, who has been her patron ('now the fleeting moon | No planet is of mine,' ll. 240-1).

However, the opposition between female/Egyptian mutability and male/Roman self-consistency is by no means as absolute as might at first appear; and while the play indubitably entertains such stereotypes it is far too restless to remain content with them. Part of this restlessness indeed arises directly from an embroilment with sceptical tendencies in late Renaissance moral philosophy that tended to call in question the very possibility of coherent selfhood, regardless of gender. The great popularizer of such ideas was Michel Eyquem de Montaigne whose footsteps can be tracked everywhere in early seventeenth-century drama, not least in Shakespeare; but

---

[1] See e.g. Jyotsna Singh, 'Renaissance Anti-theatricality, Antifeminism and Shakespeare's *Antony and Cleopatra*', *Renaissance Drama*, ns 21 (1990), pp. 99–121; Madelon Sprengnether, 'The Boy Actor and Femininity in *Antony and Cleopatra*', in Norman N. Holland, Sidney Homan, and Bernard J. Paris (eds.), *Shakespeare's Personality* (Berkeley, Calif., 1989), pp. 191–205. Jean E. Howard, 'Renaissance Anti-theatricality and the Politics of Gender and Rank in *Much Ado About Nothing*', in Jean E. Howard and Marion O'Connor (eds.), *Shakespeare Reproduced: The Text in History and Ideology* (London, 1987), 163–87; and Katherine E. Maus, ' "Playhouse Flesh and Blood": Sexual Ideology and the Restoration Actress,' *ELH* 46 (1979), pp. 595–617.

Montaigne's own thought was substantially influenced by a work that Shakespeare seems to have consulted whilst working on *Anthony and Cleopatra*, Plutarch's collection of essays, the *Moralia*.[1]

In plays like *Hamlet* and *Troilus and Cressida* Shakespeare had already shown a fascination with the discontinuous and histrionic nature of identity explored in Montaigne's *Essays*, where the 'self' was exposed as a haphazard collage of incongruous impulses. Hamlet's violent oscillations of mood, his tormented self-scrutiny and baffled questioning of the gap between motive and action, represent an attempt to explore Montaignean subjectivity from within, as Troilus's anguished confrontation with Cressida's infidelity ('This is, and is not Cressid') probes its contradictions from without. *Anthony and Cleopatra*, it could be argued, goes a step further by simply taking Montaigne's psychological paradoxes for granted, and in the process throwing the perplexity experienced by Hamlet and Troilus back upon the audience—hence the interminable (and fundamentally indeterminable) arguments about whether Cleopatra is 'really' true to Anthony, whether she is 'really' bargaining with Caesar or merely playing for time, and so on. It is essential to recognize, however, that such perplexities are by no means exclusively provoked by Cleopatra,

---

[1] Particularly important for Montaigne was the essay 'What Signifieth this Word Ei, engraven over the door of *Apollo*'s temple in the city of *Delphi*', whole sections of which are incorporated or paraphrased in the most thorough account of his sceptical philosophy, 'The Apology of Raymond Sebond'. For Plutarch the self is a creature of Heraclitan flux: 'we are engendered many, according as the matter glideth.... For were it not so, but that we continue still the same, how is it that we take delight now in these things, whereas we joyed before in others? How is it that we love and hate, praise and dispraise contrary things? ... retain not the same visage, one countenance, one mind and one thought? ... and look who is changed, he continueth not the same; and if he be not the same, he is not at all' (p. 1362). For evidence that another essay in the collection, 'Of Isis and Osiris', was among the texts which Shakespeare consulted to enlarge his knowledge of Egyptian mythology, see Commentary, notes to 3.2.20, 3.6.17, and Adelman, *Suffocating Mothers*, pp. 337–8, nn. 37, 38, 43. The two essays are related to the extent that Plutarch's Isis, who 'receiveth all forms, and becometh all manner of things' is a kind of icon of the fluid selfhood explored in 'What Signifieth this Word Ei'; and it seems plausible that Shakespeare's reading of the *Moralia* in Holland's translation (*The Philosophy, commonly called The Morals*, trans. Philemon Holland (London, 1603)) helped to reinvigorate his interest in discontinuous identity.

but involve other major characters too—Anthony, first and foremost, but also Caesar, and even, it could be argued, figures of the second rank, like Enobarbus and Pompey.

In Caesar's case, for example, we are faced with the question of how to assess his motives in the matter of Octavia: is she *simply* the tool of political expediency? Does his reaction to her abandonment by Anthony spring from genuine fraternal affection, mixed with injured family pride, or does it merely mask pleasure at Anthony's having given him the handsome occasion for war on which he has always gambled?[1] Caesar's valediction to the dead Anthony presents similar difficulties: is it merely a display of magnanimity for public consumption, or does it reveal pangs of authentic regret—an emotion as unexpected and 'strange' as the compassion which overwhelms Webster's Flamineo after the murder of his brother (*The White Devil* 5.4.111–13)?[2]

Anthony's character confronts an audience with even more puzzling uncertainties: from the moment that Philo introduces him as an Anthony who 'is not Anthony' (1.1.59), they must face the problem of distinguishing what the Roman world takes to be the 'real' man from the emasculated shadow to which Cleopatra has allegedly reduced him. There is the puzzle of reconciling his cowardice at Actium with the forlorn heroism of Alexandria (both of them, oddly enough, 'stirred by Cleopatra'); and there are the radical ambiguities that attach to his marriage with Octavia or to the assassination of Pompey. Given that the marriage is an openly political one, should we necessarily accept Enobarbus's cynical assessment that Anthony 'married but his occasion here' (2.6.129–30)? Or should we rather suppose that Anthony's wish to marry 'for my peace' is quite as genuine as the desire to abandon everything for 'my pleasure' in the East which almost instantly

---

[1] For Bradley such uncertainties reveal merely a lack of clarity in Shakespeare's conception of the character (*Oxford Lectures*, pp. 289–90)

[2] Political readings of the play usually opt for the former solution; Freudian readings, stressing the Oedipal relation between Caesar and Anthony, require the latter—see Adelman, *Suffocating Mothers*, pp. 181–3. For Adelman, however, the tone of Caesar's eulogy is complicated by the need to 'subdue Antony's magical presence' and cut him down to size. John Bayley, from a different perspective, suggests that 'Caesar *is* touched . . . but he turns his feeling, like everything else, to good use' (*Shakespeare and Tragedy*, p. 129).

succeeds it (2.3)? Should we take at face value Eros's description of Anthony's rage against 'that his officer | That murdered Pompey' (3.5.17–18), or suppose that (like Caesar's explanations for the coup against Pompey) this too is a gesture for public consumption? The text constantly presents us with such extremes of possibility, without giving us the means to decide between them; and the effect is often to leave the audience torn like Octavia between irreconcilable alternatives: 'no midway | 'Twixt these extremes at all' (3.4.19–20). The issues are made especially difficult to determine because of the fundamentally exterior, instrumental notion of selfhood implicit in the heroic ideal, its insistence that character is discovered in action—a point to which I shall return later. As in the case of Caesar, different theatrical interpretations have suggested different answers to all these questions; but it may be that the proper solution is not to resolve the ambiguities but to emphasize them. In so far as any answers are suggested in the text itself, rather than tilting towards one solution or another (or even a compromise between them), they tend towards a paradoxical insistence on the successive (or even simultaneous) truth of the contradictory alternatives.

'He whom you saw yesterday so boldly venturous,' wrote Montaigne, in a passage that might almost have been inspired by the vagaries of Anthony's career, 'wonder not if you see him a dastardly meacock tomorrow next . . . We are all framed of flaps and patches and of so shapeless and diverse a contexture, that every piece and every moment playeth his part. And there is as much difference found between us and our selves, as there is between our selves and [an]other.' The 'self', in effect, is no more than the site of endless theatrical self-inventions, and one should '*esteem it a great matter, to play but one man*'.[1] In Montaigne's analysis the self cannot be expected to 'hang together' in the fashion assumed by psychological naturalism, because it has no fixed and substantial existence. Since within them 'all is but changing, motion,

[1] 'Of the Inconstancy of our Actions,' in L. C. Harmer (ed.), *Montaigne's Essays*, trans. John Florio, 3 vols. (London, 1910), 2.1. 11, 14 (italics original). For a lucid account of Shakespeare's absorption of Montaignean ideas of 'discontinuous identity' see the first two chapters of Dollimore's *Radical Tragedy*.

and inconstancy' (2.2.9), human beings 'have no communication with being', but subsist in a perpetually fluid state of 'becoming':

In few there is no constant existence ... of our being. ... for every human nature is ever in the middle between being born and dying; giving nothing of it self but an obscure appearance and shadow. ... And if perhaps you fix your thought to take its being; it would be even, as if one should go about to grasp the water; for, how much the more he shall close and press that, which by its own nature is ever gliding, so much the more he shall loose what he would hold and fasten.[1]

It is no accident that Cleopatra, whom the language of the play repeatedly identifies with the flux of 'becoming', should be associated with water, and especially with the gliding river Nile; nor that Anthony, as he succumbs to the contradictions of his own nature, should feel his heroic identity become 'indistinct | As water is in water' (4.15.10–11).[2] For what the play does is to pit a classical 'Roman' notion of fixed and stable identity, embodied in the heroic image of Anthony, against the incarnation of its Montaignean opposite in Cleopatra, and to expose the classical ideal as chimerical and ultimately self-destructive.[3] Indeed, as Cleopatra's own assumption of 'marble constancy' in Act 5 makes perfectly explicit, the monumental singleness of being which knits together the flaps and patches of the self to 'shackle accident and bolt-up change', is something achievable only in death.

Although Anthony may sometimes speak as if there were a 'real' Cleopatra, against the 'truth' of whose being her falsehoods might be measured ('what's her name | Since she was

---

[1] Montaigne, 'The Apology of Raymond Sebond,' *Essays*, 2.12. 323. This passage is substantially lifted from Plutarch's 'What Signifieth this Word Ei', pp. 1361–2.

[2] Compare Plutarch: 'what is it (in truth) to be? Surely to be eternal—that is to say, which never had being in generation, nor shall have end by corruption; and in which time never worketh any mutation. For a movable and mutable thing is time, appearing (as it were) in a shadow with the matter which runneth and floweth continually, never remaining stable, permanent and solid', 'What Signifieth this Word Ei', p. 1362.

[3] It is the fact that Cleopatra's 'self' is so unashamedly the sum of the parts she plays that makes her 'Not know me yet?' so bafflingly opaque; it is also this which renders Mason's irritable complaints about her not being 'fully "there" ' behind the theatrical rhetoric of her role so much beside the point.

Cleopatra?' 3.13.98–9), it is of course axiomatic to the Roman fascination with her 'infinite variety' that no such stable centre should exist in her. For a culture narrowly obsessed with temperance and measure, she represents the bounty of an absolute excess in which destruction and creation are indistinguishable ('the higher Nilus swells, | The more it promises,' 2.7.20–1); for a society preoccupied with limits, control, and boundaries, she embodies a fantasy of the limitless, the 'infinite variety' of a world without end, in which desire, rather than consuming, is perpetually renewed by what it feeds on, and where more of the same is always something different:

CLEOPATRA
  If it be love indeed, tell me how much.
ANTHONY
  There's beggary in the love that can be reckoned.
CLEOPATRA
  I'll set a bourn how far to be beloved.
ANTHONY
  Then must thou needs find out new heaven, new earth.

1.1.14–17

[ENOBARBUS]
Age cannot wither her, nor custom stale
Her infinite variety; other women cloy
The appetites they feed, but she makes hungry
Where most she satisfies.

2.2.242–5

From the Roman point of view these things are the sign of Cleopatra's radical otherness—an otherness which is registered in both cultural and gender terms by a world which defines its own 'virtue', conceived as masculine, self-restrained, and rational, against an 'Eastern' voluptuousness, imagined as feminine, histrionic, capricious, and dangerously fecund. Such oppositions have been read as expressing the play's uncomplicated endorsement of racialist and sexist essentialisms.[1] However, we have only to put Cleopatra's playful sense

---

[1] Linda Fitz [Woodbridge], in 'Egyptian Queens and Male Reviewers' analyses what she takes to be male misreadings of the play's construction of femininity. But for readings of the play which see it as endorsing racial,

of herself as 'with Phoebus' amorous pinches black' (1.5.28) alongside Othello's anguished 'Haply for I am black' (*Othello* 3.3.267) to recognize how relatively insignificant (despite the early prominence of Philo's sneers at the 'tawny . . . gypsy') is the issue of racial difference in *Anthony and Cleopatra*. On the other hand, it is certainly true that gender is foregrounded throughout, and systematically associated with cultural difference. But the important point to register here is the degree to which the stereotypes involved are the product of Roman perception; and while the Roman view is given a strategic advantage by the way in which the speeches of Philo and Caesar enclose the whole action, it scarcely goes unchallenged.

Indeed Jyotsna Singh has shown how Cleopatra's theatricality, through its 'playful disruptions of . . . gender polarities' significantly undermines the Roman ideology of order, revealing it as merely 'a contingent fiction, subject to revision', and replacing its exclusive 'myth of a stable and unified male subject' with an inclusive notion of all human identity as 'multiple, varied, and protean'.[1] Singh's reading of the play, which finds Cleopatra's histrionics significantly mirrored in Anthony's own 'excellent dissembling', is supported from a slightly different angle by Gil Harris's argument that 'the relationships between Egypt and Rome, Cleopatra and Antony, are less ones of opposition than of specularity'. The point is subtly emphasized by the latent irony in Enobarbus's 'she makes hungry | Where most she satisfies', which, as Harris points out, paraphrases a famous tag from Ovid's *Metamorphoses: inopem me copia fecit* (my plenty makes me poor).[2]

---

cultural, and gender stereotypes, see Ania Loomba, *Gender, Race, Renaissance Drama* (Manchester, 1989), pp. 75–9, Leonard Tennenhouse, *Power on Display: The Politics of Shakespeare's Genres*, pp. 141–6, and (less straightforwardly) Hughes-Hallett, *Cleopatra*, pp. 132–59.

[1] Singh, 'Renaissance Anti-theatricality', 109, 117.

[2] See Jonathan Gil Harris's so-far unpublished paper ' "Hadst thou Narcissus in thy face": Rethinking Gender and Difference in *Antony and Cleopatra*'. Harris cites a number of other instances in which Ovid's plenty/poverty metaphor is transformed into one of feeding/hunger. The Narcissus allusion might be capable of a different interpretation, of course, in the light of Honigmann's observations on the mirror-like effect of the language which makes Cleopatra seem to 'bask . . . so unashamedly in self-admiration . . . as if she and sex are one, as if paying tribute to herself' (*Shakespeare: Seven Tragedies*, p. 158).

As Narcissus gazes adoringly at his own watery reflection, which at once gives back his own desire and yet bafflingly eludes his embrace, he coins this paradoxical trope of deprivation-in-abundance, which Enobarbus appropriates and transforms to evoke Cleopatra's inexhaustible desirability. Scanning Enobarbus's eulogy in the light of the play's repeated identification of desire with deprivation and absence, Harris notices how Cleopatra features in its vivid play of synaesthesic imagery only as a missing centre. Precisely because she 'beggar[s] all description', Cleopatra becomes a kind of 'gap in nature'—'a suggestive figure for the intolerable absence, or vacuum, into which Roman desire imperially projects itself'. She is, as it were, the very site of that 'vacancy' in Anthony, which, according to Octavius, he 'fill[s] . . . with his voluptuousness' (1.4.25–6). Thus Harris finds in Cleopatra's description of Pompey's rapt gaze ('great Pompey | Would stand and make his eyes grow in my brow— | There would he anchor his aspect, and die | With looking on his life', 1.5.31–4) a perfect description of the 'trajectory of narcissistic desire' apparent in Anthony himself:

This trajectory prompts a critical re-evaluation of those very qualities which audiences and readers have not only attributed to Cleopatra, but also believed to be representative of a transcending femininity. These allegedly female qualities now demand to be understood as displaced, or misrecognised, *Roman* (and hence male) characteristics. A particularly good example is Cleopatra's alleged 'infinite variety.' The impression of her 'variety' is in part created by the panoply of subject positions she is accorded by the alternately desiring and disgusted Antony . . . Cleopatra's 'variety' provides the specular image—is, perhaps, the very *effect*—of Antony's own.[1]

More speculatively, Harris proposes that the effect he describes will have been brought home to the Jacobean audience by the self-referential conceit in Act 5 when the boy-actor playing the Queen is made to envisage a theatrical travesty in which

[1] Compare Adelman's perception of how 'oddly inessential' Cleopatra comes to seem to the Oedipal struggle acted out between Caesar and Anthony: 'If we read the play backwards from [Caesar's] response to Antony's death, then the Roman official line—that Antony was destroyed by Cleopatra's entrapment—begins to look like a cover-up: if Cleopatra had not been there, *Caesar's Rome would have had to invent her*' (*Suffocating Mothers*, p. 183; my emphasis).

'some squeaking Cleopatra' will 'boy [her] greatness' (5.2.220):
here they might disconcertingly recognize 'the spectacle of an
exotic feminine Other suddenly revealed as the same'.

THE PLAY OF PERSPECTIVE: ENOBARBUS AS CHORIC FOOL

Whatever its precise effect on Jacobean playgoers, such reflexive wit has a calculatedly alienating effect which is wholly
consistent with the play's habit of estranging its audience
from the central characters in ways that suggest how much
they are indeed the products of what others see in them.[1] It
does this typically by the use of choric or pseudo-choric
characters whose commentary, not unlike the gestures of the
sprecher figure in mannerist painting, serves to push the main
action back into a perspective frame.[2] The most striking
example of this device occurs in the dramatized prologue of
the opening scene, where Philo and Demetrius act like the
presenters of an illustrative play within the play. The lovers'
entry is ushered in by Philo with an urgently demonstrative
gesture ('Take but good note . . . Behold and see', 1.1.11–13)
that gathers in the audience and invites them to view the
main action as a dramatic inset, a piece of self-conscious
performance whose rhetorical protestations they are forced to
measure against both the criticisms of these Roman onlookers
and the evidence of their own eyes.

This way of introducing the play helps to nourish a habit
of detached observation in the audience which is sustained
throughout by innumerable variations on its pseudo-choric

---

[1] The idea was by no means a new one in Shakespeare of course, but is
extensively elaborated by Ulysses in *Troilus and Cressida* (3.3.91–4) and Cassius
in *Julius Caesar* (1.2.69–72).

[2] In *Common Liar* (pp. 31–4) Adelman draws attention to the recurrence
of this device in the play, finding 'partial or complete framing' in no fewer
than twelve scenes. The resulting multiplication of quasi-choric commentary
'forcibly dissociates us from the lovers', so that *Anthony and Cleopatra*, uniquely
among Shakespeare's tragedies, compels its audience to 'live outside [the
protagonists'] immediate universe and see them from perspectives which are
alien to them' (p. 40). Cyrus Hoy's 'Jacobean Tragedy and the Mannerist
Style,' *SSu* 26 (1973), 49–67 contains a brief but suggestive analysis of
Anthony and Cleopatra comparing aspects of its technique to the conventions
of mannerist painting, including the use of the *sprecher* (pp. 62–4). Cf. also
John Greenwood, *Shifting Perspectives and the Stylish Style: Mannerism in
Shakespeare and his Jacobean Contemporaries* (Toronto, 1988), pp. 54, 80.

technique. These particularly involve Enobarbus, whose framing role is established at the beginning of 1.2 by his sardonic
interjections and equally eloquent silence during the frivolous
banter with the Soothsayer. Structurally speaking, Enobarbus's function is close to that of the satiric clowns of earlier
tragedies:[1] on one level he is a kind of civil Thersites, scoffing
at state and mocking the attitudinizing of the great. Again
and again his comments and asides, like those of Thersites,
prick the bubbles of lofty pretension to produce those moments
of comic bathos that are so characteristic of this play:

ANTHONY Fulvia is dead.
ENOBARBUS Fulvia?
ANTHONY Dead.
ENOBARBUS Why sir, give the gods a thankful sacrifice .... This grief
is crowned with consolation ...

1.2.157-67

AGRIPPA (*aside to Enobarbus*) Why, Enobarbus,
When Anthony found Julius Caesar dead
He cried almost to roaring; and he wept,
When at Philippi he found Brutus slain.
ENOBARBUS (*aside to Agrippa*)
That year, indeed, he was troubled with a rheum.

3.2.54-8

Like Thersites too, Enobarbus frequently voices a cynical
disillusionment which strips away the hyperbolic rhetoric of
love and martial prowess to expose in both the ungoverned
play of mere appetite. It is Enobarbus, more than anyone,
who gives the play's pervasive imagery of hunger and feeding
the satiric edge which we are to recognize, unmetaphored, in
the grossly competitive carousal on Pompey's galley (2.7).[2]

---

[1] It is conceivable that Enobarbus's part was actually doubled with that
of the Clown who brings the asps in 5.2, in which case it may have been
meant for Robert Armin, famous for his melancholy fools. The doubling would
give an odd comic poignancy to the Clown's puns on erotic dying, with their
recollection of Enobarbus's bawdy in 1.2, as well as to his description of
woman as 'a dish for the gods' (5.2.273) which adapts and transforms Enobarbus's offhand reference to Cleopatra as Anthony's 'Egyptian dish' (2.6.125).
[2] For a more extensive analysis of food imagery in the play, which,
however, overstresses its association with Egyptian sensuality, see Maurice
Charney's chapter on 'The Imagery of *Antony and Cleopatra*' in *Shakespeare's
Roman Plays* (Cambridge, Mass., 1961), pp. 79-141 (pp. 102-7).

It is he who identifies Cleopatra as Anthony's 'Egyptian dish' (2.6.125), 'monstrous matter of feast' to be devoured at a public banquet (2.2.189, 243–5). His dismissive satire prepares the way for Anthony's embittered travesty of Cleopatra's image of herself as 'a morsel for a monarch' (1.5.31)—'I found you as a morsel, cold upon | Dead Caesar's trencher . . . a fragment | Of Gneius Pompey's' (3.13.117–19)—much as Thersites's scorn prepares the way for Troilus's nauseated reduction of Cressida to 'The fragments, scraps, the bits and greasy relics | Of her o'ereaten faith' (*Troilus* 5.2.162–3). And it is Enobarbus who reduces the whole epic of empire to a terrifying image of omnivorous consumption, reminiscent of *Troilus and Cressida*'s 'universal wolf' of appetite which 'last eat[s] up itself' (*Troilus* 1.3.124):[1]

> Then, world, thou hast a pair of chops, no more,
> And throw between them all the food thou hast,
> They'll grind the one the other.
>
> 3.5.12–14

What such satire forces us to recognize, in a peculiarly brutal way, is the profound entanglement of sexuality and power in this play: if Cleopatra is the exotic banquet, spiced with 'cloyless sauce', on which Anthony gorges until he is poisoned, Octavia is meat tossed into the saurian maw of power. In Enobarbus's analysis, the erotic is either the helpless instrument of power, or its dangerous adversary, another form of power—as Cleopatra herself, whose hand 'kings | Have lipped, and trembled kissing' (2.5.29–30),[2] is the first to recognize. However Anthony may fantasise about living 'a private man in Athens' (3.12.16), the nostalgic notion of staking out such a private space is bound to prove chimerical in a world which, as Octavia discovers, allows 'no midway | 'Twixt these extremes at all' (3.4.19–20).

---

[1] L. C. Knights, *Some Shakespearean Themes* (London, 1959), p. 147, is inclined to see the central love-affair in this Thersitean fashion when he writes that 'the continued references to feasting . . . serve to bring out the element of repetition and monotony in a passion which, centring on itself, is self-consuming'.

[2] With its ambiguous suggestions of both eating and submission, the gesture of hand-kissing, highlighted again in Cleopatra's exchange with the 'feeder' Thidias (3.13.75–85), perfectly symbolizes the ambiguous interplay of sexuality and power on which she trades.

Yet if Enobarbus knows the play's extremes, he is far from being himself an extremist. His attitudes towards Anthony and Cleopatra, in particular, oscillate between worldly cynicism and nostalgic admiration in a way that closely matches (and partly accounts for) the wavering pulse of the play's own judgements; and if Anthony has difficulty matching his actions to the heroic rhetoric in which he is invested, Enobarbus has similar difficulty reconciling his actions with his satiric insights. In this, as in other things, he is less a Thersitean satyr-satirist (or even H. A. Mason's 'more [aristocratic and] elegant Iago')[1] than a more rational kinsman of Lear's Fool—the ambivalent spokesman of a common sense that will ultimately break his heart. Enobarbus's role as a kind of licensed fool is highlighted by his sardonic interventions in the political bartering of 2.2, where he answers Anthony's rebuke with a paraphrase of the Fool's 'Truth's a dog [that] must to kennel' (*The Tragedy of King Lear* 1.4.110), allegorizing himself as *Veritas*: 'That Truth should be silent, I had almost forgot' (2.2.113). But like the Fool's, his 'Truth' is an ambiguous thing, his troth to Anthony pulling increasingly against the arid verities of common sense, each mocking the other as a common liar. Like the Fool he knows the wisdom of letting go one's hold when a great wheel runs down the hill (*Lear* 2.2.245–6); and like the Fool he chooses to follow the fool's counsel of loyalty:

> The loyalty well held to fools does make
> Our faith mere folly; yet he that can endure
> To follow with allegiance a fall'n lord
> Does conquer him that did his master conquer,
> And earns a place i'th'story.

> 3.13.42–6

Such following, however, is a rational *non sequitur* which Enobarbus's common sense eventually forces him to recognize as self-cancelling ('Mine honesty and I begin to square ... When valour preys on reason, | It eats the sword it fights with. I will seek | Some way to leave him' 3.13.41, 199–201). Yet to leave the fool's path and follow the logic of self-interest,

---

[1] Mason, 'Angelic Strength', p. 218.

Enobarbus will discover, only entraps him in even more
destructive self-contradiction:[1]

> Throw my heart
> Against the flint and hardness of my fault,
> Which being dried with grief, will break to powder,
> And finish all foul thoughts.

4.10.15–18

When the 'foul thoughts' of a master-leaver, and the 'fool
thoughts' of a sentimental follower, indistinguishable in Elizabethan pronunciation, lead impartially to a contradictory
impasse, all that remains is for Enobarbus, like the Fool before
him, to leave the play. Unlike the Fool, however, who simply
disappears 'to bed at noon', Enobarbus is overwhelmed by a
sense of nostalgic belatedness that tints his departure with
quite different significance.

Enobarbus's frustration, his entanglement in contradiction,
mirrors the audience's own; but his despair ultimately tilts
them against the shallow resolutions of common sense. This
happens as a result of the play's most daring stroke, which
is to make this hardened old sweat the spokesman not just
for the quotidian truths associated with Demetrius's 'common
liar', but for the 'excellent falsehoods' of hyperbole. It is the
Cydnus speech which establishes the habitually prosaic Enobarbus as one of the three great poetic voices of hyperbole in
the play. In his *Arte of English Poesie*, George Puttenham,
while he identified this overreaching figure as 'the loud liar',
nevertheless insisted on its capacity to speak a paradoxical
kind of truth: 'it must needs be a great dissimulation, because
I mean nothing less than that I speak'.[2] What Enobarbus's
desertion and death bring home is how much the 'great
dissimulation' of hyperbole belongs to the realm of nostalgia,
that its 'truths' are of a kind only warrantable by deprivation
or death. From this arises the play's preoccupation with

---

[1] The play's paradoxes of 'following-in-leaving' and 'leaving-in-following'
are extensively explored in Fawkner, *Shakespeare's Hyperontology*—see esp. ch.
2, 'To Follow Faster'. Cf. also Patricia Parker's dazzling explorations of
'following', 'sequence', and the *non sequitur* in *Literary Fat Ladies: Gender,
Order, Rule* (London, 1987), ch. 6 'Motivated Rhetorics: Gender, Order, Rule',
pp. 97–125, and in 'Preposterous Events', *SQ* 43 (1992), pp. 186–213.
[2] Puttenham, p. 192, cited in Adelman, *Common Liar*, p. 114.

'leaving', its strange intoxication with 'greatness going off' (4.14.6), and its sense of the peculiar desolation of coming after, when 'there is nothing left remarkable | Beneath the visiting moon' (4.16.69–70). In an excess of magnanimity, a kind of enacted hyperbole, Anthony sends Enobarbus's treasure after him, a visible reminder of all that he has irremediably left behind, and the effect is to make this fugitive feel utterly abandoned, to destroy him. For such giving is also a calling to account (a much more exacting counterpart, in the play's thematizing of service and reward, of Cleopatra's scene of accounting with Seleucus), an invocation of the archaic code of feudal loyalty so absolute that only Enobarbus's death can answer it. Its real remorselessness is registered in a remarkable piece of word-play: as Enobarbus sees what (and where) his leaving has left him, he discovers in the rich 'mine' of Anthony's generosity the explosive undermining of an Elizabethan siege-work ('O Anthony, | Thou mine of bounty. ... This blows my heart', 4.6.31–3). The figure perfectly embodies the way in which the hyperbolic yearning of nostalgia becomes implicated in death. It is also, of course, another reworking of the Narcissus paradox, *inopem me copia fecit*; and the paradox embraces the giver as well as the receiver of this ambiguous largesse. For Anthony's gesture is at once 'full' with magnanimity, and yet as rhetorically 'empty' as the nostalgic theatre of farewell which Enobarbus recognized as designed merely 'to make his followers weep' (4.2.24).[1]

THE RHYTHMS OF NOSTALGIA

'I am so lated in the world that I | Have lost my way for ever,' Anthony laments after the catastrophic self-betrayal of Actium (3.11.3–4); and his reaction serves to remind us that the nostalgic feeling of belatedness is by no means confined to Enobarbus. It belongs to a widely noticed aspect of the play's imaginative vision which is closely connected to the pattern

---

[1] Such fullness-in-emptiness, as Rosalie Colie recognized, was inscribed even in the lavish 'Asiatic' style of oratory which Antonius was said to have preferred to the restrained 'Attic' manner favoured by Roman orators: for the Asiatic style was described as at once *superfluens* (overflowing) and *inanus* (empty). See Rosalie L. Colie, *Shakespeare's Living Art* (Princeton, NJ, 1974), pp. 168–207.

of disappointed expectation we have already explored. For all its ruthlessly end-directed efficiency, the Roman world is especially haunted by a sense of faded glories. From Cleopatra's indulgent recollections of those lovers of her 'salad days', 'broad-fronted Caesar' and 'great Pompey' (1.5), to the younger Pompey's glorification of the conspirators Brutus and Cassius as 'courtiers of beauteous freedom' (2.6), the play is full of recollections of the colossic figures of late republican Rome, in whose vanished glamour the conniving politicians of the new age seek to deck their cause. Octavius's right to rule, for example, is always implicitly linked to his inheritance of the heroic name of 'great Caesar'; while Sextus Pompey's 'name and power' are explicitly dependent on the popular yearning for his father's vanished magnificence:

> Our slippery people,
> Whose love is never linked to the deserver
> Till his deserts are past, begin to throw
> Pompey the Great and all his dignities
> Upon his son . . .
>
> 1.2.184–8

Recognizing that, in the rhetoric of Roman political life, nostalgia has become the determining condition of the heroic, Pompey, already 'Rich in his father's honour' (1.3.50), seeks to present himself as the legitimate heir to 'all-honoured, honest, Roman Brutus' and the other martyrs of republican liberty. But it is Anthony above all, as the last survivor of a heroic age, whom the play bathes in the glow of admiring retrospection[1]—not

---

[1] Janet Adelman finds nostalgic 'longing for [his] heroic masculinity . . . at the center of the play', arguing that 'though Enobarbus's great set-piece on Cleopatra at Cydnus would seem to create Cleopatra as the play's ultimate unattainable erotic object, Antony himself is the primary absent object of desire for all the major characters' (*Suffocating Mothers*, p. 177). For Jonathan Dollimore this yearning expresses a Jacobean preoccupation with the contemporary decline of 'the warrior or martial ideal': 'this "greatest prince o'th' world . . ." is becoming obsolete: the myth of martial omnipotence has served its day. In other worlds a whole history informs Antony's sexuality'; see Jonathan Dollimore, 'Shakespeare, Cultural Materialism, Feminism, and Marxist Humanism', *New Literary History*, 21 (1989–90), pp. 471–93 (p. 487). Mason, by contrast, sees this feature of the play only as a sign of dramatic failure on Shakespeare's part: 'We are *told* I don't know how many times that [Anthony] was a supreme specimen of humanity . . . that his nature partook

merely through his followers' laments at the spectacle of his 'noble ruin', or Cleopatra's yearning for a time when 'Eternity was in our lips and eyes' (1.3.35), but even through the grudging tributes of enemies and rivals. If their descent renders Caesar and Pompey 'high in name', Anthony's own name is still a 'magical word of war' (3.1.31). The mythologized warrior of Philo's opening speech lives not only in Pompey's memory ('his soldiership | Is twice the other twain', 2.1.34–5), but in Caesar's too—the reminiscence of Anthony's magnificent retreat from Modena kindling something in his sober imagination nearly as unexpected as the cynical Enobarbus's beglamoured recollection of Cleopatra at Cydnus (1.4.55–71).[1]

If this heroic Anthony figures in the play almost entirely as an object of frustrated desire, an absence at the heart of the action, 'no-one,' as Janet Adelman remarks, 'is more keenly aware of his absence than Antony himself'.[2] As the tide of events turns against him, Anthony, 'looking back what I have left behind | 'Stroyed in dishonour' (3.11.52–3), more and more seeks to fix his sense of self on 'what ... I was' not what 'I am' (3.13.143–4):

> Of late, when I cried 'Ho!',
> Like boys unto a muss, kings would start forth
> And cry, 'Your will?'
>
> 3.13.90–2

Above all his memory keeps returning him to the triumphant battle against Brutus and Cassius as the occasion that continues to define his heroic difference from Octavius:

> I struck
> The lean and wrinkled Cassius; and 'twas I
> That the mad Brutus ended. He alone

of the divine. The Anthony who is presented dramatically never makes us believe these reports'; 'Telling *versus* Showing', p. 347.

[1] Caesar's hyperbolic enthusiasm nevertheless takes, as Adelman points out, a characteristically negative turn: it is as if he can imagine heroism only as emptiness, something located in 'a landscape of absolute deprivation, at the furthest possible remove from the emasculating excess Caesar associates with Egypt' (*Suffocating Mothers*, p. 179).

[2] *Suffocating Mothers*, p. 177; Adelman further notes how 'the play is from the very beginning obsessed with gaps, absences, lacks' of all kinds (p. 342, n. 59).

> Dealt on lieutenantry, and no practice had
> In the brave squares of war; yet now—no matter.
>
> 3.11.36–40

It would be a mistake, however, to suppose that this afterglow of nostalgic reflection serves simply to invest Anthony's political decline with the pathos that Shaw found so meretricious. As Jonathan Dollimore's analysis of the play's mystification of power has demonstrated, 'the language of desire, far from transcending the power relations which structure this society, is wholly informed by them'.[1] Indeed Anthony's own recollection of Philippi, with its contemptuous dismissal of 'the lean and wrinkled Cassius' and 'the mad Brutus', is a direct reminder of how far nostalgia in this play is an agent of propaganda. Only a few scenes earlier, after all, Agrippa has reminded us of a more generous Anthony who wept for the vanquished Brutus (3.2.56–7)—only for the comic deflation of Enobarbus's reply to identify this display of magnanimity as another example of onion-eyed sentiment, locating it firmly within the cynical political manœuvring of *Julius Caesar*: 'What willingly he did confound, he wailed, | Believe't, till I wept too' (3.2.59–60).

At best Roman nostalgia may represent nothing more than a self-indulgent regret for what the mourner has happily seen destroyed—like Anthony's regret at Fulvia's passing: 'What our contempts doth often hurl from us, | We wish it ours again. . . . She's good being gone— | The hand could pluck her back that shoved her on' (1.2.123–7). The bathos of the rhyming phrase 'shoved her on' would be enough to expose the hollowness of the emotion even without Enobarbus's mocking reaction ('Why sir, give the gods a thankful sacrifice,' l. 160). The unexpected analogy which this episode establishes between aristocratic magnanimity and the despised fickleness of popular affection ('never linked to the deserver | Till his deserts are past', 1.2.185–6), creates a harshly satiric context in which to read Octavius's tributes to his vanquished enemies ('No grave upon the earth shall clip in it | A pair so famous,' 5.2.357–8). More subtly it may even affect our reaction to Cleopatra's soaring encomium upon the dead Anthony

---

[1] *Radical Tragedy*, p. 207.

(5.2.76–100)—especially since at this point Shakespeare makes the boldest use of bathos to undermine the rapturous hyperbole of her love poetry, reminding us (after the abrasive restlessness of their scenes together) that Anthony too is 'good being gone'. 'Think you there was, or might be such a man | As this I dreamt of?' Cleopatra demands of the courtly Dolabella; and the uncharacteristically frank scepticism of his reply ('Gentle madam, no') ensures that, as Dollimore puts it, 'we are never allowed to forget that the moments of sublimity are conditional upon absence, nostalgic contemplation upon the fact that the other is irrevocably gone.'[1]

Nevertheless the vehemence of Cleopatra's response, insisting on the power of hyperbolic imagination to outwork nature, transforming desire into something 'past the size of dreaming' (l. 97), ensures that the bathos is less than overwhelming. Rather than simply cancelling her pathos, the effect is to relocate it in the tension between desire and its always imperfect realization. 'This is the monstruosity in love,' Troilus warned Cressida, 'that the will is infinite, and the execution confined; that the desire is boundless, and the act a slave to limit' (*Troilus* 3.2.79–82). *Anthony and Cleopatra* figures that monstrosity, as it trades between the boundlessness of erotic ambition ('Then must thou needs find out new heaven, new earth,' 1.1.17), and a degraded awareness of limit, the 'strong necessity of time' (1.3.42), under whose regime love is no more than Enobarbus's 'monstrous matter of feast' (2.2.189). The gap between 'the promised largeness' of heroic imagination, and the 'bias and thwart' of its realization is what Cleopatra herself is made to glance at when she says of her lover, 'Though he be painted one way like a Gorgon, | The other way's a Mars' (2.5.117–18). The heroic aspect of this anamorphic portrait is the Anthony whom Philo's opening speech recalls; while its deformed (and oddly female) anti-self corresponds more closely to the Anthony,

---

[1] *Radical Tragedy*, p. 207. In a subsequent footnote to his essay, Dollimore astutely observes how 'in the valediction there is also invoked the commemorative statue, literally larger than life. . . . in death Antony becomes statuesque in a way which recalls that the statue is a literal, material embodiment of a respect for its subject which is inseparable from the obsolescence of that subject.' See 'Shakespeare, Cultural Materialism, Feminism, and Marxist Humanism', p. 487.

'most large | In his abominations' (3.6.94–5), whom for most of the play we actually *see*. A similar discrepancy opens up between the mortal Venus whom Enobarbus remembers in the water-pageant at Cydnus and the all-too-human 'gypsy', ageing, capriciously self-indulgent, and with a streak of dangerous violence, who presides over the court at Alexandria.[1]

Yet, however much anticlimax and bathos are part of the play's design, it would be misleading to suggest that the final impression of *Anthony and Cleopatra* is meant to be in any way anticlimactic. Instead, this tragedy's most extraordinary effect lies in Shakespeare's capacity to draw a superb theatrical climax out of seeming anticlimax, in much the way that Cleopatra herself transforms the most abject defeat into the paradoxical victory that renders the triumphant Caesar 'ass | Unpolicied' (5.2.306–7). Just as the Queen is translated out of time and limit by Enobarbus's awakened imagination (2.2.243–4), so her own ecstatic vision makes of Anthony an incarnation of the boundless reach of desire, and of satisfaction endlessly renewed ('For his bounty, | There was no winter in't—an autumn 'twas | That grew the more by reaping', 5.2.86–8). At such moments the lovers seem to rise to the level

---

[1] For many in Shakespeare's audience this discrepancy must have shadowed (without exactly mirroring) the gap between the public mythology of Gloriana and the far less glamorous reality of Elizabeth's old age. Broadly suggestive parallels between Cleopatra and Elizabeth have often been observed: e.g. by Helen Morris, 'Queen Elizabeth I "Shadowed" in Cleopatra,' *HLQ* 32 (1969), pp. 271–8; Kenneth Muir, 'Elizabeth I, Jodelle and Cleopatra,' *Renaissance Drama*, NS 2 (1969), pp. 197–206; and Keith Reinhart, 'Shakespeare's Cleopatra and England's Elizabeth,' *SQ* 23 (1972), pp. 81–6. However, among all the major plays, *Anthony and Cleopatra* has probably responded least well to the detailed 'local readings' of new historicist criticism. Two rare exceptions are H. Neville Davies's 'Jacobean *Antony and Cleopatra*', *SQ*. 17 (1985), pp. 123–58, and Theodora A. Jankowski, ' "As I am Egypt's Queen": Cleopatra, Elizabeth I, and the Female Body Politic', in Peggy A. Knapp (ed.), *Assays: Critical Approaches to Medieval and Renaissance Texts*, vol. v (Pittsburgh, 1989), pp. 91–110. Davies reads the play in the light of the visit to England by Christian IV of Denmark in 1606, with Anthony and Octavius as figurations of the bibulous Christian and his brother-in-law, James I. Whilst the play's emphasis on Octavius as the usher of 'universal peace' (4.6.4) was clearly well calculated to flatter the professing peacemaker and new Augustus, James, the details of Davies's argument are not especially persuasive. Jankowski's reading of *Anthony and Cleopatra* as a 'text of female political theory', allegorizing the problematic nature of female monarchy in a patriarchal culture is rather more attractive, though the argument still involves suppressing important aspects of the tragedy.

of their mythic counterparts: Enobarbus's rhapsody transforms Cleopatra at Cydnus to a mortal Venus; whilst in her
rhetorical metamorphosis of the dead Anthony, she, who once
attired herself 'In th'habiliments of the goddess Isis' (3.6.17),
symbolically enacts the goddess's re-membering of her consort,
the fertility god Osiris.[1]

THE REACH OF PARADOX: DOING AND UNDOING (1)

What gives such moments of transformation their peculiar
poignancy, however, is precisely the audience's sense of their
rhetorical momentariness. They are dramatically powerful in
exact proportion to a relentlessly forced awareness of the
frailty of the illusion on which they are based. Puttenham's
'over reacher', its 'credit' dependent upon 'incredible comparison',[2] is forever drawing attention to the peril or folly of its
own overreaching. Even at the climax of Cleopatra's ecstatic
threnody the elegiac cadences point up a subtle reminder of
death's 'pestilent scythe' (3.13.194) in her image of reaping:
Anthony's bounty, after all, now 'grows the more' *only* in
Cleopatra's imagination. No matter how intensely we are
compelled to admire the transcendental raptures of the last
act, we are never asked to surrender to them in the purely
operatic fashion that Shaw imputes to the play. Instead they
are continuously tested against countervailing comic or satiric
perspectives in a fashion that preserves the dialectical pattern
of *Anthony and Cleopatra* to the very end.[3]

The pattern, once again, is established at the very beginning
of the play in a passage of dialogue which plunges the
audience (through what amounts to a witty quibble upon the
hallowed epic formula) *in medias res*—straight into the middle
of an argument. Philo's opening words, 'Nay but' set the

[1] For a particularly suggestive account of the way in which Shakespeare
seems to replicate the configurations of the Isis/Osiris/Typhon story in which
'the male dismembers while the female remembers', see Adelman, *Suffocating
Mothers*, pp. 183–5; Michael Lloyd, 'Cleopatra as Isis,' *SSu* 12 (1959),
pp. 88–94; and Constance Brown Kuriyama, 'The Mother of the World: A
Psychoanalytic Interpretation of Shakespeare's *Antony and Cleopatra*', *ELR* 7
(1977), pp. 324–51 (pp. 335–7).

[2] Puttenham, p. 226, cited in Adelman, *Common Liar*, p. 114.

[3] The seminal account of the play's 'peculiarly Shakespearian dialectic' is
in Danby's '*Antony and Cleopatra*: A Shakespearian Adjustment', See also
Schanzer, *Problem Plays*, pp. 138–45.

keynote for this tragedy as decisively as Barnardo's 'Who's there?' at the beginning of *Hamlet*, announcing the characteristic rhetorical posture of a play always arguing with itself, in which no single argumentative position, no point of view, however passionately presented, is allowed to go unquestioned or unqualified.[1]

In part, obviously, this dialectic is a function of the perspectival play created by the technique of comic framing discussed earlier. But it is also structural to the language of the tragedy. Particularly striking is the way in which, by means of the paradoxical idiom which Janet Adelman and others have described,[2] the 'Nay but' of sceptical resistance is repeatedly stitched into the very fabric of hyperbolic or ecstatic utterance—just as the voice of satiric criticism in its turn is habitually undermined by the contradictory pull of unexpected admiration. So, for example, in Philo's opening speech the evocation of the martial firmness and restraint which characterized Anthony's soldierly past is compromised by suggestions of heroic excess ('His captain's heart . . . hath burst | The buckles on his breast') quite incompatible with the stoical 'measure' and 'temper' (temperance) that Philo professes to admire. By contrast Lepidus's acknowledgement of Anthony's faults as being like 'the spots of heaven, | More fiery by night's blackness' (1.4.12–13) produces, through its oddly inverted chiaroscuro, an effect of paradoxical celebration.

---

[1] While Philo's is the most dramatic example, an unusually high proportion of scenes begin in the middle of a conversation, and the effect of continuing discussion and debate which this creates is enhanced by the number of scenes which break off abruptly in mid-conversation, often on a short line—see George T. Wright, *Shakespeare's Metrical Art* (Berkeley, Calif., 1988), pp. 136–7.

[2] Adelman's brilliant monograph, *The Common Liar*, to which (like most subsequent critics) I am deeply indebted, offers by far the most comprehensive treatment of this aspect of the play, finding in paradox and in the related (because inherently paradoxical) figure of hyperbole a key to its whole structure. Readers are referred to the third chapter of her study in particular for its account of paradoxical strategies that I can only touch on here. Also important is Rosalie Colie's excellent chapter on *Anthony and Cleopatra* in *Shakespeare's Living Art*, pp. 168–207; and H. M. Fawkner's *Shakespeare's Hyperontology*, which ingeniously explores the paradoxical interplay of 'leaving' and 'following'. Colie's *Paradoxia Epidemica: The Renaissance Tradition of Paradox* (Princeton, NJ, 1966) is a rich account of the tradition of literary paradox on which Shakespeare and his contemporaries drew.

Cleopatra's vices are similarly transformed in Enobarbus's eyes ('for vilest things | Become themselves in her', 2.2.245–6), just as Caesar's tribute to the courage of her suicide will be qualified by his Roman disdain for 'easy ways to die': 'O, noble weakness!' (5.2.342).

Broadly speaking, there are two distinct uses of paradox in the play, which correspond to the rival perceptions of reason and imagination. In one, which we might loosely call 'Roman', it expresses only self-devouring contradiction; in the other, more typically 'Egyptian' use, it figures the inalienable doubleness of things, by which opposites flourish in mysterious complementarity. The 'Roman' use is perhaps best represented by those figures which accumulate around the hero's self-betrayal, such as Enobarbus's 'When valour preys on reason, | It eats the sword it fights with' (3.13.199–200; my emphasis). In this use for something to 'become | The opposite of itself' (1.2.125–6) can only be self-cancelling, since it is an axiom of logic that a thing cannot be both itself and another thing. In the Roman world identity (and heroic identity above all) requires the absolute self-consistency and singleness of being that is parodied in Anthony's tautological description of the crocodile: 'It is shaped, sir, like itself, and it is as broad as it hath breadth. It is just so high as it is, and moves with it own organs' (2.7.41–3).[1] As one whose very attempts to 'be himself' for Cleopatra (1.1.45) reveal to Philo and Demetrius an Anthony who 'is not Anthony' (l. 59), the hero of the opening scene appears to confound this kind of integrality; and from one point of view, of course, the subsequent action (especially of Acts 3 and 4) seems amply to confirm the self-cancelling paradox of an Anthony who 'comes too short of that great property that still should go with "Anthony" '. Yet, even in the opening scene, as Janet Adelman points out, Demetrius's perplexed regret that Anthony's behaviour seemingly confirms the libels of 'the common liar who | Thus speaks of him at Rome' (1.1.62–3), opens up a kind of Cretan Liar paradox, by which such partial and unforgiving truth

[1] Compare the stress in *Coriolanus* upon the heroic singularity of Caius Marcius, and Aufidius's remarks about the compulsion of his nature 'Not to be other than one thing' (4.7.42).

appears to give itself the lie.[1] The effect is to prepare the way for a quite different reading in which self-contradiction can flower into the sublime doubleness which Cleopatra celebrates in the 'heavenly mingle' of Anthony's 'well-divided disposition' (1.5.59, 53)—so that self-loss, through an erotic version of a familiar Christian paradox, can finally appear as a more profound kind of self-realization.

It is this second variety of paradox, with its insistence on co-existing contraries, that best represents Puttenham's characterization of the figure as 'the Wonderer';[2] and, as Adelman shows, it is the rhetorical device most typically associated with Cleopatra, whose ability to 'embrace contradictions . . . [seems] to confound all our logical categories'.[3] If Anthony often seems devoured by contradictions, Cleopatra feasts upon them. When Anthony is at his most Roman, he thinks of Egypt as a place of 'poisoned hours' where he is 'bound . . . up | From [his] own knowledge' (2.2.95–6); but Cleopatra's Egypt is a world where it is equally possible for a woman to 'feed [herself] | With most delicious poison' as for a man to 'die | With looking on his life' (1.5.27, 33–4)—without involving either in the annihilating self-contradiction of Lepidus's 'murder in healing wounds' (2.2.22).

Nowhere is the power of the Queen's paradoxical nature to excite wonder made more vivid than in the extraordinary metamorphosis it works upon Enobarbus's normally prosaic language: in the Cydnus speech it kindles his imagination through a powder-train of flashing oxymorons. In the midst of them it is possible to recognize the latent paradoxicality of Philo's contemptuous 'the bellows and the fan | To cool a gypsy's lust' transformed by the illumination of the marvellous. Enobarbus remembers the Queen surrounded by

> pretty, dimpled boys, like smiling Cupids,
> With divers-coloured fans, whose wind did seem

---

[1] Adelman, *Common Liar*, p. 39. Compare Henry Peacham's description of paradox as a 'form of speech by which the Orator affirmeth something to be true, by saying he would not have believed it . . .', *The Garden of Eloquence*, ed. William Crane (Gainesville, Fla., 1954), p. 112, cited in Adelman, p. 113.

[2] Puttenham, p. 226, cited in Adelman, *Common Liar*, p. 113.

[3] Adelman, ibid., p. 115.

To glow the delicate cheeks which they did cool,
And what they undid did.

2.2.209–12

That last phrase, 'what they undid did', with a characteristically vertiginous reflexiveness, perfectly describes the
operation of paradox in this play, undoing what it does, doing
what it seemingly undoes, until 'done' and 'undone' themselves come to seem oddly interchangeable. Its teasing reversal
of *Macbeth*'s 'What's done cannot be undone' (5.1.65) is
significant; for if that tragedy plays on a fear of doubleness,
insisting that only in the duplicitous, phantasmagoric world
of the witches can a thing be both itself and its opposite, done
and undone, 'fair and foul', *Anthony and Cleopatra*, with its
twin protagonists, dual worlds, tragi-comic design, and conspicuously divided catastrophe,[1] celebrates doubleness of all
sorts—epitomized in the figure of a Queen who quite explicitly
makes foul fair, since 'vilest things | Become themselves in
her' (2.3.245–6). It is Cleopatra who compels us to recognize
in a spectacle of absolute and abject undoing the image of
something supremely 'well done, and fitting for a princess |
Descended of so many royal kings' (5.2.324–5). And if Macbeth, tormented by the equivocation of fiends 'who palter with
us in a double sense', struggles to find in the absolute
determinacy of 'doing' a principle to counter the fearful
indeterminacy of speaking, *Anthony and Cleopatra* revels in its
equivocation upon the very idea of 'doing' itself.

'Doing' matters here as much as 'thinking' in *Hamlet*, partly
because *Anthony and Cleopatra*, with its resolute refusal of
interiority, is a tragedy that might almost have been written
to illustrate the force of Aristotle's dictum that 'the end at
which the [tragic] dramatist aims is a certain kind of activity,
not a quality'.[2] In *Hamlet* the hero's nobility is conceived as

---

[1] For an account of the way in which the tragedy 'ends twice' (with the
deaths of Anthony and Cleopatra) see Anne Barton, ' "Nature's piece 'gainst
fancy" ', cited above, p. 70, n. 3.

[2] Aristotle is arguing that plot is of more importance than character or
any of the other four constituents of tragedy (spectacle, melody, diction, and
thought): 'Tragedy is an imitation not of persons but of action and life, of
happiness and misery. Now happiness and misery take the form of action; the
end at which the dramatist aims is a certain kind of activity, not a quality.
We have certain qualities in accordance with character, but it is in our actions

a quality of mind or character; for Anthony it is a mode of action. In the opening scene Demetrius's 'hope | Of better deeds tomorrow' (1.1.63–4) is set against the challenge implicit in Cleopatra's playful reformulation of the *King Lear* love-test—'If it be love *indeed*, tell me how much' (l. 14). Together they establish the conditions for a love affair that is compelled to demonstrate and display itself over and over again. In the end the only answer to Cleopatra's 'how much' lies not in *telling* at all, no matter how hyperbolical, but in doing—a doing so extravagant that it will confound the doer:

> Let Rome in Tiber melt, and the wide arch
> Of the ranged empire fall . . .
> . . . The nobleness of life
> Is to *do thus*, when such a mutual pair
> And such a twain can do't.
>
> 1.1.35–40 (emphasis added)

The problem for Anthony is that 'to do thus'—to be himself in the terms proposed here—will involve nothing less than an absolute *undoing* of the chivalric military 'doing' that claims his allegiance back in Rome:[1]

that we are happy or the reverse. Actors do not therefore perform with a view to portraying character; no, they include character for the sake of the action. Consequently the end of tragedy is its action.' *Poetics*, trans. John Warrington (London, 1963), p. 13. In the *handling* of his plot material, however, as Bevington argues, Shakespeare is very far from Aristotelian orthodoxy ('Introduction', pp. 30–4).

[1] This style of chivalric 'doing', however, with its ideal of 'good service', is hardly the straightforward, self-consistent business that its Roman practitioners would like to believe, as we may see from Pompey's paltering in that chilling episode on his galley when Menas offers to cut the throats of the feasting triumvirs: 'Being *done unknown*, | I should have found it afterwards *well done*, | But must condemn it now.' (2.7.79–81; my emphases). As Anthony's victorious lieutenant, Ventidius, also recognizes, the deeds which in one context may seem 'well done' in another may encompass a man's undoing:

> I have *done enough.* . . .
> *Better to leave undone* than by our *deed*
> Acquire too high a fame when him we serve's away. . . .
> I could *do* more to *do* Antonius good,
> But 'twould offend him . . .
>
> 3.1.12–26 (emphases added)

In Sillius's judgement it is precisely such politic reluctance to 'make too great an act' that distinguishes a soldier from 'his sword', the sign of mere doing.

> 'Tis spoken well:
> Were we before our armies, and to fight,
> I should *do thus.*

> 2.2.25–7 (emphasis added)

The ideal of 'nobleness' is expressed at these two moments by the same gesture, an embrace; but the theatrical symmetry highlights rather than disguises the fact that two mutually inconsistent ideas of noble doing are expressed—a contradiction that will be intensified when Anthony's simple phrase is repeated for the third time at the point of his own suicide:

> I will be
> A bridegroom in my death, and run into't
> As to a lover's bed. Come then—and Eros,
> Thy master dies thy scholar: *to do thus*
> I learned of thee.

> 4.15.99–103 (emphasis added)

'The perfect type of the man of action,' wrote William Carlos Williams, 'is the suicide';[1] and it is to such a perfection that Anthony's death aspires. The language of his speech, with its simultaneous recapitulation of the first embrace with Cleopatra and the chivalric atonement with Caesar, attempts a reconciliation of the martial and the erotic, of 'Roman' and 'Egyptian' values. Anthony invites us to witness in his dying both an erotic self-sacrifice—the extreme consummation of his desire—and the stoical self-conquest of 'A Roman, by a Roman | Valiantly vanquished' (4.16.59–60). But the audience's awareness of the fictive nature of Cleopatra's 'nobleness in record' ironizes his embrace of death in a fashion calculated to draw attention to the self-cancelling nature of the paradoxes with which the hero decorates his suicide.

Despite Cleopatra's endorsement of his gallant vision of valour triumphing on itself—'So it should be, that none but

---

[1] William Carlos Williams, 'The Descent of Winter', in *Imaginations* (New York, 1970), p. 255. Williams may even have been thinking of Anthony, since the apothegm appears at the end of a poem which can be read as an ironic paraphrase of Cleopatra's death ('Before | she died she told them— | I always liked to be well dressed | I wanted to look nice— | So she asked them to dress | her well. They curled her hair . . .').

Anthony | Should conquer Anthony' (4.16.18–19)—it is not easily separable from the herculean passion in which, just a few lines earlier, Anthony had imagined himself 'subdu[ing] my worthiest self' at the thought of Cleopatra's infidelity (4.13.47). From a sceptical Roman perspective, indeed, his death does little more than carry to its logical conclusion the process of his own undoing which Caesar mockingly compelled him to act out in the battle of Alexandria: 'Plant those that have revolted in the van, | That Anthony may seem *to spend his fury* | *Upon himself*' (4.6.8–10; my emphasis). There is a grim appropriateness in the fact that the last tribute to Anthony's manner of dying should come from the last of these deserters, Dercetus. The tightly enfolded reflexiveness of Dercetus's praise aims at heroic sublimity: 'that self hand | Which writ his honour in the acts it did | Hath, with the courage which the heart did lend it, | Splitted the heart' (5.1.21–4); but Dercetus's deeply compromised position—the very instrument of honourable inscription, Anthony's sword, is what he hopes will purchase his own dishonourable advancement—places the swagger of his rhetoric in a bitterly ironic light. What, after all, do these sublime paradoxes amount to but a description of a mode of doing that spirals into undoing, the ultimate reduction of Philo's imagery of self-destructive excess?

> his captain's heart,
> Which in the scuffles of great fights hath burst
> The buckles on his breast, reneges all temper . . .
>
> 1.1.5–7

GENDER AND SELF-LOSS

Rosalie Colie remarks of suicide—the 'decision to . . . unmake . . . oneself by one's own act'—that it is 'the paradox of self-contradiction at its irrevocable extremity'.[1] Anthony's incantatory insistence that his death is a triumphant act of self-conquest, while it gestures at the Stoic idea of suicide as a victory over fortune and the passional self, remains entangled in the ambivalence Colie describes. Compared with the self-immolation of Othello, which it in some respects resembles,

[1] Colie, *Paradoxia Epidemica*, p. 486.

it is free of the self-hatred that compels the Venetian Moor
to figure his death as the annihilation of a 'malicious' and
barbarous Other; but, where Othello's killing of the 'turbaned
Turk' brutally preserves the heroic distinctions on which
(however destructively) he has founded his life, the self-
cancelling paradoxy of 'a Roman by a Roman | Valiantly van-
quished', like the dissipation of 'water . . . in water', threatens
a collapse into the very indistinction, the self-loss that the
hero most fears. Indeed the elegiac power of Cleopatra's grief
for him comes precisely from her overwhelming sense of
Anthony's death as undoing all difference:

> The crown o'th'earth doth *melt* . . .
> The soldier's pole is fall'n—young boys and girls
> Are *level* now with men; *the odds is gone*,
> And there is *nothing left remarkable*
> Beneath the visiting moon.

> 4.16.65–70 (emphases added)

Her imagery of melting catches up, with fearful poignancy,
the language of Anthony's own gathering sense of dissolution,
which climaxes in the great lament at the beginning of 4.15:

> Authority melts from me.

> 3.13.90

>   The hearts
> That spanieled me at heels, to whom I gave
> Their wishes, do discandy, melt their sweets . . .

> 4.13.20–2

> That which is now a horse, even with a thought
> The rack dislimns, and makes it indistinct
> As water is in water. . . .
> My good knave Eros, now thy captain is
> Even such a body . . .

> 4.15.9–13

It is not at all accidental that Cleopatra should imagine the
undoing of difference in such sharply gendered terms ('The
soldier's pole is fall'n; young boys and girls | Are level now
with men'); nor that the imagery of melting should link this
levelling with the proverbially feminine element, water, in

which she herself appears to move. For *Anthony and Cleopatra*, like its successor and companion piece, *Coriolanus*, is a tragedy whose exploration of heroic selfhood is bound up with a deep sense of the fragility of masculine identity in face of the female Other. The very 'overflow' of passion of which Philo convicts him is as much a sign of feminized instability as of heroic excess, and from the beginning it links him imaginatively with the flooding of the Nile, that river whose ambiguous overflow is the dominant symbol of the female realm of Egypt. From this perspective Anthony's death does no more than make real the dissolution with which his passion for Cleopatra has always threatened him: 'These strong Egyptian fetters I must break, | Or *lose my self* in dotage' (1.2.116–17, emphasis added).

The male psyche, as Walter Ong, among others, has argued, is peculiarly vulnerable to such anxieties. Pointing out that (contrary to Freud's notion of femininity as a modification of the 'natural' state of masculinity) nature's primary tendency is to produce females, Ong notes that, whether biologically or psychologically defined, 'masculinity means becoming something different, separation from [maternal] origins, a certain kind of getting away, transcendence'. As a result, he writes, 'the male's problem is one of differentiation. He must . . . prove that he is not female.'[1] Any threat to the boundaries of gender will thus be experienced as a threat to identity itself; and the collapsing of gender distinctions must entail an annihilation of the self which is ultimately no different from death.[2]

[1] Walter J. Ong, *Fighting for Life: Contest, Sexuality and Consciousness* (Ithaca, NY, 1981), pp. 66, 112.

[2] It is no doubt for this reason that the male-inflected language of sexuality characterizes the melting-away of orgasm as 'dying'. In this context we should observe that the identification of Cleopatra with the East ('I'th'East my pleasure lies,' 2.3.38) associates her not merely with the site of oriental *luxuria* but with the place of death—and that the two, as the clustering images of sunset, death, and erotic consummation at the end of the play insist, are essentially the same. As Enobarbus's satire suggests, the threat posed by Cleopatra is expressed not merely in her capacity to undo Anthony's masculine identity, but in the mysterious female affinity with Death which allows her (like the lying 'honest woman' of the Clown's anecdote) to die and die again: 'Cleopatra, catching but the least noise of this, dies instantly; I have seen her die upon far poorer moment. I do think there is mettle in death which commits some loving act upon her, she hath such celerity in dying' (1.2.139–43).

Yet, of course, the very act of separation produces a kind of incompleteness, which it is possible to see emblematized in the traditional symbols of gender difference: for while 'the received symbol for woman, Venus' mirror . . . signifies self-possession' and wholeness, its male counterpart, Mars's spear, has no such connotations, but 'signifies conflict, change, stress, dissection, division'.[1] In so far as male sexuality is profoundly entangled with the psychic incompleteness implicit in successful self-differentiation, the struggle to distinguish the self from the female (m)other is in principle unending and must be endlessly renewed. The result, according to Ong, is that 'human males tend to feel [their] environment as a kind of againstness, something to be fought with and altered';[2] and this agonistic compulsion is typically satisfied in competition with other males:

the only adversary who can enable one to establish male identity is another male . . . if he is not to be woman, a boy must venture into the all-male world. That is to say he must face the threat of masculinity within himself by facing it in others like himself. To be a man, the male must be able to face insecurity—for that is what maleness implies—existence in an environment that is both needed and hostile. The male carries this insecurity within himself. So does the other male, who is thus a surrogate for himself. If [he] can stand off the male restlessness, the adversativeness of the other, he can live with himself.[3]

The heroic ideal with its profoundly agonistic ethos is the classic expression of this male urge to differentiation; and it is significant that Shakespeare's experiments in heroic tragedy, *Anthony and Cleopatra* and *Coriolanus*, despite their great contrasts of mood and tone, should both be constructed around an agonistic triangle of the sort that Ong describes. In each case the hero struggles to separate himself from a female figure (Volumnia, Cleopatra) whose dominance threatens to undo his masculine identity (though he remains radically incomplete without her); in each case he seeks to prove his masculinity in homosocial rivalry with a male antagonist

---

[1] Ong, *Fighting for Life*, p. 77. The archetypal myth of gender difference as incompleteness is Aristophanes' famous account in Plato's *Symposium* of sexual desire as the expression of human longing to restore the primal unity of beings whom the gods divided.

[2] Ong, ibid., p. 77.

[3] Ong, ibid., p. 78.

('competitor' is Shakespeare's nicely ambiguous term in *Anthony*) who is identified precisely as a kind of other self or surrogate (Tullus Aufidius, Octavius Caesar);[1] in each case the cost of the struggle to maintain the heroic self and remain 'oneself alone'[2] proves ironically to be nothing less than annihilation of the self. Each hero feels himself unmanned by the female who at once makes and unmakes him; each falls victim to his male antagonist; and in the fate of each we are invited to recognize the operation of profoundly self-destructive contradictions lying at the very heart of the heroic masculine ideal. A major difference between the two plays, however, consists in the fact that in *Coriolanus* the influence of the domineering female is almost entirely malign, while in *Anthony* it is much more ambiguously regarded, and may even (as Janet Adelman has suggested) represent a fantasy of escape from the prison of rigidly bounded male selfhood.[3] In so far as Anthony's desire for Cleopatra is figured as a reckless longing for dissolution of the self in the Other ('Let Rome in Tiber melt') it is established from the beginning as amounting to a thinly sublimated death wish. 'If I lose mine honour, | I lose my self' (3.4.22–3), Anthony confesses to Octavia; yet he also insists that to be himself at all he must be 'stirred by Cleopatra'; and paradoxically the play is never more insistent that we take that claim seriously than at the point of death. How this can be so is perhaps best approached by reflecting on the significance of that weapon which is the received symbol of masculinity, the spear of Mars—or rather upon its equivalent in the play, Anthony's 'sword Philippan'.

[1] Coriolanus says of Aufidius 'were I anything but what I am, | I would wish me only he' (*Coriolanus* 1.1.231–2), while Caesar salutes the dead Anthony as 'The arm of mine own body, and the heart | Where mine his thoughts did kindle' (*Anthony* 5.1.45–6).

[2] The desire for such singularity and aloneness is more apparent in Coriolanus, whose wish to be 'author of himself' carries it to violent excess, but it is also an essential part of Anthony's ideal of heroic 'authority', as witness his challenge to Octavius to answer him 'sword against sword, | Ourselves alone' (3.13.27–8).

[3] Adelman finds in Anthony's death a 'letting go', a willingness to abandon 'the boundaries of his selfhood' which becomes regenerative: 'Antony can be recreated in and through his merger with Cleopatra; and in her recreation of him, the play reaches toward a new kind of masculinity . . . founded on incorporation of the female. . . . For one fragile moment, Shakespeare is able to imagine the possibility of a maternal space that is neither suffocating nor deforming' (*Common Liar* pp. 190–1).

THE PROPERTIES OF THE SELF

If the spear of Mars stands for 'conflict . . . stress [and] division', it also expresses the fundamentally instrumental conception of selfhood which is implicit in the heroic idea of masculinity.[1] In a fashion that Aristotle well understood, this kind of self realizes itself in 'doing'—as though it were capable of recognizing itself only as an entity projected into the outside world. While the vertigo of self-loss is a persistent theme in Shakespearian tragedy from *Hamlet* onwards, it becomes especially intense in *Anthony and Cleopatra* and *Coriolanus*. Even more absolutely than Othello, Anthony feels his identity as a public thing, a matter of 'occupation' (4.4.17), a function of power and authority—less the *locus* of subjectivity than a species of 'property'. To be without authority is to be without authenticity, 'unqualitied', in Iras's phrase (3.11.43), and radically amorphous: 'here I am Anthony, | Yet cannot hold this visible shape' (4.15.13–14). When Philo in the opening scene complains that the besotted Anthony already comes 'too short of that great property | Which still should go with Anthony' (1.1.60–1), he uses the term 'property' with a peculiarly seventeenth-century inflection: it includes all those qualities and attributes that serve to differentiate a man's 'proper person'—both those innate 'properties' that define his biological nature, and those acquired 'properties' that express his social identity. It was a concept closely related, as James Calderwood has pointed out, both to our notion of 'propriety' and to 'property' in the modern sense of 'possessions';[2] and by that very fact, in a society where proprietorship was imagined as 'properly' the prerogative of males, it was first and foremost a term of male definition. In *Anthony and Cleopatra* the fiercely determined boundaries of masculinity are marked by 'property/propriety', while the indeterminate limits of femininity are nominated by the elasticity of 'becoming'—to use the term that so frequently attaches itself to Cleopatra.[3]

---

[1] Spear and sword are also eloquent metaphors for the 'rigidity [and] brittleness' which Peter Erickson, thinking of Othello as well as Anthony, sees as characteristic of a 'masculine self based entirely on martial toughness', *Patriarchal Structures in English Drama* (Berkeley, Calif., 1985), p. 131.

[2] James L. Calderwood, *The Properties of Othello* (Amherst, Mass., 1989), p. 10.

[3] On 'becoming', which links the ideas of process and decorum, as the key to Cleopatra's nature, see Adelman, *Common Liar*, pp. 144–5: 'If everything

Thus the abbreviation of Anthony's 'property' bespeaks a truncation of his manhood that renders explicit the emasculation suggested by the fanning eunuchs of the lovers' first entry: Anthony 'comes too short' in Philo's estimate exactly as Mardian's 'good will . . . come[s] too short' for Cleopatra in the bawdy badinage of Act 2, scene 5 (4–9). From a contemporary point of view, a eunuch was precisely not a 'proper man', since he was defined, as Cleopatra cruelly reminds Mardian, by his want of sexual property ('I take no pleasure | In aught an eunuch has', 1.5.9–10). The effect of such emasculation was less to render its victims neuter, than to feminize them—'to make them more effeminate, transforming them as near might be into women'.[1] Mardian and his fellow eunuchs (whose visible presence makes them bulk much more significantly in performance than they do in a printed text) stand for the threat of such effeminate metamorphosis. For in the patriarchal Roman world of *Anthony and Cleopatra* the fear of being undone, of losing oneself in dotage is always, more or less explicitly, the fear of joining the company of 'woman's men' (3.7.70), of being somehow transformed to a woman (as Enobarbus feels himself transformed by the water that leaches treacherously from his eyes in 4.2).[2] In gender, as in politics, there is no midway between extremes: to be stripped of the properties of masculinity is to become feminine.

becomes Cleopatra, she also becomes everything' (p. 144); in *Suffocating Mothers* (p. 185) Adelman notes how this notion links Cleopatra with the Isis described in Plutarch's essay 'Of Isis and Osiris'.

[1] William Prynne, *Histrio-mastix: The Player's Scourge or Actor's Tragedy* (1633; New York, 1974), p. 209, cited in Laura Levine, 'Men in Women's Clothing: Anti-theatricality and Effeminization from 1579 to 1642', *Criticism* 28 (1986), pp. 121–43 (p. 134). The passage is worth quoting at greater length: Prynne is describing the practices of sodomites who 'clothed their Galli, Succubi, Ganymedes and Cynadi in women's attire, whose virilities they did often dissect, to make them more effeminate, transforming them as near might be into women, both in apparel, gesture, speech, behaviour'. Significantly the word 'neuter' does not appear to have been used in a sexual sense before the later eighteenth century (*OED*, *neuter* sb. A4).

[2] For enlightening comment on the fearful permeability attributed to women's bodies, see Gail Kern Paster, 'Leaky Vessels: The Incontinent Women of Jacobean City Comedy', *Renaissance Drama* NS 18 (1987), pp. 43–64. From this perspective the 'leakiness' which Enobarbus attributes to Anthony when his dearest quit him, is another sign of his feminization (like the 'melting' of his authority), and a sorry travesty of the 'overflow' attributed to him by Philo.

Such anxiety about the stability of masculine identity, while it accords well with Ong's account of gender difference, may seem paradoxical in a period when biology and theology alike defined the female as an imperfect derivative of the male. But Laura Levine's work on anti-theatricality and effeminization suggests a patriarchal culture shot through with ontological uncertainty—haunted by 'an unmanageable anxiety that there is no such thing as a masculine self'.[1] In the contradictory discourse of the polemicists she discusses, this creature emerges both as something dangerously 'pliable, manipulable, easily unshaped', so far from being a fixed essence that it is 're-ally nothing at all', *and* as a monster of passionate and barely governable will whose nature is essentially womanish.[2] Hence the particular fear aroused by cross-dressing, since it might either mould the amorphous masculine 'self' to fatal effemin-acy, or give dangerous play to the womanish monster 'locked away "inside" ' the incautious transvestite.[3]

It is no coincidence that Cleopatra's teasing erotic 'play' with Mardian should seem to trigger her reminiscence of the drunken debauch in which she and Anthony exchanged cos-tumes—a game involving both the effeminate surrender of specifically masculine properties, and the adulteration of mas-culinity with feminine attire. Transvestism, like eunuchism (and for the same reasons), is symbolically central to *Anthony and Cleopatra*, being inscribed in the very mythic structure on which its action is grounded. When Cleopatra recalls the dress-ing of her 'Herculean Roman' in her own 'tires and mantles' whilst she strutted in his 'sword Philippan' (1.3.84, 2.5.22–3), the anecdote is undoubtedly meant to recall, as it did for Plutarch (see Appendix A), the unmanning of Anthony's ancestor by another Eastern queen. According to the legend, Omphale compelled Hercules to assume her robes and distaff, after surrendering to her his lion pelt, bow, and club.[4] Allegorized by classical writers as an exemplum of masculine strength overcome by female lechery and ambition, this epi-

[1] Levine, 'Men in Women's Clothing,' p. 136.

[2] Ibid., pp. 126–8, 136.

[3] Ibid., p. 135.

[4] The Omphale story is no doubt what Caesar means to recall when he complains that Anthony in Egypt 'is not more manlike | Than Cleopatra, nor the queen of Ptolemy | More womanly than he' (1.4.5–7). John Coates, ' "The

sode became a commonplace in the Renaissance for female usurpation and the subversiveness of erotic passion.[1] Spenser reworked the episode in Book 5, Cantos 5–6 of *The Faerie Queene*, where the Knight of Justice, Artegall, is diverted from his imperial mission by falling into the clutches of the Amazon queen, Radigund, who strips him of the trappings of heroic fame, breaks his sword, and dresses him 'In womans weedes, that is to manhood shame' (Canto 5, stanza 20).[2] For the Puritan polemicist William Prynne, Hercules's transvestism illustrated the dreadful vulnerability of heroic identity:

Doth not that valiant man, that man of courage who is admirable in his arms, and formidable to his enemies degenerate into a woman with his veiled face? he lets his coat hang down to his ankles, he twists a girdle about his breast, he puts on woman's shoes, and after the manner of women, he puts a caul upon his head; moreover he carries a distaff with wool, and draws a thread with his right hand, wherewith he had formerly borne a trophy, and he extenuateth his spirit and voice into a shriller and womanish sound.[3]

'There is nothing essential about this "valiant man's" identity,' Levine notes: 'it slips away from him with his clothes.'[4] As with Hercules, so it proves with Anthony; and Cleopatra's playful, but none the less disturbing, reminder of masculine

Choice of Hercules" in *Antony and Cleopatra*', *SSu* 31 (1978) pp. 45–52, stresses the additional relevance of an iconographical tradition in which Hercules was presented as having to choose between two women, representing Virtue and Vice (or Pleasure). See also Richard Hillman, 'Antony, Hercules, and Cleopatra: "the bidding of the gods" and "the subtlest maze of all"', *SQ* 38 (1987), pp. 442–51.

[1] See e.g. Henry Peacham's *Vis Amoris* (Love's Power), from *Minerva Britannia, or a Garden of Heroical Devices* (1612) reproduced in Bevington's edition, p. 10. Interestingly enough, in the context of the symbolism of female power in *Anthony*, the border of Peacham's emblem is made up of intertwined serpents.

[2] Spenser returns to the Omphale story in the opening stanzas of Canto 8, where Hercules is cited along with Samson and Antony himself, as examples of martial 'rigour' undone by 'beauty's lovely bait':

> And so did warlike *Antony* neglect
> The world's whole rule for *Cleopatra's* sight,
> Such wondrous power hath women's fair aspect,
> To captive men, and make them all the world reject.
>
> (5.8.2).

[3] *Histrio-mastix*, p. 197, cited in Levine, 'Men in Women's Clothing', p. 135.
[4] Levine, ibid., p. 135.

instability gathers suggestiveness, as the action unfolds, from its association with a specific set of properties—the trappings that represent Anthony's 'proper' self, the sword and armour in which he once 'glowed like plated Mars' (1.1.4).

The emblematic significance of these arms is substantially determined by a second mythic archetype which underlies the whole action of the play. This is the story of the adulterous infatuation of Mars and Venus,[1] which Mardian is made to invoke when he apologizes for his want of the masculine power of 'doing'. 'Hast thou affections?' Cleopatra asks him; 'yes,' he replies, but

> Not in deed, madam, for I can do nothing
> But what indeed is honest to be done;
> Yet have I fierce affections, and think
> What Venus did with Mars.

1.5.15–18

The eunuch's affections might seem fiercer if he thought what *Mars* did with *Venus*; but his unlucky emphasis only succeeds in reminding us that what the goddess of love did with the god of war was to *undo* him, as Cleopatra undoes Anthony, by taming his martial ferocity. For the Renaissance, the triumph of Venus, whether positively or negatively understood, was essentially an allegory of emasculation;[2] and in the iconographic tradition it was expressed by the stripping of the armour and weapons, the proper instruments which represented the god's phallic power and aggressivity (Fig. 11).

---

[1] For a discussion that usefully links the Mars/Venus and Hercules/Omphale stories with Samson and Delilah and other allegoric representations of female usurpation, see Patricia Parker, 'Suspended Instruments: Lyric and Power in the Bower of Bliss,' in *Literary Fat Ladies*, pp. 54–66.

[2] The emasculation might be understood in a straightforwardly negative way as an allegory of (masculine) virtue overwhelmed by (feminine) softness and emotion; or positively as the taming of destructive passion and violence by the principles of generative love and harmony—a union of opposites whose offspring was the goddess Harmonia. For helpful accounts of the various meanings available in the Renaissance, see Edgar Wind, *Pagan Mysteries of the Renaissance* (London, 1967), pp. 86–96; Raymond B. Waddington, '*Antony and Cleopatra*: "What Venus did with Mars" ', *Shakespeare Studies* 2 (1966), pp. 210–27, and pp. 78–101 of Adelman's chapter on 'Tradition as Source' in *The Common Liar*. Wind and Waddington consider only the positive Neoplatonic interpretations of Venus's triumph as an allegory of harmony (*discordia concors*), while Adelman stresses the paradoxical coexistence of contrary readings.

abad union, material maternal

11. Veronese, *Mars and Venus United by Love*

fruitful a productive union of 2 forces; harmonious

So, in Shakespeare's play, Anthony's undoing is expressed in the symbolic degradation and stripping away of the 'property which still should go with "Anthony" '—above all in the usurpation of his 'sword Philippan'.

Taking its name from the battle that is the focus for so much of Anthony's nostalgic self-recollection, this sword is the instrument with which he hyperbolically 'quartered the world' (4.15.58)—as much the sign of his martial virtue as the 'conquering sword' of Tamburlaine. With it, even after Actium, he envisages himself earning 'our chronicle' (3.13.176). It is the weapon which, in his imagination at least, can transform even abject defeat into the moral victory of suicide; and it is the emblem of all that distinguishes from him the 'boy' Octavius, who 'at Philippi kept | His sword e'en like a dancer' (3.11.35-6). Unlike his canny subordinate, Ventidius, Anthony (or the heroic image embodied in his name, 'that magical word of war', 3.1.31) seems barely distinguishable from his sword; but (as Sillius implies) the hero's identification with this property of martial virtue is also the measure of his vulnerability, for the externally defined self is always peculiarly susceptible to the constructions and appropriations of others.[1] In practice the gap between the symbolic properties of the self and the (often emblematically conceived) 'properties' of the tiring house is dangerously narrow and unstable. Thus Anthony's sword is twice reduced to a mere stage property, the equipment of a prize-fighter or some braggart-captain in comedy—first in 1.3, when Cleopatra has her 'Herculean Roman' swear by his sword 'and target' (1.3.82); and again in 3.13, when Enobarbus, dismissing Anthony's 'sword against sword' challenge to Caesar, identifies it with the braggadocio of a professional 'sworder' (ll. 27, 31). From this it is only a short step to its final debasement as a woman's plaything. After Actium, Anthony himself imagines his weapon as 'made weak by my affection' (3.11.66); and when Cleopatra seem-

---

[1] This is the point that Ulysses makes in *Troilus and Cressida*, when he reminds Achilles 'that man, how dearly ever parted, | How much in having, or without or in, | Cannot make boast to have that which he hath, | Nor feels not what he owes but by reflection' (*Troilus* 3.3.91-4). It partly accounts for what Bayley calls 'the general helplessness of external and exterior life' in the play (*Shakespeare and Tragedy*, p. 137).

ingly betrays him a second time at Alexandria, it is as if the playful usurpation of the cross-dressing episode is being repeated in humiliating earnest, completing the hero's identification with the emasculated phallic warriors of the governing myths:[1] 'O, thy vile lady, | She has robbed me of my sword' (4.15.22–3)

The main action of Act 4, in what amounts to a nostalgic recapitulation of his heroic career, is framed by two pieces of stage business in which Anthony is symbolically made and unmade, reinvested with the properties of martial selfhood, and then formally stripped of them. The sequence begins with a scene that deliberately recalls one of the great conventional set-pieces of classical epic, as Cleopatra helps to arm the hero for his last encounter with his antagonist (4.4). But the belated rearguard heroics at Alexandria (4.7–8) serve only as a prelude to the utter undoing that concludes this sequence, when Anthony acts out the dismantling of his identity with the squire whose very name seems ironically to recall the *putti* who strip the war god of his trappings in the paintings of Mars and Venus:

> Unarm, Eros, the long day's task is done,
> And we must sleep. . . .
> Lie down and stray no farther. Now all labour
> Mars what it does; yea, very force entangles
> Itself with strength. Seal then, and all is done.
>
> 4.15.35–49

The doffing of his arms announces the exhaustion of heroic action; and his language makes it seem as if, for Anthony,

---

[1] Of this line Adelman remarks 'the presence of [Mardian] the eunuch on stage makes it impossible [not to recognize it] as a description of emasculation', *Common Liar*, p. 91. Compare Spenser's description of the warrior Verdant's subjection to the enchantress Acrasia in *The Faerie Queene*, where emasculation is figured in the stripping of martial properties, and a self-spending that results in fatal blurring of identity:

> His warlike arms, the idle instruments
>   Of sleeping praise, were hung upon a tree,
> And his brave shield, full of old moniments,
> Was foully 'rased, that none the signs might see;
> Ne for them, ne for honour cared he . . .
> But in lewd loves, and wastful luxury,
> His days, his goods, his body he did spend:
> O horrible enchantment, that him did so blend.
>
> (2.12.80)

all his 'doing', heroic or erotic, has amounted to nothing more
than an utter using up or spending of the self, until there
remains only the extreme self-cancellation of 'Ourselves to end
ourselves' (4.15.22). The Anthony whom we first glimpsed in
Philo's imagery of a heroic self so excessive that it seemed to
'burst the buckles on his breast', as if visibly rupturing the
continent of self, now enacts his sense of gathering indistinction by finally discarding the carapace of properties, leaving only his sword to complete the process of 'dissection,
[and] division'. From this perspective, for Anthony to run upon
his sword like a 'bridegroom ... to a lover's bed' (4.15.100–1)
is a gesture that perfectly expresses the self-consuming nature
of the passion to which that 'property that still should go with
Anthony' is mortgaged.

Yet the play marvellously resists this reductive reading. By
a sharply calculated irony, it is not, after all, Cleopatra, but
Dercetus, a denizen of the masculine world and the pseudo-
choric chronicler of Anthony's suicide, who steals the hero's
sword. 'Robb[ing] Anthony's wound' (5.1.25) in a piece of
shameless thievery which outdoes the disillusioned master-
leaving of those thieves by sea and land, Menas and Enobarbus, Dercetus turns his back on the ethics of honourable
martyrdom to pursue his interest in the new world of triumphant *realpolitik*: 'This sword, but shown to Caesar with this
tidings, | Shall enter me with him' (4.15.114–15). It is the last
of a series of episodes in the play—we may think particularly
of the peculiar arithmetic of 'honour' and murderous policy
that underlies the display of chivalric hospitality on Pompey's
galley in 2.7, or of the careful calculation of self-interest
behind the panoply of Ventidius's entry 'as it were in triumph'
in 3.1—that expose the gap between martial rhetoric and
political reality, revealing the ultimate hollowness of those
properties in which Roman masculinity is publicly invested.
It helps to make way for an ending in which the calculus of
the propertied self, with its rhetoric of spending and saving,
is severely (if by no means absolutely) discounted.

Against its 'Roman' ideology of identity as a species of
property, to be bound in and guarded against the 'waste' that
Octavius so deplores in Anthony, the play sets its 'Egyptian'
ethos of spontaneity and bounty in which consuming, spend-

ing, giving, and largesse of all kinds are celebrated.[1] The contemptuous stratagem by which Octavius forces Anthony to 'spend his fury on himself' in the last battle merely gives a satiric literalness to what Caesar perceives as his rival's profligate self-spending. For Caesar, to waste time as Anthony 'wastes | The lamps of night in revel' (1.4.4–5) *is* to squander oneself—hence the 'lightness' and 'vacancy' to which Anthony is reduced in his eyes (ll. 25–6). For the 'Egyptian' Anthony, by contrast, to defy 'the strong necessity of time' (1.3.42) to 'mock the midnight bell' (3.13.185) and 'burn this night with torches' (4.2.41) is to engage in a kind of conspicuous self-consumption which is paradoxically enlarging ('There's not a minute of our lives should *stretch* | Without some pleasure now,' (1.1.48–9; emphasis added). As the latent sexual pun in 'spend' suggests,[2] for Anthony to be 'spent' in the fashion that Cleopatra acknowledges ('Our lamp is spent, it's out,' 4.16.86), is not merely to be used up, but to achieve a kind of fulfilment beyond the comprehension of the conqueror whom Thidias calls 'the fullest man' (3.13.87). Proculeius's glozing tongue may dwell on Caesar's fullness and overflow in his attempt to persuade Cleopatra to surrender ('Make your *full* reference freely to my lord, | Who is so *full* of grace that it *flows over* | On all that need,' 5.2.23–5); but it is the overplus of Anthony's generosity to which both Enobarbus and Cleopatra testify—the careless opulence which drops 'realms and islands' like small coin from his pocket, a winterless bounty whose ability to 'grow the more by reaping' recalls Cleopatra's magic renewals of desire.[3]

In this seductive fantasy of self-renewing bounty, as recent feminist criticism has argued, the play gestures at the 'liberatory, subversive' potential of 'a more inclusive definition

---

[1] It is for this reason that Adelman pairs *Anthony* with *Timon of Athens*, finding in its celebration of 'male bounty' an answer to a play which 'shrunk to the limits of Timon's masculine self, founded in scarcity . . . itself becomes parsimonious' (*Suffocating Mothers*, pp. 174–5). Caesar, whose most generous sentiments are characterized by 'narrow measure' and uttered 'from his teeth', is this play's arch-representative of Timonian parsimony. For Erickson (*Patriarchal Structures*, p. 140) the disarming of Anthony climaxes the process of 'divesting himself of power' to which his 'bounty overplus' commits him.

[2] Cf. 5.2.301.

[3] The point is nicely made by Fawkner, *Shakespeare's Hyperontology*, pp. 105–7.

of masculinity'—one that imitates the absolute generosity of 'the ideal all-giving mother',[1] and by incorporating aspects of the feminine, 'can overflow its own rigid boundaries'.[2] It remains true, of course, that this is a quality discovered only in nostalgic retrospect, celebrated as absence and loss. But the paradoxical logic of the play ensures that loss itself is redefined in the closing scenes. Reversing Narcissus's oxymoronic formula, Anthony's self-spending produces a poverty that makes him rich. For if Ventidius's ambition prefers loss to a 'gain which darkens him' (3.1.24), in a much more profound fashion Anthony is made to claim from 'the very heart of loss' a kind of gain, in which the undoing of the self is figured as a terminal act of self-realization. It is a discovery confirmed, significantly enough, at the point of extreme self-abandon when, submitting to the instruction of Eros, Anthony chooses death as the final consummation of his love for Cleopatra[3]—making of his suicide a paradox that goes beyond mere stoic self-assertion to embrace those transcendent antinomies which, in Shakespeare's enigmatic threnody *The Phoenix and Turtle*, seem to confound the very notion of 'property', difference, and identity:[4]

> Property was thus appalled
> That the self was not the same:
> Single nature's double name
> Neither two nor one was called.
>
> Reason, in itself confounded,
> Saw division grow together.

[1] Erickson, *Patriarchal Structures*, pp. 131, 134, 135.

[2] *Suffocating Mothers*, p. 190.

[3] Adelman writes acutely about the paradoxes here: for her the play 'fulfils the dangerous desire at the heart of masculine selfhood, the dream of reunion with the maternal matrix. And fulfilment of this dangerous dream seems to require no less than all: Anthony can be cured only with a wound' (*Suffocating Mothers*, p. 187)

[4] James Calderwood uses the paradoxes of this poem as a way of approaching love's violation of property in *Othello*, see *The Properties of 'Othello'*, ch. 3, 'Appalling Property', pp. 38–9; but Wilson Knight had already remarked on the 'mutually illuminating' qualities of *The Phoenix and Turtle* and *Anthony and Cleopatra* in *The Imperial Theme*, p. 349. The Anthony whom Cleopatra eulogizes, his voice 'propertied | As all the tunèd spheres', is a figure whose miraculous excess typically overreaches his natural 'properties', a creature who hyperbolically revels in breaking the limits of his proper self ('His delights | Were dolphin-like; they showed his back *above* | *The element they lived in*', 5.2.89–91; emphasis added).

Anthony still has to cope with the terrible anticlimax of his botched suicide ('I have done my work ill') and the ensuing indignities of the monument scene; but his subsuming of the heroic in the erotic sets the pattern for Cleopatra's more sustained exercise in self-undoing which, like his, is figured as at once an act of self-surrender (in which she will be 'taken' by a highly eroticized Death, whose stroke is 'as a lover's pinch', 5.2.294), and a form of paradoxically heroical self-fashioning, something done 'after the high Roman fashion' (4.16.88).[1]

FINIS CORONAT OPUS: DOING AND UNDOING (2)

Superficially the ending of *Anthony and Cleopatra* is bound to recall that of Shakespeare's first love tragedy, *Romeo and Juliet*, with its setting in the Capulet tomb. In each play, the death of a female protagonist leaves the stage to be commanded by spokesmen of patriarchal authority who lend their ambiguous voices to the monumentalization of transgressive passion. In each play the place of death has been imaginatively transformed, in a fashion that echoes the play's own probing of the relation between death and desire, to a site of erotic consummation:

> Shall I believe
> That unsubstantial death is amorous,
> And that the lean abhorrèd monster keeps
> Thee here in dark to be his paramour?
>
> *Romeo* 5.3.102–5

> Now boast thee, Death, in thy possession lies
> A lass unparalleled.
>
> *Anthony* 5.2.313–14

---

[1] Erickson's term for the cross-gender identification exemplified in her death and Anthony's is '*heterosexual androgyny*', *Patriarchal Structures*, p. 133. See also James J. Greene, 'Antony and Cleopatra: The Birth and Death of Androgyny,' *Hartford Studies in Literature*, 19 (1987), pp. 24–44. Carol Thomas Neely, on the other hand, has argued that 'in *Antony and Cleopatra* . . . gender roles are not exchanged or transcended, but are played out in more variety than in the other tragedies'; 'Gender and Genre in *Antony and Cleopatra*' in *Broken Nuptials in Shakespeare's Plays* (New Haven, Conn., 1985), 136–65 (p. 137). Although she insists that gender distinctions are ultimately 'ratified' by the play Neely nevertheless finds that this enlargement of gender roles is sufficient to expand its genre in a way that partially anticipates the mixed form of the romances.

In each play the death of the lovers confirms the excited drive to self-consumption with which their forbidden liaison has always been entangled:

> These violent delights have violent ends,
> And in their triumph die like fire and powder,
> Which as they kiss consume.

Romeo 2.5.9–11

Yet, although the streak of self-destructive perversity apparent in Romeo's compulsive attraction to Capulet women is writ large in Anthony's consuming desire for a foreign queen, his fatal passion produces a very different kind of catastrophe, whose keynotes are of relaxation, glad self-abandon, and ultimate triumph. Cleopatra's royal mausoleum is conspicuously without the sepulchral grotesquerie with which the Capulet tomb emblematizes the implication of sexuality in the processes of mortal change.

In his first exchange with Anthony, Enobarbus had mocked Cleopatra's erotic hyperbole with his own sardonic version of the Death and the Maiden trope: 'I do think there is mettle in death, which commits some loving act upon her, she hath such a celerity in dying' (1.2.141–3). Now the Queen produces her own strangely metamorphosed version of this well-worn conceit, endowing it with an astonished (and astonishing) literalness: 'The stroke of death is as a lover's pinch, | Which hurts, and is desired' (5.2.294–5). The agent of that stroke, the asp, is delivered by a Clown whose eldritch humour identifies him as the antic voice of mortality; and the Clown's description of his 'worm' that feeds on woman's flesh associates it with the maggots of vermiculation. From the perspective that he supplies, this image of a queen with a worm at her breast resembles a tomb-sculpture in the *macabre* tradition. Yet the gothic horror of Romeo's 'worms that are thy chambermaids' (*Romeo* 5.3.109), is here transmuted to the strangely passive submission of a 'pretty worm | Of Nilus' (ll. 242–4) which becomes the 'baby at my breast, | That sucks the nurse asleep' (ll. 308–9); and in an oddly touching recollection of the maternal *pietà* in which she cradled her dying lover, Cleopatra's imagination transforms the asp to a surrogate for Anthony himself: 'As sweet as balm, as

soft as air, as gentle. | O Anthony! Nay, I will take thee too.'
(ll. 310–11).[1]

If this suckling creature is on one level a substitute for
Anthony—the lover as helpless infant, or phallic warrior
reduced to 'pretty worm'—it is also, more conspicuously, a
diminutive or infant version of her personal emblem, 'the
serpent of old Nile', which symbolizes her peculiar intimacy
with the processes of life and death.[2] It thus acts (as a
nursing baby properly should) as a kind of Venus's mirror,
the mysterious female property which gives back to its owner
the image of her own perfection. Yet if Cleopatra's triumph
registers as a kind of completeness—something that renders
her disdainfully impervious to 'the luck of Caesar'—it is not
simply of the archetypally female kind. To the contrary, what
she claims is the androgynous wholeness at which Anthony's
end gestures only falteringly. It is not for nothing that, in
handing over to Cleopatra almost the whole last act, Shakespeare accords her the structural privilege conventionally
granted to the male protagonist. For Cleopatra's triumph is
ultimately dependent on her assumption of a propertied 'self'

---

[1] The complex word-play on 'gentle' (emphasized by Cleopatra's aposiopesis, and the dying fall of her feminine ending) deserves notice here:
picking up the soothing suggestions of 'balm', it also seems to send her mind
back to the 'gentle' Anthony; applied to a worm, however, it must recall her
fantasy earlier in the scene of her own fly-blown corpse in a 'gentle grave',
with its grotesque play on *gentle* as a word for maggot. What results is a
rhetorical metamorphosis in which the worm of corruption becomes itself the
balm of preservation. The transformation is entirely appropriate to a creature
associated with the ambivalent river Nile, whose 'mud' and 'slime' are at
once the signs of mortal corruption and the philoprogenitive source of spon-
taneous life.

[2] Shakespeare deliberately departed from Plutarch's account, where Cleopatra dies from bites to the arm, in favour of the several medieval and
Renaissance versions which have her applying the asps to her breasts. The
resulting tableau is powerfully suggestive, and critics have variously seen in
it echoes of the ancient iconography of the Earth Goddess (see Adelman,
Common Liar, pp. 64, 205), hints of mother Eve, or suggestions of 'a Satanic
Virgin Mary, suckling a viper at her breast . . . [an] age-old image . . . of sin
and repentance' (Barroll, pp. 182–3). Hughes-Hallett usefully points both to
the significance of serpents in the Egyptian Isis cult (where their symbolism
includes immortality), and to nineteenth-century sado-erotic responses to
Cleopatra (where her snakes represent a decadent fascination with evil and
death): see Hughes-Hallett, *Cleopatra*, pp. 106–9, 239–40. The power of the
scene probably depends on its capacity to evoke a variety of such contradictory
associations whilst resisting containment by any one of them.

which allows her to play out a superb mastery of the masculine vocabulary of 'doing'.

In the tightly enfolded paradoxes of Act 5 where Cleopatra's 'desolation does begin to make | A better life' (5.2.1–2) doing and undoing at last become, to all intents and purposes, one. The act that Proculeius superficially dismisses as 'Th' undoing of yourself' (5.2.44) becomes for Cleopatra the triumphant doing that 'ends all other deeds' (5.2.5), liberating its performer from the contingency of mere action in a world where the politician Caesar (like the Clown's worm of mortality) is condemned to 'do his kind'. The theatrical metaphor which Shakespeare chose to embody this arresting sublimation of doing and undoing involves a marvellously anachronistic borrowing from the language of contemporary political pageantry. Cleopatra stages her suicide as a ceremonious reversal of Anthony's: her followers dress her in the properties of Egyptian royalty as Eros had stripped Anthony of the trappings of Roman soldiership. The full meaning of this formal re-membering of her regal self is best understood, however, by contrast with the symbolic self-dismemberment performed by Richard II when he consents to 'undeck the pompous body of a king':

> Now mark me how I will undo myself.
> I give this heavy weight from off my head,
> And this unwieldy sceptre from my hand,
> The pride of kingly sway from out my heart.
>
> *Richard II* 4.1.193–6

As Richard mimes the stripping away of his 'body politic' to expose his 'body natural' in all its mortal frailty,[1] so Cleopatra, discarding her elements of 'baser life', mimes the assumption of a royal identity, the immortal body symbolized by the regalia in which her women deck her:[2] 'Give me my robe, put on my crown—I have | Immortal longings in me' (5.2.279–80).

---

[1] For an account of the political doctrine on which this scene depends, see Ernst H. Kantorowicz, *The King's Two Bodies: A Study in Medieval Theology* (Princeton, NJ, 1957).

[2] Of course Shakespeare found the detail of Cleopatra's corpse 'attired and arrayed in her royal robes' in North's Plutarch; but with this act of formal investiture he completely transformed its significance.

From one point of view (which the play by no means suppresses) Cleopatra's is an empty gesture, of course—depending as it does on the audience's willingness to submit to a political illusion that has been given no real substance by the preceding action. This 'royal' Cleopatra barely exists elsewhere, outside Enobarbus's beglamoured imagination. What endows her 'noble act' with its theatrical power, however, saving it from the self-deceiving narcissism that compromises Richard's display, is precisely its self-conscious paradoxicality—the fine effrontery that allows the Queen to exploit the iconography of immortal royal authority at precisely the point where the utter dissipation of her own political power has mortally undone her.

In the process Cleopatra converts her suicide into an extraordinary unmetaphoring of the stoic proverb which, in its several forms, traditionally expressed the paradoxical splendour of the good death: *Finis coronat opus*—the end crowns the work. This favourite tag, and its English proverbial variant, 'the evening crowns the day, and death crowns life',[1] enjoy a strange subterranean life through the play's closing scenes.[2] They surface progressively through the recurrent imagery of crowns and crowning,[3] and the persistent identification of death with the ending of day ('the long day's task is done', 4.15.35; 'Our lamp is spent, it's out', 4.16.86; 'the bright day is done', 5.2.193), to emerge full blown in the staging of Cleopatra's coronation-in-death:

---

[1] See e.g. *2 Henry VI* (Folio version) 5.3.10; *Troilus* 4.7.107; *All's Well* 4.4.35–6. Richard Nochimson's essay 'The End Crowns All' seems to hint at the significance of the tag with the title it borrows from *Troilus*, only to read the ending ironically. However, the theatrical potency of Shakespeare's unmetaphoring of the proverb is suggested by Ford's imitation of it in the coronation-in-death which concludes *The Broken Heart*, where Cleopatra's 'Husband, I come' is formalized as a rite of marriage: 'Thus I new marry him whose wife I am' (*Broken Heart* 5.3.66). In Webster's *The Duchess of Malfi*, the Duchess's deliberate undoing of her royal self, as she submits to death upon her knees, looks like a conscious reversal of Shakespeare's conceit.

[2] Anthony's magnanimity, for example, ironically 'crowns' Enobarbus's disgraceful end with gold (4.6.33); Anthony identifies the bosom of his 'grave charm', Cleopatra, as 'my crownet, my chief end' (4.13.27)—both the focus of his desire, and his place of death; Cleopatra figures Anthony's death as the melting of 'the crown o'th'earth' (4.16.65).

[3] For an analysis of this imagery, see Wilson Knight, *Imperial Theme*, pp. 248–9.

> Show me, my women, like a queen. Go fetch
> My best attires. . . . bring our crown and all. . . .
> My resolution's placed, and I have nothing
> Of woman in me—now from head to foot
> I am marble constant; now the fleeting moon
> No planet is of mine.

5.2.227–41

Death crowns life by translating it out of the realm of the contingent into the immutability of monumental marble. A double paradox is involved here, since the turning of human flesh to stone is conventionally a sign of death's arrest, an 'essential metaphor for the body's undoing' in Leonard Barkan's words[1]—as it is in *The Winter's Tale*, for example. But Cleopatra makes it the sign for a different kind of arrest, the shackling of accident and bolting up of the arbitrary change associated not just with her infinite variety, but with mutability and death itself. It is an essential part of the sublime paradox through which the Queen aims to 'remake past time' and to deny death itself, that the final scene of her tragedy should be played out in a funerary monument, as a tableau of constancy whose self-conscious theatricality (emphasized by the iteration of words like 'show', 'play', 'act', 'perform') produces perhaps the most splendid elaboration in all drama of the ancient trope of art-as-monument.[2]

Cleopatra's is a triumph which presses even Octavius Caesar into the reluctant service of her fame:

> She shall be buried by her Anthony—
> No grave upon the earth shall clip in it
> A pair so famous.

5.2.356–8

---

[1] Leonard Barkan, *The Gods Made Flesh: Metamorphosis and the Pursuit of Paganism* (New Haven, Conn., 1986), p. 90.

[2] This aspect of the ending is stressed by Robert Ornstein, 'The Ethic of the Imagination: Love and Art in *Antony and Cleopatra*', in John Russell Brown and Bernard Harris (eds.), *Later Shakespeare*, Stratford-upon-Avon Studies 8 (London, 1966), pp. 31–46. See also Anne Barton, 'The Divided Catastrophe', pp. 11, 17, 20. For a discussion of the funerary iconography of the scene which compares the figure of the dead Cleopatra to a piece of mortuary sculpture in a chantry chapel, see John M. Bowers, 'Cleopatra's Monumental End', *Huntington Library Quarterly*, 46 (1983), pp. 283–97. For a reading of the play which resists as inappropriately 'comic' the notion of Cleopatra's end

Caesar's valedictory tribute turns upon a word-play of un-characteristic delicacy: 'clip' first hints at the arbitrary cutting off, the sudden arrest of death, only to reveal itself as a word from Anthony's amatory vocabulary ('clip your wives', 4.9.8) which serves to prolong the erotic glow that the lovers' own rhetoric has cast over their end. In this it once again recalls the ending of *Romeo and Juliet*, where the golden statues promised by the grieving fathers will monumentalize forever the erotic embrace of the lovers' death ('As rich shall Romeo's by his lady's lie,' 5.3.303). The parallel serves as reminder of another aspect of the play's double nature—the generic ir-regularity that allows a political history-play to preserve, in the teeth of its own scepticism, the qualities of both heroic drama and love tragedy. It is important that the stage property on which Cleopatra's death is performed should be, after all, a bed and not a throne. The 'fame' of which Octavius speaks attaches the dead to his public realm of 'high events' and 'solemn shows'; but the embrace of the grave belongs to that conspicuously private domain in which Caesar is ren-dered 'ass | Unpolicied' (5.2.306–7).[1]

However powerfully Cleopatra is allowed to make her claims on us, the play does not, of course, end on a note of unam-biguous triumph.[2] Whatever her imagination makes of it, 'the worm will do his kind'; and we are not allowed to forget

as in any sense triumphant, see J. Leeds Barroll, *Shakespearean Tragedy: Genre, Tradition, and Change 'Antony and Cleopatra'* (Washington, DC, 1984). For Barroll, if Cleopatra is to be seen as tragic in the same way as Shakespeare's male protagonists, she must be seen as 'losing all, like Lear and Richard stripped literally and figuratively to a nakedness' (p. 134); just as Anthony is tragic because he abandons his 'one great truth . . . his loving and the love he causes in others' in favour of 'two lies', Rome and the idea of 'himself as hero and soldier' (p. 272).

[1] Stanley Wells has drawn my attention to the way in which 'ass un-policied' forms 'a curious half-rhyme' with 'lass unparalleled'.

[2] Honigmann (whose reading is more sceptical than mine) but who never-theless confesses to being at a certain point 'swept along' by Cleopatra's performance, puts the matter nicely: 'Shakespeare built so many contrary impressions into the fifth act that Cleopatra's motives and self-awareness are much harder to assess than those of the typical tragic hero, or of Antony. Ennoblement remains a possibility, though not one that we can fully believe in. It is merely a possibility—and *Antony and Cleopatra* differs from the other tragedies in leaving this all-important point unresolved' (*Shakespeare: Seven Tragedies*, p. 169).

that the fulfilment of Cleopatra's 'immortal longings' is dependent on an 'immortal' biting that cuts off her speech upon an enigmatic half line (5.2.312). Cleopatra may choose to think of Octavius as the relict of her transformation, a cast-off creature of sublunary Fortune (5.2.2–4); but even if he is bilked of his triumphal centrepiece, the closing moments of the play belong to him. However much Anthony and Cleopatra may seem to elude the ends that Caesar designs for them, the ending is nevertheless practically at his disposal. It is Caesar's rhetoric which forces the Queen's monumental spectacle to submit to one of those potentially self-cancelling oxymorons familiar from the earlier part of the play: 'O, noble weakness' (l. 342). The phrase is curiously reminiscent of Cleopatra's dismissal of Antony's 'excellent falsehood' and 'excellent dissembling' (1.1.42; 3.79); and a kind of excellent falsehood—'lies, | Alas, unparalleled' in the pun that Charmian's fine tribute cannot quite exclude (5.2.313–14)—is all that Caesar tempts us to see in the exquisite dissembling of Cleopatra's end. By the same token, however, theatrical dissembling of another kind is what we are bound to recognize in the 'solemn show' of a funeral that expresses the victor's 'pity' for the defeated only in so far as it proclaims 'his [own] glory which | Brought them to be lamented' (ll. 360–1). In its meticulous rendering unto Caesar of that which is his, *Anthony and Cleopatra* is careful to acknowledge the limitations attendant on the poetry of transcendence as well as upon the prosaic 'measure' of policy. But, then, as I have argued, its power to move us is at every point dependent on just such awareness of the fragile nature of the artifice on which it stakes everything—an awareness that is never more beautifully registered than in the gesture of extraordinary tenderness with which Charmian registers her allegiance to the end that crowns the masterpiece: 'Your crown's awry, | I'll mend it, and then play—' (ll. 316–17).

EDITORIAL PROCEDURES

The text of this edition is based on the sole authoritative text of the play, the Folio of 1623, using the version prepared by Charlton Hinman for the Norton Facsimile, which I have checked against the copy held in the Auckland public library.[1] The text has been thoroughly modernized in broad accordance with the principles adumbrated by the General Editor of the series,[2] and quotations from other sixteenth and seventeenth-century texts are similarly treated—the only exception being at 3.7.13–15, where the editorial argument requires a literal reproduction of North's punctuation. Modernization of the text is generally silent, except where it may be contentious, or where the modern spelling obscures significant word-play, when the alteration is collated and (if necessary) discussed in the commentary—as for example at 1.2.154 (travel/Trauaile). In some few cases I have chosen to preserve such forms as 'my self', where simple substitution of the modern pronoun 'myself', as well as disturbing the metre, tends to obscure the anxious preoccupation with role and identity conveyed by the original (as for example at 1.2.117, or 3.4.23). This seems of particular importance in a play which renders the constitution of the 'self' so intensely problematic.

Only in the treatment of proper names, however, will the edition depart significantly from the usual principles of modernization observed in the series. This is because such names present special barriers to consistency. Arguing the need for a wholesale modernizing of historical and significant names, Jürgen Schäfer acidly observes that they have never been 'subjected to the principle of modernization nor to any other editorial principle'.[3] Schäfer's position is strongly supported

[1] Charlton Hinman (ed.), *The First Folio of Shakespeare: The Norton Facsimile* (New York, 1968).

[2] See Stanley Wells, 'Modernizing Shakespeare's Spelling', in Wells and Gary Taylor, *Modernizing Shakespeare's Spelling, with Three Studies in the Text of Henry V* (Oxford, 1979); and Wells, *Re-Editing Shakespeare for the Modern Reader* (Oxford, 1984). The editorial procedures adopted for the whole series are fully laid out in Gary Taylor's edition of *Henry V*, pp. 75–81.

[3] Jürgen Schäfer, 'The Orthography of Proper Names in Modern-spelling Editions of Shakespeare,' *SB* 23 (1970), pp. 1–19 (p. 1).

by Stanley Wells (*Re-Editing Shakespeare*, pp. 22–4); but Wells's own edition (like every other) bears witness to the virtual impossibility of devising any completely consistent method of rendering the names in *Anthony and Cleopatra* or any of Shakespeare's Roman plays. It is true that, since the beginning of the eighteenth century, editors have routinely attempted to regularize the Folio spellings of Roman names in accordance with current popular and scholarly practice; but none has managed a completely consistent procedure—*Varrius*, for example, is rarely, if ever, corrected to the proper form, *Varius*; and *Scarrus*, though usually emended to *Scarus*, is never replaced by the strictly correct *Scaurus*. Indeed, if rigorously applied, the principle would produce such metrical impossibilities as *Ahenobarbus* for *Enobarbus*. Early editors felt little compunction in simply using North's Plutarch to 'correct' F: thus Theobald replaced F's *Thidias* with North's *Thyreus* (though Plutarch himself had given the name as *Thyrsus*); even more oddly Pope chose to render as *Dercetas* the name which F gives variously as *Dercetus* (1), *Decretas* (2), *Decre.* (1), and *Dec.* (3), on the grounds that this odd hybrid, while preserving the metre, was orthographically closer to Plutarch's *Dercetaeus*. Modern editors, by contrast, have complicated the business of regularization by acknowledging that some Folio names, rather than representing irregular, phonetically influenced seventeenth-century spellings, or compositorial misreadings, may actually be deliberate authorial alterations. Thus, for example (despite the ambiguous evidence of the text), Dover Wilson defended *Decretas* as a genuine Shakespearian coinage. More recently the Oxford editors have elected to restore F's *Camidius* in place of the almost universally accepted and historically correct *Canidius*, apparently on the grounds that it too represents a deliberate alteration of the source name.

The Oxford decision is a puzzling one since the substitution of *-m-* for *-n-* could easily be accounted for as a scribal or compositorial minim-error; while in the one case where there are reasonably good grounds for believing that a rejected F form represents a genuine Shakespearian preference, the editors accept the usual latinizing *Antony* for *Anthony*. In most cases, of course, the problem is a purely technical one, the alternatives being phonetically indistinguishable. But it is not necessarily for that reason a completely trivial matter, since the 'look' of such crucial details can be of some importance in determining the 'feel' of the text; and it can be argued that the attempt to give the names in their 'correct' form is a textual counterpart of the theatrical attempts to archaeologize the play which reached their disastrous apogee in the spectacular nineteenth-century productions that boasted their pedigree from 'the splendid Collection of Roman and Egyptian Antiquities in the British Museum'.

A good argument can be made, then, for simply printing all the characters' names in the form apparently preferred by Shakespeare—especially since the defamiliarizing effect of restoring these spellings can serve as a useful reminder that the characters are not, after all, Romans, but Jacobean representations of Romans, personages substantially of Shakespeare's own invention, in many ways as unlike their historical models as the classical figures in Renaissance painting, or the anachronistically costumed actors in Henry Peacham's illustration of *Titus Andronicus*. Unfortunately, however, the problem is not so easily resolved, since there can be no certainty that the F spellings always represent what Shakespeare wrote. F was set from good copy close to the dramatist's own foul papers, but its universal preference for 'Oh' rather than 'O' suggests, as John Jowett and Gary Taylor have shown, that it may have been manuscript in someone else's hand.[1] Thus, in considering how to render the name *Dercetus/Decretas*, for example, apart from possible authorial inconsistency, we need to take into account the possibility of both scribal and compositorial misreading. *Decretas* is a perfectly conceivable misreading for *Dercetus* or *Dercetas*; and since *Dercetus*, the form in which the name first appears in F, is phonetically a little closer to North and virtually identical to *Dircetus*, the form adopted in the Countess of Pembroke's *The Tragedy of Antonie*, which Shakespeare may have known, I have chosen to use it here. Bevington, who makes the same decision, further

[1] See Gary Taylor and John Jowett, ' "With New Additions": Theatrical Interpolation in *Measure for Measure*', in their *Shakespeare Reshaped, 1606–1623*. For a suggestion that the copy-text may have been a private transcript, see H. R. Woudhuysen, 'The Year's Contributions to Shakespeare Studies: 3. Editions and Textual Studies', *SSu* 45 (1992), pp. 193–204 (p. 196).

argues that 'Compositor B could not have happened on the historically correct *Dercetus* . . . unless it was in his copy'.

The alteration of *Dercetaeus* is probably explicable as a metrical convenience. But since Shakespeare seems to have worked with a copy of North's Plutarch beside him, one might otherwise expect him, where he was not deliberately modernizing, to have stuck fairly closely to North's spellings—a practice evident, for example, in F's preference of *Ptolomy* for *Ptolemy*, and perhaps also in 'Brandusium' (echoing North's 'Brundusium') for *Brundisium* (3.7.21). However, names like *Towrus* and *Thidias* call this assumption into question. While 'Towrus' is certainly a possible misreading for *Taurus*, it is equally explicable as a phonetic mistranscription; and only some sort of phonetic confusion can plausibly account for the otherwise arbitrary-seeming transformation of *Thyreus* into *Thidias*—since (as Marvin Spevack has pointed out to me) if *Thyreus* was pronounced with a short -*y*- and a rolled -*r*- the two forms would have sounded almost indistinguishable. It is difficult, however, to imagine any circumstances in the transmission of the text that could produce such consistent phonetic mistakes, so that one must assume that the transformations somehow took place in the dramatist's own head, and that the spellings are therefore authentically Shakespearian.[1]

The hero's own name ought to present fewer difficulties. F is quite consistent in spelling it with an -*h*- (except at 4.16.12–13 where abbreviation is required by the exigencies of typesetting). In speech-prefixes the preferred form is '*Ant.*', but appearance of '*Anth.*' and '*Antho.*' in a significant minority of cases lends weight to the supposition that the manuscript spelt the name with an -*h*-. Since this form is almost invariably favoured elsewhere in the canon, we can be reasonably certain that (unlike *Oh*) it represents the dramatist's own preference;[2] and since it also corresponds to the most common

---

[1] It may be worth noting, however, that there are other apparent phonetic errors in F whose presence is less easily explained: e.g. *vouchsafe to/Vouchsafed to* at 1.4.8; *places vnder us/place is under us* at 1.2.194; *Ventigius/Ventidius* in 2.3; *Action/Actium* at 3.7.51; *Mine/My* at 4.9.18.

[2] The sole, rather confusing exception is *Julius Caesar*, whose most recent editor, however, takes its preference for 'Antony' as significant evidence of scribal transmission of the manuscript; see Arthur Humphreys (ed.), *Julius Caesar* (Oxford, 1984), pp. 73–4.

modern form of the name, only a misleading antiquarian habit (and a desire to be consistent with the orthography of *Julius Caesar*, where *Antony* is preferred) can justify the retention of Rowe's spelling. Accordingly I have chosen to retain *Anthony*—even at the risk of some inconsistency, since on the few occasions where Shakespeare uses the Latin or Italian form of the name, retention of the bastard forms *Anthonius* and *Anthonio* would probably constitute an unnecessary distraction for the modern reader.

In general then, and despite the principles of modernization applied to other parts of the text, this edition seeks to preserve characters' personal names in the forms that F suggests were favoured by the dramatist. There would seem to be little point, however, in extending this practice to the names of persons who are not included in the action (i.e. to historical personages who enjoy no separate existence as characters in Shakespeare's drama, such as Cleopatra's brother, *Ptolemy*—*Ptolomy* in F), where it might seem like a new kind of antiquarian fussiness. Equally, in the case of familiar geographical names it could only be a source of pointless confusion.

The Folio contains no act or scene divisions, after the initial heading '*Actus Primus. Scœna Prima*'; the divisions followed here are those adopted by nearly all editions since the eighteenth century, except in Act 4, scene 7, where logic demands that the clearing of the stage after Agrippa's three-line speech should mark the beginning of a new scene. Nevertheless it needs to be remembered that such scene divisions are wholly editorial, deriving (like the misleading indications of locale still found in some editions) from the stage practice of a later era, and bear no relation to the continuous staging of Shakespeare's playhouse. Even act divisions, though common in Jacobean texts, were a mainly literary convention—except in the so-called 'private' theatres, where music was normally played between the acts. Accordingly both act and scene divisions are rendered as inconspicuous as possible in this edition; while discussion of locale is confined to the commentary on those few scenes (notably the episodes in Cleopatra's monument in Acts 4 and 5) where the imagined location requires particular stage effects.

All significant alterations to F's stage directions are collated, but only those likely to be regarded as contentious are distinguished in the text by the use of half-brackets and discussed in the commentary. Directions for characters to speak 'aside' or 'to' another character are entirely editorial and are therefore not collated. In the text the ending of an aside, like a speaker's change of addressee, is indicated by a dash. Speech-prefixes are silently normalized and given in full.

The collation employs the format outlined by Gary Taylor in his edition of *Henry V*:

What's . . . Jupiter?] OXFORD; Whats *Anthony*, the . . . *Iupiter*? F; What's *Antony*? The . . . *Jupiter*. JOHNSON

where the lemma, representing the chosen reading, is followed by the source of the reading, then by the rejected Folio reading, and finally by the proposals of other editors, if any. The latter are recorded only when they seem particularly plausible or interesting. The early folios are cited *literatim*, ignoring only long *s* and diagraphs. In addition to collating emendations, contentious modernizations, and significant changes in punctuation, the edition also records realignments of verse and prose. Since these have a bearing upon sometimes contentious issues of versification, they are best studied as a group and are therefore consigned to a special appendix.

The commentary employs *OED*'s abbreviations for different parts of speech and its numbering system for different definitions and usages, which are often paraphrased without acknowledgement. Proverbs and proverbial expressions have been checked against both Tilley and Dent. References to other works of Shakespeare are keyed to the Oxford edition of *The Complete Works*, ed. Stanley Wells and Gary Taylor (Oxford, 1986); while biblical citations, unless otherwise indicated, are to the Geneva Bible (1560).

Because Shakespeare's use of Plutarch's 'Life of Marcus Antonius' is so extensive and detailed, it has been thought better to include an abbreviated text of North's translation in an appendix, rather than clog up the commentary with long quotations. The commentary does, however, alert the reader to the more significant borrowings from North, and North's text in turn is annotated with act, scene, and line numbers to make cross-referencing as easy as possible. For other possible sources the reader is referred, as appropriate, to Bullough's magisterial collection. Further appendices are devoted to the vexed question of the staging of Act 4, scene 16 and Act 5, scene 2, and to a discussion of the nuances of pronoun usage in the play, overlooked by most commentators.

This edition was prepared independently of Stanley Wells's in the Oxford *Complete Works*; though I have, of course consulted that text, and am indebted to it at several points.

Abbreviations and References

Place of publication, except where otherwise specified, is London.

EDITIONS OF SHAKESPEARE

F	The First Folio, 1623 (F*a* and F*b* denote variant states of this text)
F2	The Second Folio, 1632
F3	The Third Folio, 1663
F4	The Fourth Folio, 1685
Alexander	Peter Alexander, *Complete Works* (1951)
Arden	M. R. Ridley, *Antony and Cleopatra*, The Arden Shakespeare (1954), based on the edition of R. H. Case (1906)
Bevington	David Bevington, *Antony and Cleopatra* (Cambridge, 1990)
Cambridge	W. G. Clark and W. A. Wright, *Works*, The Cambridge Shakespeare, 9 vols. (Cambridge, 1863–6)
Capell	Edward Capell, *Comedies, Histories, and Tragedies*, 10 vols. (1767–8)
Case	See Arden
Collier	John Payne Collier, *Works*, 8 vols. (1842–4)
Collier 1853	John Payne Collier, *Works*, 8 vols. (1853)
Collier 1858	John Payne Collier, *Comedies, Histories, Tragedies, and Poems*, 6 vols. (1858)
Craig	W. J. Craig, *The Complete Works of Shakespeare* (1891)
Delius	Nicolaus Delius, *Werke*, 7 vols. (Elberfeld, 1854–60)

Dyce	Alexander Dyce, *Works*, 6 vols. (1857)
Furness	Horace Howard Furness, *The Tragedie of Anthonie, and Cleopatra*, New Variorum (Philadelphia, 1907)
Hanmer	Thomas Hanmer, *Works*, 6 vols. (Oxford, 1743–4)
Harrison	G. B. Harrison, *Antony and Cleopatra*, The Penguin Shakespeare (Harmondsworth, 1951)
Hudson	H. N. Hudson, *The Complete Works of William Shakespeare*, 20 vols. (1880–1)
Irving	H. Irving and F. Marshall, *The Henry Irving Shakespeare* (1888)
Johnson	Samuel Johnson, *Plays*, 8 vols. (1765)
Jones	Emrys Jones, *Antony and Cleopatra*, The New Penguin Shakespeare (Harmondsworth, 1977)
Keightley	Thomas Keightley, *Plays*, 6 vols. (1864)
Kittredge	George Lyman Kittredge, *Complete Works* (Boston, 1936)
Knight	Charles Knight, *Comedies, Histories, Tragedies, and Poems*, Pictorial Edition, 7 vols. (1838–43)
Mack	Maynard Mack, *Antony and Cleopatra*, The Pelican Shakespeare (New York, 1970)
Malone	Edmond Malone, *Plays and Poems*, 10 vols. (1790)
Norton	Charlton Hinman, *The First Folio of Shakespeare* (New York, 1968)
Oxford	Stanley Wells, *Antony and Cleopatra* in Stanley Wells and Gary Taylor (gen. eds.), *The Complete Works*, The Oxford Shakespeare (Oxford, 1986), together with textual notes in Wells and Taylor, *A Shakespeare Companion*, The Oxford Shakespeare (Oxford, 1987)
Pope	Alexander Pope, *Works*, 6 vols. (1725)
Pope 1728	Alexander Pope, *Works*, 10 vols. (1728)
Ridley	See Arden
Riverside	G. Blakemore Evans, *The Riverside Shakespeare* (Boston, Mass., 1974)
Rowe,	Nicholas Rowe, *Works*, 6 vols. (1709)
Rowe 1709(2)	Nicholas Rowe, *Works*, 6 vols. (1709), 2nd ed.
Rowe 1714	Nicholas Rowe, *Works*, 8 vols. (1714)
Singer	S. W. Singer, *Dramatic Works*, 10 vols. (1826)
Singer 1856	S. W. Singer, *Dramatic Works*, 10 vols. (1856)
Spevack	Marvin Spevack (ed.), *Antony and Cleopatra*, a New Variorum Edition (MLA, 1990)

Staunton	Howard Staunton, *Plays*, 3 vols. (1858–60)
Steevens	Samuel Johnson and George Steevens, *Plays*, 10 vols. (1773)
Steevens 1778	Samuel Johnson and George Steevens, *Plays*, 10 vols. (1778)
Steevens 1785	Samuel Johnson, George Steevens, and Isaac Reed, *Plays*, 10 vols. (1785)
Steevens 1793	George Steevens and Isaac Reed, *Plays*, 15 vols. (1793)
Theobald	Lewis Theobald, *Works*, 7 vols. (1733)
Theobald 1740	Lewis Theobald, *Works*, 8 vols. (1740)
Warburton	William Warburton, *Works*, 8 vols. (1747)
Wilson	John Dover Wilson, *Antony and Cleopatra*, The New Shakespeare (Cambridge, 1950)

OTHER WORKS AND ABBREVIATIONS

Barroll	J. Leeds Barroll, 'Scarrus and the Scarred Soldier', *HLQ* 22 (1958), pp. 31–9
Bullough	Geoffrey Bullough, *Narrative and Dramatic Sources of Shakespeare*, 8 vols (1957–75)
Collier MS	Manuscript emendations in Collier's copy of F2 (the 'Perkins Folio'), generally assumed to be in Collier's hand
Daniel	Samuel Daniel, *The Tragedy of Cleopatra*, in Bullough, vol. v, pp. 406–49.
Deighton	Kenneth Deighton, *The Old Dramatists: Conjectural Readings* (1896)
Dent	R. W. Dent, *Shakespeare's Proverbial Language: An Index* (Berkeley, Calif., 1981)
ELR	English Literary Renaissance
Garnier	Robert Garnier, *The Tragedy of Antony*, trans. Mary Herbert (1595) in Bullough, vol. v, pp. 358–406.
Granville-Barker	H. Granville-Barker, *Prefaces to Shakespeare: Antony and Cleopatra, Coriolanus* (1931; pb. edn. 1963)
Greg	W. W. Greg, *The Shakespeare First Folio* (Oxford, 1955)
Hinman	Charlton Hinman, *The Printing and Proof-Reading of the First Folio of Shakespeare*, 2 vols. (Oxford, 1963)

HLQ	Huntington Library Quarterly
Hughes-Hallett	Lucy Hughes-Hallett, *Cleopatra: Histories, Dreams, Distortions* (1990)
Jackson	Zachariah Jackson, *Shakespeare's Genius Justified* (1819)
Lamb	Margaret Lamb, *Antony and Cleopatra on the English stage* (Rutherford, NJ, 1980)
Lowen	Tirzah Lowen, *Peter Hall Directs 'Antony and Cleopatra'* (1990)
Mason	John Monck Mason, *Comments on the Last Edition of Shakespeare's Plays* (1785)
Miola	Robert S. Miola, *Shakespeare's Rome* (Cambridge, 1983)
Montaigne	John Florio (trans.), *Essays*, 3 vols. (1910)
N&Q	*Notes and Queries*
Naylor	E. W. Naylor, *Shakespeare and Music* (1931)
North	Plutarch, *The Lives of the Noble Grecians and Romans . . . Translated out of the Greek into French by James Amyot . . . and out of French into English by Thomas North* (1579 and 1603). The augmented 1603 edition contains Simon Goulart's translation of the spurious 'Life of Octavius Caesar Augustus.' See also Bullough.
OED	*Oxford English Dictionary*
Oxford . . . Proverbs	Oxford Dictionary of English Proverbs, revised F. P. Wilson (Oxford, 1970)
Partridge	Eric Partridge, *Shakespeare's Bawdy* (1947)
Plutarch	'The Life of Marcus Antonius' in the Loeb Edition of *Plutarch's Lives*, with a translation by Bernadette Perrin, 11 vols. (1914–26), vol. ix; and see North
Plutarch's *Morals*	Plutarch, *The Philosophy, commonly called The Morals*, trans. Philemon Holland (1603)
Puttenham	George Puttenham, *The Arte of English Poesie* (1559)
RES	*Review of English Studies*
Revenger's Tragedy	Cyril Tourneur, *The Revenger's Tragedy*, ed. Brian Gibbons (1967)
SB	*Studies in Bibliography*

Schäfer	Jürgen Schäfer, *Documentation in the O.E.D.: Shakespeare and Nashe as Test Cases* (Oxford, 1980)
Schmidt	Alexander Schmidt, *Shakespeare Lexicon and Quotation Dictionary*, 3rd edn., rev. Gregor Sarrazin (New York, 1971)
Sisson (*New Readings*)	C. J. Sisson, *New Readings in Shakespeare*, 2 vols. (Cambridge, 1956)
SQ	*Shakespeare Quarterly*
SSu	*Shakespeare Survey*
subs.	substantively
Textual Companion	Stanley Wells and Gary Taylor (eds.), *William Shakespeare: A Textual Companion* (Oxford, 1987)
Thirlby	Styan Thirlby's unpublished annotations of Pope's 1725 edition, extensively consulted by Theobald for his 1733 edition, Yale University Library
Thirlby 2	Styan Thirlby's unpublished annotations of Theobald's 1733 edition, Folger Shakespeare Library
Thirlby 3	Styan Thirlby's unpublished annotations of Warburton's 1747 edition, Folger Shakespeare Library
Thiselton	Alfred Edward Thiselton, *Some Textual Notes on The Tragedy of Anthony and Cleopatra* (1899)
Tyrwhitt	Thomas Tyrwhitt, *Observations and Conjectures upon Some Passages of Shakespeare* (1766)
Tilley	M. P. Tilley, *A Dictionary of Proverbs in England in the Sixteenth and Seventeenth Centuries* (Ann Arbor, Mich., 1950)
Wells	Stanley Wells, *Re-Editing Shakespeare for the Modern Reader* (Oxford, 1984)
Wright	George T. Wright, *Shakespeare's Metrical Art* (Berkeley, Calif., 1988)

The Tragedy of Anthony
and Cleopatra

THE PERSONS OF THE PLAY

Romans

MARK ANTHONY (Marcus Antonius)
CAESAR (Octavius Caesar) } triumvirs of Rome
LEPIDUS

DEMETRIUS

PHILO

ENOBARBUS (Domitius Enobarbus)

RANNIUS

LUCILLIUS

VENTIDIUS } friends and followers of Anthony

SILLIUS

CAMIDIUS

SCARRUS

EROS

DERCETUS

AMBASSADOR, formerly Anthony's schoolmaster

OCTAVIA (Caesar's sister)

MECENAS

AGRIPPA

TOWRUS

DOLABELLA } friends and followers of Caesar

THIDIAS

GALLUS

PROCULEIUS

POMPEY (Sextus Pompeius)

MENECRATES

MENAS } friends and followers of Pompey

VARRIUS

Egyptians

CLEOPATRA, Queen of Egypt

CHARMIAN
IRAS } ladies attendant on Cleopatra

ALEXAS
MARDIAN, a eunuch
DIOMEDES
SELEUCUS, Cleopatra's treasurer } followers of Cleopatra

A SOOTHSAYER ('Lamprius')

AN EGYPTIAN

A CLOWN

A BOY who sings

A SENTRY and men of his WATCH

MESSENGERS

SOLDIERS

GUARDS

SERVITORS

Eunuchs, courtiers, attendants, captains, servants.

THE PERSONS OF THE PLAY] *list not in* F

PERSONS OF THE PLAY For a discussion of the problematic spelling of many of the names, see Editorial Procedures, pp. 131–5.

Rannius, Lucillius Since they appear only in 1.2 and have no speaking parts, these may be merely 'ghost' characters surviving from Shakespeare's MS draft; the same may be true of 'Lamprius', unless (as this edition supposes—see notes to 1.2.1–4 and 2.2.186 below), this is intended as the name of the Soothsayer in Cleopatra's court.

The Tragedy of Anthony and Cleopatra

1.1 *Enter Demetrius and Philo*

PHILO

Nay, but this dotage of our General's

O'erflows the measure: those his goodly eyes,

That o'er the files and musters of the war

Have glowed like plated Mars, now bend, now turn

The office and devotion of their view   5

Upon a tawny front; his captain's heart,

Which in the scuffles of great fights hath burst

The buckles on his breast, reneges all temper,

And is become the bellows and the fan

To cool a gypsy's lust.

> *Flourish. Enter Anthony, Cleopatra, her ladies, the*
> *train, with eunuchs fanning her*

1.1] F (*Actus Primus. Scœna Prima.*); *Acts and scenes not otherwise marked in* F.

1.1.0 *Enter Demetrius and Philo* These characters (neither of whom is actually named in the dialogue) act both as a chorus and as a stage audience for the ensuing action, which is framed by their dialogue. The effect is to place the lovers' first scene together in theatrical quotation marks, almost as if it were a kind of play-within-the-play, emphasizing the histrionic and public aspect of their love, and establishing an unusual distance between the theatre audience and the stage action. The device is typical of a play in which the impulse to identify with the protagonists is constantly checked by the requirement to 'behold and see'—to compare what is said with what is done, to set one perspective against another, and to weigh action against action.

1–13 Nay . . . see Cf. Plutarch's assessment, Appendix A.

1 dotage imbecility; foolish behaviour; excessive love

2 O'erflows the measure exceeds the mean

3 files and musters ranks of assembled troops

4 plated armoured

5 office attention; service; duty

6 front forehead; countenance

7 scuffles The word must have had a colloquial immediacy, since this is its first recorded occurrence in *OED*.

7–8 burst . . . buckles Ironically, for one so concerned with temperance and the mean, Philo's hyperbole suggests something excessive even in the heroic Anthony he means to praise.

8 reneges all temper abandons all restraint (temperance); but the 'temper' or hardness of steel may also be suggested

9 the bellows and the fan Since the heating and cooling functions of bellows and fan seemed incompatible, this metaphor has puzzled some editors,

> Look where they come: 10
> Take but good note, and you shall see in him
> The triple pillar of the world transformed
> Into a strumpet's fool. Behold and see.

CLEOPATRA

If it be love indeed, tell me how much.

ANTHONY

There's beggary in the love that can be reckoned.   15

CLEOPATRA

I'll set a bourn how far to be beloved.

ANTHONY

Then must thou needs find out new heaven, new earth.
> *Enter a Messenger*

MESSENGER   News, my good lord, from Rome.

---

including Johnson, who thought that
Shakespeare must originally have
written something like '*To kindle and* to
cool'. But the compression serves to
create an effect of deliberate paradox—
Anthony arouses Cleopatra's desire
even as he satisfies it, just as 'she
makes hungry | Where most she satis-
fies' (2.2.244–5). Cf. also Enobarbus's
description of the fans on Cleopatra's
barge at 2.2.210–12.

10 **gypsy** Gypsies were believed to have
originated in Egypt—hence a contemptuous term for an Egyptian; but also a
cunning, deceitful, or fickle woman,
hussy, whore. Cleopatra actually belonged to the Macedonian Ptolemaic
dynasty, established by one of Alexander the Great's generals, but Shakespeare seems to have thought of her
as a 'tawny' North African.
train retinue
eunuchs fanning her (an ironic enactment of Philo's metaphor)

12 **triple pillar** i.e. one of the three triumvirs who controlled the Roman world.
The heavens, and sometimes the
earth itself, were poetically represented as supported by gigantic pillars,
to which the two pillars supporting the
so-called 'heavens' above the Elizabethan stage must have given a physical
presence.

13 **strumpet's fool** one whom a whore has

made a fool of; but also a mere jester
in a strumpet's household; significantly the
question-and-answer game
played by Cleopatra and Anthony in
the ensuing section bears a generic
resemblance to the standard repartee
between Lady and Fool—see e.g.
Twelfth Night 1.5.

15 **There's beggary . . . reckoned** love that
can be counted is of no value; cf.
Romeo 2.5.32, 'They are but beggars
that can count their worth'

16 **bourn** limit, boundary

17 **new heaven, new earth** Echoing Rev.
21: 1 'And I saw a new heaven, and
a new earth' (cf. also Isa. 65: 17, and
2 Pet. 3: 13); this allusion to the mil-
lennial vision of a New Jerusalem should
be compared with Caesar's later anticipation of 'the time of universal peace'
(4.6.4); each in its different way is
ironic, but the exact effect on Shakespeare's audience is difficult to calculate. The most extensive treatment of
this pattern of allusions is by Andrew
Fichter, '*Antony and Cleopatra*: "The
Time of Universal Peace" ', *SSu* 33
(1980), pp. 99–111. At the same time
Anthony's 'find out' associates his
hyperbole with the expanding horizons
of New World discovery, glancingly
identifying Cleopatra's 'bourn' with
the traditional limits of the ancient
world, the Pillars of Hercules with
their motto *Ne plus ultra* ('no further').

ANTHONY Grates me—the sum!

CLEOPATRA Nay, hear them, Anthony.   20
  Fulvia perchance is angry; or who knows
  If the scarce-bearded Caesar have not sent
  His powerful mandate to you: 'Do this, or this;
  Take in that kingdom, and enfranchise that.
  Perform't, or else we damn thee.'   25

ANTHONY How, my love?

CLEOPATRA Perchance? Nay, and most like.
  You must not stay here longer. Your dismission
  Is come from Caesar; therefore hear it, Anthony.
  Where's Fulvia's process?—Caesar's, I would say—   30
  both?
  Call in the messengers. As I am Egypt's queen,
  Thou blushest, Anthony, and that blood of thine
  Is Caesar's homager—else so thy cheek pays shame,
  When shrill-tongued Fulvia scolds. The messengers!

ANTHONY
  Let Rome in Tiber melt, and the wide arch   35
  Of the ranged empire fall! Here is my space.
  Kingdoms are clay. Our dungy earth alike

---

19 **Grates me—the sum** this is irksome:
give me the gist of it

21 **Fulvia** Anthony's wife. Shakespeare's
character of 'shrill-tongued Fulvia'
derives from Plutarch (see below, Appendix A).

22 **scarce-bearded Caesar** a teasing hyperbole. Octavius Caesar, great-nephew
and adopted heir of Julius Caesar, was
in fact 23 at the time; but the twenty-
year difference in their ages is persistently galling to Anthony.

23-32 **you . . . thou** The change of pro-
nouns is significant. For commentary
on the nuances of pronoun usage here
and elsewhere in the play, see Appendix C.

24 **Take in** conquer

25 **we** Cleopatra compounds the imaginary insult by having Caesar condes-
cend to Anthony with the 'royal we'.

28 **dismission** deprivation of office; discharge from service

30 **process** summons or writ; legal action
or suit

33 **homager** vassal

33-4 **else so . . . scolds** or (even more ri-

diculously) it must be Fulvia's scolding
that makes you blush like this

35-6 **Rome . . . space** the wit of the hyperbolic compliment depends on the familiar Rome/room pun: cf. *Caesar*
1.2.157, 'Now is it Rome indeed, and
room enough'. Granville-Barker's description of this speech as 'heroic, yet
fustian-flavoured' nicely catches its
paradoxical effect (p. 67).

35 **arch** As Emrys Jones points out, the
image is of a Roman triumphal arch
(frequently imitated in Renaissance
street pageantry as an emblematic representation of the city or realm); it
initiates the play's important triumph
motif.

36 **ranged** ordered; the metaphor may be
from architecture—where buildings
can 'range' (stretch out in a line)—or
from military parlance (where 'ranged'
means set out in ranks or battle array).
In this context, both connotations may
be appropriate.

37 **dungy** of the nature of dung; abound-
ing in dung

Feeds beast as man. The nobleness of life
Is to do thus, ⌈*embracing Cleopatra*⌉
        when such a mutual pair
And such a twain can do't—in which I bind,   40
On pain of punishment, the world to weet
We stand up peerless.
CLEOPATRA   Excellent falsehood!
Why, did he marry Fulvia and not love her?
I'll seem the fool I am not; Anthony
Will be himself.
ANTHONY   But stirred by Cleopatra.   45
Now for the love of Love and her soft Hours,
Let's not confound the time with conference harsh;
There's not a minute of our lives should stretch

39–42 thus, when . . . do't—in . . . weet | We] This edition; thus: when . . . doo't, in . . . weete | We F; thus; when . . . do't—in . . . weet— | We OXFORD   39 *embracing Cleopatra*] POPE (*subs.*); *not in* F   43 Why, did . . . Fulvia and] This edition (*after* Ridley *conj.*); Why did . . . *Fuluia*, and F

39 *embracing Cleopatra* Recent editors, following Granville-Barker's strenuous objections (p. 83 n. 40), have tended to discard Pope's once widely accepted s.d., but 'to do thus' is repeated at 2.2.27 in a context which makes it sound even more insistently like an implied stage direction. I think that the repetition of the phrase is meant to be ironic, and the gestural repetition would give it the required theatrical emphasis. **mutual** intimate; closely bonded

41 **weet** know. The archaic form suits the pompous manner of official proclamations which Anthony imitates here.

42–4 **Excellent . . . not** Oxford treats this as an extended aside; but that seems inappropriate to Cleopatra's 'wrangling' mood, and the antithetical point of her irony is lost if only 'Anthony | Will be himself' is directed to her lover.

42 **Excellent falsehood** what an outrageous lie. But (as with 'Excellent dissembling', 1.3.79) an oxymoronic sense, conveying half-mocking admiration, is also appropriate. Cf. Puttenham's description of the *'loud* liar', hyperbole: 'when I speak that which neither I myself think to be true, nor would have any other body believe, it must needs be *a great dissimulation*, because I mean nothing less than that I

speak' (pp. 159–60; emphasis added).

44–5 **Anthony | Will be himself** Cleopatra probably intends 'the fool he really is' (Jones), but Anthony chooses to understand 'his true heroic self' or 'his usual loving self' (Arden). Together with Demetrius's 'sometimes when he is not Anthony' (l. 59) Cleopatra's remark begins the process by which the question of Anthony's 'true' identity is rendered intensely problematic.

45 **But stirred by Cleopatra** usually taken to mean 'only if excited to it by Cleopatra'; and the context ('Love and her soft hours') suggests that the bawdy sense of 'stirred' (= sexually aroused) is also present. But Johnson (understanding 'Anthony will be himself' to mean 'Anthony will recollect himself') took the sense as 'Unless kept in commotion by Cleopatra'.

46 **love of Love** 'Love' is allegorized here as the goddess Venus, attended by her handmaids the Hours, as in Spenser's *Epithalamium*, ll. 98–109.

47–9 **confound the time . . . what sport tonight?** Plutarch castigates Antonius's Egyptian revelry as a waste of 'the most precious thing a man can spend . . . and that is, time' (see Appendix A).

47 **confound** waste
    conference talk

Without some pleasure now. What sport tonight?

CLEOPATRA

Hear the ambassadors.

ANTHONY   Fie, wrangling Queen,   50
Whom everything becomes—to chide, to laugh,
To weep—how every passion fully strives
To make itself in thee fair and admired!
No messenger but thine; and all alone
Tonight we'll wander through the streets, and note   55
The qualities of people. Come, my queen,
Last night you did desire it. (*To the Messenger*) Speak
    not to us.

> *Exeunt Anthony and Cleopatra with the train,* ⌈*and*
> *the Messenger by another door*⌉

DEMETRIUS

Is Caesar with Antonius prized so slight?

PHILO

Sir, sometimes when he is not Anthony
He comes too short of that great property   60
Which still should go with Anthony.

DEMETRIUS   I am full sorry
That he approves the common liar who
Thus speaks of him at Rome; but I will hope
Of better deeds tomorrow. Rest you happy.   *Exeunt*

I.2   *Enter* ⌈*by one door*⌉ *Enobarbus, a Soothsayer*
        (*'Lamprius'*), *Rannius* ⌈*and*⌉ *Lucillius;* ⌈*by*
        another,⌉ *Charmian, Iras, Mardian the Eunuch,*
        and Alexas

CHARMIAN Lord Alexas, sweet Alexas, most anything
    Alexas, almost most absolute Alexas, where's the

---

49 now] F; new WARBURTON   52 how] ARDEN; who F1; whose F2   57.1 *Anthony
and Cleopatra*] CAPELL; *not in* F   57.2 *and . . . Messenger*] OXFORD; *not in* F
    1.2.0.1 *by one door*] This edition (*after* Arden); *not in* F   0.1–2 *a Soothsayer* ['*Lamprius*']
after F ('*Lamprius, a Southsayer*')   0.2 *and*] This edition; *not in* F   0.2–3 *by another*]
This edition (*after* Arden); *not in* F   1 Lord] JOHNSON; L. F

---

56 **qualities** characters. The detail is from
    Plutarch (see Appendix A).
60 **property** includes the ideas of both
    'propriety' and 'possession'—i.e. 'the
    distinctive attributes proper to his na-

ture'. Cf. *Phoenix* ll. 36–7: 'Property
was thus appalled | That the self was
not the same'; and see Introduction,
pp. 112–23.
1.2.0.1–4 This stage direction has been

soothsayer that you praised so to th'Queen? O, that I
knew this husband, which you say must change his
horns with garlands!   5
ALEXAS Soothsayer!
SOOTHSAYER Your will?
CHARMIAN Is this the man? Is't you, sir, that know
things?
SOOTHSAYER
In nature's infinite book of secrecy   10
A little I can read.
ALEXAS *(to Charmian)* Show him your hand.
ENOBARBUS *(calling)* Bring in the banquet quickly: wine
enough Cleopatra's health to drink!
⌈*Enter servants with food and wine, and exeunt*⌉
CHARMIAN Good sir, give me good fortune.
SOOTHSAYER I make not, but foresee.   15
CHARMIAN Pray then, foresee me one.

---

4 change] F; charge THEOBALD *(conj.* Warburton *and* Southern MS) 12 *calling*] OXFORD;
not in F   13.1 *Enter . . . exeunt*] OXFORD; *not in* F

the subject of much debate: since Rannius, Lucillius, and perhaps Lamprius
(if he is not the Soothsayer) speak no
lines and appear nowhere else in the
play, they are often excised by editors;
moreover since Enobarbus has nothing
to say until l. 12, the direction for his
entry is often postponed to l. 11. The
form of entry adopted here follows Ridley's suggestion that the order of Shakespeare's stage direction indicates that
the characters should enter in two
groups. Two worlds are juxtaposed in
this scene: the banter between the
courtiers establishes the sophistication
and frivolity of Cleopatra's predomi-
nantly feminine court; the largely silent presence of the group of Romans
establishes the taciturn, consciously
masculine presence of a very different
culture, sardonically dismissive of
Egyptian play (ll. 44–5), and impatiently
businesslike even in debauch (ll. 12–13).
If the Soothsayer enters with the Roman
group, the arrangement has the additional merit of explaining Charmian's
enquiry at ll. 2–3 and Alexas's summons at l. 6. Perhaps a small private

joke is involved in naming the Soothsayer after one of Plutarch's informants, 'my grandfather Lampryas' (see
Appendix A and note to 2.2.186).

1–5 Lord . . . garlands The lineation of
this speech and of several others in the
scene is in dispute. For a discussion of
the problems see Appendix D.
4–5 change . . . garlands This passage has
been the subject of much comment
and conjecture. Assuming the F reading to be correct, the best explanation
seems to be Thiselton's 'take his horns
in exchange for [wedding] garlands'; if
'charge' was what Shakespeare wrote,
then Alexas may either have envisaged
the cuckolded husband as a bull with
its horns garlanded for sacrifice
(Arden), or have envisaged the garlands as an ironic sign of contentment
(Malone) or triumph (Steevens).
12 banquet not, here, a sumptuous feast,
nor even the more usual light meal of
sweetmeats, fruit and wine, but probably 'a wine-drinking carousal' (*OED
banquet* sb. 4)
15 but only

SOOTHSAYER

You shall be yet far fairer than you are.

CHARMIAN He means in flesh.

IRAS No, you shall paint when you are old.

CHARMIAN Wrinkles forbid!   20

ALEXAS Vex not his prescience, be attentive.

CHARMIAN Hush!

SOOTHSAYER

You shall be more beloving than beloved.

CHARMIAN I had rather heat my liver with drinking.

ALEXAS Nay, hear him.   25

CHARMIAN Good now, some excellent fortune! Let me be
married to three kings in a forenoon, and widow them
all; let me have a child at fifty, to whom Herod of
Jewry may do homage; find me to marry me with
Octavius Caesar, and companion me with my mistress.   30

SOOTHSAYER

You shall outlive the lady whom you serve.

CHARMIAN O, excellent! I love long life better than figs.

SOOTHSAYER

You have seen and proved a fairer former fortune
Than that which is to approach.

CHARMIAN Then belike my children shall have no names.   35
Prithee, how many boys and wenches must I have?

SOOTHSAYER

If every of your wishes had a womb,

17–19 **fairer ... old** The lines quibble on three available senses of 'fair': 'fortunate', 'plump', and 'beautiful'.

24 **heat my liver** Love was also supposed to inflame the liver, the presumptive source of human passions.

26 **Good now** all right then

28–9 **Herod of Jewry** a playfully anachronistic semi-blasphemy is involved: Cleopatra's enemy, Herod, was to become infamous for his Massacre of the Innocents, committed in an attempt to kill the infant Christ, to whom he should have offered adoration. Charmian's child will thus command the homage due to Jesus, while her 'three kings' irreverently echo the Three Kings at Christ's birth.

32 **I ... figs** According to Plutarch, the fig 'seemeth naturally to resemble the member of generation' (*Morals*, 'Of Isis and Osiris', p. 1301). For Elizabethans, the bawdy connotations of this supposed resemblance to female genitalia were enhanced by the well-known Italian pun on *fico* (fig) and *fica* (female genitalia); the pun was also available in Spanish (*higo/higa*)—hence the indecent gesture known as the 'Spanish fig' in which a thumb was thrust into the mouth, or between two fingers of a closed fist. For those familiar with the details of Cleopatra's death, the joke will also seem uncannily proleptic.

33 **proved** experienced

35 **have no names** be bastards

And fertile every wish, a million.

CHARMIAN   Out, fool! I forgive thee for a witch.

ALEXAS   You think none but your sheets are privy to   40
your wishes.

CHARMIAN   (*to Soothsayer*) Nay come, tell Iras hers.

ALEXAS   We'll know all our fortunes.

ENOBARBUS   Mine, and most of our fortunes tonight, shall
be drunk to bed.   45

IRAS   (*showing her hand to Soothsayer*) There's a palm
presages chastity, if nothing else.

CHARMIAN   E'en as the o'erflowing Nilus presageth
famine.

IRAS   Go, you wild bedfellow, you cannot soothsay.   50

CHARMIAN   Nay, if an oily palm be not a fruitful prognostication, I cannot scratch mine ear. (*To Soothsayer*) Prithee, tell her but a workaday fortune.

SOOTHSAYER   Your fortunes are alike.

IRAS   But how, but how? Give me particulars.   55

SOOTHSAYER   I have said.

IRAS   Am I not an inch of fortune better than she?

CHARMIAN   Well, if you were but an inch of fortune better than I, where would you choose it?

IRAS   Not in my husband's nose.   60

CHARMIAN   Our worser thoughts heavens mend! Alexas—come, his fortune, his fortune? O, let him marry a

---

38 fertile] THEOBALD (Warburton); *foretell* F   46 *showing . . . Soothsayer*] OXFORD; *not in*
F   61–2 Alexas—come] THEOBALD; *Alexas. Come* F ('*Alexas*' *as speech-prefix*)

39 **forgive thee for a witch** i.e. you will
never be arraigned as a witch if this is
a sample of your talent (most editors);
or (possibly) a playful acknowledgement of the accuracy of his perception
(Herford, cited in Arden).
48–9 **Nilus . . . famine** For the Nile floods
as the source of Egypt's fertility, see
below 2.7.16–23.
50 **wild** licentious
    soothsay The earliest recorded example
    of this verb in *OED*.
51 **oily palm** a supposed symptom of sensuality; for Othello Desdemona's hand
'argues fruitfulness and liberal heart. |
Hot, hot and moist' (*Othello* 3.4.38–

9) and in *Venus and Adonis* the hero's
'sweating palm' is 'the precedent of
pith and livelihood' (ll. 25–6).
51–2 **fruitful prognostication** sign of fertility
56 **I have said** I have nothing more to say;
a deliberate Latinism, imitating the
standard formula of rhetorical closure,
dixi, it has an ominously final ring here
60 **nose** The phallic significance of noses
was a common folk belief. Arden cites
Massinger's *The Unnatural Combat* 4.2:
'It hath just your eyes; and such a
promising nose, | That, if the sign
deceive me not, in time | 'Twill prove
a notable striker, like his father'.

woman that cannot go, sweet Isis, I beseech thee; and
let her die too, and give him a worse; and let worse
follow worse till the worst of all follow him laughing to   65
his grave, fiftyfold a cuckold. Good Isis, hear me this
prayer, though thou deny me a matter of more weight;
good Isis, I beseech thee.

IRAS Amen, dear goddess, hear that prayer of the
people. For as it is a heart-breaking to see a handsome   70
man loose-wived, so it is a deadly sorrow to behold a
foul knave uncuckolded. Therefore, dear Isis, keep
decorum, and fortune him accordingly.

CHARMIAN Amen.

ALEXAS Lo now, if it lay in their hands to make me a   75
cuckold, they would make themselves whores but
they'd do't.

          Enter Cleopatra

ENOBARBUS

Hush, here comes Anthony.

CHARMIAN   Not he, the Queen.

CLEOPATRA

Saw you my lord?

ENOBARBUS   No, lady.

CLEOPATRA   Was he not here?

CHARMIAN No, madam.   80

CLEOPATRA

He was disposed to mirth, but on the sudden
A Roman thought hath struck him. Enobarbus!

79 Saw you my lord?] F2; Saue you, my Lord. F1

63 **cannot go** as we should say 'cannot
come' (see Partridge, pp. 121–2, who
suggests 'cannot copulate' as an alternative possibility). Arden proposes 'cannot carry a child'.
Isis Egyptian moon and earth goddess,
patroness of fertility
69–70 **hear ... people** Iras's mock-piety is
emphasized by this liturgical formula,
which recalls the standard versicle and
response from the Anglican Prayer
Book: 'O Lord hear our prayer ... And
let our cry come unto thee.'
76–7 **they ... do't** they would do it even if
it meant making whores of themselves
78 **here comes ... the Queen** Enobarbus's

mistake creates a slight ironic bathos
at the expense of Anthony's authority.
Gordon P. Jones has suggested that his
error may arise from the lovers' having cross-dressed in the opening scene
('The Strumpet's Fool in *Antony and
Cleopatra*', *SQ* 34 (1983), pp. 62–8).

82 **a Roman thought** a thought of Rome;
but the epithet must also suggest the
moral qualities associated with Roman
ideals of virtue—sobriety, temperance,
piety, etc. Plutarch's Alexandrians praise
Antonius for showing them 'a comical
face—to wit, a merry countenance—
and the Romans a tragical face—to
say, a grim look' (see Appendix A)

ENOBARBUS Madam?

CLEOPATRA

Seek him, and bring him hither. Where's Alexas?

ALEXAS

Here, at your service. My lord approaches.   85

Enter Anthony, with a Messenger

CLEOPATRA

We will not look upon him. Go with us.

Exeunt all but Anthony and the Messenger

MESSENGER

Fulvia thy wife first came into the field.

ANTHONY

Against my brother Lucius?

MESSENGER Ay.

But soon that war had end, and the time's state   90

Made friends of them, jointing their force 'gainst

    Caesar,

Whose better issue in the war from Italy

Upon the first encounter drave them.

ANTHONY   Well, what worst?

MESSENGER

The nature of bad news infects the teller.   95

ANTHONY

When it concerns the fool or coward. On.

Things that are past are done. With me 'tis thus:

Who tells me true, though in his tale lie death,

I hear him as he flattered.

MESSENGER   Labienus—

This is stiff news—hath with his Parthian force   100

---

84 Alexas] F2; *Alexias* F1   86.1 *all ... Messenger*] *not in* F   97 done. With me 'tis
thus:] WILSON (*conj.* E. G. Spencer-Churchill); done, with me. 'Tis thus F

87 **Fulvia ... field** See Appendix A.
88–111 **Lucius ... earing** In Plutarch
   Antonius reacts to the news from
   Rome and Parthia like a man roused
   from deep sleep or prolonged drunkenness (see Appendix A).
90 **time's state** force of circumstances
92 **better issue** greater success
95 **The nature ... teller** This truism,
   which has a proverbial ring (cf. *2
   Henry IV* 1.1.100–1), will be comically
   illustrated in Cleopatra's scenes with
   the Messenger (2.5, 3.3).

99 **as** as if
   Labienus Roman general who defected
   to the Parthians after the defeat of
   Brutus and Cassius at Philippi
100 **Parthian** An Asiatic people of Scy-
   thian origin whose kingdom, south-
   east of the Caspian Sea, came to
   include much of Persia and Mesopotamia. They were in continual conflict
   with the expanding power of Rome
   from the middle of the first century BC
   until the collapse of their empire at the
   beginning of the third century AD.

Extended Asia; from Euphrates
His conquering banner shook, from Syria
To Lydia, and to Ionia,
Whilst—
ANTHONY   'Anthony', thou wouldst say?
MESSENGER   O, my lord!
ANTHONY

Speak to me home. Mince not the general tongue—   105
Name Cleopatra as she is called in Rome;
Rail thou in Fulvia's phrase, and taunt my faults
With such full licence as both truth and malice
Have power to utter. O, then we bring forth weeds,
When our quick winds lie still; and our ills told us   110
Is as our earing. Fare thee well awhile.
MESSENGER   At your noble pleasure.

Exit Messenger

Enter a Second Messenger

110 winds] F; minds HANMER (*conj.* Warburton)   112.2 *a Second Messenger*] This
edition; *another Messenger* F

101 **Extended** seized
  Asia (usually trisyllabic in Shakespeare's time)
  Euphrates (accent on first syllable)
105 **home** bluntly
  Mince . . . tongue don't gloss over what
  people are saying about me
108 **full licence** absolute liberty (perhaps
  even to the point of abusing it)
109–11 **we . . . earing** Dent W241 'Weeds
  come forth on the fattest soil if it is
  untilled'.
110 **quick winds** Most editors have accepted the Hanmer/Warburton emendation, which makes easy sense, but
  disrupts the line of agricultural metaphor: as Johnson saw, 'the sense is
  that man, like soil not ventilated [or
  perhaps, rather, *scoured*] by *quick
  winds*, produces more evil than good'.
  Cf. also *3 Henry VI* 2.6.21: 'For what
  doth cherish weeds, but gentle air?'
111 **earing** ploughing
112.1 *Exit Messenger* The stage directions involving the Messengers in this
  scene are difficult to resolve. F includes an exit for the first Messenger
  who brings news of Fulvia at l. 112;
  and then indicates the entry of 'another Messenger'; however, that entry

is immediately followed by a passage
of dialogue in which *two* Messengers,
labelled '1.*Mess.*' and '2.*Mess.*' in the
speech-headings, take part, their sole
function being to clarify the existence
of a further Messenger, 'the man from
Sicion'; finally at l. 117 there enters
'*another Messenger*', the man from Sicyon himself, labelled '3.*Mess.*'. Even
in a play as profligate with super-
numerary characters as *Anthony*, this
seems a redundancy of Messengers.
The most economical solution so far
proposed is that of Stanley Wells: he
argues (Wells, pp. 39–41) that the
words 'Is there such an one?', given
to 1.*Mess.* in F, properly belong to
Anthony, whose speech-prefix was
either missing or illegible in the MS.
Puzzled by the appearance of two adjacent speeches apparently ascribed to
the Messenger, the compositor then
divided this character into two. The
missing direction for the messenger's
exit provides no special problem, since
these are often omitted from the Folio,
and Anthony's 'Let him appear' seems
like a clear instruction for the messenger to fetch his colleague from Sicyon.

ANTHONY
From Sicyon how the news? Speak there.
SECOND MESSENGER The man from Sicyon—
⌈ANTHONY⌉   Is there such an one?
SECOND MESSENGER
He stays upon your will.
ANTHONY   Let him appear.   115
                    ⌈*Exit Second Messenger*⌉
These strong Egyptian fetters I must break,
Or lose my self in dotage.
                Enter Third Messenger, with a letter
                              What are you?
THIRD MESSENGER
Fulvia thy wife is dead.
ANTHONY   Where died she?
THIRD MESSENGER In Sicyon.
Her length of sickness, with what else more serious   120
Importeth thee to know, this bears.
                              He gives Anthony the letter
ANTHONY   Forbear me.
There's a great spirit gone. Thus did I desire it.
What our contempts doth often hurl from us,
We wish it ours again; the present pleasure,

113 Sicyon how the news?] F (*Scicion . . . newes?*); Sicyon, ho, the news COLLIER 1858
114 SECOND MESSENGER] OXFORD; I. *Mes.* F   ANTHONY] OXFORD; *not in* F   115.1 *Exit
. . . Messenger*] OXFORD; *not in* F   117 *Third Messenger*] This edition; ANOTHER MESSENGER
F   121 *He . . . letter*] JOHNSON (*subs.*); *not in* F   123 contempts doth] F1; contempts
do F2

115 stays . . . will awaits your command
117–19 Or . . . Sicyon The matter of lin-
    eation is critical to the dramatic
    effect here: F as usual does not indi-
    cate which half-lines are to be re-
    garded as part of a single shared line,
    which as broken lines, and which as
    'amphibious', notionally completing
    both the line that precedes them and
    the one that follows. If, for example,
    as most editors assume, Anthony and
    the Messenger are meant to share l. 18
    ('Fulvia . . . she?'), the quick cueing
    will suggest an Anthony briskly in-
    different to Fulvia's death. Arguably
    the pausing suggested by linking An-
    thony's 'What are you?' with the
    Messenger's 'Fulvia . . . dead' (which is
    metrically possible) and leaving 'Or . . .

dotage' to stand alone, is dramatically preferable in that it allows more
room for the actor playing Anthony to
establish the ambiguities developed in
the soliloquy which follows, and serves
to highlight the slight oddity of the
question ('where' when one might expect 'how'). It has the additional advantage of giving a more meditative
close to l. 117, making better sense of
Anthony's 'What are you?'—as though
he were jerked out of reverie.
123 contempts doth Despite F2, the use
    of a plural noun with a singular verb
    is not uncommon in Shakespeare and
    Elizabethan English generally.
123–4 What . . . again Dent W924 'The
    worth of a thing is best known by the
    want'.

By revolution low'ring, does become   125
The opposite of itself. She's good being gone—
The hand could pluck her back that shoved her on.
I must from this enchanting queen break off:
Ten thousand harms, more than the ills I know,
My idleness doth hatch.
        Enter Enobarbus
                        How now, Enobarbus!   130
ENOBARBUS What's your pleasure, sir?
ANTHONY   I must with haste from hence.
ENOBARBUS Why then, we kill all our women. We see
how mortal an unkindness is to them: if they suffer
our departure death's the word.
ANTHONY I must be gone.   135

130 *Enter Enobarbus*] F; *after* 'Enobarbus' DYCE   How now] F; ho now CAPELL

125 **by revolution low'ring** revolving
downwards as upon a wheel; as in the
traditional icon of the Wheel of Fortune, the wheel is a familiar symbol of
arbitrary change. Renaissance micro-
cosmic thinking typically associates
the arbitrariness of passion and opinion in the little world of man with
the whimsical activity of Fortune in
the great world. This is the earliest
instance of the verb *lower* recorded in
OED.
126 **opposite of itself** In the light of the
play's fascination with paradoxes of
self-contradiction and self-annihilation, it is probably worth remembering
that 'opposite' also meant 'enemy'.
  good being gone Dent G298.1 'The
  good is not known until lost'.
128 **enchanting** Stronger than in modern
English: the implication is that (literally or metaphorically) Cleopatra has
entrapped him with magic. The language of the play frequently associates
Cleopatra ('this great fairy', 4.9.12)
with enchantment, probably reflecting
both popular superstitions about the
supernatural powers of gypsies and the
learned regard for Egypt as the supposed source of hermetic wisdom and
magic. Cf. Josephus's comment that
Anthony 'was in such sort possessed
by this woman that he seemed not
only to be bewitched by her words, but
also enchanted by her poisons, to obey

her' (Bullough, p. 332).
130 **idleness** Jones suggests that 'as well
as its obvious sense, the word probably
has the further connotation of "lasci-
viousness"'. Cf. 1.3.92–3; and Dent
I13 'Idleness is the mother of all evil'.
130–1 I can see no reason to follow the
Dyce/Capell rearrangement followed
by most editors. As Arden notes (only
to reject the parallel), Enobarbus's
entry here breaks into Anthony's
speech exactly as Varrius's does Pompey's at 2.1.27; Arden is wrong to
argue, however, that Enobarbus's line
'is almost nonsensical as a reply to a
question', since 'how now' is often
used in a purely exclamatory fashion
(as in e.g. *Twelfth Night* 1.3.42), and
can thus quite properly be followed by
a question (as in *Hamlet* 3.4.13). Lineation is once again ambiguous in F:
'How now, Enobarbus!' might be
treated as completing the line 'My . . .
hatch', or as beginning a new line,
ending at '. . . sir?', depending on
whether or not an actor felt the need
for a pause before registering Enobarbus's presence.
132–74 **Why then . . . your abode** The
basis for Enobarbus's easy bantering
relation with his general is to be found
in Plutarch's comments on Antonius's
relaxed relationship with his subordinates (see Appendix A).

ENOBARBUS Under a compelling occasion let women die.
  It were pity to cast them away for nothing—though
  between them and a great cause, they should be
  esteemed nothing. Cleopatra catching but the least
  noise of this, dies instantly—I have seen her die   140
  twenty times upon far poorer moment. I do think there
  is mettle in death, which commits some loving act
  upon her, she hath such a celerity in dying.
ANTHONY She is cunning past man's thought.
ENOBARBUS Alack, sir, no—her passions are made of   145
  nothing but the finest part of pure love. We cannot call
  her winds and waters sighs and tears: they are greater
  storms and tempests than almanacs can report. This
  cannot be cunning in her; if it be, she makes a shower
  of rain as well as Jove.   150
ANTHONY Would I had never seen her!
ENOBARBUS O sir, you had then left unseen a wonderful
  piece of work, which not to have been blest withal,
  would have discredited your travel.
ANTHONY Fulvia is dead.   155
ENOBARBUS Sir?
ANTHONY Fulvia is dead.
ENOBARBUS Fulvia?
ANTHONY Dead.
ENOBARBUS Why sir, give the gods a thankful sacrifice.   160
  When it pleaseth their deities to take the wife of a man
  from him, it shows to man the tailors of the earth;

---

136 a compelling occasion] ROWE; a compelling an occasion F; so compelling an
occasion NICHOLSON (*cited in* Cambridge)   154 travel] F (Trauaile)

---

136 **compelling** The first use of this participle recorded in *OED*.
140 **die** The sexual sense of the word ('to
  have orgasm') becomes inescapable in
  this line, but hovers about all Enobarbus's uses of 'die' and related words
  ('kill', 'death') in these speeches, so
  that the pun climaxes a slow-burn
  joke. In this context the repetition of
  'nothing' (ll. 137, 139, 146) may also
  involve bawdy word-play as in *Hamlet*
  3.2.112–13 and (almost certainly) in
  the title of *Much Ado About Nothing*.
141 **upon far poorer moment** for much
  less cause. 'Moment' has a possible

bawdy sense (Partridge, p. 155:
  momentary trick = copulation).
142 **mettle** natural ardour, vigour; 'abundance (and vigour) of semen' (Partridge, p. 153)
143 **celerity** quickness
150 **Jove** As Jupiter Pluvius, the chief of
  the gods was also tutelary of rain.
153 **piece of work** masterpiece
154 **travel** The F spelling 'Trauaile', as
  well as suggesting the different connotations of travel for a seventeenth-
  century audience, preserves the
  word-play on 'piece of work'.
162–4 **it shows . . . new** it shows man

comforting therein, that when old robes are worn out,
there are members to make new. If there were no more
women but Fulvia, then had you indeed a cut, and the   165
case to be lamented. This grief is crowned with consolation; your old smock brings forth a new petticoat—
and indeed the tears live in an onion that should water
this sorrow.

ANTHONY
The business she hath broachèd in the state   170
Cannot endure my absence.

ENOBARBUS And the business you have broached here
cannot be without you, especially that of Cleopatra's,
which wholly depends on your abode.

ANTHONY
No more light answers. Let our officers   175
Have notice what we purpose. I shall break
The cause of our expedience to the Queen,
And get her leave to part. For not alone
The death of Fulvia, with more urgent touches
Do strongly speak to us, but the letters too   180
Of many our contriving friends in Rome
Petition us at home. Sextus Pompeius

178 leave] POPE; loue F

how the gods have organized the
world for his comfort like a tailor's
shop where new clothes are always
made to replace old ones when they
wear out. Jones suggests that 'members' has a bawdy significance, picking
up the familiar phallic suggestiveness
of the tailor's needle. In the context
'tailors of the earth' also seems to have
a more sinister resonance, perhaps
remembering the so-called 'nine tailors'
of the passing bell, or jokingly alluding
to the three classical Fates, the chthonic
deities who spun, measured, and cut
the thread of each individual's life.

165 **cut** blow; but Jones draws attention
  to the train of bawdy puns in which
  'members' refers to male genitalia, and
  'cut' and 'case' to the female organs.
167 **smock** female undergarment, shift
168 **tears ... onion** Cf. Dent O67: 'to
  weep with an onion' (cf. also P391 'to

water one's plants' as an expression
for weeping).
170 **broached** Enobarbus plays bawdily
  on *broach* = to open and begin to use
  [a cask].
174 **your abode** your remaining here
175 **light** frivolous, bawdy
  our Anthony shifts to the royal plural,
  putting a formal distance between
  himself and Enobarbus.
177 **expedience** haste, expedition; also expediency
179 **touches** motives
181 **many ... Rome** the many friends
  busying themselves on our behalf in
  Rome
  contriving (the first use of this participle recorded in *OED*)
182 **Petition ... home** urge me to return
  home; identified by Schäfer as the earliest recorded use of the verb *petition*.
  Sextus Pompeius younger son of Julius
  Caesar's defeated rival, Pompey the Great

Hath given the dare to Caesar, and commands
The empire of the sea. Our slippery people,
Whose love is never linked to the deserver   185
Till his deserts are past, begin to throw
Pompey the Great and all his dignities
Upon his son, who high in name and power—
Higher than both in blood and life—stands up
For the main soldier; whose quality, going on,   190
The sides o'th'world may danger. Much is breeding,
Which, like the courser's hair, hath yet but life,
And not a serpent's poison. Say our pleasure
To such whose place is under us; require
Our quick remove from hence.   195
ENOBARBUS I shall do't.

I.3   *Enter Cleopatra, Charmian, Alexas, and Iras*
CLEOPATRA
Where is he?
CHARMIAN   I did not see him since.
CLEOPATRA (*to Alexas*)
See where he is, who's with him, what he does:
I did not send you. If you find him sad,
Say I am dancing; if in mirth, report
That I am sudden sick. Quick, and return.   5
                                                Exit Alexas
CHARMIAN
Madam, methinks if you did love him dearly,
You do not hold the method to enforce

183 Hath] F2; Haue F1   192 hair] F (heire)   193 pleasure] This edition; pleasure,
F   194 place is under us; require] This edition; places vnder vs, require F1; place is
under us, requires F2 *and most eds.*; places under us require, ARDEN
     1.3.5.1 *Exit Alexas*] CAPELL; *not in* F

186–7 **throw ... dignities** heap all of
   Pompey the Great's titles and honours
189 **blood and life** temper and vigour
189–90 **stands up ... soldier** presents
   himself as the most powerful soldier [in
   the world]
190–1 **whose quality ... danger** whose
   abilities, if they continue to meet with
   success, may come to endanger the
   very frame of the world
191–3 **breeding ... poison** Referring to
   the folk-belief, recorded by William

Harrison, *Description of England* (in
Holinshed's *Chronicles*, 1587) 1.3.224)
that horsehairs thrown into stagnant
water would turn into small eels or
serpents. According to Coleridge the
phenomenon is produced when 'an
immense number of small slimy water-
lice' attach themselves to the hair,
making it seem to metamorphose into
a worm.
1.3.1 **I ... since** I have not seen him recently

The like from him.

CLEOPATRA   What should I do, I do not?

CHARMIAN

In each thing give him way, cross him in nothing.

CLEOPATRA

Thou teachest like a fool—the way to lose him.   10

CHARMIAN

Tempt him not so too far. I wish forbear—
In time we hate that which we often fear.

> *Enter Anthony*

But here comes Anthony.

CLEOPATRA   I am sick and sullen.

ANTHONY

I am sorry to give breathing to my purpose.

CLEOPATRA

Help me away, dear Charmian, I shall fall.   15
It cannot be thus long, the sides of nature
Will not sustain it.

ANTHONY   Now, my dearest queen.

CLEOPATRA

Pray you, stand farther from me.

ANTHONY   What's the matter?

CLEOPATRA

I know by that same eye there's some good news.
What, says the married woman you may go?   20

---

11 I wish] F; Iwis WILSON (anon. *conj. in* Cambridge)   20 What, says ... go?] F4 (*subs.*);
What sayes ... goe? F1; What ... Woman? you may go; ROWE

---

11 **I wish forbear** I beg you to lay off; as
Spevack suggests, the phrase is a colloquial ellipsis for 'I wish [you would]
forbear'. The amendment favoured by
Dover Wilson, Oxford, and others
('iwis' = certainly) does not make the
sense any easier.

12 **In time ... fear** Cf. Dent L556: 'He
cannot love me that is afraid of me'.

13 **I am ... sullen** The line can be played
either as a defiant announcement to
Anthony, or as an aside to Charmian
and Iras, cueing them into the kind of
performance she is about to produce.
Cf. Dent S964: 'To be sick of the sul-
lens'.

14 **breathing** utterance. Anthony's style

is one of courtly circumlocution.

16–17 **the sides ... sustain it** my constitution will surely crack under the strain.
Cf. 1.2.191 'the sides o'th'world'.

20–1 **What ... come** Jones suggests that
Shakespeare is consciously imitating
Ovid's version of the Dido and Aeneas
story here: 'The two lines are probably
based on a line in the verse epistle sent
by Dido to Aeneas in Ovid's *Heroides*
(7.139), which Shakespeare is likely to
have read at school: "*Sed iubet ire
deus." Vellem vetuisset adire ...* '("But
your god orders you to go." I wish he
had forbidden you come).'

20 **married woman** Cleopatra's emphasis
upon 'married' is at once sarcastic and

Would she had never given you leave to come!
Let her not say 'tis I that keep you here—
I have no power upon you; hers you are.

ANTHONY
The gods best know—

CLEOPATRA   O, never was there queen
So mightily betrayed! Yet at the first   25
I saw the treasons planted.

ANTHONY   Cleopatra—

CLEOPATRA
Why should I think you can be mine and true—
Though you in swearing shake the thronèd gods—
Who have been false to Fulvia? Riotous madness,
To be entangled with those mouth-made vows   30
Which break themselves in swearing.

ANTHONY   Most sweet Queen—

CLEOPATRA
Nay, pray you seek no colour for your going,
But bid farewell and go. When you sued staying,
Then was the time for words—no going then:
Eternity was in our lips and eyes,   35
Bliss in our brows bent; none our parts so poor,
But was a race of heaven. They are so still,
Or thou, the greatest soldier of the world,
Art turned the greatest liar.

ANTHONY   How now, lady?

resentful. Cf. Claudio's sneer in *Much Ado*, 'Here dwells Benedick, the married man' (5.1.179-80).

31 **break . . . swearing** are broken as soon as uttered. But the condensed figure produces a self-cancelling paradox, as though the oath were violated by the very act of swearing it. Cf. 2.2.212 'And what they undid did'.

32 **colour** pretext

33 **sued staying** begged to stay

35-7 **Eternity . . . heaven** Cleopatra is quoting Anthony's past hyperboles back at him; an actor may play the lines as pure sarcastic parody, or allow them a tinge of nostalgic pathos.

36 **brows bent** arched eyebrow. Some editors prefer to read 'brows' bent' ('the arch of your eyebrows'), but *OED* records 'brows bent' or 'bent brow' as a standard formula from the 14th cent.

36-7 **none . . . heaven** my most ordinary feature (or quality) was a thing of divine origin

37 **race of heaven** Either 'offspring of heaven' or 'mark of divine origin' (*OED race* sb.[2] I, 1 and sb.[5]); but Warburton, supported by Johnson, proposed 'smack or flavour of heaven' (*OED race* sb.[1] II, 10).

38 **thou** The stress, emphasized by the following pause, highlights Cleopatra's shift to the singular pronoun (see Appendix C).

CLEOPATRA I would I had thy inches, thou shouldst
　　know   40
There were a heart in Egypt.
ANTHONY   Hear me, Queen:
The strong necessity of time commands
Our services awhile; but my full heart
Remains in use with you. Our Italy
Shines o'er with civil swords: Sextus Pompeius   45
Makes his approaches to the port of Rome;
Equality of two domestic powers
Breed scrupulous faction; the hated, grown to strength,
Are newly grown to love; the condemned Pompey,
Rich in his father's honour, creeps apace   50
Into the hearts of such as have not thrived
Upon the present state, whose numbers threaten;
And quietness, grown sick of rest, would purge
By any desperate change. My more particular,
And that which most with you should safe my going,   55
Is Fulvia's death.

---

43 services] F2; Servicles F1

41 **There . . . Egypt** Egypt's queen has a
heart; or, there's *one* person in Egypt
with a heart. Both senses may be felt.
heart Probably both as the seat of
courage and of (outraged) love.
42 **necessity of time** This 'Roman' emphasis on the demands of time is a
deliberate counter to the rhetoric of
eternity which Cleopatra has quoted
back at him.
44 **in use with you** Either 'invested, in
trust with you' or 'yours to enjoy'
(Arden).
45 **civil swords** swords drawn in the cause
of civil war
46 **port** Either 'gate' or 'seaport' (i.e.
Ostia, at the mouth of the Tiber—an
obvious target for Pompey's powerful
fleet).
47 **Equality . . . powers** the equal division
of power in the state (i.e. between Octavius and Lepidus)
48 **Breed . . . faction** leads to factional dispute over the most trivial matters
48–9 **the hated . . . love** those who were
formerly hated, as a result of their new

power, now find themselves loved
49 **the condemned Pompey** Pompey's de-
predations had led to his being pro-
scribed by the Senate.
52 **Upon . . . state** under the present political dispensation
53–4 **quietness . . . change** Purging, whether by bloodletting, laxative, or
enema, was the principal technique of
Renaissance medicine, its purpose
being to restore the four humours to
their proper balance in the body; the
metaphor here depends on the habit of
analogical thinking which conceives
the 'body politic' of the state as liable
to the same dangerous imbalances;
thus an excess of peace leads to the
outbreak of disorders which can be
cured only by the purgative violence
of war. Cf. *2 Henry IV* 4.1.54–8 and
Hamlet Additional Passage J, 18–20.
54 **My more particular** what especially
concerns me
55 **with you . . . going** should make my
departure seem safe as far as you are
concerned

CLEOPATRA

Though age from folly could not give me freedom,
It does from childishness. Can Fulvia die?

ANTHONY She's dead, my queen.

He shows her letters

Look here, and at thy sovereign leisure read   60
The garboils she awaked. At the last, best—
See when and where she died.

CLEOPATRA   O most false love!
Where be the sacred vials thou shouldst fill
With sorrowful water? Now I see, I see,
In Fulvia's death how mine received shall be.   65

ANTHONY

Quarrel no more, but be prepared to know
The purposes I bear—which are, or cease,
As you shall give th'advice. By the fire
That quickens Nilus' slime, I go from hence
Thy soldier-servant, making peace or war   70
As thou affects.

59.1 *He . . . letters*] OXFORD (*subs.*): *not in* F   61 best—] This edition; best, F
70 soldier-servant] STAUNTON (*conj.* Delius); Souldier, Seuant F

60 **at . . . leisure** at your majesty's leisure;
perhaps also 'alluding to the lachrymatory
at leisure'
61 **garboils** tumults
At the last, best Either 'lastly, and best
news of all', or 'she showed herself at
her best in the last moments of her
life'—Cf. Anthony's ambiguous tribute
'she's good being gone' (1.2.126), and
Caesar's to Cleopatra 'Bravest at the
last' (5.2.333).
63 **sacred vials** Johnson rightly explained
this as 'alluding to the lachrymatory
vials, or bottles of tears, which the
Romans sometimes put into the urn of
a friend' (Cf. *Kinsmen* 1.5.5)—although it is now known that such
vials contained only unguents.
64–5 'The neat rhyme suggests something of the artificiality of Cleopatra's
behaviour here' (Jones).
67 **which are, or cease** which I shall
either persist with or abandon
68–9 **fire . . . slime** sun which brings life
to the Nile mud; Anthony is thinking
not merely of agricultural fertility, but
of the process whereby scarabs, ser-

pents, and crocodiles were supposed to
hatch spontaneously from the Nile
mud through the action of the sun. Cf.
2.7.25–6.
70–1 **Thy . . . thou** Anthony's temporary
recourse to the intimate pronoun
marks his conciliatory tone; it does not
long survive Cleopatra's provocation
(see l. 80), but returns for his farewell
(ll. 104–5). Cf. Appendix D.
70 **soldier-servant** warrior-lover and obedient subordinate, *servant* here means
both chivalric lover and feudal vassal.
Delius's conjecture suggests a courtly
formulation, analogous to French *cavalier servant* or Italian *cavaliere ser-
vante* (both of which appear to be
later); and it is possible that *servant*
should be taken as an obsolete adjective (*OED servant* a.), since such forms
(deriving from French present parti-
ciples) are common in heraldic language. The F punctuation assumes two
nouns in apposition, stressing their
links with the alternative occupations
of war and peace.
71 **As . . . affects** as you desire

CLEOPATRA   Cut my lace, Charmian, come—
But let it be: I am quickly ill, and well,
So Anthony loves.
ANTHONY   My precious queen, forbear,
And give true evidence to his love which stands
An honourable trial.
CLEOPATRA   So Fulvia told me.   75
I prithee turn aside, and weep for her;
Then bid adieu to me, and say the tears
Belong to Egypt. Good now, play one scene
Of excellent dissembling, and let it look
Like perfect honour.
ANTHONY   You'll heat my blood. No more!   80
CLEOPATRA
You can do better yet; but this is meetly.
ANTHONY Now by my sword—
CLEOPATRA   And target. Still he mends.
But this is not the best. Look, prithee, Charmian,
How this Herculean Roman does become
The carriage of his chafe.   85
ANTHONY I'll leave you, lady.
CLEOPATRA Courteous lord, one word:

---

72 ill, and well,] F; ill and well; OXFORD   80 blood. No more!] ROWE; blood no
more? F   82 my] F2; *not in* FI

lace i.e. the lace fastening the tight
corset (of whalebone, wood, or steel)
affected by fashionable women of
Shakespeare's day, which needed to be
loosened in moments of emotional
stress. The detail is a reminder of the
anachronistic look which 'Roman'
plays were expected to have in the
Jacobean theatre.
72–3 I am . . . loves Either 'I am well,
provided that Anthony loves me', or 'I
veer between sickness and health in
just the erratic fashion of Anthony's
love for me'.
74 give . . . evidence bear true witness
his . . . stands his love which is able to
stand; or, 'the love of him who is
prepared to stand'
78 Egypt i.e the Queen of Egypt
79 excellent dissembling cf. 'excellent
falsehood' 1.1.42
81 this is meetly that was not a bad
performance

82 by my sword This is more than a casual exclamation; throughout the play
Anthony's sword is made the emblem
of his heroic masculinity.
target small shield. Cleopatra turns
Anthony's angry oath into the kind of
bluster one might expect from the
braggart soldier of stage convention;
perhaps a suggestion of the sword-and-
buckler fights, popular as enter-
tainments in the public theatres, is
also intended (cf. 'sworder', below
3.13.30).
84 Herculean (accent on the second syllable) prodigiously strong, heroic; but
also referring literally to his supposed
descent from Hercules, whom, according to Plutarch, Antonius resembled
(see Appendix A)
84–5 become . . . chafe plays according to
the decorum of his angry part (i.e.
Hercules Furens)

Sir, you and I must part, but that's not it;
Sir, you and I have loved, but there's not it—
That you know well. Something it is I would—   90
O, my oblivion is a very Anthony,
And I am all forgotten.

ANTHONY   But that your royalty
Holds Idleness your subject, I should take you
For Idleness itself.

CLEOPATRA   'Tis sweating labour
To bear such idleness so near the heart   95
As Cleopatra this. But sir, forgive me,
Since my becomings kill me when they do not
Eye well to you. Your honour calls you hence—
Therefore be deaf to my unpitied folly,
And all the gods go with you. Upon your sword   100
Sit laurel victory, and smooth success
Be strewed before your feet.

ANTHONY   Let us go. Come:
Our separation so abides and flies
That thou residing here, goes yet with me,
And I hence fleeting, here remain with thee.   105
Away.   *Exeunt*

91–2 **my oblivion ... forgotten** Harrison
rightly calls this densely compacted
conceit 'untranslatable'; the meaning
seems to include: (1) my memory is as
negligent as Anthony, and I can remember nothing; (2) I am altogether
forgotten, since his forgetful neglect of
me is as absolute as Anthony's own
character; (3) my mind is so possessed
by Anthony to the exclusion of everything else, that even my forgetfulness
is stamped with his character, overwhelming me with oblivion. The last
meaning carries a strong suggestion of
erotic possession and its mutual transformations.

92–3 **But ... subject** 'if it were not clear
that you are in perfect control of these
follies, as a queen is of her subjects'
(Jones). 'Idleness' here includes the
sense of 'theatrical pretence', as in
Hamlet 3.2.88: 'They are coming to
the play. I must be idle'; and cf. note
to 1.2.130.

94 **labour** Cleopatra imagines the emotion
which Anthony dismissively calls 'idle-

ness' as a child that she is struggling
to bring to birth.

97 **my becomings** those things which befit
me; my transformations. Throughout
the play Cleopatra is associated with
metamorphosis and the idea of 'becoming' (as opposed to 'being'); perhaps
Shakespeare was influenced in this by
Plutarch's description of Isis, the goddess whose earthly incarnation Cleopatra affects to be (see note to 3.6.17).

98 **Eye** look

100–2 **Upon ... feet** The imagery suggests a 'triumph' of the sort accorded
to victorious Roman generals who
wore the laurel wreath as a symbol of
victory.

103–5 **Our separation ... thee** since our
separation is something that will be
experienced equally by you here in
Alexandria and by me on my journey,
it is paradoxically the very thing that
links us, so that you may be said to
accompany me, even as I remain here
with you. Despite the metaphysical
ingenuity of Anthony's conceit, its

I.4 *Enter Octavius Caesar reading a letter, Lepidus,*
       and their train

CAESAR

You may see, Lepidus, and henceforth know
It is not Caesar's natural vice to hate
Our great competitor. From Alexandria
This is the news: he fishes, drinks, and wastes
The lamps of night in revel; is not more manlike   5
Than Cleopatra, nor the queen of Ptolemy
More womanly than he; hardly gave audience, or
Vouchsafed to think he had partners. You shall find
       there
A man who is the abstract of all faults
That all men follow.

LEPIDUS   I must not think there are   10
Evils enough to darken all his goodness.
His faults in him seem as the spots of heaven,
More fiery by night's blackness—hereditary
Rather than purchased, what he cannot change
Than what he chooses.   15

CAESAR

You are too indulgent. Let's grant it is not
Amiss to tumble on the bed of Ptolemy,

1.4.0.1 *Caesar*] ROWE; *not in* F   3 Our] SINGER (*conj.* Thirlby); one F   8 Vouchsafed]
JOHNSON; vouchsafe F1; did vouchsafe F2   9 the abstract] F3; th' abstracts F1;
th'abstract F2

brevity and the patness of his couplet
give it a slightly perfunctory air.

1.4.3 **competitor** literally, 'one who seeks
   the same object as oneself—therefore
   suitably ambiguous, either 'partner' or
   'rival'. Like Anthony, Caesar employs
   the royal plural.

3–33 **From Alexandria . . . judgement** This
   passage draws extensively on Plutarch,
   both in its historical detail and in the
   judgements which Caesar passes on
   Anthony's frivolity (see Appendix A).

6 **queen of Ptolemy** At Julius Caesar's
   behest, Cleopatra married her younger
   brother, the child-prince Ptolemy, and
   was generally supposed to have poisoned him.

9 **abstract** epitome

12–13 **His faults . . . blackness** like stars

against the night sky, his faults appear
more pronounced by virtue of their
contrast with his predominant goodness. Arden explains that 'the simile
aims only at force of contrast, disre-
garding correspondence of quality in
the things compared'; but in fact the
paradoxical inversion of the normal
symbolism of light and dark, combined
with the striking double stress on
'More fiery', has the effect of suggesting a kind of splendour even in
Anthony's vices. The self-cancelling
contradictions of Anthonius's personality and paradoxical attractiveness of
his vices are themes developed by Plutarch (see Appendix A).

16–21 **Let's . . . him** The force of Caesar's
   revulsion and disdain is caught in the
   spitting alliteration of these lines.

To give a kingdom for a mirth, to sit
And keep the turn of tippling with a slave,
To reel the streets at noon, and stand the buffet   20
With knaves that smells of sweat. Say this becomes
    him—
As his composure must be rare indeed
Whom these things cannot blemish—yet must Anthony
No way excuse his foils when we do bear
So great weight in his lightness. If he filled   25
His vacancy with his voluptuousness,
Full surfeits and the dryness of his bones
Call on him for't. But to confound such time
That drums him from his sport and speaks as loud
As his own state and ours, 'tis to be chid—   30
As we rate boys who, being mature in knowledge,
Pawn their experience to their present pleasure,
And so rebel to judgement.
          Enter a Messenger

LEPIDUS   Here's more news.

MESSENGER

Thy biddings have been done, and every hour,
Most noble Caesar, shalt thou have report   35
How 'tis abroad. Pompey is strong at sea,
And it appears he is beloved of those
That only have feared Caesar. To the ports

---

18 **give . . . mirth** reward a joke with the prize of a kingdom
19 **keep the turn of** take turns in
20 **stand the buffet** exchange blow for blow
22–3 **As . . . blemish** and, after all, it would take a man of remarkable character to remain untainted by such things
24 **foils** blemishes
24–5 **when . . . lightness** 'his trifling levity throws so much burden on us' (Johnson); but 'lightness' suggests sexual profligacy as well as triviality
26 **vacancy** leisure; but the heavy stressing required by the alliteration perhaps suggests a more contemptuous nuance—'empty frivolity', 'idleness'
27 **surfeits** diseases of intemperance
dryness . . . bones a consequence of old age or debauchery (Jones suggests sy-

philis), or both. Cf. Vindice's satire of the lecherous old Duke in *The Revenger's Tragedy* (1606–7): 'O that *marrowless* age | Would stuff the *hollow bones* with damned desires, | And stead of heat kindle infernal fires | Within the veins of a *dry* duke, a *parched and juiceless luxur*' (1.1.5–8; emphases added).
28 **Call on him** bring him to book
confound waste
29–30 **speaks . . . ours** makes demands as pressing as those imposed by his public eminence and mine
30 **'tis to be chid** invites reproof
31 **rate** scold
33 **to** against
34–5 **Thy . . . thou** For the significance of the singular pronoun here, see Appendix C.

The discontents repair, and men's reports
Give him much wronged.
CAESAR   I should have known no less: 40
It hath been taught us from the primal state
That he which is was wished until he were;
And the ebbed man, ne'er loved till ne'er worth love,
Comes deared by being lacked. This common body,
Like to a vagabond flag upon the stream,   45
Goes to and back, lackeying the varying tide
To rot itself with motion.
       ⌈*Enter a Second Messenger*⌉
SECOND MESSENGER   Caesar, I bring thee word,
Menecrates and Menas, famous pirates,
Makes the sea serve them, which they ear and wound
With keels of every kind. Many hot inroads   50
They make in Italy; the borders maritime
Lack blood to think on't, and flush youth revolt.
No vessel can peep forth but 'tis as soon
Taken as seen—for Pompey's name strikes more
Than could his war resisted.
CAESAR   Anthony,   55
Leave thy lascivious wassails. When thou once
Was beaten from Modena, where thou slew'st
Hirtius and Pansa, consuls, at thy heel

---

44 deared] THEOBALD (*conj.* Warburton); fear'd F   46 lackeying] THEOBALD (*conj.* Warburton); lacking F   47 *Enter . . . Messenger*] CAPELL; *not in* F   SECOND MESSENGER] CAPELL; *Mes.* F   56 wassails] POPE; *Vassailes* F1; *Vassals* F4   58 Hirtius and Pansa] F2; *Hirsius, and Pausa* F1

39 **discontents** malcontents
40 **Give him** speak of him as
41 **primal state** very beginning of the world; the earliest organized society
42 **he . . . were** the man now in power was always longed for by the populace until he actually achieved power
43–4 **the ebbed . . . lacked** the man now out of power, who never enjoyed favour while he actually deserved it, becomes adored as soon as he is missed. Cf. notes to 1.2.123, 126. The first recorded occurrence of the participial adjective *ebbed* (Schäfer).
44 **deared** adored; the F reading would make sense if 'fear'd' were understood to mean 'revered' (*OED fear,* v.6); but, as Bevington points out, the opposition

of 'beloved' and 'feared' just a few lines earlier (ll. 37–8) would tend to confuse this meaning.
common body common people
45 **flag** water iris; or often, any kind of reed or rush
46 **lackeying** following with lackey-like subservience
48–54 **Menecrates . . . seen** The details derive from Plutarch (see Appendix A).
49 **ear** plough
52 **flush** lusty
54 **Pompey's name** Cf. Ventidius's reference to Anthony's 'name, | That magical word of war' (3.1.31).
56 **wassails** carousings
56–68 **When thou . . . die to look on** The details here again derive from Plutarch

Did Famine follow, whom thou fought'st against—
Though daintily brought up—with patience more   60
Than savages could suffer. Thou didst drink
The stale of horses, and the gilded puddle
Which beasts would cough at. Thy palate then did deign
The roughest berry on the rudest hedge.
Yea, like the stag, when snow the pasture sheets,   65
The barks of trees thou browsed. On the Alps
It is reported thou didst eat strange flesh,
Which some did die to look on. And all this—
It wounds thine honour that I speak it now—
Was borne so like a soldier that thy cheek   70
So much as lanked not.

LEPIDUS 'Tis pity of him.

CAESAR Let his shames quickly
Drive him to Rome. 'Tis time we twain
Did show ourselves i'th'field; and to that end   75
Assemble we immediate council. Pompey
Thrives in our idleness.

LEPIDUS   Tomorrow, Caesar,
I shall be furnished to inform you rightly
Both what by sea and land I can be able
To front this present time.

CAESAR   Till which encounter   80
It is my business too. Farewell.

LEPIDUS Farewell, my lord. What you shall know mean-
    time

---

66 browsed] F1 (brows'd); browsed'st F2   76 we] F2; me F1   council] F (counsell)

(see below, Appendix A). In the battle
at Mutina, shortly after the assassination of Julius Caesar, Antonius was
beaten by Octavius's forces, and rescued from total defeat only by striking
an alliance with Lepidus.

59 **Famine** F's capitalization points up the
allegory: Famine is imagined in its
apocalyptic guise as one of the Four
Horsemen of Rev. 6: 1–8.
62 **stale** urine
gilded covered with iridescent scum
63 **deign** not refuse
64 **rudest** wildest
65 **sheets** The earliest example of this verb
recorded in *OED*.

66 **barks . . . browsed** Arden cites Nashe,
Christ's Tears, Works (ed. R. B. McKer-
row) II, p. 70 ('All the bushes and
boughs . . . were hewed down and
felled, for men (like brute beasts) to
browse on') and Browne, *Britannia's
Pastorals*, Book II (1616), Song 1,
663–7 ('As in a forest well complete
with deer | We see the hollies, ashes,
everywhere | Robb'd of their clothing
by the browsing game').
71 **lanked** grew thin
78–9 **I . . . able** I shall be in a position to
let you know what land and sea forces
I can assemble
80 **front** confront

Of stirs abroad, I shall beseech you, sir,
To let me be partaker.
CAESAR   Doubt not, sir,
I knew it for my bond.   *Exeunt ⌈severally⌉*   85

1.5   *Enter Cleopatra, Charmian, Iras, and Mardian*
CLEOPATRA Charmian!
CHARMIAN Madam?
CLEOPATRA
Ha, ha! Give me to drink mandragora.
CHARMIAN Why, madam?
CLEOPATRA
That I might sleep out this great gap of time   5
My Anthony is away.
CHARMIAN   You think of him too much.
CLEOPATRA
O, 'tis treason.
CHARMIAN   Madam, I trust not so.
CLEOPATRA
Thou, eunuch Mardian!
MARDIAN   What's your highness' pleasure?
CLEOPATRA
Not now to hear thee sing. I take no pleasure
In aught an eunuch has. 'Tis well for thee   10
That, being unseminared, thy freer thoughts
May not fly forth of Egypt. Hast thou affections?
MARDIAN Yes, gracious madam.

85 knew] F; know DYCE 2 (*conj.* Thirlby)
    1.5.5 time] ROWE; time: F

85 **I ... bond** I have always understood
   the obligations of our alliance. Some
   editors follow Walker in emending
   'knew' to 'know'; but the cool tone of
   Caesar's reassurance is emphasized by
   the unexpected past tense, as well as
   by the slightly enigmatic way in which
   it is left hanging upon a half-line. The
   scene is already laying the ground for
   Caesar's casually announced coup
   against Lepidus (3.5–6).
1.5.3 **Ha, ha!** Most editors take this to
   represent a yawn.
   mandragora mandrake, a plant with
   strong narcotic properties

9 **Not ... sing** Castrati were frequently
   employed in Renaissance courts (and
   churches) as singers, the quality of
   voice resembling that of a male alto or
   counter-tenor; Cleopatra's gibe anachronistically confuses the functions of
   Renaissance castrati with the powerful
   offices often assigned to eunuchs in
   Roman and oriental courts. The an-
   achronism is probably deliberate, a
   metatheatrical joke at Mardian's expense.
11 **unseminared** gelded
   freer unfettered; lustful
12 **affections** desires

CLEOPATRA Indeed?

MARDIAN

Not in deed, madam, for I can do nothing   15
But what indeed is honest to be done;
Yet have I fierce affections, and think
What Venus did with Mars.

CLEOPATRA   O, Charmian,
Where think'st thou he is now? Stands he, or sits he?
Or does he walk? Or is he on his horse?   20
O happy horse, to bear the weight of Anthony!
Do bravely horse, for wot'st thou whom thou mov'st?—
The demi-Atlas of this earth, the arm
And burgonet of men. He's speaking now,
Or murmuring, 'Where's my serpent of old Nile?'—   25
For so he calls me. Now I feed myself

15–16 Not...done The word-play here ('in deed...do...indeed...done'), picking up Anthony's 'The nobleness of life is to *do* thus', foregrounds the significance of the verb *do* in a play which repeatedly opposes heroic *deeds* to erotic *doing*. Cf. also 5.2.5, 324.

16 honest chaste

18 What...Mars The love affair between Mars and Venus was perhaps the most celebrated adultery of classical myth and (together with their entrapment by the cuckolded Vulcan) a favourite subject with painters and poets alike. The analogy between Anthony and Mars has already been established (1.1.4); and the myth is an important part of the play's frame of reference (see Introduction pp. 116–19).

20–2 horse The context of erotic yearning makes explicit the *horse/whores* pun here. Riding is traditional bawdy for intercourse.

22 wot'st thou do you know

23 demi-Atlas Formed by analogy with demi-god; the Titan Atlas supported the earth (or the heavens) upon his shoulders, and in this case the demi-god, or hero, in Cleopatra's mind is Hercules, whom Atlas once tricked into taking over his burden. The legend of Hercules provides a second important frame of mythological reference in the play (see Introduction, pp. 114–15 and cf. 1.3.84); Daniel's Cleopatra similarly calls Antony 'My

Atlas, and supporter of my pride | That did the world of all my glory sway' (1.15–16; Bullough, p. 408).

24 burgonet light steel helmet (of an outstandingly effective Burgundian design)

25 serpent Cleopatra is repeatedly associated with serpents. Conceivably Shakespeare knew that the cobra was an Egyptian royal emblem, displayed on the headpieces of the Pharaohs. In Renaissance beast lore the serpent was a fittingly ambiguous creature, a symbol of treachery and cunning, the vehicle chosen by Satan for his seduction of Eve and so the author of human misery and of death itself. But the serpent ('more subtle than any beast of the field' Gen. 3: 1) was also a symbol of wisdom ('be ye therefore as wise as serpents', Matt. 10: 15)—as in the famous Rainbow Portrait of Queen Elizabeth, which shows an embroidered snake coiled upon her left sleeve (see Roy Strong, *Gloriana: The Portraits of Queen Elizabeth* (1987), pp. 156, 159). As a symbol of renovation (its young, hatching from buried eggs, appearing to be born spontaneously from the earth) the serpent had been sacred to Aesculapius, the God of Medicine. In the accommodating taxonomy of the time, crocodiles, emblematic of hypocrisy, could be included in the category of serpents.

With most delicious poison. Think on me,
That am with Phoebus' amorous pinches black,
And wrinkled deep in time. Broad-fronted Caesar,
When thou wast here above the ground, I was   30
A morsel for a monarch; and great Pompey
Would stand and make his eyes grow in my brow—
There would he anchor his aspect, and die
With looking on his life.

> *Enter Alexas*

ALEXAS   Sovereign of Egypt, hail.

CLEOPATRA

How much unlike art thou Mark Anthony!   35
Yet coming from him, that great medicine hath
With his tinct gilded thee.
How goes it with my brave Mark Anthony?

ALEXAS Last thing he did, dear queen,
He kissed—the last of many doubled kisses—   40
This orient pearl. His speech sticks in my heart.

34 *Enter Alexas*] ROWE; *Enter Alexas from Caesar* F; *Enter Alexas from Antony* COLLIER
MS.

27 **delicious poison** Dent P456.1 'Love is
a sweet poison'.
28 **with . . . black** Cleopatra's conceit wittily ascribes her dark (sunburned)
complexion to bruising caused by the
love-play of the sun-god, Phoebus.
29 **wrinkled . . . time** perhaps more than
a playfully hyperbolical reference to
her age; in the mouths of some actresses, at least, 'deep in time' develops
a mysterious resonance that seems to
link it with the serpent of Nile. Daniel's
Cleopatra is similarly frank about 'this
autumn of my beauty': 'thou cam'st
but in my beauty's wane, | When new
appearing wrinkles of declining |
Wrought with the hand of years,
seemed to detain | My graces light'
(1.181, 171–4; Bullough, p. 412).
Broad-fronted usually interpreted as
referring to Julius Caesar's high (bald-
ing) forehead; but perhaps it means
something like 'amply countenanced',
referring to his noble demeanour or
public 'face'
31 **great Pompey** Cleopatra's lover had
actually been Gnaeus Pompeius, elder
brother of Sextus Pompeius; but Shakespeare, whose play is populated by

shadows of an heroic past, deliberately
confuses him with his more famous
father, Pompey the Great. Plutarch
mentions in passing Cleopatra's earlier
liaisons (Appendix A).
33 **aspect** gaze
die suffer erotic ecstasy
34 *Enter Alexas* the F stage direction, although misleading, is the kind of fossil
to be expected in a text deriving from
foul papers—presumably Shakespeare
wrote *'from Caesar'* in error for *'from
Antony'* and the annotation represents
the dramatist's reminder to himself in
the course of composition of why he
needed to introduce Alexas at this point.
36–7 **great medicine . . . thee** i.e. Alexas
seems to be transformed into something finer than he is by mere contact
with Anthony, as base metals might
be transformed into gold by virtue of
the philosopher's stone (the 'great medicine', 'tincture', 'tinct', or 'elixir').
38 **brave** magnificent (as at l. 67)
41 **orient** lustrous—either because pearls
from the East were supposed to be
of the finest quality, or 'because of the
clearness which resembleth the colour
of the clear air before the rising of the

CLEOPATRA

Mine ear must pluck it thence.

ALEXAS   'Good friend,' quoth he,

'Say the firm Roman to great Egypt sends

This treasure of an oyster—at whose foot,

To mend the petty present, I will piece   45

Her opulent throne with kingdoms. All the East,

Say thou, shall call her mistress.' So he nodded,

And soberly did mount an arm-gaunt steed,

Who neighed so high that what I would have spoke

Was beastly dumbed by him.

CLEOPATRA   What, was he sad, or merry?   50

ALEXAS

Like to the time o'th'year between th'extremes

Of hot and cold, he was nor sad nor merry.

CLEOPATRA

O, well divided disposition! Note him,

Note him, good Charmian, 'tis the man, but note him:

He was not sad, for he would shine on those   55

That make their looks by his; he was not merry,

Which seemed to tell them his remembrance lay

In Egypt with his joy; but between both.

48 an arm-gaunt] F (Arme-gaunt); an arm-girt HANMER; a termagaunt MASON; war-gaunt JACKSON; arrogaunt BOADEN (*conj., in* Singer); arm-jaunced OXFORD   50 dumbed] THEOBALD; dumbe F   What, was he sad,] ROWE *subs.*; What was he sad, F; What was he, sad WILSON (*conj.* Furness)

sun' (Harrison, *Description of England* 1.3.240)

43 **firm** constant, resolute

45 **To . . . present** Bevington glosses 'To improve upon the trivial or ordinary state of things as they are at present'; but the sense is surely rather that when Anthony returns to Cleopatra in person he will 'make amends for this trivial gift' (of a mere pearl) by heaping her throne with new kingdoms.

45–6 **piece . . . throne** complete her kingdom (by adding further pieces to it)

48 **arm-gaunt** A celebrated crux to which Ridley devotes an entire appendix, and the Variorum editors very lengthy notes. 'Arm-gaunt', reluctantly accepted by most editors, is taken to mean 'lean and hardened' from long war service—perhaps with the additional sense of

'fierce-looking in armour' or 'hungry for battle' (Bevington). Of the various proposed emendations, Hanmer's 'arm-girt' has the merit of clarity, whilst Oxford makes a strong case for 'arm-jaunced', from *jaunce* (also spelt *gaunce*) = make a horse prance up and down. A possibility so far uncanvassed is 'argeaunt', i.e. *argent* = clad in silver armour.

50 **beastly dumbed** (1) silenced or drowned out by the animal's noise; (2) reduced to beast-like inarticulacy

51 **extremes** (stress on the first syllable)

51–61 Alexas describes Anthony as a model of Roman temperance and the *via media*; Cleopatra characteristically reinterprets this as a paradoxical mixture of opposites ('mingle').

56 **make their looks by his** model their demeanour on his

O heavenly mingle! Be'st thou sad, or merry,
The violence of either thee becomes,   60
So does it no man else. Met'st thou my posts?
ALEXAS
Ay, madam, twenty several messengers.
Why do you send so thick?
CLEOPATRA   Who's born that day
When I forget to send to Anthony
Shall die a beggar. Ink and paper, Charmian!   65
Welcome, my good Alexas! Did I, Charmian,
Ever love Caesar so?
CHARMIAN   O, that brave Caesar!
CLEOPATRA
Be choked with such another emphasis!
Say 'the brave Anthony'.
CHARMIAN   The valiant Caesar.
CLEOPATRA
By Isis, I will give thee bloody teeth,   70
If thou with Caesar paragon again
My man of men.
CHARMIAN   By your most gracious pardon,
I sing but after you.
CLEOPATRA   My salad days,
When I was green in judgement, cold in blood,
To say as I said then. But come, away!   75
Get me ink and paper,
He shall have every day a several greeting,
Or I'll unpeople Egypt.   *Exeunt*

61 man] F2; mans F1

60 **The violence . . . becomes** the most extravagant display of either emotion
would seem becoming in you. Compare Anthony's 'Fie, wrangling queen!
| Whom everything becomes—to
chide, to laugh, | To weep' (1.1.50–2).
61 **posts** messengers
71 **paragon** compare
73–4 **My salad . . . blood** paraphrasing Plutarch (Appendix A)
74 **blood** desire
76–8 **Get . . . Egypt** The compositor evidently had difficulty with the versifica-

tion here, setting the last line-and-
a-half as prose. The point might seem
of little consequence when the metre
is so broken, but the half-lines are used
to significant dramatic effect: l. 76
allows for a pause after 'come, away!'
highlighting one of Cleopatra's characteristically sudden switches of direction; while the incomplete line at the
end of the speech (where convention
tended to favour a full rhyming
couplet) suits the hurry and informality of the scene's conclusion.

2.1   *Enter Pompey, Menecrates, and Menas, in
            warlike manner*

POMPEY

If the great gods be just, they shall assist
The deeds of justest men.

MENECRATES   Know, worthy Pompey,
That what they do delay they not deny.

POMPEY

Whiles we are suitors to their throne, decays
The thing we sue for.

MENECRATES   We, ignorant of ourselves,   5
Beg often our own harms, which the wise powers
Deny us for our good; so find we profit
By losing of our prayers.

POMPEY   I shall do well:
The people love me, and the sea is mine;
My powers are crescent, and my auguring hope   10
Says it will come to th'full. Mark Anthony
In Egypt sits at dinner, and will make
No wars without doors. Caesar gets money where

2.1.2, 5 MENECRATES] F (*Mene.*), MALONE; *Menas* JOHNSON

2.1.2, 5, 17, 19 MENECRATES Dr Johnson's
testy comment, 'I know not why *Menecrates* appears; *Menas* can do all without him' initiated a lengthy debate
about this character. F assigns to
'*Mene.*' all the speeches traditionally
apportioned between Menas and Menecrates; and since it also prints Menas
as *Menes* in 2.7, '*Mene.*' can plausibly
be construed as an abbreviation of
either name. Since Menas is the only
character directly addressed by Pompey in the scene, some editors assign
all the speeches to him, treating Menecrates as a 'ghost' character, like Rannius and Lucillius in 1.2. However, the
first two speeches, as Granville-Barker
noted, belong to 'a philosophical pirate' (p. 106) quite unlike the rather
ruthless Menas; and it seems possible
that Menecrates' unwelcome news at
ll. 16–17 leads an irritated Pompey to
turn from him to Menas at l. 32.

3 That ... deny the fact that they delay
granting a request does not mean
that they are refusing it. Proverbial:

'Delays are (not) denials' (Dent
D198.1).

4–5 Whiles ... for the thing we beg the
gods for loses its value even as we beg
for it

10 powers military forces
crescent growing
auguring prescient; the first recorded
usage of this participle, according to
OED, which gives 1601 as the earliest
appearance of the verb *augur*

11 it Usually explained as referring to the
metaphoric moon of Pompey's power,
implicit in 'crescent'; but in fact there
is no reason why 'crescent' (from Latin
crescere to grow) should involve a
metaphor; in this context it is equally
likely to be a conscious Latinism, and
'it' may just as well be reflexive: i.e.
Pompey's hope of victory is confident
of fulfilment.

13 No ... doors As opposed to his erotic
wars indoors (playing on the conventional metaphors of sexual combat in
Petrarchan love-poetry).

He loses hearts. Lepidus flatters both,
Of both is flattered; but he neither loves,   15
Nor either cares for him.

MENECRATES   Caesar and Lepidus
Are in the field, a mighty strength they carry.

POMPEY
Where have you this? 'Tis false.

MENECRATES   From Silvius, sir.

POMPEY
He dreams: I know they are in Rome together
Looking for Anthony. But all the charms of love,   20
Salt Cleopatra, soften thy waned lip!
Let witchcraft join with beauty, lust with both,
Tie up the libertine in a field of feasts,
Keep his brain fuming! Epicurean cooks
Sharpen with cloyless sauce his appetite,   25
That sleep and feeding may prorogue his honour,
Even till a Lethe'd dullness—
    Enter Varrius

                    How, now, Varrius?

16, 18 MENECRATES] F (*Mene.*); *Menas* JOHNSON   21 waned] STEEVENS 1793 ('wan'd';
conj. Thirlby 2); wand F; wan POPE; wann'd IRVING (*conj.* Steevens 1773)

20 **charms** magic (like 'witchcraft' at
l. 22, this may echo Josephus; cf.
above 1.2.128)
21 **Salt** lecherous
waned 'faded, ageing'. Jackson, followed by Collier, sought to justify the
F reading 'wand' (= 'potent as a
wand'); but though it would link with
'charms' and 'witchcraft', the metaphor seems too strained, and Collier
abandoned it in 1858 in favour of the
reading adopted by Steevens 1793,
'wan'd', which has the advantage of
not distinguishing between the two
principal rivals, 'waned' which most
editors favour, and 'wanned' (made
pale—with age) which is spelt 'wand'
in the Q2 version of Hamlet's Hecuba
speech (*Hamlet* 2.2.555); it would also
allow for word-play on Jackson's
'wand'. The *Hamlet* evidence is ambiguous, however, since F substitutes
'warm'd' for 'wand'; and 'warm'd' or
'warme' (= heated with lust) are
equally possible readings here, fitting

Pompey's emphasis on libertine luxury. However, the case for 'waned'
seems to be clinched by a passage in
Elizabeth Cary's *The Tragedy of Mariam*
(1613), which speaks of Anthony's
love for Cleopatra's 'wayned face'
(1.2.200, sig. B1ᵛ). The Oxford editor
and Spevack both note that a case can
also be made for 'wan' (= 'dusky';
spelt 'wane').
22–3 **Let . . . tie up** i.e. let witchcraft,
beauty, and lust combine to tie up
23 **field** i.e. like a beast confined to a fat
pasture; but it also contrasts with the
field of battle where Caesar and Lepidus are to be found.
24 **fuming** clouded with the fumes of
liquor
25 **cloyless** never-cloying; apparently a
Shakespearian neologism (*OED*)
26 **prorogue his honour** postpone the
fulfilment of his debt to honour
27 **till** This may be construed, as in modern English, as the equivalent of *until*,
in which case Pompey's sentence is

VARRIUS
This is most certain that I shall deliver:
Mark Anthony is every hour in Rome
Expected. Since he went from Egypt, 'tis   30
A space for farther travel.
POMPEY   I could have given less matter
A better ear. Menas, I did not think
This amorous surfeiter would have donned his helm
For such a petty war; his soldiership
Is twice the other twain—but let us rear   35
The higher our opinion, that our stirring
Can from the lap of Egypt's widow pluck
The ne'er lust-wearied Anthony.
MENAS   I cannot hope
Caesar and Anthony shall well greet together:
His wife that's dead did trespasses to Caesar;   40
His brother warred upon him—although, I think,
Not moved by Anthony.
POMPEY   I know not, Menas,
How lesser enmities may give way to greater:
Were't not that we stand up against them all,
'Twere pregnant they should square between themselves,   45
For they have entertainèd cause enough
To draw their swords; but how the fear of us

---

38 MENAS] ROWE 1709 (2); MENE. F   39 greet] F; gree RIDLEY (*conj.* Furness)
41 warred] F2 (warr'd); wan'd FI.

incomplete; or it may represent an archaic usage (still current in Ulster,
Scots, and Northern dialects), where
till replaces *to* before a vowel, in which
case the sentence is complete. F's dash
probably favours the first alternative.
27 **Lethe'd** In the classical underworld,
Lethe was the river whose waters
brought oblivion to the souls of the
dead. Apparently the adjective is a
Shakespearian coinage (*OED*).

30-1 **'tis...travel** enough time has
elapsed for him to have travelled even
further
34-5 **his soldiership...other twain** For
Plutarch's emphasis on Antonius's military talents and popularity amongst
his troops, see Appendix A.
35-6 **rear...opinion** think the better of

ourselves
37 **lap** (sexually explicit; cf. *Hamlet*
3.2.107-15)
39 **well greet together** meet each other on
friendly terms. Though intransitive
uses of 'greet' are rare, 'together' is a
not uncommon substitute for the reci-
procal pronoun 'each other'. However,
it is possible that Furness was right in
supposing that the compositor had
simply tacked the 't' of 'together' onto
'gree' (an obsolete form of 'agree').
45 **pregnant** obvious; not, as Arden supposes, a 'figurative use' of 'pregnant'
= 'with child' which derives from late
Latin *praegnare* (to be with child), but
a wholly distinct adjective, deriving
from Latin *premere* (to press).
square between quarrel amongst

May cement their divisions and bind up
The petty difference, we yet not know.
Be't as our gods will have't. It only stands   50
Our lives upon to use our strongest hands.
Come, Menas.   *Exeunt*

2.2   *Enter Enobarbus and Lepidus*

LEPIDUS
　Good Enobarbus, 'tis a worthy deed,
　And shall become you well, to entreat your captain
　To soft and gentle speech.
ENOBARBUS   I shall entreat him
　To answer like himself: if Caesar move him,
　Let Anthony look over Caesar's head   5
　And speak as loud as Mars. By Jupiter, /
　Were I the wearer of Antonio's beard, |
　I would not shave't today.
LEPIDUS   'Tis not a time
　For private stomaching.
ENOBARBUS   Every time serves
　For the matter that is then born in't.   10
LEPIDUS
　But small to greater matters must give way.
ENOBARBUS
　Not if the small come first.
LEPIDUS   Your speech is passion:
　But pray you stir no embers up—here comes
　The noble Anthony.
　　　Enter ⌈at one door⌉ Anthony and Ventidius
ENOBARBUS   And yonder Caesar

2.2.7 Antonio's] F (Anthonio's); Antonius' STEEVENS (*conj.* Thirlby 3)   14, 14.1 *at one
door . . . at another door*] OXFORD; *not in* F

48 **cement** repair; the accent falls on the
　first syllable
49 **difference** quarrel
50–1 **It . . . use** our lives depend upon our
　using
2.2.4 **like himself** This seemingly casual
　phrase has already been rendered
　problematic by the conflicting versions

of Anthony's character offered by
Philo, Cleopatra, Caesar, Lepidus, and
Pompey; Enobarbus now offers a version of his own.
7–8 **Were I . . . shave't** i.e. I would dare
　Caesar to pluck it
9 **stomaching** cherishing bitterness

Enter ⌈*at another door Caesar,*⌉ *Mecenas, and*
    Agrippa
ANTHONY (*to Ventidius*)
    If we compose well here, to Parthia.   15
    Hark, Ventidius. (*They talk aside*)
CAESAR   I do not know,
    Mecenas; ask Agrippa.
LEPIDUS (*to Caesar and Anthony*) Noble friends,
    That which combined us was most great, and let not
    A leaner action rend us. What's amiss,
    May it be gently heard. When we debate   20
    Our trivial difference loud, we do commit
    Murder in healing wounds. Then, noble partners,
    (The rather for I earnestly beseech)
    Touch you the sourest points with sweetest terms,
    Nor curstness grow to th'matter.
ANTHONY   'Tis spoken well: 25
    Were we before our armies, and to fight,
    I should do thus.
        ⌈*Anthony and Caesar embrace*⌉. *Flourish*
CAESAR Welcome to Rome.
ANTHONY Thank you.
CAESAR Sit.   30
ANTHONY Sit, sir.
CAESAR Nay then.
        ⌈*Caesar sits and then Anthony*⌉

27.1 *Anthony . . . embrace*] OXFORD (*conj.* Nicholson); *not in* F   32.1 *Caesar . . . Anthony*]
This edition; *not in* F

13 compose settle our dispute
16–17 **Hark, Ventidius . . . ask Agrippa**
    As Bevington points out, the rival
    leaders studiously ignore one another
    until Lepidus brings them together.
24 **Touch** (1) touch upon; (2) probe (a
    wound), apply a remedy
25 **Nor . . . matter** 'Let not *ill-humour*
    [curstness] be added to the real *subject*
    of our difference' (Johnson); in addi-
    tion Bevington suggests a continuation
    of the medical metaphors in 'healing
    wounds' and 'touch': 'And do not
    allow the present infection to come to
    a head' (*matter* = pus).
27.1 *Anthony . . . embrace* For the im-

plicit stage direction in 'do thus' see
above 1.1.39. The flourish of trumpets
here points up the formal difference
between the two superficially similar
gestures.
28–32 Many editors arrange these short
speeches as a single verse line, but such
rapid cueing is doubtfully appropriate
to the dramatic situation. Steevens and
Johnson both detected an edginess in
the exchange; Malone (and later Ridley) thought it no more than an exchange of 'after you' courtesies. But in
a society where courtiers might fight
and kill over matters of precedence it
is difficult to believe that the exchange

ANTHONY

I learn you take things ill which are not so:
Or being, concern you not.

CAESAR   I must be laughed at,
If or for nothing, or a little, I   35
Should say myself offended, and with you
Chiefly i'th'world; more laughed at, that I should
Once name you derogately, when to sound your name
It not concerned me.

ANTHONY

My being in Egypt Caesar, what was't to you?   40

CAESAR

No more than my residing here at Rome
Might be to you in Egypt—yet if you there
Did practise on my state, your being in Egypt
Might be my question.

ANTHONY   How intend you 'practised'?

CAESAR

You may be pleased to catch at mine intent   45
By what did here befall me. Your wife and brother
Made wars upon me, and their contestation
Was theme for you: you were the word of war.

ANTHONY

You do mistake the business: my brother never

49 the] HANMER (y^e) (conj. Thirlby); your F

could have appeared merely neutral. Some awkward pausing is almost certainly required. Cyrus Hoy comments 'it looks to me like an uneasy testing of the ground in which Anthony refuses to accept Octavius' taking the initiative in the encounter.... Octavius, the younger man, accepts having his bluff called. It dramatically illustrates the problem of having two people trying to rule the world.'

38 **derogately** disparagingly; the accent falls on the first syllable. Evidently a Shakespearian coinage (OED).

43 **practise on my state** plot against my power and authority

44 **question** occasion for dispute

48 **theme for you** Sometimes explained as 'Had you for theme'; Jones suggests 'was a debate on your behalf'; the

most plausible suggestion is from Steevens (citing Coriolanus 1.1.217-18 'throw forth greater themes | For insurrection's arguing'). He glosses 'Was proposed as an example for you to follow on a yet more extensive plan, as *themes* are given for a writer to dilate upon'; cf. also Hamlet 5.1.264, 'Why I will fight with him upon this theme'.

word of war war-cry (cf. Ventidius's description of Anthony's name as 'that magical word of war' (3.1.31); in Renaissance warfare it was still customary for troops to go into battle shouting the name of their commander (see e.g. 1 Henry VI 2.1.39, 79, 3 Henry VI 5.1.59-80).

49 **the business** Hanmer's 'the', which assumes the easy misreading of 'y^r' for the manuscript's abbreviated 'y^e',

Did urge me in his act; I did inquire it,   50
And have my learning from some true reports
That drew their swords with you. Did he not rather
Discredit my authority with yours,
And make the wars alike against my stomach,
Having alike your cause? Of this, my letters   55
Before did satisfy you. If you'll patch a quarrel—
As matter whole you have to make it with—
It must not be with this.

CAESAR   You praise yourself
By laying defects of judgement to me; but
You patched up your excuses.

ANTHONY   Not so, not so: 60
I know you could not lack—I am certain on't—
Very necessity of this thought, that I,
Your partner in the cause 'gainst which he fought,
Could not with graceful eyes attend those wars
Which fronted mine own peace. As for my wife,   65
I would you had her spirit in such another!
The third o'th'world is yours, which with a snaffle
You may pace easy, but not such a wife.

ENOBARBUS Would we had all such wives, that the men
might go to wars with the women.   70

---

64 graceful] F; grateful POPE

makes easier sense and has a more
idiomatic ring.

50 **urge . . . act** cite me as the pretext for
his actions
51-2 **true . . . you** reliable sources on
your side
51 **reports** informants
54 **stomach** desire
55 **Having . . . cause** either, 'having as
much reason to resent his behaviour
as you'; or, 'since I shared equally in
the cause for which your fought'
56 **patch** patch together, contrive
57 **As** given that. Bevington, however,
prefers to understand 'as if', assuming
that Anthony, far from tendering an
implicit apology, is denying all wrong-
doing.
matter whole plentiful reasons (Caesar
continues the tailoring metaphor)
60-8 Jones comments, 'The style of this

and Anthony's next speech seems deliberately tortuous, evasive, and grace-
less. Shakespeare no doubt meant it to
express the double-talk of politicians.'
61-2 **I . . . thought** Elaborately emphatic
circumlocution for 'You absolutely
must have been aware'.
64 **with . . . attend** look favourably upon
65 **fronted** opposed
65-160 **As for my wife . . . amen** Much of
the detail here derives from Plutarch
(see Appendix A).
67 **snaffle** a simple bridle-bit, less harsh
than one with a curb; the implicit
reference is to the 'scold's bridle' or
'branks', a device used in the punishment of unruly women, consisting of
an iron cage for the head with a sharp
metal bit to restrain the tongue.
68 **pace** train to walk at a steady pace
70 **go . . . women** (with a sexual innuendo)

ANTHONY
So much uncurbable, her garboils, Caesar,
Made out of her impatience—which not wanted
Shrewdness of policy too—I grieving grant
Did you too much disquiet: for that, you must
But say I could not help it.

CAESAR   I wrote to you: 75
When rioting in Alexandria you
Did pocket up my letters, and with taunts
Did gibe my missive out of audience.

ANTHONY   Sir,
He fell upon me ere admitted, then:
Three kings I had newly feasted, and did want   80
Of what I was i'th'morning; but next day
I told him of myself, which was as much
As to have asked him pardon. Let this fellow
Be nothing of our strife: if we contend
Out of our question wipe him.

CAESAR   You have broken   85
The article of your oath, which you shall never
Have tongue to charge me with.

LEPIDUS Soft, Caesar.

ANTHONY No, Lepidus, let him speak.
The honour is sacred which he talks on now,   90
Supposing that I lacked it—but on, Caesar:
The article of my oath?

CAESAR
To lend me arms, and aid when I required them,

74 disquiet: for that, you] This edition; disquiet: for that you F; disquiet, for that you OXFORD

71 **uncurbable** Continues the horse-break-ing figure; the only example of this adjective recorded in *OED* and appar-ently a Shakespearian coinage.
   garboils tumults (also at 1.3.61)
72 **not wanted** did not lack
73 **policy** Often, in Elizabethan English, with a suggestion of political cunning, deviousness, or dissimulation; machia-vellian intrigue.
74–5 **for that ... say** as far as that's con-cerned, you must at least admit
78 **missive** messenger
80–1 **did want ... morning** was not the man I had been in the morning
83–4 **Let ... strife** don't let's quarrel about this insignificant person
85 **question** dispute
87 **Have tongue** have the gall; the sense derives from the verbal use of 'tongue' = to reproach, to speak injuriously about
91 **Supposing ... it** Either 'imagining me to be deficient in such honour'; or 'Even supposing me to be deficient in honour [the way in which he now impugns my honour is so outrageous as to demand a response].'

The which you both denied.

ANTHONY   Neglected rather—
And then when poisoned hours had bound me up   95
From mine own knowledge. As nearly as I may,
I'll play the penitent to you; but mine honesty
Shall not make poor my greatness, nor my power
Work without it. Truth is that Fulvia,
To have me out of Egypt, made wars here,   100
For which myself, the ignorant motive, do
So far ask pardon as befits mine honour
To stoop in such a case.

LEPIDUS   'Tis noble spoken.

MECENAS

If it might please you to enforce no further
The griefs between ye: to forget them quite   105
Were to remember that the present need
Speaks to atone you.

LEPIDUS   Worthily spoken, Mecenas.

ENOBARBUS Or, if you borrow one another's love for the
instant, you may, when you hear no more words of
Pompey, return it again. You shall have time to   110
wrangle in when you have nothing else to do.

ANTHONY

Thou art a soldier only: speak no more.

ENOBARBUS That Truth should be silent, I had almost forgot.

ANTHONY You wrong this presence; therefore speak no
    more!

ENOBARBUS Go to, then—your considerate stone.   115

---

112 soldier only: speak] THEOBALD (*subs.*), Souldier, onely speake F

95–6 **bound . . . knowledge** drugged self-
    knowledge into oblivion
98–9 **nor . . . without it** nor shall I exer-
    cise my power without the control of
    honesty
99–100 **Truth . . . here** Anthony's excuse
    is supported by Plutarch's account of
    Fulvia's motives for making trouble in
    Italy (see Appendix A).
101 **ignorant motive** unconscious cause
104–5 **enforce . . . griefs** not to harp any
    more on the grievances
107 **atone** make at one, reconcile
113 **truth . . . silent** apparently proverbial,
    though Tilley and Dent list no exact

equivalent; cf. 'Truth has no need of
rhetoric' and 'All truths must not be
told' (Dent T575, T594). The nearest
parallel is perhaps the Fool's 'Truth's a
dog must to kennel' *Lear* 1.4.110—one
of many details that link him with Enobarbus (see Introduction, pp. 89–94).
115 **your . . . stone** Dent S878.1, S879:
'As mute/still as a stone'. Given that
Enobarbus's role in this scene is that
of licensed fool (see Introduction, p.
92), a punning allusion to 'Stone the
fool', whose death is recorded in *Vol-
pone* (2.1.53), may be intended.
considerate An ironic quibble: the

CAESAR

I do not much dislike the matter, but
The manner of his speech; for't cannot be
We shall remain in friendship, our conditions
So diff'ring in their acts. Yet, if I knew
What hoop should hold us staunch, from edge to edge   120
O'th'world I would pursue it.

AGRIPPA Give me leave, Caesar.

CAESAR Speak, Agrippa.

AGRIPPA

Thou hast a sister by the mother's side,
Admired Octavia. Great Mark Anthony   125
Is now a widower.

CAESAR   Say not so, Agrippa;
If Cleopatra heard you, your reproof
Were well deserved of rashness.

ANTHONY

I am not married, Caesar: let me hear
Agrippa further speak.   130

AGRIPPA

To hold you in perpetual amity,

119–21 Yet . . . staunch, from . . . world] POPE; Yet if I knew, . . . Ath' world: I F; Yet, if . . . world, I ARDEN   126 not so,] ROWE; not, say F   127 reproof] HANMER (*conj.* Warburton); proofe F; Approof THEOBALD

ostensible meaning is 'showing consideration for others' (here close to 'obedient'), but Enobarbus also intends the older sense of 'thoughtful' ('I may act the stone, but that won't prevent me having my own thoughts').

118 **our conditions . . . acts** our dispositions producing such different behaviour

119–21 **Yet . . . it** Pope's punctuation has been almost universally accepted by recent editors, even though the Folio with its unpunctuated l. 120 and semi-colon after 'world' unambiguously associates 'from edge to edge | Ath' world' with 'hold us staunch'; not only does this make perfect sense, it also fits with the pervasive imagery of a splitting world, its warring extremes held together only by the political will of its great competitors.

120 **hold us staunch** hold fast together,

render watertight; the metaphor is from the craft of cooperage in which metal hoops are used to bind together the wooden staves of a barrel or other wooden container.

124–5 **sister . . . Octavia** Octavius had two sisters named Octavia; Plutarch mistakenly assigned the elder, born from the father's first wife, to Antonius; in fact he was married to the younger, Octavius's full sister. Shakespeare seems to compound the confusion by making her a half-sister on the mother's side.

127–8 **your . . . rashness** you would justly be accused of rashness

131–4 Wilson compares Countess of Pembroke's *Antony* (1592), whose 'Argument' announces that 'Antonius, who for knitting a straiter bond of amity between them had taken to wife Octavia.'

To make you brothers, and to knit your hearts
With an unslipping knot, take Anthony
Octavia to his wife, whose beauty claims
No worse a husband than the best of men,   135
Whose virtue and whose general graces speak
That which none else can utter. By this marriage
All little jealousies which now seem great,
And all great fears which now import their dangers,
Would then be nothing; truths would be tales,   140
Where now half-tales be truths; her love to both
Would each to other and all loves to both
Draw after her. Pardon what I have spoke,
For 'tis a studied, not a present thought,
By duty ruminated.

ANTHONY   Will Caesar speak?   145
CAESAR
Not till he hears how Anthony is touched
With what is spoke already.

ANTHONY
What power is in Agrippa,
If I would say 'Agrippa, be it so',
To make this good?

CAESAR   The power of Caesar, and   150
His power unto Octavia.

ANTHONY   May I never
To this good purpose, that so fairly shows,
Dream of impediment. Let me have thy hand
Further this act of grace; and from this hour

153–4 hand | Further] F; hand; | Further THEOBALD

133 **unslipping** The first example of this
   participial adjective recorded in *OED*.
140–1 **truths ... truths**   uncomfortable
   truths would seem insignificant fic-
   tions, where now mere malicious
   rumours are taken as truth
144 **present** spur-of-the-moment
147–8 **With what ... Agrippa** Most editors treat these two half lines as a
   single hypermetrical line. But a significant pause is appropriate after Caesar's
   probing evasion of Anthony's question.
152 **so fairly shows** seems so hopeful
153 **impediment** Echoing the language of
   the Anglican marriage service: 'If

either of you do know any impediment
why ye may not lawfully be joined
together in matrimony' (*Book of Common Prayer*, 1559); cf. Sonnet 116:
'Let me not to the marriage of true
minds | Admit impediments'.
153–4 **hand | Further** Theobald's inser-
tion of a semicolon after *hand* is accepted by many editors, but it alters
the sense of F, and obscures the careful
rhetorical balance of 'hand | Further
... heart govern'. The sense is 'give
me your hand as a pledge of this reconciliation'.
154 **act of grace** not merely 'gracious,

The heart of brothers govern in our loves   155
And sway our great designs.
CAESAR   There's my hand:
Anthony and Caesar clasp hands
A sister I bequeath you, whom no brother
Did ever love so dearly. Let her live
To join our kingdoms and our hearts; and never
Fly off our loves again.
LEPIDUS   Happily, amen.   160
ANTHONY
I did not think to draw my sword 'gainst Pompey,
For he hath laid strange courtesies and great
Of late upon me. I must thank him only,
Lest my remembrance suffer ill report—
At heel of that, defy him.
LEPIDUS   Time calls upon's: 165
Of us must Pompey presently be sought,
Or else he seeks out us.
ANTHONY   Where lies he?
CAESAR About the Mount Misena.
ANTHONY   What is his strength
By land?
CAESAR   Great, and increasing; but by sea
He is an absolute master.
ANTHONY   So is the fame.   170

156.1 *Anthony . . . hands*] OXFORD; *not in* F   169 By land] F; *given to Caesar* HANMER
(*conj.* Thirlby)

generous action', but also 'act imbued
with divine grace'

155 **heart of brothers** 'Heart' is singular
because of the familiar conceit that
lovers and friends share a single heart
(cf. Dent B503.1).
160 **Fly off** desert
161–8 **Pompey . . . strange courtesies . . .
Misena** The detail is from Plutarch (see
Appendix A).
162 **strange** unusual
164 **remembrance** gratitude
168 **Mount Misena** 'the mount of Misena'
in North (properly Misenum, a southern Italian port)
168–9 **What . . . land** Hanmer's emendation, adopted by most recent editors,

is attractive, but (as Oxford recognizes)
by no means as 'certain' as Ridley
claimed. Ridley writes 'Anthony was
not likely to narrow the scope of his
question to the enemy's land forces,
whereas the two abrupt questions from
him, with Caesar's itemized reply to
the second, seem to me much more
effective and in character'; but so
much has already been made of Pompey's strength by sea that it might
seem only natural for Anthony to seek
specific intelligence about his land
forces. In that case 'So is the fame' may
contain a tinge of irony at the expense
of Caesar's redundant information.
170 **fame** rumour

Would we had spoke together! Haste we for it—
Yet ere we put ourselves in arms, dispatch we
The business we have talked of.
CAESAR   With most gladness;
And do invite you to my sister's view,
Whither straight I'll lead you.
ANTHONY   Let us, Lepidus,   175
Not lack your company.
LEPIDUS   Noble Anthony,
Not sickness should detain me.
          Flourish. Exeunt all but Enobarbus, Agrippa, Mecenas
MECENAS Welcome from Egypt, sir.
ENOBARBUS Half the heart of Caesar, worthy Mecenas!
My honourable friend, Agrippa!   180
AGRIPPA Good Enobarbus!
MECENAS We have cause to be glad that matters are so
well digested. You stayed well by't in Egypt.
ENOBARBUS Ay, sir, we did sleep day out of countenance,
and made the night light with drinking.   185
MECENAS Eight wild boars roasted whole at a breakfast,
and but twelve persons there—is this true?
ENOBARBUS This was but as a fly by an eagle. We had

177.1 *Exeunt all but*] F (*Exit omnes.* | *Manet*)   183 digested] F2; disgested F1

171 **spoke together** Either 'joined battle'
with Pompey, as Case (citing 2.6.25)
supposed; or 'consulted with one another' (i.e. Anthony with Caesar) as
Dover Wilson and Ridley argued.
'Haste we for it' favours the former
interpretation.
174 **to my sister's view** to see my sister
179 **Half the heart** Metaphorically, close
friends, like lovers, shared a single
heart.
182–3 **matters . . . digested** affairs have
been so satisfactorily arranged. But the
sudden switching of the conversation
to the topic of Egyptian feasts suggests
a quibble here, so that a sense like 'our
disputes have been so thoroughly
swallowed' may also be appropriate.
F's 'disgested' is cited by *OED* as 'a
parallel form' which continues to survive in dialect, and is therefore retained by most editors; but the
difference is insignificant, and the

word-play makes it desirable to use the
standard form.
183 **stayed well by't** stuck it out well
184 **sleep . . . countenance** upset the day
by sleeping through it (thus turning it
to night)
185 **made . . . light** Puns on several senses
of 'light'—merry, light-headed, debauched, bright (as day).
186 **Eight . . . breakfast** This detail derives
from an anecdote told by Plutarch's
grandfather, Lampryas (see Appendix
A). Such debauches were perhaps part
of Antonius's consciously assumed
Herculean character; Hercules was famous for his gigantic appetite (being
supposedly capable of devouring an
entire ox at a sitting); amongst his
Twelve Labours, moreover, was included the slaying of the terrible wild
boar of Eurymanthus.
188 **a fly by an eagle** Bevington cites Dent
E190 ('The eagle does not catch flies').

much more monstrous matter of feast, which worthily
deserved noting.   190

MECENAS She's a most triumphant lady, if report be
square to her.

ENOBARBUS When she first met Mark Anthony, she
pursed up his heart upon the River of Cydnus.

AGRIPPA

There she appeared triumphantly indeed—   195
Or my reporter devised well for her.

ENOBARBUS I will tell you:
The barge she sat in, like a burnished throne

---

195 appeared triumphantly indeed] This edition (*conj.* Wilson); appeared indeed, F

191–2 Mecenas's apparent *non sequitur*
perhaps suggests that Enobarbus's
'much more monstrous matter of feast'
should be played as a sexual innuendo
(consistent with the play's repeated association of sexuality and food—cf. ll.
231–2, 243–5).

191 **triumphant** magnificent; but perhaps
also with a hint of a more literal sense,
'given to triumphal display', since Enobarbus will go on to describe the most
celebrated of her 'triumphs' (see also
note to l. 195).

192 **square** fair

194 **Cydnus** (the river in Asia Minor on
which Tarsus was situated)

195 **triumphantly** The F sense seems incomplete, or at the least inappropriately weak; Dover Wilson's plausible
conjecture, as well as converting the
prose to two pentameter lines, picks up
Mecenas's 'triumphant' and under-
lines the presentation of Cleopatra's
royal entry as a triumphal water-
pageant in a play where the idea of
formal 'triumph' develops a gathering
imaginative importance. Kittredge,
however, interpreted 'appeared indeed', on the basis of its emphatic construction, as meaning 'made a truly
magnificent spectacle'.

196 **reporter** informant
    devised invented

197 **I will tell you** The translation of
North's glittering description of Cleopatra's water-triumph into the mouth
of Enobarbus is an extraordinary dramatic stroke: not only does it deepen
his character by its quite unexpected

imaginative richness; it transforms the
audience's sense of Cleopatra herself
by her ability to evoke this response
from Anthony's normally sceptical and
prosaic lieutenant. The speech has
been played in various ways: Patrick
Stewart's first Enobarbus for the RSC
(1972) sought to convey the sense
that 'all of this was traveller's tales',
something concocted by 'an old sweat'
for the benefit of gullible listeners; but
when he took the part again in 1978,
he sought to convey the feeling that
'a genuine *transformation* occurred on
that river; and that neither Anthony
nor Enobarbus would ever be the same
again' (RSC Workshop, *The South Bank
Show*, ITV 1978). Michael Bryant in
the 1987–8 National Theatre production worked against the grain of lyricism in the verse for most of the
speech, suggesting a purveyor of high-
class pornography, but his imagination suddenly caught fire on 'I saw
her once | Hop forty paces through
the public street' (ll. 235–6).

198–233 **The barge . . . eat** only Arden
cites the description of the Battle of
Actium in Fairfax's Tasso, *Godfrey of
Boulogne* (1600), 16.4: 'The waters
burnt about their vessels good, | Such
flames the god therein enchased
threw'; but much of the detail of the
passage derives from Plutarch, and is
often closely indebted to the wording of
North's translation. The two passages
are worth detailed comparison in order
to see how fine prose is alchemized
into great poetry (see Appendix A).

Burned on the water; the poop was beaten gold,
Purple the sails, and so perfumèd that   200
The winds were lovesick with them; the oars were silver,
Which to the tune of flutes kept stroke, and made
The water which they beat to follow faster,
As amorous of their strokes. For her own person,
It beggared all description: she did lie   205
In her pavilion—cloth-of-gold of tissue—
O'er-picturing that Venus where we see
The fancy out-work nature; on each side her
Stood pretty, dimpled boys, like smiling Cupids,
With divers-coloured fans, whose wind did seem   210
To glow the delicate cheeks which they did cool,
And what they undid did.

AGRIPPA   O, rare for Anthony!

ENOBARBUS

Her gentlewomen, like the Nereides,
So many mermaids, tended her i'th'eyes,
And made their bends adornings. At the helm   215
A seeming mermaid steers; the silken tackle
Swell with the touches of those flower-soft hands

201 lovesick with them; the] POPE ('with 'em'); Loue-sicke. With them the F   211 glow]
ROWE (*after* F1 'gloue'); glove F2

204 **strokes** Enobarbus quibbles on three
senses of the word: the strokes of the
oars are simultaneously blows (cf.
'beat') and erotic caresses (cf. Cleopatra's 'The stroke of death is as a lover's
pinch', 5.2.294).

206 **cloth-of-gold of tissue** 'Cloth-of-gold'
and 'tissue' (= 'a rich kind of cloth,
often interwoven with gold or silver',
OED) are often virtual synonyms; but
OED cites 'A gown of tawny cloth of
gold of tisshue' (1501) which presumably refers to an especially luxurious
cloth-of-gold, woven as 'tissue'—apparently made from twisted rather
than plain thread (Bevington).

207–8 **O'er-picturing . . . nature** outdoing
the Venus portrayed in works of art
whose imaginative splendour goes beyond anything in the world of nature.
The earliest instance of *overpicture*
cited in OED.

209, 213 **like** As Kittredge noted, in Elizabethan usage 'like' can mean 'in the
guise of'.

210–12 **wind . . . did** (a transformed version of Philo's paradox, 1.1.9–10)

213 **Nereides** Sounded as four syllables.
These beautiful sea-nymphs, fifty
daughters of the sea-god Nereus, were
normally represented as fully human
in shape, unlike mermaids, though a
Pompeian fresco shows one riding a
lion with a tail like a sea-horse.

214 **tended . . . eyes** waited in her sight

215 **made . . . adornings** adorned the
spectacle with their graceful postures.
Since this appears to be his equivalent
for Plutarch's comparison with the
Graces, Shakespeare perhaps has in
mind the elegant *contraposto* and serpentine line of the figures in Renaissance representations of the Three
Graces.

216–17 **tackle | Swell** 'Tackle' is treated
as a collective noun; it includes sails
as well as ropes—hence *swell*. The
erotic mood of the whole speech brings
out the suggestion of sexual tumes-
cence in 'swell'.

That yarely frame the office. From the barge
A strange invisible perfume hits the sense
Of the adjacent wharfs. The city cast   220
Her people out upon her; and Anthony,
Enthroned i'th'market- place, did sit alone,
Whistling to th'air, which but for vacancy
Had gone to gaze on Cleopatra too,
And made a gap in Nature.

AGRIPPA   Rare Egyptian!   225

ENOBARBUS

Upon her landing, Anthony sent to her,
Invited her to supper. She replied,
It should be better he became her guest,
Which she entreated. Our courteous Anthony,
Whom ne'er the word of 'no' woman heard speak,   230
Being barbered ten times o'er, goes to the feast,
And for his ordinary pays his heart
For what his eyes eat only.

AGRIPPA   Royal wench!
She made great Caesar lay his sword to bed,
He ploughed her, and she cropped.

218 **yarely ... office** nimbly perform the
task
220 **wharfs** Usually glossed as 'river
banks'; however, the gloss is dependent on *OED*, which cites only Hamlet's
'Lethe wharf' (*Hamlet* 1.5.33) to warrant the existence of anything like this
meaning before 1867. It is possible that
Shakespeare, by confusing Lethe with
Acheron, the river across which souls
were ferried into the underworld, imagined it with a wharf. On balance the
modern meaning of the word seems appropriate to the scene of Cleopatra's
triumph, which the dramatist is likely
to have imagined as resembling the
water-pageants of contemporary London.
223 **but for vacancy** except that 'nature
abhors a vacuum' (Dent N42)
225 **Rare Egyptian** Since *Egyptian* was
often used as a synonym for *gypsy* (see
note to 1.1.10), Agrippa's exclamation, like his 'Royal wench!' below,
involves an oxymoron; Cyrus Hoy suggests a further play on the association
of both gypsies and Egyptians with
magic, since 'Enobarbus is suggesting
she almost performed the miracle of

creating a natural vacuum'; and in
this context a complicated quibble on
rare as the opposite of *dense* may be
involved, since the creation of such a
vacuum would amount to a miracle of
absolute rarefaction, glancing forwards
to Cleopatra's final self-metamorphosis
into the rarer elements of 'fire and air'
(5.2.288).
231 **barbered** (*OED*'s first recorded instance of this verb)
232 **ordinary** public dinner, held in an
inn or eating-house
233 **Royal wench** A quibble is involved:
'royal' was often used to mean little more
than 'splendid'; but Cleopatra's literal
royalty creates an oxymoron, since
'wench' was usually applied to girls of
low breeding, sometimes with an impu-
tation of wantonness. Cf. note to l. 239.
234 **lay his sword to bed** Like much of the
imagery describing Anthony's subjugation to Cleopatra, this draws on the
mythological imagery of Mars subdued
by Venus; the sword, which becomes
the play's most insistent symbol of
Anthony's masculinity, is presented
here in explicitly phallic terms.

ENOBARBUS   I saw her once   235
Hop forty paces through the public street;
And having lost her breath, she spoke, and panted,
That she did make defect perfection,
And breathless, power breathe forth.

MECENAS
Now Anthony must leave her utterly.   240

ENOBARBUS Never. He will not:
Age cannot wither her, nor custom stale
Her infinite variety; other women cloy
The appetites they feed, but she makes hungry
Where most she satisfies; for vilest things   245
Become themselves in her, that the holy priests
Bless her when she is riggish.

MECENAS
If beauty, wisdom, modesty, can settle
The heart of Anthony, Octavia is
A blessèd lottery to him.

---

239 breathless, power breathe] HANMER; breathlesse powre breath F1; breathlesse
power breath F2; breathless power breathe F3 and F4; breathless, pour breath OXFORD
(*conj.* Daniel)

235 **ploughed her** Agrippa, wittily recalling the Neoplatonic interpretation of
the Mars and Venus myth as an allegory of Violence subdued by Love
(Caritas), plays on the proverbial
image of swords cast into plough-
shares.
  cropped Cleopatra bore Julius Caesar a
son, Caesarion (see note to 3.13.163).
239 **breathless . . . forth** Since 'powre' occurs elsewhere in F as a spelling for
'pour', while 'breath' and 'breathe'
were not properly distinct in Elizabethan English, the F reading is deeply
ambiguous, as the efforts of successive
Folio printers and of subsequent editors show. The difficulty is that each
reading creates a paradox appropriate
to the style of Enobarbus's speech. On
balance 'power' seems the more reson-
ant of the two readings, because by reminding his audience of the queen (and
perhaps also the enchantress) behind
the playful schoolgirl performance
it catches up Agrippa's oxymorons
'Royal wench' and 'Rare Egyptian'.
242 **stale** make stale. Bevington notes a
play on the proverbial 'as stale as cus-

tom' (Dent C930), adding that 'both
"custom" and "stale" may have risible
suggestions of prostitution'.
243–5 **variety . . . satisfies** Echoing the
proverb 'variety takes away satiety'
(Dent V18); cf. also Plutarch, *Morals*,
'Of Isis and Osiris', p. 1309, where Isis
is credited with 'an infinite number of
names, for that she receiveth all forms
and shapes'.
244–5 **she . . . satisfies** For Jonathan Gil
Harris's suggestion that Enobarbus
echoes a famous tag from Ovid's account of Narcissus, *inopem me copia
fecit* (my plenty makes me poor), see
Introduction, pp. 87–9.
246 **Become themselves** achieve a paradoxical decorum; but there may also
be a hint of the pervasive metamorphic
sense of 'become'—'she transforms the
most degraded things back to their
pristine ideal condition'; cf. the transformations attributed to love in *Dream*
1.1.232–3: 'Things base and vile,
holding no quantity, | Love can trans-
form to form and dignity.'
247 **riggish** licentious
250 **lottery** prize

AGRIPPA   Let us go.   250
　Good Enobarbus, make yourself my guest
　Whilst you abide here.
ENOBARBUS   Humbly, sir, I thank you.

Exeunt

2.3   *Enter Anthony, Caesar; Octavia between them*
ANTHONY
　The world and my great office will sometimes
　Divide me from your bosom.
OCTAVIA   All which time,
　Before the gods my knee shall bow my prayers
　To them for you.
ANTHONY   Good night, sir. My Octavia,
　Read not my blemishes in the world's report.   5
　I have not kept my square, but that to come
　Shall all be done by th'rule. Good night, dear lady.
　Good night, sir.
CAESAR   Good night.

Exeunt Caesar and Octavia

　Enter Soothsayer

ANTHONY
　Now, sirrah—you do wish yourself in Egypt?
SOOTHSAYER
　Would I had never come from thence, nor you   10
　Gone thither.
ANTHONY   If you can, your reason?

2.3.8 Good night, sir.] F1; *assigned to Octavia in* F2   8.1 *Exeunt . . . Octavia*] ROWE;
Exit F   10–11 you | Gone thither] OXFORD; you thither F.

2.3.0 The stage direction emblematically points towards Octavia's emotional division between husband and brother (see 3.4).
1–2 **The world . . . bosom** Ironically Anthony is made to begin his first dialogue with Octavia by foreshadowing the rupture between them: in the context of the previous scene, an audience is likely to interpret 'the world' as referring (consciously or unconsciously) to the lure of Egypt.
6 **kept my square** kept to the straight and narrow; 'a golden set square was an

emblem of temperance' (Jones)
7 **by th' rule** according to the rule (of temperance); but also punning on rule = ruler, and so continuing the carpentry metaphor in 'square'
11–15 The irregularities in the verse and the uncertainties of the F lineation (where ll. 10–11 and perhaps 13–16 are treated as prose) make the verse difficult to reconstruct here, and editors have attempted several different solutions. It might be better to treat the first five speeches as cadenced prose.

SOOTHSAYER

I see it in my motion, have it not in my tongue.
But yet hie you to Egypt again.

ANTHONY   Say to me,

Whose fortunes shall rise higher: Caesar's or mine?

SOOTHSAYER Caesar's.   15

Therefore, O Anthony, stay not by his side.
Thy daemon, that thy spirit which keeps thee, is
Noble, courageous, high, unmatchable,
Where Caesar's is not; but near him, thy angel
Becomes afeard, as being o'erpowered—therefore   20
Make space enough between you.

ANTHONY   Speak this no more.

SOOTHSAYER

To none but thee; no more but when to thee.
If thou dost play with him at any game,
Thou art sure to lose; and of that natural luck,
He beats thee 'gainst the odds. Thy lustre thickens,   25
When he shines by—I say again, thy spirit
Is all afraid to govern thee near him;
But he away, 'tis noble.

ANTHONY   Get thee gone.

Say to Ventidius I would speak with him.
He shall to Parthia.

                                    Exit Soothsayer

                    Be it art or hap,   30

---

18 high, unmatchable] F3; high vnmatchable F1; high-unmatchable (*conj.* anon. *cited in Spevack*)   20 afeard,] COLLIER 1853 (*conj.* Thirlby); a feare: F   o'erpowered—therefore] This edition; o'repower'd, therefore F   22 thee; no more ... thee] THEOBALD; thee no more but: when to thee F   18 away, 'tis] FOPE, alway 'tis F   29, 38 Ventidius] F2; *Ventigius* F1   30 Parthia. Be] HANMER; Parthia, be F   *Exit Soothsayer*] This edition; F *prints* 'Exit.' *after* 'speak with him.'

---

12 **motion** inward prompting
13–14 **Say ... Caesar's or mine** The Sooth-sayer's intervention is described by Plutarch (see Appendix A). In Plutarch this episode follows the triumvirs' encounter with Pompey at Misenum; by placing it earlier Shakespeare creates an ironic context for their diplomatic triumph.
17 **daemon** guardian spirit, angel; genius
22 **no more ... thee** only when I'm talk-

ing to you in person
24 **of** as a result of
25 **thickens** dims, becomes clouded
29 **Ventidius** Spelt 'Ventigius' throughout in this scene. Even though F consistently uses 'Ventidius' elsewhere, the recurrence of the error here suggests that it is less likely to represent a simple compositorial misreading than Shakespeare's own phoneticization of the name.

He hath spoken true: the very dice obey him,
And in our sports my better cunning faints,
Under his chance; if we draw lots he speeds;
His cocks do win the battle still of mine,
When it is all to nought; and his quails ever   35
Beat mine, inhooped, at odds. I will to Egypt;
And though I make this marriage for my peace,
I'th'East my pleasure lies.
         Enter Ventidius
                            O come, Ventidius.
You must to Parthia, your commission's ready—
Follow me, and receive't.   *Exeunt*   40

2.4   *Enter Lepidus, Mecenas, and Agrippa*
LEPIDUS
Trouble yourselves no further. Pray you hasten
Your generals after.
AGRIPPA   Sir, Mark Anthony
Will e'en but kiss Octavia, and we'll follow.
LEPIDUS
Till I shall see you in your soldier's dress,
Which will become you both, farewell.
MECENAS   We shall,   5
As I conceive the journey, be at the Mount
Before you, Lepidus.
LEPIDUS   Your way is shorter;
My purposes do draw me much about:
You'll win two days upon me.
MECENAS *and* AGRIPPA   Sir, good success!
LEPIDUS Farewell.   *Exeunt severally*   10

38 *Enter Ventidius*] DYCE; *after* 'O come Ventigius' F
   2.4.6 at the Mount] F2; at Mount, F1   9 MECENAS *and* AGRIPPA] *Both.* F

32 **better cunning** greater skill
33 **speeds** wins
35 **When . . . nought** i.e. no matter how
   overwhelming the odds
36 **inhooped** confined in a tight circle so
   as to force them to fight; apparently a
   Shakespearian coinage, since *OED* records no other occurrence of the verb,

though John Davies's *Epigrams* speaks
of the current vogue for 'cocking in
hoops' ('Upon English Proverbs', no. 287 in
Works, ed. Alexander Grosart (1869–76),
ii. 47)

2.4.6 **Mount** i.e. 'the Mount Misena' (see
   2.2.168)

2.5   *Enter Cleopatra, Charmian, Iras, and Alexas*

CLEOPATRA

Give me some music—music, moody food

Of us that trade in love.

ALL   The music, ho!

Enter Mardian the Eunuch

CLEOPATRA

Let it alone, let's to billiards—come, Charmian.

CHARMIAN

My arm is sore. Best play with Mardian.

CLEOPATRA

As well a woman with an eunuch played,   5

As with a woman. Come, you'll play with me, sir?

MARDIAN   As well as I can, madam.

CLEOPATRA

And when good will is showed, though't come too
    short,

The actor may plead pardon. I'll none now—

Give me mine angle, we'll to th'river; there,   10

My music playing far off, I will betray

Tawny-fine fishes, my bended hook shall pierce

Their slimy jaws; and as I draw them up,

I'll think them every one an Anthony,

And say 'Ah, ha! you're caught.'

CHARMIAN   'Twas merry when   15

2.5.2 ALL] *Omnes.* F   10–11 river; there, | My . . . off,] F4 (*subs.*); Riuer there | My
. . . off. F1   12 Tawny-fine] F3; Tawny fine F1; Tawny fin ROWE; Tawny-finn'd,
THEOBALD (*conj.* Thirlby)

2.5.3 **billiards** In *The Blind Beggar of Alex-*
andria (1598), from which Shake-
speare may have derived the notion,
George Chapman also has Egyptian
ladies playing at billiards (4.12–13).

8–9 **And . . . pardon** Jones rightly suggests
'a good-humoured parody of a senten-
tious maxim'; there are bawdy quibbles on 'will' (sexual desire; penis),
'come too short', and 'actor' (act =
sexual act).

10 **angle** fishing tackle

12 **Tawny-fine** Most editors have accepted
Theobald's amendment, assuming an
e/d error such as occurs at 1.4.8 and
1.5.50; but a rich yellowish red cloth
was often described as 'tawny' (cf.
note to 2.2.206), and there is no reason

why Cleopatra should not imagine her
fish as if tricked out in cloth-of-gold
finery.

15–18 **'Twas merry when . . . drew up**
The anecdote is closely derived from
Plutarch (see Appendix A). Fish often
have erotic connotations in Shakespeare (see Partridge, p. 112), and because of their pungent aroma an
especially bawdy symbolism attaches
to salt fish in many cultures—one
which the common Elizabethan sense
of *salt* (= lascivious) was likely to emphasize. The context of erotic yearning
to which Shakespeare assigns Plutarch's story probably activates its la-
tent suggestiveness.

You wagered on your angling, when your diver
Did hang a salt fish on his hook which he
With fervency drew up.

CLEOPATRA   That time? O times!
I laughed him out of patience, and that night
I laughed him into patience, and next morn,   20
Ere the ninth hour, I drunk him to his bed—
Then put my tires and mantles on him, whilst
I wore his sword Philippan.

    Enter a Messenger

                  O, from Italy!
Ram thou thy fruitful tidings in mine ears,
That long time have been barren.

MESSENGER   Madam, madam—   25

CLEOPATRA

Antonio's dead! If thou say so, villain,
Thou kill'st thy mistress. But well and free,
If thou so yield him, there is gold, and here
My bluest veins to kiss, a hand that kings
Have lipped, and trembled kissing.   30

---

23 *Enter a Messenger*] COLLIER; *after* 'from Italie' F   24 Ram] F ('Ramme'); Rain
HANMER   26 Antonio's] F1 (*Anthonyo's*); *Anthony's* F2; Antonius, DELIUS   28 him,
there] POPE 1728; him. There F

22–3 **Then ... Philippan** As well as
glancing at the familiar imagery of
Venus subduing Mars, this episode
seems designed to recall the behaviour
of Anthony's ancestor, Hercules: when
he fell in love with Omphale (to whom
he had been sold by Hermes), Hercules
put on her garments and spun wool,
whilst she assumed his lion skin and
club. The comparison was a favourite
one in Roman propaganda (Hughes-
Hallett, pp. 53–4), and the episode is
glanced at by Plutarch in 'The Comparison of Demetrius with Antonius'
where he accuses Antonius of 'delaying time to follow his own pleasure—as we see in painted tables,
where Omphale secretly stealeth away
Hercules' club, and took his lion's skin
from him. Even so Cleopatra oftentimes
unarmed Antonius and enticed him to
her, making him lose matters of great
importance and very needful journeys,
to come and be dandled with her' (Bul-

lough, p. 319); cf. also Garnier's *The
Tragedy of Antony*, 11. 1210–31 (Bullough, pp. 388–89).
Philippan i.e. the sword which Anthony wore in his victory over Brutus
and Cassius at Philippi (see note to
2.6.10–23; and cf. also 2.2.234). Theobald may be correct in supposing that
'Philippan' is intended as a name, following the medieval practice of naming swords after famous victories.
24–5 **Ram ... barren** In opting for Hanmer's emendation, Capell was disturbed by 'a grievous and striking
indelicacy [in *ram*] that could not
come from Cleopatra', but the metaphor carries on the vein of bawdy
quibbling from the first part of the
scene—Anthony's messenger is greeted
as though he promised to be a more
satisfactory substitute for his master
than Charmian or Mardian.
28 **yield** report

MESSENGER First, madam, he is well.

CLEOPATRA

Why, there's more gold! But, sirrah, mark, we use
To say the dead are well—bring it to that,
The gold I give thee will I melt and pour
Down thy ill-uttering throat.   35

MESSENGER Good madam, hear me!

CLEOPATRA Well, go to—I will.

But there's no goodness in thy face if Anthony
Be free and healthful: so tart a favour
To trumpet such good tidings! If not well,   40
Thou shouldst come like a Fury crowned with snakes,
Not like a formal man.

MESSENGER   Will't please you hear me?

CLEOPATRA

I have a mind to strike thee ere thou speak'st.
Yet if thou say Anthony lives, is well,
Or friends with Caesar, or not captive to him,   45
I'll set thee in a shower of gold, and hail
Rich pearls upon thee.

MESSENGER   Madam, he's well.

CLEOPATRA   Well said.

MESSENGER

And friends with Caesar.

CLEOPATRA   Thou'rt an honest man.

MESSENGER

Caesar and he are greater friends than ever.

CLEOPATRA

Make thee a fortune from me.

MESSENGER   But yet, madam   50

---

44 is] CAPELL (*conj.* Thirlby); 'tis F

---

33 **the dead are well** (semi-proverbial eu-
   phemism, Dent H347 'He is well since
   he is in heaven'. Dent cites only Shakespearian sources for this formulation,
   including *Romeo* 5.1.17 and *Macbeth*
   4.3.180; but cf. also Dent D142.3
   'Death is a physician').
34–5 **The gold . . . throat** imitating the
   torture of the wealthy Roman, Crassus, by King Orodes of Scythia (see

note to 3.1.2).
37 **go to** all right then
39 **so . . . favour** so sour an expression
41 **Fury** one of the Furies (Erinnyes or
   Eumenides), avenging deities of classical myth who produced frenzy in
   their victims. They were represented as
   winged females with snakes for hair.
42 **formal** in his natural shape, normal
48 **honest** worthy (as well as 'truthful')

CLEOPATRA
  I do not like 'But yet', it does allay
  The good precedence—fie upon 'But yet'!
  'But yet' is as a jailer to bring forth
  Some monstrous malefactor. Prithee, friend,
  Pour out the pack of matter to mine ear,   55
  The good and bad together: he's friends with Caesar,
  In state of health, thou sayst; and, thou sayst, free.
MESSENGER
  Free, madam? No, I made no such report:
  He's bound unto Octavia.
CLEOPATRA   For what good turn?
MESSENGER
  For the best turn i'th'bed.
CLEOPATRA   I am pale, Charmian.   60
MESSENGER
  Madam, he's married to Octavia.
CLEOPATRA
  The most infectious pestilence upon thee!
      She strikes him down
MESSENGER
  Good madam, patience!
CLEOPATRA   What say you?
      She strikes him

                              Hence
  Horrible villain, or I'll spurn thine eyes
  Like balls before me; I'll unhair thy head;   65
      She hales him up and down
  Thou shalt be whipped with wire and stewed in brine,
  Smarting in ling'ring pickle.
MESSENGER   Gracious madam,
  I that do bring the news made not the match.
CLEOPATRA
  Say 'tis not so, a province I will give thee,

62.1 *She*] *not in* F   63.1 *She*] *not in* F

51 **allay** alloy (and so diminish the worth
   of)
52 **good precedence** preceding good news
55 **Pour . . . matter** tell me everything
   (Cleopatra speaks as though his news

were material contained in a pedlar's
pack)
64 **spurn** kick
65.1 **hales** drags

And make thy fortunes proud. The blow thou hadst   70
Shall make thy peace for moving me to rage,
And I will boot thee with what gift beside
Thy modesty can beg.
MESSENGER   He's married, madam.
CLEOPATRA
Rogue, thou hast lived too long!
        She draws a knife
MESSENGER   Nay then, I'll run.
What mean you, madam? I have made no fault.   *Exit*   75
CHARMIAN
Good madam, keep yourself within yourself:
The man is innocent.
CLEOPATRA
Some innocents scape not the thunderbolt.
Melt Egypt into Nile! And kindly creatures
Turn all to serpents! Call the slave again—   80
Though I am mad, I will not bite him. Call!
CHARMIAN
He is afeard to come.
CLEOPATRA   I will not hurt him,
These hands do lack nobility that they strike
A meaner than myself, since I myself
Have given myself the cause. Come hither, sir.   85
        Enter the Messenger again
Though it be honest, it is never good
To bring bad news. Give to a gracious message
An host of tongues, but let ill tidings tell
Themselves, when they be felt.
MESSENGER   I have done my duty.
CLEOPATRA Is he married?   90
I cannot hate thee worser than I do,
If thou again say 'Yes'.

---

74 *She . . . knife*] OXFORD; *Draw a knife.* F

72 **boot** enrich
73 **Thy modesty** one as humble as you
78 **innocents** Case suggests a play on *in-
    nocent* = fool.
79 **Melt . . . Nile** Cf. 1.1.35.
84–5 **since . . . cause** since I myself am re-
    sponsible for what has upset me

88 **host of tongues** Fame was traditionally
    represented (like Rumour in *2 Henry
    IV*) as 'full of tongues'.
88–9 **but . . . felt** it is time enough for bad
    news to reveal itself, when its effects
    are felt

MESSENGER   He's married, madam.

CLEOPATRA

The gods confound thee. Dost thou hold there still?

MESSENGER

Should I lie, madam?

CLEOPATRA   O, I would thou didst,

So half my Egypt were submerged and made   95

A cistern for scaled snakes. Go, get thee hence!

Hadst thou Narcissus in thy face, to me

Thou wouldst appear most ugly. He is married?

MESSENGER

I crave your highness' pardon.

CLEOPATRA   He is married?

MESSENGER

Take no offence that I would not offend you.   100

To punish me for what you make me do

Seems much unequal. He's married to Octavia.

CLEOPATRA

O, that his fault should make a knave of thee,

That act not what thou'rt sure of! Get thee hence—

The merchandise which thou hast brought from Rome   105

Are all too dear for me. Lie they upon thy hand,

And be undone by 'em!

Exit Messenger

---

97 face, to me] F2; face to me, F1   104 act not] OXFORD (*conj.* Case); art not F; say'st but HANMER   107 *Exit Messenger*] ROWE; *not in* F

95 **submerged** The earliest use of this verb recorded in *OED*.

97 **Narcissus** In classical mythology a youth of astonishing beauty whose self-infatuation caused the nymph Echo to die of unrequited love.

100 **Take . . . you** The Messenger is caught in a double bind, since the Queen now appears enraged that he will *not* tell the truth that formerly so upset her.

102 **unequal** unjust

104 **That act . . . sure of** Either 'you who are after all innocent of this offence that you know about'; or 'you who are unable even to convey the news [cf. "what you make me do"] that you know only too well'. Since Hanmer's first attempt at emending this passage, editors have suggested numerous alter-

natives, some extremely elaborate, while several recent editions, including the New Cambridge, have attempted more or less contorted justifications of F. The Oxford reading (discussed in Wells, pp. 37–9) has the advantage of simplicity and clarity, as well as being graphically plausible.

105–6 **merchandise . . . Are** 'Merchandise' was often treated as a plural noun in seventeenth-century English. Though deriving from the French *marchandise*, it was quite commonly spelt 'merchandies' and perhaps therefore regarded as a plural of the obsolete 'merchandy' (= trade, traffic; mercantile commodities).

106 **Lie . . . hand** may you be unable to sell them. In this speech Cleopatra picks up the pedlar metaphor from l. 55.

CHARMIAN   Good your highness, patience.
CLEOPATRA
  In praising Anthony, I have dispraised Caesar?
CHARMIAN Many times, madam.
CLEOPATRA
  I am paid for't now. Lead me from hence,   110
  I faint—O Iras, Charmian!—'Tis no matter.
  Go to the fellow, good Alexas, bid him
  Report the feature of Octavia, her years,
  Her inclination—let him not leave out
  The colour of her hair. Bring me word quickly.   115
                                Exit Alexas
  Let him for ever go—let him not, Charmian!
  Though he be painted one way like a Gorgon,
  The other way's a Mars. (*To Mardian*) Bid you Alexas
  Bring me word how tall she is.—Pity me, Charmian;
  But do not speak to me. Lead me to my chamber.   120
                                   Exeunt

2.6 *Flourish. Enter Pompey and Menas at one door,*
     with drummer and trumpeter; at another Caesar,
     Lepidus, Anthony, Enobarbus, Mecenas, Agrippa,
     with soldiers marching
POMPEY
  Your hostages I have, so have you mine;
  And we shall talk before we fight.

---

108 Caesar?] This edition; Caesar. F   115.1 *Exit Alexas*] CAPELL; *not in* F   116 Let
... Charmian!] This edition; Let ... go, let him not *Charmian*, F
  2.6.0.1 *and Menas*] ROWE; *not in* F *which lists Menas after 'Agrippa'*

---

113 **feature** physical appearance (not merely face)

117-18 **Though ... Mars** Cleopatra compares the contradictions of Anthony's character to a type of 'perspective' or anamorphosis which represents different images according to the angle from which it is viewed. A great variety of these popular pictures and toys were produced in the Renaissance, but Cleopatra seems to have in mind one of the simpler sorts, still familiar today, in which a conventional-seeming portrait can be inverted to reveal the head of a grotesque.

117 **Gorgon** The Gorgons were three mythological creatures, of whom Medusa is the best known, whose hideous faces, wreathed in snakes, had the power to turn all who gazed on them to stone.

2.6. The veiled ironies of this scene are nicely caught in Peter Hall's note to his actors at the National: 'this scene is about politicians who never say what they are thinking ... conceal your hostility beneath a veil of utmost charm. Make it sound perfectly genuine. The art is to show how "nice" you can be' (Lowen, p. 64).

CAESAR   Most meet
That first we come to words, and therefore have we
Our written purposes before us sent,
Which if thou hast considered, let us know   5
If 'twill tie up thy discontented sword,
And carry back to Sicily much tall youth
That else must perish here.
POMPEY   To you all three,
The senators alone of this great world,
Chief factors for the gods: I do not know   10
Wherefore my father should revengers want,
Having a son and friends; since Julius Caesar,
Who at Philippi the good Brutus ghosted,
There saw you labouring for him. What was't
That moved pale Cassius to conspire? And what   15
Made all-honoured, honest, Roman Brutus,
With the armed rest, courtiers of beauteous freedom,
To drench the Capitol, but that they would

16 all-honoured] F1; the all-honor'd, F2

2 **meet** fit
3 **come to words** playing on the familiar 'come to blows'
4 **purposes** proposals
7 **tall** brave
10 **factors** agents, deputies, representatives
10–23 **I . . . father** Pompey the Great, having been defeated by the forces of Julius Caesar at Pharsalia in Thessaly (48 BC), fled to Egypt, where he was assassinated by agents of the boy-king Ptolemy (Cleopatra's half-brother). Caesar himself was assassinated by the republican conspirators Brutus and Cassius, who were defeated and killed in their turn by Antonius and Octavius at the battle of Philippi in Macedonia (42 BC). These latter events had provided the subject of Shakespeare's earlier Roman tragedy, *Julius Caesar*.
10–14 **I . . . him** if Julius Caesar, whose spirit haunted the virtuous Brutus at Philippi, had the satisfaction of seeing you working to revenge him in that battle, I do not see why my father should go unrevenged, when he has a son and friends ready to perform the task

15 **pale** Like the 'lean and hungry look' attributed to Cassius in *Julius Caesar* (1.2.195), pallor is one of the traditional marks of envy.
16 **honest** honourable (as well as 'honest' in the modern sense)
Roman Brutus F2 treats 'Roman' as a noun; but 'Roman Brutus' is perfectly acceptable, invoking Brutus as the incarnation of the Roman ideal of virtue. Cf. *Henry V* 2.4.37, where 'Roman Brutus' describes Brutus's putative ancestor, the regicide Lucius Junius Brutus, distinguishing him from 'Trojan Brutus', the supposed founder of Britain.
17 **courtiers** wooers (but the more usual sense of the word is probably also present, being applied with deliberate irony to these determined republicans); compare Plutarch's comment on Antonius's victory at Philippi: 'the greatest and most famous exploit Antonius ever did in wars (to wit, the war in which he overthrew Cassius and Brutus) was begun to no other end but to deprive his countrymen of their liberty and freedom' (Bullough, p. 319).
18 **drench** drown in blood

Have one man but a man? And that is it
Hath made me rig my navy, at whose burden   20
The angered Ocean foams, with which I meant
To scourge th' ingratitude that despiteful Rome
Cast on my noble father.

CAESAR   Take your time.

ANTHONY

Thou canst not fear us, Pompey, with thy sails.
We'll speak with thee at sea. At land thou know'st   25
How much we do o'ercount thee.

POMPEY   At land indeed
Thou dost o'ercount me of my father's house—
But since the cuckoo builds not for himself,
Remain in't as thou mayst.

LEPIDUS   Be pleased to tell us—
For this is from the present—how you take   30
The offers we have sent you.

CAESAR   There's the point.

ANTHONY

Which do not be entreated to, but weigh
What it is worth embraced.

CAESAR   And what may follow,
To try a larger fortune.

POMPEY   You have made me offer

19 is] F2; his, F1

21 **Ocean** The sea is allegorized here as the god Ocean (Oceanus).

24–9 **Thou . . . Thou** The edge of prickly hostility between Anthony and Pompey is partly registered in their use of the singular pronoun, which is otherwise clearly felt to be inappropriate to the formality of this occasion. By the same token Lepidus's more courteous *you* at ll. 30–1 marks an attempt to soothe Pompey's rising temper. Cf. Appendix C.

24 **fear** frighten

25 **speak** fight (picking up Caesar's wordplay at l. 3)

27 **o'ercount . . . house** Pompey's complaint is explained in Plutarch who records that the expropriation was an occasion of widespread resentment (see Appendix A).

28–9 **cuckoo . . . mayst** The insulting

comparison of Anthony to the cuckoo who appropriates the nests of others is combined with an implied threat, 'keep it while you can'.

30 **from the present** beside the point

32–3 **Which . . . embraced** don't let yourself be cajoled into accepting our terms, but think seriously about the great advantages in accepting them

33–4 **what . . . fortune** Ambiguous (perhaps deliberately so): it may involve either further inducement ('what further benefits may accrue, if you are prepared to test the full possibilities of what fortune has granted you'); or (as most editors assume) threatening ('think of the consequences if you push your luck too far').

34–81 **offer | Of Sicily . . . Aboard my galley** The terms of the treaty and the

Of Sicily, Sardinia; and I must   35
Rid all the sea of pirates; then to send
Measures of wheat to Rome—this greed upon,
To part with unhacked edges, and bear back
Our targes undinted.

CAESAR, ANTHONY, *and* LEPIDUS That's our offer.

POMPEY   Know then,   40
I came before you here a man prepared
To take this offer; but Mark Anthony
Put me to some impatience. Though I lose
The praise of it by telling, you must know,
When Caesar and your brother were at blows,   45
Your mother came to Sicily and did find
Her welcome friendly.

ANTHONY   I have heard it, Pompey,
And am well studied for a liberal thanks,
Which I do owe you.

POMPEY   Let me have your hand—
I did not think, sir, to have met you here.   50

ANTHONY
The beds i'th'East are soft; and thanks to you
That called me timelier than my purpose hither—
For I have gained by't.

CAESAR   Since I saw you last,
There's a change upon you.

POMPEY   Well, I know not
What counts harsh Fortune casts upon my face,   55
But in my bosom shall she never come
To make my heart her vassal.

LEPIDUS   Well met here!

POMPEY
I hope so Lepidus, thus we are agreed.
I crave our composition may be written

---

meeting on the galley are described by
Plutarch (see Appendix A).

37 **greed** agreed (obsolete verb)
39 **targes** shields
   undinted *OED*'s first recorded occurrence of this participial adjective.

48 **studied** prepared
55 **What . . . face** how my misfortunes
   may have scarred my face. 'To cast
   counts' is to make a reckoning (originally with tally marks or 'counts' on
   a stick).
59 **composition** agreement, reconciliation

And sealed between us.

CAESAR   That's the next to do.   60

POMPEY

We'll feast each other ere we part, and let's
Draw lots who shall begin.

ANTHONY   That will I, Pompey.

POMPEY

No, Anthony take the lot. But first or last,
Your fine Egyptian cookery shall have
The fame—I have heard that Julius Caesar   65
Grew fat with feasting there.

ANTHONY   You have heard much.

POMPEY I have fair meanings, sir.

ANTHONY   And fair words to them.

POMPEY

Then so much have I heard. And I have heard
Apollodorus carried—

ENOBARBUS

No more o' that. He did so.

POMPEY   What I pray you?   70

ENOBARBUS

A certain queen to Caesar in a mattress.

---

67 meanings] MALONE (*conj.* Thirlby); meaning F   70 o'that] F3 (of that); that FI

62–70 For some discussion on the problems of lineation in this passage, see
Appendix D.
67 **fair words** Jones reads Anthony's line
as flatteringly placatory, but a number
of proverbial formulations suggest the
tone may be sarcastic ('Fair words and
ill deeds deceive both wise and fools',
'Fair words butter no parsnips', 'Fair
words make fools fain'. 'Fair words
make me look to my purse'; Tilley
W788, W791, W794, W795; Dent
W794; and cf. Tilley W792, W800,
W804, W809, W812). It is Enobarbus
who acts as the lightning conductor in
this tense exchange.
68–9 **Then . . . carried** Pompey apparently
responds to Anthony with a dead bat,
as though to close the discussion, but
then cannot resist further goading. A
director will have to decide whether
Anthony should walk away at this
point (as Jones suggests), or whether

he remains throughout the ensuing
dialogue, reining himself in.
69 **Apollodorus** The incident is recounted
in Plutarch's 'Life of Julius Caesar':
'[Caesar] secretly sent for Cleopatra,
which was in the country, to come
unto him. She, only taking Apollodorus Sicilian of all her friends, took a
little boat and went away with him in
it in the night, and came and landed
hard by the foot of the castle. Then,
having no other mean to come into
the court, without being known, she
laid herself down upon a mattress or
flock bed, which Apollodorus her
friend tied and bound up together like
a bundle with a great leather thong;
and so took her up on his back, and
brought her thus hampered in this far-
del unto Caesar in at the castle gate.
This was the first occasion (as it is
reported) that made Caesar to love her'
(Bullough, p. 74).

POMPEY
    I know thee now. How far'st thou, soldier?
ENOBARBUS
    Well—and well am like to do, for I perceive
    Four feasts are toward.
POMPEY   Let me shake thy hand,
    I never hated thee. I have seen thee fight,   75
    When I have envied thy behaviour.
ENOBARBUS   Sir,
    I never loved you much, but I ha' praised ye
    When you have well deserved ten times as much
    As I have said you did.
POMPEY   Enjoy thy plainness,
    It nothing ill becomes thee.   80
    Aboard my galley I invite you all.
    Will you lead, lords?
CAESAR, ANTHONY *and* LEPIDUS Show's the way, sir.
POMPEY   Come.
                    Exeunt all but Enobarbus and Menas
MENAS (*aside*) Thy father, Pompey, would ne'er have
    made this treaty.—You and I have known, sir.
ENOBARBUS At sea, I think.   85
MENAS We have, sir.
ENOBARBUS You have done well by water.
MENAS And you by land.
ENOBARBUS I will praise any man that will praise me,
    though it cannot be denied what I have done by land.   90
MENAS Nor what I have done by water.
ENOBARBUS Yes, something you can deny for your own
    safety: you have been a great thief by sea.
MENAS And you by land.
ENOBARBUS There I deny my land service. But give me   95

---

82 CAESAR . . . LEPIDUS] CAPELL; *All.*, F   82.1 *Exeunt . . . Menas*] *Exeunt. Manet Enob. &*
Menas F

72–80 **thou . . . you** Pompey's and Eno-
    barbus's pronouns carefully reflect the
    difference in status between them,
    though in this case Pompey's tone sug-
    gests that his condescension is tinged
    with a gracious hint of intimacy. Cf.

Appendix C.
74 **toward** impending
79 **Enjoy thy plainness** indulge your
    plain-speaking. Kent, in *Lear*, is also
    identified with 'plainness' (1.1.147).
84 **known** met, been acquainted

your hand, Menas. If our eyes had authority, here
they might take two thieves kissing.
　　They shake hands
MENAS All men's faces are true, whatsome'er their
hands are.
ENOBARBUS But there is never a fair woman has a true　　100
face.
MENAS No slander—they steal hearts.
ENOBARBUS We came hither to fight with you.
MENAS For my part, I am sorry it is turned to a drinking.
Pompey doth this day laugh away his fortune.　　105
ENOBARBUS If he do, sure he cannot weep't back again.
MENAS You've said, sir. We looked not for Mark
Anthony here. Pray you, is he married to Cleopatra?
ENOBARBUS Caesar's sister is called Octavia.
MENAS True, sir, she was the wife of Caius Marcellus.　　110
ENOBARBUS But she is now the wife of Marcus Antonius.
MENAS Pray ye, sir?
ENOBARBUS 'Tis true.
MENAS Then is Caesar and he forever knit together.
ENOBARBUS If I were bound to divine of this unity, I　　115
would not prophesy so.
MENAS I think the policy of that purpose made more in
the marriage than the love of the parties.
ENOBARBUS I think so too. But you shall find the bond
that seems to tie their friendship together will be the　　120
very strangler of their amity: Octavia is of a holy, cold,
and still conversation.

---

97 1 *They . . . hands*] OXFORD; *not in* F

97 **take** arrest
　　two thieves kissing This may suggest
　　that the handclasp is followed by an
　　embrace; or (as the apparent identifi-
　　cation of hands with dishonesty in ll.
　　98–9 would suggest) it may refer play-
　　fully to their clasping hands them-
　　selves.
98, 100 **true** honest; Enobarbus puns on
　　the meanings 'faithful' and 'genuine'
　　(i.e. without cosmetics)
115 **divine of** make predictions about
117 **policy of that purpose** politics of that

alliance
　　made more counted for more
119 **bond** Shakespearian English did not
　　distinguish between 'band' (the F spell-
　　ing) and 'bond'; Enobarbus quibbles
　　on several senses of the word: security,
　　pledge; wedding bond; binding rope
　　(mod. 'band').
122 **still** quiet, calm; gentle, meek
　　conversation behaviour; perhaps Eno-
　　barbus also plays on the bawdy sense,
　　'sexual intercourse'

MENAS Who would not have his wife so?

ENOBARBUS Not he that himself is not so—which is Mark
  Anthony. He will to his Egyptian dish again; then shall   125
  the sighs of Octavia blow the fire up in Caesar; and, as
  I said before, that which is the strength of their amity
  shall prove the immediate author of their variance.
  Anthony will use his affection where it is. He married
  but his occasion here.   130

MENAS And thus it may be. Come, sir, will you aboard? I
  have a health for you.

ENOBARBUS I shall take it sir—we have used our throats
  in Egypt.

MENAS Come, let's away.   *Exeunt.*   135

2.7   *Music plays. Enter two or three Servants with a*
        banquet.

FIRST SERVANT Here they'll be, man. Some o'their plants
  are ill rooted already—the least wind i'th'world will
  blow them down.

SECOND SERVANT Lepidus is high-coloured.

FIRST SERVANT They have made him drink alms-drink.   5

2.7.1 ff. FIRST SERVANT] ROWE; 1 F   4 ff. SECOND SERVANT] ROWE; 2 F   4 high-coloured]
F2; high Conlord F1

128 **variance** falling out
129 **use . . . is** indulge his passions where
  they are really engaged
130 **occasion** opportunity
133 **used our throats** had plenty of drinking practice
2.7.0.1 *two or three Servants* The vague-
  ness is characteristic of authorial stage
  directions.
0.2 *banquet* course of sweetmeats, fruit,
  and wine
1 **Here . . . man** Oxford rightly draws attention to this as a suspect reading,
  since it does not lead naturally
  into what follows; but the suggested
  emendations 'Here they'll lie, man'
  or 'Here they'll be unmanned' are
  not really convincing. 'Here they'll be
  wan' (pale, sick with drinking) is another outside possibility; but it seems
  more likely that something has been
  dropped out after 'be' ('undone'? 'laid

flat'?).
  plants (1) soles of the feet (Latin *planta*);
  (2) newly planted trees, shrubs etc.
  (i.e. the new agreements between the
  political rivals)
5 **alms-drink** *OED* glosses 'the remains of
  liquor reserved for alms-people' (i.e. in
  this case dregs, likely to make Lepidus
  ill), but also gives *alms-wine* 'wine
  given in alms' (which might be meant
  ironically of the liquor pressed upon
  Lepidus); alternatively Case suggested
  it might mean 'drink taken as a work
  of charity' (to further the reconciliation process), a suggestion which the
  Second Servant's following speech
  makes plausible. Mack proposes 'drink
  drunk on behalf of one too far gone to
  continue his toasts' (i.e. Lepidus is
  tricked into drinking more than the
  others).

SECOND SERVANT As they pinch one another by the disposition, he cries out 'No more!', reconciles them to his
entreaty, and himself to th'drink.

FIRST SERVANT But it raises the greater war between him
and his discretion.   10

SECOND SERVANT Why, this it is to have a name in great
men's fellowship. I had as lief have a reed that will do
me no service, as a partisan I could not heave.

SECOND SERVANT To be called into a huge sphere, and not
to be seen to move in't, are the holes where eyes   15
should be, which pitifully disaster the cheeks.

> *A sennet sounded. Enter Caesar, Anthony, Pompey,*
> *Lepidus, Agrippa, Mecenas, Enobarbus, Menas,*
> *with other Captains, ⌈ and a Boy ⌉.*

ANTHONY
Thus do they, sir: they take the flow o'th'Nile

---

12 lief] F (liue)   16.3 *and a Boy*] JONES; *not in* F

---

6 **pinch ... disposition** Much disputed: it
might mean that Anthony and Caesar
stint one another in dispensing alms-
drink to Lepidus; or that they find
themselves irked by each other's tem-
peraments. Lepidus's 'No more' can
thus be a request to stop pouring him
drinks, or an appeal to the other two
to cease quarrelling. The First Servant's 'greater war' seems to favour
the second possibility.

13 **partisan** military spear of the halberd
type
heave lift

14–16 **To ... cheeks** An awkwardly condensed and complex figure: in the
Ptolemaic astronomy the universe was
made up of a series of concentric
spheres with the earth at their centre,
each of the first seven containing a
planet, whose movement around the
earth it controlled; Lepidus in his role
as triumvir is like a planet which remains motionless and invisible within
its sphere; in a further mocking analogy, the apparently empty sphere is
compared to empty eye- sockets.

16.1 *sennet* set of notes on the trumpet,
presumably distinct from a 'flourish'

16.3 *and a Boy* Enobarbus at l. 109 calls
for 'the boy' to sing the bacchic song.

17–23 **Thus ... harvest** The dependence
of Egyptian agriculture upon the an-
nual flooding of the Nile was well
known, but Shakespeare's notion that
'the *higher* Nilus swells, | The *more* it
promises' seems to derive specifically
from Garnier, the 'fat slime' of whose
Nile makes '*greatest* grow ... when his
floods do *highest* flow' (ll. 768–73, Bullough, p. 377; my emphases). The detail of Anthony's account suggests that
he also drew on John Pory's translation of Leo Africanus's *A Geographical
History of Africa* (1600). Leo records
that the Egyptians used 'the inunda-
tion of Nilus' to 'foresee the plenty or
scarcity of the year following' by
means of 'a kind of device invented by
the ancient Egyptians ... a certain pillar ... marked and divided into ... cu-
bits ... If the water reacheth only to
the fifteenth cubit ... they hope for a
fruitful year following; but if [it]
stayeth between the twelfth cubit and
the fifteenth, then the increase ... will
prove but mean. But if it ariseth to the
eighteenth cubit, there is like to follow
great scarcity' (p. 312). The transformation of 'pillar' into pyramid can
probably be explained by the habitual
Elizabethan confusion of pyramids
with obelisks.

By certain scales i'th'pyramid; they know
By th'height, the lowness, or the mean, if dearth
Or foison follow. The higher Nilus swells,   20
The more it promises: as it ebbs, the seedsman
Upon the slime and ooze scatters his grain,
And shortly comes to harvest.

LEPIDUS   You've strange serpents there?

ANTHONY Ay, Lepidus.

LEPIDUS Your serpent of Egypt is bred now of your mud   25
by the operation of your sun; so is your crocodile.

ANTHONY They are so.

POMPEY Sit, and some wine! A health to Lepidus!
          [*They sit and drink*]

LEPIDUS I am not so well as I should be—but I'll ne'er
out.   30

ENOBARBUS Not till you have slept—I fear me you'll be in
till then.

LEPIDUS Nay, certainly, I have heard the Ptolemies' py-
ramises are very goodly things; without contradiction
I have heard that.   35

MENAS (*aside to Pompey*)
    Pompey, a word.

POMPEY (*aside to Menas*) Say in mine ear: what is't?

MENAS (*aside to Pompey*)
    Forsake thy seat I do beseech thee, captain,
    And hear me speak a word.

POMPEY (*aside to Menas*)   Forbear me till anon.
    (*Aloud*) This wine for Lepidus.
    Menas begins whispering in Pompey's ear

28.1 *They . . . drink*] BEVINGTON; *not in* F   39.1 *Menas . . . ear*] OXFORD; *Whispers in's*
Eare. F

20 **foison** plenty
25 **bred . . . mud** The ancient belief that
   certain reptilian, amphibian, and in-
   sect life-forms were spontaneously produced by the action of the sun upon
   inorganic matter was based upon incomplete observation: young crocodiles can appear to hatch from the
   mud in which their eggs were buried.
29–30 **I'll ne'er out** I won't back out, or
   leave
31 **be in** (1) remain here (2) be in your

cups
36–81 **Pompey, a word . . . condemn it
   now** Menas's *realpolitik* is recorded by
   Plutarch (see Appendix A).
39.1 **Menas . . . ear** Most editors take this
   to refer simply to Pompey's final aside;
   but, as Oxford points out, it is not used
   for the previous asides and is an odd
   way of describing words intended for
   the audience. It seems clear that
   Menas's whispering is meant to continue until Pompey's outburst at l. 53.

LEPIDUS What manner o'thing is your crocodile?   40
ANTHONY It is shaped, sir, like itself, and it is as broad as
    it hath breadth. It is just so high as it is, and moves
    with it own organs. It lives by that which nourisheth
    it, and the elements once out of it, it transmigrates.
LEPIDUS What colour is it of?   45
ANTHONY Of it own colour too.
LEPIDUS 'Tis a strange serpent.
ANTHONY 'Tis so, and the tears of it are wet.
CAESAR (*aside to Anthony*) Will this description satisfy
    him?   50
ANTHONY (*aside to Caesar*) With the health that Pompey
    gives him, else he is a very epicure.
POMPEY (*aside to Menas*)
    Go hang, sir, hang! Tell me of that? Away,
    Do as I bid you! (*Aloud*) Where's this cup I called for?
MENAS (*aside to Pompey*)
    If for the sake of merit thou wilt hear me,   55
    Rise from thy stool.
POMPEY (*aside to Menas*) I think thou'rt mad.
                   He rises and they walk aside
                          The matter?
MENAS I have ever held my cap off to thy fortunes.
POMPEY
    Thou hast served me with much faith: what's else to
    say?—
    (*Aloud*) Be jolly, lords.
ANTHONY   These quicksands, Lepidus,   60
    Keep off them, for you sink.

43, 46 **It own** archaic form of 'its own'—
    often teasingly used in Shakespeare to
    create an effect of mock-childishness.
44 **elements** the four elements of earth,
    water, air, and fire of which all matter
    was supposedly made up; here stand-
    ing for the crocodile's material body.
    Cf. 5.2.288–9.
    transmigrates Referring playfully to
    Pythagoras's doctrine of metempsy-
    chosis, according to which the souls of
    animals and humans transmigrated at
    death into other new-born creatures.
48 **tears ... wet** Behind the continued
    play with tautology there is probably

an ironic allusion to the proverbial
hypocrisy of the crocodile's tears (Dent
C831). Perhaps an ironically unconscious commentary on Pompey's behaviour in the scene is involved.
52 **epicure** Here 'glutton' (whom nothing
    can satisfy).
55 **thou** Menas's persistent *thou*ing of his
    leader here is worth observing, it may
    be a way of registering as much impa-
    tience as presumed intimacy.
57 **held ... off** deferred to
60 **quicksands** Lepidus is beginning to
    totter.

MENAS
Wilt thou be lord of all the world?

POMPEY   What sayst thou?

MENAS
Wilt thou be lord of the whole world? That's twice.

POMPEY
How should that be?

MENAS   But entertain it,
And though thou think me poor, I am the man   65
Will give thee all the world.

POMPEY   Hast thou drunk well?

MENAS
No, Pompey, I have kept me from the cup.
Thou art, if thou dar'st be, the earthly Jove:
Whate'er the ocean pales, or sky inclips,
Is thine, if thou wilt ha't.

POMPEY   Show me which way?   70

MENAS
These three world-sharers, these competitors
Are in thy vessel. Let me cut the cable;
And when we are put off, fall to their throats.
All then is thine.

POMPEY   Ah, this thou shouldst have done,
And not have spoke on't: in me 'tis villainy;   75
In thee 't had been good service. Thou must know,
'Tis not my profit that does lead mine honour;
Mine honour, it. Repent that e'er thy tongue
Hath so betrayed thine act. Being done unknown,
I should have found it afterwards well done,   80
But must condemn it now. Desist, and drink.

MENAS (*aside*)
For this, I'll never follow thy palled fortunes more.

74 then] POPE; there F

69 **pales** encloses
   inclips embraces
71 **competitors** partners; but as at 1.4.3
   the word is also bound to suggest an
   edge of rivalry.
80 **I should . . . well done** The natural pausing of the line requires a caesura between
   the fourth and fifth feet; this, together
   with the spondaic double-stressing of

'well done', has the effect of italiciz-
ing the final phrase. The verb *do* takes
an unusual stress in this play,
emphasizing its preoccupation with incompatible ideas of virtuous action—
moral-philosophical, political, martial,
heroic, erotic (see Introduction pp.
104–7, 126–8).

82 **palled** dwindled

Who seeks and will not take, when once 'tis offered,
Shall never find it more.

POMPEY   This health to Lepidus!

ANTHONY (*to a servant*)
Bear him ashore—I'll pledge it for him, Pompey.   ,   85

ENOBARBUS
Here's to thee, Menas!

MENAS   Enobarbus, welcome!

POMPEY
Fill till the cup be hid!

ENOBARBUS (*pointing to the Servant who is carrying off Lepidus*)
There's a strong fellow, Menas.

MENAS   Why?

ENOBARBUS   A bears
The third part of the world, man: seest not?

MENAS
The third part then he is drunk—would it were all,   90
That it might go on wheels!

ENOBARBUS   Drink thou, increase the reels.

MENAS Come.

POMPEY
This is not yet an Alexandrian feast.

ANTHONY
It ripens towards it. Strike the vessels, ho!
Here's to Caesar.

---

88 *pointing . . . Lepidus*] ROWE (*subs.*); *not in* F   90 then he is drunk] F (then, he); then is drunk, ROWE

83–4 **Who seeks . . . more** Proverbial: cf. 'He that will not when he may, when he would he shall have nay' (Dent N54)

86 **thee** The developing friendship between Menas and Enobarbus is registered in their shift from *you* (which they had used throughout their previous encounter) to *thou*—a pronoun which Enobarbus never uses with his Roman acquaintance in 2.2, for example. Cf. Appendix C.

88 **A** colloquial form of 'he'

90 **then . . . drunk** most eds. follow Rowe in omitting 'he' in order to rearrange Menas's speech as verse ('all | That'). But the emendation is syntactically un-

necessary, and the additional syllable can readily be elided to fit the metre.

91 **go on wheels** go fast (with a suggestion of running dizzily out of control); a semi-proverbial formulation ('The world goes on wheels', Dent W893).
reels whirling or staggering movement; revels; dancing

93 **Alexandrian** The earliest recorded usage of this adjective, according to Schäfer.

94 **Strike the vessels** Clearly part of Anthony's toast, but there is no agreement as to its precise meaning: 'broach the casks', 'fill the cups', 'clink the cups', and 'sound the kettle-drums' have all been suggested. Perhaps drinking vessels were sometimes

CAESAR   I could well forbear't: 95
  It's monstrous labour when I wash my brain,
  An it grow fouler.
ANTHONY Be a child o'th'time.
CAESAR Possess it, I'll make answer.
  But I had rather fast from all, four days,   100
  Than drink so much in one.
ENOBARBUS (*to Anthony*) Ha, my brave emperor!
  Shall we dance now the Egyptian bacchanals,
  And celebrate our drink?
POMPEY Let's ha't, good soldier.
ANTHONY Come, let's all take hands   105
  Till that the conquering wine hath steeped our sense
  In soft and delicate Lethe.
ENOBARBUS   All take hands.
  Make battery to our ears with the loud music.
  The while I'll place you, then the boy shall sing.
  The holding every man shall beat as loud   110
  As his strong sides can volley.
      Music plays. Enobarbus places them hand in hand
⌈BOY⌉ (*sings*)
      Come, thou monarch of the vine,
      Plumpy Bacchus, with pink eyne!

97 An it grow] F1 ('And it grow'); And it grows F2   110 beat] F; bear, THEOBALD
112 BOY] COLLIER MS; *not in* F ('The Song')

rhythmically struck with knives, as
they are on some modern occasions.

95 ff. **I could well forbear't** Shakespeare's
  characterization of Octavius, especially
  in this scene, seems to owe something
  to the 'Life of Octavius Caesar Augustus' in North's Plutarch: 'He was very
  modest and continent in all the parts
  of his life, saving that he was somewhat given to women and play . . . It
  pleased him well to make feasts . . .
  and oftentimes he sat down at the
  table a long time after everybody, and
  would rise before others, which remained after he was up. In his ordinary diet he banished superfluity of
  meats . . . Also he drunk very little
  wine' (Bullough, pp. 321–2).
97 **An . . . fouler** if it only grows fouler as
  a result

99 **Possess . . . answer** my answer is, one
  should rather possess (control) the
  time than submit to the dictates of the
  moment
102 **bacchanals** wild dances in honour of
  Bacchus. Earliest *OED* citation (*baccha-
  nal* sb. 5)
103 **celebrate** (1) consecrate; (2) honour
  with religious festivities (*OED celebrate*
  v. 2,3)
107 **Lethe** Cf. note to 2.1.27.
108 **Make battery** to batter
110 **The holding . . . beat** every man shall
  beat out the refrain (*holding*); an instruction for all the revellers to join in
  the final chorus as they stamp out the
  rhythm
113 **Plumpy** *OED*'s first recorded example
  of this variant of 'plump'.
  pink half-closed; but perhaps also red-
  dened by drink

In thy vats our cares be drowned,
With thy grapes our hairs be crowned!   115
⌈*All join in the chorus*⌉
   Cup us till the world go round,
   Cup us till the world go round!

CAESAR
What would you more? Pompey, good night. Good
    brother,
Let me request you off: our graver business
Frowns at this levity. Gentle lords, let's part—   120
You see we have burnt our cheeks. Strong Enobarb
Is weaker than the wine, and mine own tongue
Splits what it speaks. The wild disguise hath almost
Anticked us all. What needs more words? Good night.
Good Anthony, your hand.
POMPEY   I'll try you on the shore.   125
ANTHONY And shall, sir—give's your hand.
POMPEY   O Anthony,
You have my father's house. But what, we are friends?
Come down into the boat.
ENOBARBUS   Take heed you fall not.
         Exeunt all but Enobarbus and Menas
Menas, I'll not on shore.
MENAS   No, to my cabin.
These drums, these trumpets, flutes—what!   130
Let Neptune hear, we bid a loud farewell

---

114 vats] F ('fattes')   115.1 *All . . . chorus*] STAUNTON (*after Collier MS* 'the burden');
not in F   118 Good brother] F; Good-brother OXFORD (*after* Gerald A. Smith)   119 off:
our] ROWE 1714; of our F   127 father's] F2; Father F1   128.1 *Exeunt   Menas*]
CAPELL; *not in* F   128–9 *not.* | Menas, I'll] CAPELL; *not Menas.* Ile F; 'Menas' as
speech-prefix ROWE   129 MENAS] CAPELL; *not in* F   131 a loud] ROWE 1714; aloud F

---

114 **vats** F 'Fattes' is merely a dialectal
   variation.
116 **Cup us** ply us with drink. Cf. Dent
   W885.1 '(To drink until) the world
   goes round'.
118 **Good brother** Oxford follows Gerald
   Smith's suggestion (' "Good Brother"
   in *King Lear* and *Antony and Cleopatra*',
   SQ 25 (1974), p. 284) that Caesar
   uses an Elizabethan alternative to
   brother-in-law ('good-brother') and
   hyphenates accordingly. The difficulty
   is that 'brother' is in any case the

usual form of address between brothers-
in-law, and that the distinction would
be difficult to establish vocally without a metrically awkward stressing of
'Good'.

123 **wild disguise** i.e. the transformations
   brought about by drink which he has
   just described
124 **Anticked** made fools or grotesques of
125 **try you** test your (drinking) prowess
131–2 **farewell . . . hanged** Cf. Dent
   H130.1 'Farewell (Come away) and be
   hanged'.

To these great fellows! Sound and be hanged, sound
    out!   *Sound a flourish, with drums*
ENOBARBUS Hoo! says a; there's my cap.
   ⌈*Enobarbus throws his cap in the air*⌉
MENAS   Hoo! Noble captain, come.   133
                                Exeunt

3.1   *Enter Ventidius,* ⌈*with Sillius and other Roman*
      soldiers⌉, *as it were in triumph; the dead body of*
      Pacorus borne before him
VENTIDIUS
Now, darting Parthia, art thou struck, and now
Pleased Fortune does of Marcus Crassus' death
Make me revenger. Bear the King's son's body
Before our army. Thy Pacorus, Orodes,   4

---

133 says a] F; sessa, RIDLEY (*conj.*)   *Enobarbus . . . air*] WILSON (*subs.*); *not in* F   Hoo!]
ARDEN; Hoa, F
  3.1.0.1–2 *with . . . soldiers*] CAPELL (*subs.; after* THEOBALD); *not in* F   4 army. Thy] F2
('Army, thy'); Army thy F1

---

133 **Hoo** *OED*'s earliest occurrence of this
exclamation (probably a variant of *ho!*
or *whoo!*).
3.1 For the historical basis of this scene,
see Plutarch (Appendix A). Plutarch
uses Ventidius's exploits to illustrate a
point he makes again in 'The Comparison of Demetrius with Antonius' (Bullough, p. 321)—that Antonius (like
Octavius Caesar) enjoyed greater military success through his subordinates
than in his own person.
0.2 **In triumph** The s.d. indicates that this
short scene, often cut in modern productions for its seeming insignificance,
was intended to provide the single
most lavish spectacle in the play. Plutarch is at pains to emphasize that
'Ventidius was the only man that ever
triumphed of the Parthians', and
North's text drew attention to this distinction with a marginal note (Appendix A). As if transposing the triumphal
procession from Rome to Syria, Shakespeare requires his company to
stretch all their resources to imitate
the effect of a triumph *all'antica*; such
a procession would normally include
(in addition to the ceremonially
presented body of Pacorus) displays of
chained prisoners, captured weapons,

and other trophies. The *triumphans*
himself might ride in a chariot (such
as we know to have been used in *2
Tamburlaine* and *Titus*.) The mounting
of such a heroic spectacle helps to
make vivid the persistently invoked
idea of 'triumph' in the play, whilst
setting up powerful ironic contrasts
with the debauchery on Pompey's galley and with the hard-headed political
realism of Ventidius's own speeches (ll.
11–34).
1 **darting Parthia . . . struck** word-play,
alluding to the well-known Parthian
cavalry tactic, in which their horsemen advanced hurling darts, and
then swung away from engagement,
shooting arrows behind them as they
retired.
2 **Marcus Crassus** Member, with Pompey
and Julius Caesar, of the First Triumvirate, and governor of Syria; defeated
by the Parthians on the Mesopotamian
plains in 53 BC; his head was taken to
King Orodes, who ordered molten gold
to be poured in the mouth, mocking
the notoriously avaricious Crassus:
'Sate yourself with what you desired
so greedily in life.'
4 **army. Thy** The F punctuation here is
uncertain, editors disagreeing as to

Pays this for Marcus Crassus.
SILLIUS   Noble Ventidius,   5
    Whilst yet with Parthian blood thy sword is warm,
    The fugitive Parthians follow. Spur through Media,
    Mesopotamia, and the shelters whither
    The routed fly. So thy grand captain, Anthony,
    Shall set thee on triumphant chariots and   10
    Put garlands on thy head.
VENTIDIUS   O Sillius, Sillius,
    I have done enough. A lower place, note well,
    May make too great an act. For learn this, Sillius:
    Better to leave undone than by our deed
    Acquire too high a fame when him we serve's away.   15
    Caesar and Anthony have ever won
    More in their officer than person. Sossius,
    One of my place in Syria, his lieutenant,
    For quick accumulation of renown,
    Which he achieved by th'minute, lost his favour.   20
    Who does i'th'wars more than his captain can
    Becomes his captain's captain; and ambition,
    The soldier's virtue, rather makes choice of loss
    Than gain which darkens him.
    I could do more to do Antonius good,   25
    But 'twould offend him, and in his offence
    Should my performance perish.
SILLIUS   Thou hast, Ventidius, that
    Without the which a soldier and his sword
    Grants scarce distinction. Thou wilt write to Anthony?

5, 27, 34 SILLIUS] THEOBALD; *Romaine* (or 'Rom.'), F   14 to] Fa; too Fb

whether the small and rather faint
mark between 'Army' and 'thy' is to
be read as a comma. If Bevington is
right in supposing that it is not, then
F (which prints a comma after 'body')
appears to attach the prepositional
phrase 'Before our Army' to 'Paies'
rather than to 'Beare'.

7 The ... follow pursue the fleeing Parthians
9 grand captain great commander
10 triumphant triumphal
12 lower place subordinate officer
18 place rank

lieutenant deputy, an officer acting in
the place of his commander (cf. the
modern 'lieutenant-general')
23–4 rather ... darkens   him   would
rather sacrifice his ambition than fulfil
it at the cost of bringing himself into
disfavour
26 in his offence as a result of his taking
offence
28–9 Without ... distinction i.e. discretion, without which a soldier would be
no better than the (mindless) instrument of killing in his hand. Compare
the persistent identification of Anthony
with his sword.

VENTIDIUS

    I'll humbly signify what in his name,   30

    That magical word of war, we have effected;

    How with his banners and his well paid ranks

    The ne'er-yet-beaten horse of Parthia

    We have jaded out o'th'field.

SILLIUS   Where is he now?

VENTIDIUS

    He purposeth to Athens—whither, with what haste   35

    The weight we must convey with's will permit,

    We shall appear before him.—On there, pass along!

                            Exeunt

3.2   *Enter Agrippa at one door, Enobarbus at another*

AGRIPPA What, are the brothers parted?

ENOBARBUS

    They have dispatched with Pompey: he is gone,

    The other three are sealing. Octavia weeps

    To part from Rome, Caesar is sad, and Lepidus

    Since Pompey's feast, as Menas says, is troubled   5

    With the green-sickness.

AGRIPPA   'Tis a noble Lepidus.

ENOBARBUS

    A very fine one. O, how he loves Caesar!

AGRIPPA

    Nay, but how dearly he adores Mark Anthony!

ENOBARBUS

    Caesar? Why, he's the Jupiter of men!

AGRIPPA

    What's Anthony—the god of Jupiter?   10

37 there] Fb; their Fa

  3.2.3 are] Fb; art Fa   10 AGRIPPA] ROWE; *Ant.*, F   What's . . . Jupiter?] OXFORD; Whats *Anthony*, the . . . Iupiter? F; What's *Antony*? The . . . *Jupiter.* JOHNSON

31 **word of war** battle cry (see 2.2.48)

34 **jaded** 'driven like worn-out nags' (Kittredge)

36 **weight** burden (i.e. their spoils and baggage)

3.2.3 **sealing** making their agreements final and binding

  6 **green-sickness** Lepidus appears so besotted with his fellow triumvirs that the symptoms of his hangover are mockingly explained as resulting from a form of anaemia normally attributed to lovesick girls.

  7 **fine one** Ridley suggests a word-play on the Latin meaning of *lepidus* = elegant, fine.

ENOBARBUS

Spake you of Caesar? How, the nonpareil!

AGRIPPA

O Anthony, O thou Arabian bird!

ENOBARBUS

Would you praise Caesar? Say 'Caesar!'; go no
          further.

AGRIPPA

Indeed he plied them both with excellent praises.

ENOBARBUS

But he loves Caesar best—yet he loves Anthony.   15
Hoo! Hearts, tongues, figures, scribes, bards, poets,
          cannot
Think, speak, cast, write, sing, number—hoo!—
His love to Anthony. But as for Caesar,
Kneel down, kneel down, and wonder!

AGRIPPA   Both he loves.

ENOBARBUS

They are his shards, and he their beetle.
                              ⌈*Trumpet within*⌉
                              So—   20

This is to horse. Adieu, noble Agrippa.

AGRIPPA

Good fortune, worthy soldier, and farewell.
          Enter Caesar, Anthony, Lepidus, and Octavia

---

16 figures] HANMER; Figure, F   20 *Trumpet within*] ROWE (*subs.*); *not in* F

12 **Arabian bird** The phoenix, mythical
   bird of which only one was supposed
   to exist at any one time; the phoenix
   perpetuated itself by burning itself to
   death and then rising out of its own
   ashes.
16 **figures** Usually glossed as 'figures
   of speech', but since it is linked to
   'cast' it probably refers to mathemat-
   ical or astrological figures; perhaps a
   quibble is involved in both words.
17 **cast** Either 'calculate, conjecture', or
   (if 'figures' refers to figures of speech)
   'form, articulate'.
   number versify (put into 'numbers' or
   metre)—with a subsidiary play on
   'count'
20 **shards** Often glossed as 'wings' (strict-

ly 'wing cases'—presumably by extension from 'shard' = scale) but there is
no real warrant for this. Jones (following *OED*) interprets: 'they are the dung
patches (*shards*) between which the
beetle Lepidus crawls to and fro'; perhaps the image is founded in Plutarch's description of the loving
concern for its brood exhibited by the
Egyptian scarab or dung-beetle: 'in
that kind there is no female, but they
be all males: they blow or cast their
seed, in the form of a pellet or round
ball, under dung, which they prepare
to be a place not for their food more
than for their brood' ('Of Isis and
Osiris', *Morals*, p. 1291).

ANTHONY (*to Caesar*) No further, sir.

CAESAR

You take from me a great part of my self—
Use me well in't. Sister, prove such a wife   25
As my thoughts make thee, and as my farthest bond
Shall pass on thy approof. Most noble Anthony,
Let not the piece of virtue which is set
Betwixt us, as the cement of our love
To keep it builded, be the ram to batter   30
The fortress of it; for better might we
Have loved without this mean, if on both parts
This be not cherished.

ANTHONY   Make me not offended
In your distrust.

CAESAR   I have said.

ANTHONY   You shall not find,
Though you be therein curious, the least cause   35
For what you seem to fear. So the gods keep you,
And make the hearts of Romans serve your ends.
We will here part.

CAESAR

Farewell, my dearest sister, fare thee well.
The elements be kind to thee, and make   40
Thy spirits all of comfort. Fare thee well.

OCTAVIA (*weeping*) My noble brother!

ANTHONY

The April's in her eyes; it is love's spring,

---

42 *weeping*] JONES (*subs.*); *not in* F

26–7 **As . . . approof** as I am sure you will be, and [especially] considering that [the worth of] my most solemn undertaking will be assessed by ('shall pass on') your ability to make it good ('your approof'). The meaning of the sentence is obscured by Shakespeare's rather free syntax, which involves two different uses of *as*. The language used is that of a commercial property transaction in which Caesar has offered a surety for the quality of his goods.

28 **piece** masterpiece, paragon

29 **cement** uniting medium, principle of union. The accent falls on the first syllable.

32 **mean** means, vehicle

34 **In** by

35 **curious** over-exacting (determined to find justification)

37 **make the hearts . . . ends** may the Roman people remain loyally committed to your purposes. But, given the way in which Octavia's heart (and indeed Anthony's own) is being made to serve political ends, this complimentary flourish is ironic; and, in the light of Caesar's distrust of Anthony, the irony is no doubt partly intentional.

43–4 **April . . . on** Cf. Dent S411: 'April showers bring May flowers'.

And these the showers to bring it on. Be cheerful.

OCTAVIA

Sir, look well to my husband's house; and—　　　45

CAESAR

What, Octavia?

OCTAVIA　　　　　I'll tell you in your ear.

　　She whispers in Caesar's ear

ANTHONY

　　Her tongue will not obey her heart, nor can
　　Her heart inform her tongue. The swan's-down feather
　　That stands upon the swell at the full of tide,
　　And neither way inclines.　　　50

ENOBARBUS　*(aside to Agrippa)*

　　Will Caesar weep?

AGRIPPA　*(aside to Enobarbus)* He has a cloud in's face.

ENOBARBUS　*(aside to Agrippa)*

　　He were the worse for that were he a horse—
　　So is he being a man.

AGRIPPA　*(aside to Enobarbus)* Why, Enobarbus,
　　When Anthony found Julius Caesar dead　　　55
　　He cried almost to roaring; and he wept,
　　When at Philippi he found Brutus slain.

ENOBARBUS　*(aside to Agrippa)*

　　That year, indeed, he was troubled with a rheum.
　　What willingly he did confound, he wailed,
　　Believe't, till I wept too.

CAESAR　　　　　No, sweet Octavia,　　　60
　　You shall hear from me still; the time shall not
　　Outgo my thinking on you.

ANTHONY　　　　　Come, sir, come,
　　I'll wrestle with you in my strength of love.

46.1 *She . . . ear*] CAPELL (subs.); *not in* F　　49 at the full] F1; at full F2　　60 wept]
THEOBALD; weepe F

48–50 **swan's-down . . . inclines**　Jones
　　notes how this figure of tensely poised
　　indecision corresponds to the mid-
　　point of the play's action.
53 **He . . . horse**　It was supposed to be a
　　bad sign if a horse had a dark patch
　　on its face; the best horses reputedly
　　carried a white patch.
58 **rheum**　head-cold, running eyes
59 **What . . . wailed**　he lamented for what

　　he deliberately destroyed
61 **still**　constantly
61–2 **time . . . you**　no matter how fast
　　time runs, I shall not forget you
63 **I'll . . . love**　The embrace enacts An-
　　thony's determination to vie with Oc-
　　tavius in love. Cf. *Troilus* 4.7.90 where
　　Nestor describes his embrace of Hector
　　as *contending* with him in courtesy.

Look, here I have you (*embracing Caesar*); thus I let
   you go,
And give you to the gods.
CAESAR   Adieu, be happy.   65
LEPIDUS Let all the number of the stars give light
   To thy fair way.
CAESAR   Farewell, farewell.   *Kisses Octavia*
ANTHONY   Farewell.
              Trumpets sound. Exeunt severally

3.3   *Enter Cleopatra, Charmian, Iras, and Alexas*
CLEOPATRA
  Where is the fellow?
ALEXAS   Half afeard to come.
CLEOPATRA Go to, go to. Come hither, sir.
   Enter the Messenger as before
ALEXAS   Good majesty,
  Herod of Jewry dare not look upon you,
  But when you are well pleased.
CLEOPATRA   That Herod's head
  I'll have—but how, when Anthony is gone,   5
  Through whom I might command it?
  (*To the Messenger*)   Come thou near.
MESSENGER
  Most gracious majesty.
CLEOPATRA   Didst thou behold Octavia?
MESSENGER
  Ay, dread queen.
CLEOPATRA   Where?
MESSENGER   Madam, in Rome.
  I looked her in the face, and saw her led
  Between her brother and Mark Anthony.   10
CLEOPATRA
  Is she as tall as me?

---

64 *embracing Caesar*] HANMER (*subs.*); *not in* F   67.1 *severally*] OXFORD; *not in* F

3.3.3 **Herod of Jewry** See 1.2.28–9; perhaps, since Herod was also the proverbial ranting tyrant of the mystery plays,
  Alexas anachronistically suggests that
  Cleopatra 'out-Herods Herod'.
4 **Herod's head** No doubt alluding to the

presentation of John the Baptist's head
to Salome by Herod Antipas, son of Cleopatra's Herod the Great. The two Herods,
not always clearly distinguishable in
the Gospels, were regularly confused
by medieval and Renaissance writers.

MESSENGER   She is not, madam.

CLEOPATRA

Didst hear her speak? Is she shrill-tongued or low?

MESSENGER

Madam, I heard her speak: she is low-voiced.

CLEOPATRA

That's not so good—he cannot like her long.

CHARMIAN

Like her? O Isis, 'tis impossible!   15

CLEOPATRA

I think so, Charmian—dull of tongue and dwarfish!
What majesty is in her gait? Remember,
If e'er thou look'st on majesty.

MESSENGER   She creeps:
Her motion and her station are as one.
She shows a body rather than a life,   20
A statue than a breather.

CLEOPATRA   Is this certain?

MESSENGER

Or I have no observance.

CHARMIAN   Three in Egypt
Cannot make better note.

CLEOPATRA   He's very knowing,
I do perceive't—there's nothing in her yet.
The fellow has good judgement.

CHARMIAN   Excellent.   25

CLEOPATRA (to the Messenger)
Guess at her years, I prithee.

3.3.18 look'st] F; lookdst POPE

14 **That's . . . good** It was thought desirable for women to be 'low-voiced'
(soft-spoken), as Cordelia, for example
is: 'Her voice was ever soft, | Gentle,
and low, an excellent thing in woman'
(*Lear* 5.3.246–7); Cleopatra, by contrast, is presented much as the chronicler Stowe described her, 'her voice
loud and shrill'. Her response here
may simply represent a characteristically unconventional response
from a queen who takes some pleasure
in confounding gender roles; or she
may register an initial dismay ('That's

not so good'), followed by hasty self-
reassurance and satiric mockery ('dull
of tongue').
18 **creeps** moves in an abject and servile
fashion
19 **Her motion . . . one** when she moves it
is barely distinguishable from her
standing still
20 **shows** appears
21 **A . . . breather** more like a statue than
a living creature
22–3 **Three . . . cannot** few in Egypt can
24 **in her** to her
26–7 **Guess . . . widow** The   lineation

MESSENGER   Madam,
  She was a widow—
CLEOPATRA   Widow? Charmian, hark.
MESSENGER
  And I do think she's thirty.
CLEOPATRA
  Bear'st thou her face in mind? Is't long or round?
MESSENGER
  Round, even to faultiness.   30
CLEOPATRA
  For the most part too, they are foolish that are so.
  Her hair what colour?
MESSENGER   Brown, madam—and her forehead
  As low as she would wish it.
CLEOPATRA   There's gold for thee:
  Thou must not take my former sharpness ill;
  I will employ thee back again—I find thee   35
  Most fit for business. Go, make thee ready;
  Our letters are prepared.   *Exit Messenger*
CHARMIAN   A proper man.
CLEOPATRA Indeed he is so—I repent me much
  That so I harried him. Why, methinks, by him,
  This creature's no such thing.
CHARMIAN   Nothing, madam.   40
CLEOPATRA
  The man hath seen some majesty, and should know.
CHARMIAN
  Hath he seen majesty? Isis else defend!
  And serving you so long?

---

37 *Exit Messenger*] HANMER; *not in* F

adopted by most editors seems exactly
right; it leaves l. 26 one syllable short;
and this, together with the natural
pausing created by the end-stopped
line, is enough to dictate the slight
pause required as the Messenger tries
to construct a suitably evasive answer.
He is less successful at l. 28, where the
long pause after 'thirty' suggests Cleopatra's displeasure (the Queen was
38); but the evasion has sufficiently
softened the blow to allow her to sim-

ply change tack.

30–1 **Round ... foolish** a commonplace of
  seventeenth-century physiognomy; the
  prejudice survives in the use of 'moon-
  faced' as a term of opprobrium.
33 **As ... wish it** a colloquial sarcasm
37 **proper** excellent; good-looking
39 **by him** from what he says
40 **no such thing** nothing remarkable
42 **Isis ... defend** i.e. I should say he
  has!

CLEOPATRA

I have one thing more to ask him yet, good Char-
    mian—
But 'tis no matter, thou shalt bring him to me   45
Where I will write. All may be well enough.

CHARMIAN I warrant you, madam.   *Exeunt.*

3.4   *Enter Anthony and Octavia.*

ANTHONY

Nay, nay Octavia, not only that—
That were excusable, that and thousands more
Of semblable import—but he hath waged
New wars 'gainst Pompey; made his will, and read it
To public ear!   5
Spoke scantly of me; when perforce he could not
But pay me terms of honour, cold and sickly
He vented them, most narrow measure lent me;
When the best hint was given him, he not took't,
Or did it from his teeth.

OCTAVIA   O, my good lord,   10
Believe not all, or if you must believe,
Stomach not all. A more unhappy lady,

3.4.7–8 honour, cold . . . them, most . . . lent me; | When . . . him,] ROWE (*subs.*);
Honour: cold . . . then most . . . measure: lent me, | When . . . him: F   8 them] ROWE;
then F   9 took't] THEOBALD (*conj.* Thirlby); look't, F

3.4 The action here is closely based on
    Plutarch (see Appendix A).
3 **semblable** similar
4 **New wars 'gainst Pompey** Plutarch
    places this detail after Octavia's meet-
    ing with her brother and the tempor-
    ary reconciliation with Antonius
    which she effected (see Appendix A).
    made his will In Plutarch, it is *Caesar*
    who, in order to rouse ill-feeling
    against his rival, reads *Anthony's* will,
    drawing public attention to the provi-
    sion that even if he dies in Rome he
    must be buried in Egypt (see Appendix
    A). Accordingly editors have suspected
    textual corruption here, which might
    account also for some of the speech's
    oddities of punctuation and lineation.
6 **scantly** grudgingly, meanly
8 **narrow . . . me** treated me most un-
    generously
10 **from his teeth** i.e. merely outwardly,

insincerely; a common expression
(more usually 'from the teeth outward'—see *OED tooth* sb. 8*b*)
11 **you** The tone of Anthony's relation
    with Octavia is indicated by the way
    in which both continue to use the
    respectful but distant plural pronoun
    to one another (as they did upon their
    first meeting in 2.3); cf. Appendix C.
12 **Stomach** resent
12–20 **A more . . . at all** Octavia's speech
    closely parallels that of Blanche, an-
    other victim of political marriage torn
    between warring kin, at a similar point
    in the action of *King John* (3.1.253–
    62). Here, as at 3.2.48–50, the figur-
    ative language emphasizes the tense
    balancing of opposite forces at this
    critical turning-point in the action. In
    Plutarch Octavia's final parting from
    Antonius takes place in Athens; al-
    though Athens is not specified until

If this division chance, ne'er stood between,
Praying for both parts.
The good gods will mock me presently   15
When I shall pray, 'O bless my lord and husband!',
Undo that prayer by crying out as loud,
'O bless my brother!' Husband win, win brother
Prays, and destroys the prayer—no midway
'Twixt these extremes at all.
ANTHONY   Gentle Octavia,   20
Let your best love draw to that point which seeks
Best to preserve it. If I lose mine honour,
I lose my self: better I were not yours
Than yours so branchless. But as you requested,
Yourself shall go between's. The meantime, lady,   25
I'll raise the preparation of a war
Shall stain your brother. Make your soonest haste;
So your desires are yours.
OCTAVIA   Thanks to my lord.
The Jove of power make me, most weak, most weak,
Your reconciler. Wars 'twixt you twain would be   30
As if the world should cleave, and that slain men
Should solder up the rift.
ANTHONY
When it appears to you where this begins,
Turn your displeasure that way, for our faults
Can never be so equal that your love   35
Can equally move with them. Provide your going,

24 yours] F2; your, F1   30 Your] F2; You, F1

3.6, it is important that this scene be imagined as taking place at some *midpoint* between Rome and Egypt.
15 **presently** immediately; inevitably
17 **undo** (1) unmake, cancel, rescind; (2) ruin, destroy
19 **prayer** Octavia probably quibbles on the secondary sense, 'she who utters the prayer'.
20-4 **Gentle ... branchless** 33-6 **When ... them** There is something deliberately equivocal about the way in which Anthony approaches the question of apportioning love and blame here, as if (while being careful to preserve the decencies) he were actually inviting Octavia to leave him.
21 **draw ... point** move to that extreme (i.e. one of the two extremes represented by Caesar and himself)
24 **branchless** maimed, diminished
27 **Shall stain** that will damage the reputation of
33 **When ... begins** when it is clear to you who began this quarrel
34-6 **our faults ... with them** it is impossible that Caesar's faults and mine can be so evenly balanced that your love can remain impartially attached to both
36 **Provide your going** get ready to leave

Choose your own company, and command what cost
Your heart has mind to.   *Exeunt*

3.5   *Enter Enobarbus and Eros, meeting*
ENOBARBUS How now, friend Eros?
EROS There's strange news come, sir.
ENOBARBUS What, man?
EROS Caesar and Lepidus have made wars upon Pompey.
ENOBARBUS This is old. What is the success?   5
EROS Caesar, having made use of him in the wars 'gainst
   Pompey, presently denied him rivality, would not let
   him partake in the glory of the action, and, not resting
   here, accuses him of letters he had formerly wrote to
   Pompey; upon his own appeal seizes him—so the poor   10
   third is up, till death enlarge his confine.
ENOBARBUS
   Then, world, thou hast a pair of chops, no more,
   And throw between them all the food thou hast,
   They'll grind the one the other. Where's Anthony?

---

38 has] F2; he's, F1
3.5.0 *meeting*] CAPELL.; *not in* F   12 world, thou hast] HANMER; would thou hadst F
14 the one] CAPELL (*conj.* Johnson); *not in* F

3.5. The historical basis for this scene is
to be found in Plutarch's 'Life of Octavius Caesar Augustus'. Shakespeare
omits the charge, which he would
have found there, that Lepidus was
guilty of treachery in the wars against
Pompey. Moreover, while Plutarch emphasizes Caesar's relative lenience in
sparing Lepidus's life and placing him
under a kind of house-arrest, Shakespeare's 'till death enlarge his confine'
strikes a note of sinister ambivalence.
At the same time, while North ('Life
of Octavius Caesar Augustus', p. 59)
made it clear that Antonius gave the
order for Pompey's murder, Shakespeare is deliberately vague about his
involvement: Anthony's threats may
either be sincere, or resemble Bolingbroke's hypocritical display of indignation against Exton at the end of
Richard II. In this way the balance of
the two events is tipped in Anthony's
favour.

5 **success** outcome
7 **rivality** the equal rights and status of
  a partner
10 **upon . . . seizes him** arrests him purely
  on the basis of his own accusation
11 **is up** is kept up, imprisoned. Perhaps
  also with the sense 'his time is up, he's
  finished'.
  till . . . confine A slight sardonic
  quibble is involved: (1) till death sets
  him free from imprisonment; (2) till he
  finds a more commodious place of imprisonment in the grave (with a subdued pun on *confine/coffin*).
12–14 **Then world . . . the other** The
  metaphor reduces all action in the political world to the grinding of two
  voracious jaws: the ambitions of
  Anthony and Caesar have come to resemble the 'universal wolf' of self-
  devouring appetite in *Troilus* (1.3.121–
  4)—no matter how much food is
  thrown to them, each in the end must
  consume the other.

EROS

He's walking in the garden—thus (*imitating An-*
    thony)—and spurns   15
The rush that lies before him; cries 'Fool Lepidus!',
And threats the throat of that his officer
That murdered Pompey.

ENOBARBUS   Our great navy's rigged.

EROS

For Italy and Caesar. More, Domitius:
My lord desires you presently. My news   20
I might have told hereafter.

ENOBARBUS   'Twill be naught—
But let it be: bring me to Anthony.

EROS   Come, sir.

                        Exeunt.

3.6   *Enter Caesar, Agrippa, and Mecenas*

CAESAR

Contemning Rome, he has done all this and more
In Alexandria. Here's the manner of't:
I'th'market-place on a tribunal silvered,
Cleopatra and himself in chairs of gold
Were publicly enthroned; at the feet sat   5

---

15 *imitating Anthony*] This edition; *not in* F
   3.6.0 *Enter . . . Mecenas*] This edition; *Enter Agrippa, Mecenas, and Cæsar.* F

15 **spurns** kicks

17–18 **threats . . . Pompey** In the 'Life of
Octavius Caesar', Pompey is put to
death on the island of Samos by Antonius's lieutenant, Titius; however, the
assassination is explicitly 'by Antonius's commandment, for which fact
he was . . . hated by the people of
Rome' (*Lives*, 1612, p. 1167). By suppressing Anthony's involvement
Shakespeare deliberately plays down
the machiavellism of his historical original, while leaving the question of his
possible complicity obscure.

20 **presently** immediately

21 **'Twill be naught** *Naught* is ambiguous,
meaning either 'bad' (cf. *naughty*) or
'nothing' (*nought*). The most probable
sense is 'the outcome will be disas-

trous'; but Arden favours ' 'Twill be
something of no consequence he wants
me for'.

3.6. For the historical basis of this scene,
see Appendix A.

0 *Enter . . . Mecenas* Ridley notes that F's
stage direction, which lists Caesar last,
is peculiar, not only because it breaks
the usual order of precedence, but also
because Caesar actually speaks first.

1–37 **Contemning Rome . . . the like** Cf.
Plutarch who describes the rising tide
of popular resentment against Antonius in Rome, after his abandonment
of Octavia (see Appendix A).

1   **Contemning** scorning

3   **tribunal** dais

5   **enthroned** *OED* records this as the first
known occurrence of the verb.

Caesarion, whom they call my father's son,
And all the unlawful issue that their lust
Since then hath made between them. Unto her
He gave the stablishment of Egypt, made her
Of lower Syria, Cyprus, Lydia,   10
Absolute queen.

MECENAS   This in the public eye?

CAESAR

I'th' common show-place where they exercise.
His sons he there proclaimed the kings of kings;
Great Media, Parthia, and Armenia
He gave to Alexander; to Ptolemy he assigned   15
Syria, Cilicia, and Phoenicia. She
In th'habiliments of the goddess Isis
That day appeared, and oft before gave audience,
As 'tis reported, so.

MECENAS   Let Rome be thus informed.

AGRIPPA

Who, queasy with his insolence already,   20
Will their good thoughts call from him.

CAESAR

The people knows it, and have now received

13 he there] JOHNSON; hither F   kings of kings] ROWE; King of Kings, F   19 reported,
so] F2; reported so FI   22 knows] FI; know F3

6 **Caesarion** Cleopatra's son, supposedly by Julius Caesar
  my father Octavius had been adopted as Julius Caesar's son.
9 **stablishment** confirmed possession
12 **show-place** arena. The detail once again derives from North's translation (see Appendix A), but in seventeenth-century London 'show-place' would also have suggested *theatre* (as in John Stockwood's 1578 *A Sermon Preached at Paul's Cross* which denounces the Theatre as 'a show-place of all beastly and filthy matters').
17 **habiliments of . . . Isis** The change from North's 'apparel' to the rare 'habiliments' (which occurs only three times elsewhere in Shakespeare) suggests that the dramatist was remembering a passage from Philemon Holland's translation of 'Of Isis and Osiris', whose description of the symbolism of the goddess's attire may have

helped to shape the idea of Cleopatra's mysterious variety, her capacity for metamorphic 'becoming': 'Moreover the habiliments of *Isis* be of different tinctures and colours, for her whole power consisteth and is employed in matter which receiveth all forms, and becometh all manner of things—to wit, light, darkness, day, night, fire, water, life, death, beginning and end. But the robes of *Osiris* have neither shade nor variety, but are of one simple colour, even that which is lightsome and bright. For the first and primitive cause is simple; the principle or beginning is without all mixture, as being spiritual and intelligible' (Plutarch, *Morals*, p. 1318).
19 **so** in the fashion I have described
20 **queasy** unsettled
21 **their good thoughts call** withdraw their support

His accusations.

AGRIPPA   Who does he accuse?

CAESAR

Caesar, and that having in Sicilia
Sextus Pompeius spoiled, we had not rated him   25
His part o'th'isle. Then does he say he lent me
Some shipping unrestored. Lastly, he frets
That Lepidus of the triumvirate
Should be deposed; and being, that we detain
All his revenue.

AGRIPPA   Sir, this should be answered.   30

CAESAR

'Tis done already, and the messenger gone.
I have told him Lepidus was grown too cruel,
That he his high authority abused,
And did deserve his change. For what I have conquered,
I grant him part; but then in his Armenia,   35
And other of his conquered kingdoms, I
Demand the like.

MECENAS   He'll never yield to that.

CAESAR

Nor must not then be yielded to in this.

        Enter Octavia with her train

OCTAVIA

Hail, Caesar and my lord! Hail, most dear Caesar!

CAESAR

That ever I should call thee castaway!   40

---

24 Sicilia] This edition; Cicilie F; Sicily ROWE   28 triumvirate] F (Triumpherate)
29 being, that] ROWE 1714; being that, F   39 my lord] F3; my L. F1; my lords,
RIDLEY (*conj.* Brooks)

24 **Sicilia** F's 'Sicilie' normally stands for
modern *Sicily*, but the metre here suggests that the Latin form, which Shakespeare uses in *The Winter's Tale*, was
probably intended: *e* and *a* are easily
confused in Elizabethan handwriting.
25 **rated** allotted
28 **triumvirate** The F spelling 'triumpherate' may suggest a conscious or unconscious etymological confusion on
Shakespeare's part, identifying the victorious *triumvirs* of Philippi as 'trium-
phers' (cf. the note to 3.1.0.2).

29 **we** Here, as often elsewhere in the
scene, Caesar employs the royal plural
30 **revenue** (accent on second syllable)
32 **too cruel** There is authority for Lepidus's cruelty in Plutarch (see Appendix A) and indeed in *Julius Caesar*; but
Shakespeare's treatment of Lepidus in
this play makes Caesar's claim seem
an improbable piece of political chi-
canery.
38.1 *Enter Octavia* For the historical basis
of the episode that follows, see Appendix A.

OCTAVIA

You have not called me so, nor have you cause.

CAESAR

Why have you stol'n upon us thus? You come not
Like Caesar's sister: the wife of Anthony
Should have an army for an usher, and
The neighs of horse to tell of her approach   45
Long ere she did appear. The trees by th'way
Should have borne men, and expectation fainted,
Longing for what it had not. Nay, the dust
Should have ascended to the roof of heaven,
Raised by your populous troops. But you are come   50
A market-maid to Rome, and have prevented
The ostentation of our love; which, left unshown,
Is often left unloved. We should have met you
By sea and land, supplying every stage
With an augmented greeting.

OCTAVIA   Good my lord,   55
To come thus was I not constrained, but did it
On my free will. My lord, Mark Anthony,
Hearing that you prepared for war, acquainted
My grievèd ear withal; whereon I begged
His pardon for return.

CAESAR   Which soon he granted,   60
Being an obstruct 'tween his lust and him.

OCTAVIA

Do not say so, my lord.

CAESAR   I have eyes upon him,
And his affairs come to me on the wind.
Where is he now?

OCTAVIA   My lord, in Athens.

---

61 obstruct] THEOBALD (*conj.* Warburton); abstract, F

42–55 **why . . . greeting** Cf. Caesar's lament for the dead Anthony (5.1.14–
19), with its similar parade of
anticlimax.
51–2 **prevented . . . ostentation** arrived
too soon to allow for the proper public
display
52–3 **left . . . unloved** if not shown is often

assumed not to exist
61 **obstruct** obstruction
62 **eyes** i.e. spies. Caesar's reliance upon
superior intelligence is several times
emphasized (e.g. 3.7.75–7), contributing to the play's sense of him as a
somewhat machiavellian character.

CAESAR
No, my most wrongèd sister. Cleopatra   65
Hath nodded him to her. He hath given his empire
Up to a whore, who now are levying
The kings o'th'earth for war. He hath assembled
Bochus, the King of Libya; Archilaus
Of Cappadocia; Philadelphos, King   70
Of Paphlagonia; the Thracian King, Adullas;
King Manchus of Arabia; King of Pont;
Herod of Jewry; Mithridates, King
Of Comagene; Polemen and Amintas,
The Kings of Mede and Licaonia;   75
With a more larger list of sceptres.

OCTAVIA Ay me, most wretched,
That have my heart parted betwixt two friends,
That does afflict each other!

CAESAR   Welcome hither.
Your letters did withhold our breaking forth   80
Till we perceived both how you were wrong led,
And we in negligent danger. Cheer your heart—
Be you not troubled with the time, which drives
O'er your content these strong necessities;
But let determined things to destiny   85
Hold unbewailed their way. Welcome to Rome,
Nothing more dear to me. You are abused
Beyond the mark of thought; and the high god,
To do you justice, makes his ministers

---

72 Manchus] WILSON (*after* North); Mauchus F; Malchus, THEOBALD (*after* Plutarch)
74 Comagene] ROWE; Comageat F   88 god] KEIGHTLEY; Gods F   89 makes his] F;
make their THEOBALD; make them CAPELL

68–76 **He hath assembled ... sceptres** For
this roll-call of oriental potentates, see
Plutarch's description of the forces arrayed at Actium (Appendix A).

72 **Manchus** North's spelling of the name
that Plutarch gives as *Malchus*; Oxford
follows Sisson's suggestion that F's
'Mauchus' is a plausible alternative
spelling of Plutarch's version; but it
seems more likely to result from foul
case or a simple misreading.

81 **wrong led** misled. Some editors, however, finding the sense unsatisfactory
and the rhythm of the line awkward,

emend to 'Till we perceivèd both how
you were wronged'.

82 **in negligent danger** in danger as a
result of our negligence

85–6 **let determined ... way** let predestined events move to their fated conclusion without lamenting for them

87 **Nothing ... me** dearest one
abused taken advantage of, deceived;
mistreated

88 **mark** reach
high god i.e. Jove

89 **ministers** agents, deputies

Of us and those that love you. Best of comfort,   90
And ever welcome to us.
AGRIPPA   Welcome, lady!
MECENAS   Welcome, dear madam!
    Each heart in Rome does love and pity you,
    Only th'adulterous Anthony, most large
    In his abominations, turns you off,   95
    And gives his potent regiment to a trull
    That noises it against us.
OCTAVIA   Is it so, sir?
CAESAR
    Most certain. Sister, welcome—pray you,
    Be ever known to patience. My dear'st sister!   *Exeunt*

3.7   *Enter Cleopatra and Enobarbus*
CLEOPATRA
    I will be even with thee, doubt it not.
ENOBARBUS   But why, why, why?
CLEOPATRA
    Thou hast forspoke my being in these wars,
    And sayst it is not fit.
ENOBARBUS   Well, is it, is it?
CLEOPATRA
    Is't not denounced against us? Why should not we   5
    Be there in person?

3.7.4 it is] F2; it it F1   5 Is't not denounced] ROWE; If not, denounc'd F; If not, denounce't MALONE; Is't not? Denounce STEEVENS 1793 (*conj.* Tyrwhitt)

94 **large** prodigal; licentious
96 **regiment** rule
   trull whore
97 **noises it** kicks up a row
99 **Be . . . patience** accustom yourself to patience
3.7.1–19 **I will . . . behind** Cleopatra's insistence on participating in the war is documented by Plutarch (see Appendix A).
2–4 **why . . . is it** Enobarbus's open impatience contrasts strikingly with the deferential tone normally expected of commoners addressing princes.
3 **forspoke** spoken against
5 **Is't not . . . us** Hasn't the war been declared on me personally? To 'denounce war' is a standard locution (*OED denounce* v. 1b). 'Is't' would have been an easy misreading for 'if', and Rowe's emendation gives the easiest sense. Some editors preserve the F reading by repunctuating 'If not denounced against us, why . . .' meaning 'Even if the war had *not* been declared against me, why . . .'; but perhaps the repunctuation is unnecessary, since, allowing for the laxity of Elizabethan syntax, F as it stands could be taken to mean 'Well, even supposing it's not fitting (for a woman to be involved in the war), considering that it was declared against me personally, why then . . .'.

ENOBARBUS (*aside*)   Well, I could reply,
  If we should serve with horse and mares together,
  The horse were merely lost: the mares would bear
  A soldier and his horse.
CLEOPATRA   What is't you say?
ENOBARBUS

  Your presence needs must puzzle Anthony,   10
  Take from his heart, take from his brain, from's time,
  What should not then be spared. He is already
  Traduced for levity; and 'tis said in Rome
  That Photinus, an eunuch, and your maids
  Manage this war.
CLEOPATRA   Sink Rome, and their tongues rot   15
  That speak against us! A charge we bear i'th'war,
  And as the president of my kingdom will
  Appear there for a man. Speak not against it,
  I will not stay behind.
    Enter Anthony and Camidius
ENOBARBUS   Nay, I have done—
  Here comes the Emperor.
ANTHONY   Is it not strange, Camidius,   20

14 Photinus, an] CAMBRIDGE (*conj.* Delius); Photinus an F   19 *Camidius*] F2; *Camidias*
F1; Canidius ROWE

7 **serve** With a play on the bawdy sense
  (as a stallion 'serves' a mare).
7, 9 **horse** stallion(s); a pun is probably
  also intended on *horse/whores* (cf.
  1.5.20–2).
8 **horse** (1) cavalry (2) stallion(s)
  merely utterly (as at l. 47). Perhaps
  also punning on 'marely'—see Gordon
  J. Ross, 'Enobarbus on Horses', *SQ* 31
  (1980), pp. 386–7.
10 **puzzle** perplex, confuse
11 **heart** courage
13–15 **'tis said … Photinus … war** The
  relevant passage in North's Plutarch
  makes it clear that F's punctuation is
  almost certainly wrong, the eunuch
  being Mardian: 'they that should make
  war with them should be Mardian the
  Eunuch, Photinus, Iras, a woman of
  Cleopatra's bedchamber that frizzled
  her hair, and dressed her head, and
  Charmian, the which were those that
  ruled all the affairs of Antonius' empire' (Bullough, p. 295; cf. Appendix A).

16 **charge** cost
17 **president** ruler (perhaps tinged by the
  sense 'presiding deity')
18 **for a man** in the capacity of a man.
  Jacobean reactions to the indecorum
  of Cleopatra's usurpation of masculine
  prerogative might have been complicated by recollections of the ostentatiously masculine role adopted by
  Queen Elizabeth when addressing her
  troops at Tilbury at the time of the
  Armada.
19 *Camidius* Although F consistently
  spells this name with an -*m*-, 'Camidius' may represent a minim-error in
  transmission of the text rather than
  an authentic Shakespearian spelling
  (see the 'Editorial Procedures' above,
  pp. 132–3). Bevington argues that
  Compositor B tended to resolve his evident difficulty with unfamiliar proper
  names by sticking to his preferred
  spelling once he had tentatively
  arrived at it.

That from Tarentum, and Brundisium,
He could so quickly cut the Ionian Sea,
And take in Toryne. You have heard on't, sweet?
CLEOPATRA
Celerity is never more admired
Than by the negligent.
ANTHONY   A good rebuke,   25
Which might have well becomed the best of men,
To taunt at slackness. Camidius, we
Will fight with him by sea.
CLEOPATRA   By sea, what else?
CAMIDIUS
Why will my lord do so?
ANTHONY   For that he dares us to't.
ENOBARBUS
So hath my lord dared him to single fight.   30
CAMIDIUS
Ay, and to wage this battle at Pharsalia,
Where Caesar fought with Pompey. But these offers,
Which serve not for his vantage, he shakes off,
And so should you.
ENOBARBUS   Your ships are not well manned—
Your mariners are muleters, reapers, people   35
Engrossed by swift impress. In Caesar's fleet
Are those that often have 'gainst Pompey fought,
Their ships are yare, yours heavy. No disgrace
Shall fall you for refusing him at sea,
Being prepared for land.
ANTHONY   By sea, by sea.   40

23 Toryne] F2 (Torine); Troine F   35 muleters] F2 (Mulliers); Militers F1

21 **Tarentum . . . Brundisium** Modern Ta-
ranto and Brindisi, ports in southern
Italy. Plutarch again provides much of
the detail for this part of the scene (see
Appendix A).
22 **Ionian Sea** name given to that part of
the Adriatic which lay between the
boot of Italy and the western shore of
Greece
23 **take in** occupy; conquer
Toryne town north of Actium on the
western Greek coast
27 **we** The pronoun takes an extra stress
from its unusual position at the end of

the line: the effect is to highlight a
significant ambivalence in Anthony's
use of the plural. Here, as for most of
the scene, it appears to be an orthodox
plural, associating Camidius and the
other followers with his decisions; but
a telling shift at l. 48, suggests that it
is really a thinly disguised royal plural,
as instinctively autocratic as Cleopatra's own. Cf. Appendix C.
35 **muleters** muleteers, mule-drivers
36 **Engrossed . . . impress** recruited by
press-gang
38 **yare** swift, manœuvrable

ENOBARBUS

Most worthy sir, you therein throw away
The absolute soldiership you have by land;
Distract your army, which doth most consist
Of war-marked footmen; leave unexecuted
Your own renownèd knowledge; quite forgo   45
The way which promises assurance, and
Give up yourself merely to chance and hazard
From firm security.

ANTHONY   I'll fight at sea.

CLEOPATRA I have sixty sails, Caesar none better.

ANTHONY Our overplus of shipping will we burn;   50
And with the rest full manned, from th'head of Actium
Beat th'approaching Caesar. But if we fail,
We then can do't at land.
        Enter a Messenger
                    Thy business?

MESSENGER

The news is true, my lord, he is descried:
Caesar has taken Toryne.   55

ANTHONY

Can he be there in person? 'Tis impossible—
Strange that his power should be. Camidius,
Our nineteen legions thou shalt hold by land,
And our twelve thousand horse. We'll to our ship:
Away, my Thetis!
        Enter ⌈ Scarrus ⌉, a soldier
                    How now, worthy soldier?   60

⌈ SCARRUS ⌉

O noble Emperor, do not fight by sea;

---

51 Actium] F2; Action F1   56 impossible—] POPE (*subs.*); impossible F   60, 61, 67,
70, 75, 78 Scarrus] This edition (*conj.* Barroll)

---

43 **Distract** (1) divide; (2) confuse, demor-
   alize. The second sense is felt as following from the first.
44 **leave unexecuted** fail to capitalize on
51 **head** headland
57 **power** army
58–9 **nineteen . . . horse** See Appendix A.
   As Bevington notes, Shakespeare uses
   the detail to suggest Anthony's bravado in deciding to fight by sea, where
   Plutarch cites the numbers to emphas-

ize Anthony's disgrace in deserting so
large a force.
60 **Thetis** sea-nymph, one of the Nereids
   (see note to 2.2.213). Like Proteus,
   Thetis had the power of assuming any
   shape she wished.
   Scarrus For a persuasive argument
   that F's Soldier and Scarrus (who is
   never named except in speech-prefixes)
   are the same character, see Barroll.

Trust not to rotten planks. Do you misdoubt
This sword, and these my wounds? Let th'Egyptians
And the Phoenicians go a-ducking—we
Have used to conquer standing on the earth,   65
And fighting foot to foot.
ANTHONY   Well, well, away!

Exeunt Anthony, Cleopatra, and Enobarbus

⌜SCARRUS⌝
By Hercules, I think I am i'th'right!
CAMIDIUS
Soldier, thou art; but his whole action grows
Not in the power on't—so our leader's led,
And we are women's men.
⌜SCARRUS⌝   You keep by land   70
The legions and the horse whole, do you not?
CAMIDIUS
Marcus Octavius, Marcus Justeus,
Publicola, and Celius are for sea;
But we keep whole by land. This speed of Caesar's
Carries beyond belief.
⌜SCARRUS⌝   While he was yet in Rome   75
His power went out in such distractions
As beguiled all spies.
CAMIDIUS   Who's his lieutenant, hear you?
⌜SCARRUS⌝
They say one Towrus.
CAMIDIUS   Well, I know the man.

Enter a Messenger

MESSENGER The Emperor calls Camidius.

66.1 *Exeunt . . . Enobarbus*] F2; *exit Ant. Cleo. & Enob.* F1   72 CAMIDIUS] POPE; *Ven.*, F
78 Well, I] F; Well I ROWE 1714

64 **a-ducking** (1) plunging in the sea; (2) cringing (Wilson)
68–9 **his . . . on't** his strategy has been conceived without any regard to the real source of his military strength
70–8 **You keep by land . . . Towrus** The details here derive from Plutarch (see Appendix A).
72 CAMIDIUS F's *Ven.* may represent a change of intention on Shakespeare's part; or may simply be an indication

that he envisaged the parts of Camidius and Ventidius being doubled by the same actor.
75 **Carries** sweeps him forward (as a weapon is said to 'carry' its projectile towards a target)
76 **His power . . . distractions** his army left in such small units (*OED distraction* 1*b*, citing only this passage; but might it not mean 'with such diversionary tactics'?)

CAMIDIUS
    With news the time's in labour, and throws forth   80
    Each minute some.   *Exeunt*

3.8   *Enter Caesar with his army, and Towrus, marching*
CAESAR
    Towrus!
TOWRUS   My lord?
CAESAR   Strike not by land, keep whole,
    Provoke not battle till we have done at sea.
    Do not exceed the prescript of this scroll—
        Gives him a scroll
    Our fortune lies upon this jump.   4
      Exit Caesar and his army at one door, Towrus at another

3.9   *Enter Anthony and Enobarbus*
ANTHONY
    Set we our squadrons on yon side o'th'hill,
    In eye of Caesar's battle, from which place   2
    We may the number of the ships behold,
    And so proceed accordingly.   *Exeunt*

3.10   *Camidius marcheth with his land army one way*
        over the stage, and Towrus, the Lieutenant of
        Caesar, with his army the other way. After their
        going in is heard the noise of a sea-fight. Alarum.
        Enter Enobarbus
ENOBARBUS
    Naught, naught, all naught! I can behold no longer.
    Th'*Antoniad*, the Egyptian admiral,   2

---

80 in labour] ROWE; with Labour, F   throws] F (throwes); throes THEOBALD
    3.8.0 *and Towrus*] CAPELL.; *not in* F   3.1 *Gives . . . scroll*] OXFORD (*subs.*); *not in* F
4.1 *Exit . . . another*] OXFORD (*after* Pope); *exit.* F
    3.9.4 *Exeunt*] POPE; *exit,* F
    3.10.0.3 *with his army*] OXFORD; *not in* F   0.5 *Enter Enobarbus*] ROWE 1714; *Enter Enobarbus and Scarus.* F

---

80 **throws forth** (as an animal is said to 'throw' a litter of offspring)
3.8.4 **jump** hazard
3.9.2 **battle** line of battle
3.10. Here again the detail derives sub-

stantially from Plutarch (see Appendix A).
1 **Naught** ruined, come to nothing
2 **admiral** flagship

With all their sixty, fly and turn the rudder—
To see't mine eyes are blasted.

Enter Scarrus

SCARRUS   Gods and goddesses,
    All the whole synod of them!
ENOBARBUS   What's thy passion?   5
SCARRUS The greater cantle of the world is lost
    With very ignorance; we have kissed away
    Kingdoms and provinces.
ENOBARBUS   How appears the fight?
SCARRUS
    On our side like the tokened pestilence,
    Where death is sure. Yon ribanded nag of Egypt—   10
    Whom leprosy o'ertake!—i'th'midst o'th'fight,
    When vantage like a pair of twins appeared,
    Both as the same, or rather ours the elder,
    The breese upon her, like a cow in June,
    Hoists sails and flies.
ENOBARBUS   That I beheld—   15
    Mine eyes did sicken at the sight, and could not
    Endure a further view.
SCARRUS   She once being luffed,

---

10 ribanded] This edition (*conj.* Gould in Arden); ribaudred] F1; ribauldred F4; ribald-rid KNIGHT (*conj.* Steevens 1778); riband-red OXFORD (*conj.* Thiselton)   14 June] F2; Inne F1

4 **blasted** as if struck by lightning
5 **synod** assembly
  What's thy passion what is the cause of your distress; but a *passion* was also a technical term for a passionate speech in a play, so there may be a hint here of the theatrical self-consciousness characteristic of some of the most intense moments in this tragedy.
6 **cantle** portion (usually a segment of a circle or sphere)
9 **tokened pestilence** The plague when revealed by plague spots (often thought to be 'tokens' of God's wrath) was reckoned to be fatal.
10 **ribanded** decked out with ribbons (like a race-horse, or a horse at a fair); as Case suggested, the figure probably refers to Cleopatra's beflagged ship on which Enobarbus comments (3.13.11), but it must also suggest the gaudy costume of some over-dressed

whore. Thiselton's 'riband red', adopted by Oxford, strikes me as over-ingenious and difficult to speak. Some recent editions, including New Cambridge, prefer to retain F's *ribaudred* (= 'lewd, debauched'?)—otherwise unknown and listed in *OED* as 'a corrupt reading in Shakespeare . . . which has not yet been satisfactorily emended'.
14 **breese** gadfly; but, in the nautical context, inevitably punning upon 'breeze' as well. Miola (pp. 139–41) argues that the passage echoes the 'gentle breezes' (*levis auras*) by which animals are excited in mating-time, according to Virgil's *Georgics* 3. 274. Cf. the proverbial 'To have a breeze in his breech' (Dent B651).
17 **luffed** with the head of the ship brought round into the wind (here, preparatory to flight); Ridley, arguing for the preservation of F's spelling,

The noble ruin of her magic, Anthony,
Claps on his sea-wing and, like a doting mallard,
Leaving the fight in height, flies after her.   20
I never saw an action of such shame—
Experience, manhood, honour, ne'er before
Did violate so itself.

ENOBARBUS   Alack, alack!

Enter Camidius

CAMIDIUS

Our fortune on the sea is out of breath,
And sinks most lamentably. Had our general   25
Been what he knew himself, it had gone well.
O, he has given example for our flight
Most grossly by his own.

ENOBARBUS (*aside*)

Ay, are you thereabouts? Why then, good night
          indeed!

CAMIDIUS

Toward Peloponnesus are they fled.   30

SCARRUS

'Tis easy to't, and there I will attend
What further comes.

CAMIDIUS   To Caesar will I render
My legions and my horse—six kings already
Show me the way of yielding.

ENOBARBUS   I'll yet follow
The wounded chance of Anthony, though my reason   35
Sits in the wind against me.   *Exeunt severally*

26 he] F2; his F1   36 *Exeunt severally*] OXFORD (*after* Theobald); *not in* F

'loofed', notes that North uses 'loof off' for 'disengage', as though the word were related to 'aloof'.

18–23 **The noble . . . itself** Scarrus's speech reintroduces the themes of Philo's opening denunciation—dotage, self-violation, and Cleopatra's malign power of metamorphosis.

19 **Claps . . . sea-wing** hurriedly hoists sail **doting mallard** love-sick wild drake

21 **action** If, as seems probable, F's spelling 'Action' for Actium (3.7.51) is a phonetic error, then we should probably find a pun here.

25 **our general . . . himself** Cf. Philo's 'sometimes when he is not Anthony . . .' (1.1.59).

29 **are you thereabouts** is that the way you're thinking?
good night indeed it's all up with us

31 **'Tis easy to't** it's within easy reach

35–6 **reason . . . against me** A condensed and difficult figure, though the general sense is clear enough. Bevington explains: 'To "sit in the wind" is to be in the downward side, having the scent coming towards you. Thus Enobarbus's reason is scenting and tracking him down as a victim.' But

3.11 *Enter Anthony with Attendants*

ANTHONY

Hark, the land bids me tread no more upon't,
It is ashamed to bear me. Friends, come hither.
I am so lated in the world that I
Have lost my way for ever. I have a ship,
Laden with gold—take that, divide it; fly,　　　　5
And make your peace with Caesar.

ALL　　　　　　　　　　　　　　　Fly? Not we.

ANTHONY

I have fled myself, and have instructed cowards
To run and show their shoulders. Friends, be gone.
I have myself resolved upon a course
Which has no need of you. Be gone.　　　　　10
My treasure's in the harbour—take it. O,
I followed that I blush to look upon;
My very hairs do mutiny, for the white
Reprove the brown for rashness, and they them
For fear and doting. Friends, be gone—you shall　　　15
Have letters from me to some friends that will
Sweep your way for you. Pray you, look not sad,
Nor make replies of loathness; take the hint
Which my despair proclaims. Let that be left
Which leaves itself. To the seaside straightway!　　　20
I will possess you of that ship and treasure.
Leave me, I pray, a little—pray you now—
Nay, do so; for indeed I have lost command—
Therefore I pray you—I'll see you by and by.

⌈*Attendants stand aside*⌉

3.11.6 ALL] *Omnes*, F　19 that] CAPELL.; them F　24.1 *Attendants stand aside*] This edition (*after* OXFORD '*Exeunt Attendants*'); *not in* F

'against me' surely suggests that Enobarbus imagines himself beating into a contrary wind (the wind of fortune which has turned against him); his own reason 'sits in' or rides this wind.

3.11.3 **lated** (like a traveller overtaken by darkness)
4–11 **I have ... treasure** The details of Anthony's magnanimity derive from Plutarch (see Appendix A).
9–10 **a course ... you** i.e. suicide
18 **loathness** reluctance

19–20 **Let ... itself** abandon a man who has ceased to be himself; but perhaps also glancing at the 'course | Which has no need of you' (ll. 9–10)—i.e. suicide.

23 **lost command** Literally, 'lost the power to command others'; but the full sense is more absolute, the equivalent of 'Othello's occupation's gone' (*Othello* 3.3.362). 'Command' here is the equivalent of *authority*, the ground of a certain kind of selfhood.

24.1 *Attendants stand aside* Oxford sup-

Anthony sits down.
Enter Cleopatra led by Charmian, ⌈Iras⌉ and Eros

EROS

Nay, gentle madam, to him, comfort him.   25

IRAS Do, most dear queen.

CHARMIAN Do! Why, what else?

CLEOPATRA Let me sit down. O Juno!

⌈*Cleopatra sits down*⌉

ANTHONY No, no, no, no, no.

EROS See you here, sir?   30

ANTHONY O fie, fie, fie!

CHARMIAN Madam!

IRAS Madam, O good empress!

EROS Sir, sir—

ANTHONY

Yes, my lord, yes!—He at Philippi kept   35
His sword e'en like a dancer, while I struck
The lean and wrinkled Cassius; and 'twas I
That the mad Brutus ended. He alone
Dealt on lieutenantry, and no practice had
In the brave squares of war; yet now—no matter.   40

24.2 *Anthony*] CAPELL; *not in* F   24.3 *Iras*] POPE; *not in* F   28.1 *Cleopatra . . . down*]
COLLIER 1853 (*subs.*); *not in* F

plies an *exeunt* for the servants here,
but since Anthony will apparently address them again at l. 71, it seems
better to have them move to the rear
or side of the stage.

24.2-69 *Sits down . . . Give me a kiss* This
scene, though imagined as taking
place on land, is based on Plutarch's
description of Antonius's behaviour
after he was taken on board Cleopatra's fleeing ship (see Appendix A); a
further passage describing Antonius's
behaviour after their return to Alexandria is also relevant (Appendix A).

29 *No . . . no* Surely not directed at Cleopatra, as the Oxford editors seem to
suggest, but part of the distracted
monologue that continues down to l.
49.

35 *my lord* Perhaps identifies Caesar as
Anthony's imaginary interlocutor—in
which case it is furious mock-

deference.
kept kept undrawn; for Plutarch's
account of their conduct at Philippi,
see Appendix A.

37 *lean . . . Cassius* Cf. *Caesar* 1.2.195.
Cassius's 'lean and hungry look'
identifies him with conventional representations of Envy.

38 *mad Brutus* The contemptuous term
says something about Anthony's attitude to the republican ideals celebrated
in Pompey's tribute to the 'courtiers of
beauteous freedom' (2.6.17); it contrasts with Agrippa's claim at 3.2.56–
7 that Anthony wept for the dead
Brutus at Philippi.

38-9 *alone . . . lieutenantry* fought the
battle entirely through his subordinates

40 *squares* Usually glossed as 'squad-
rons'; but Elizabethan infantry were
regularly drawn up for battle in
squares.

CLEOPATRA Ah, stand by!

EROS   The Queen, my lord, the Queen!

IRAS
Go to him, madam, speak to him,
He's unqualitied with very shame.

CLEOPATRA ⌈*rising*⌉ Well then, sustain me. O!

EROS
Most noble sir, arise: the Queen approaches,   45
Her head's declined, and death will seize her, but
Your comfort makes the rescue.

ANTHONY
I have offended reputation,
A most unnoble swerving.

EROS   Sir, the Queen.

ANTHONY ⌈*rising*⌉
O whither hast thou led me, Egypt? See   50
How I convey my shame out of thine eyes,
By looking back what I have left behind
'Stroyed in dishonour.

CLEOPATRA   O my lord, my lord,
Forgive my fearful sails! I little thought
You would have followed.

ANTHONY   Egypt, thou knew'st too well   55
My heart was to thy rudder tied by th'strings,
And thou shouldst tow me after. O'er my spirit
Thy full supremacy thou knew'st, and that
Thy beck might from the bidding of the gods
Command me.

CLEOPATRA   O, my pardon!

ANTHONY   Now I must   60

---

44 *rising*] This edition; OXFORD *at* l. 41; *not in* F   46 seize] F2; cease F1   50 *rising*]
OXFORD; *not in* F   57 tow] ROWE (towe); stowe F   58 Thy] THEOBALD 1740 (*conj.*
Thirlby); The F

41 **stand by** help
43 **unqualitied** (1) stripped of his nobility;
   (2) drained of all his essential and
   distinguishing characteristics
44 **sustain** support, hold upright
46 **but** unless
48 **reputation** honour; pronounced here
   as five syllables

51–3 **I . . . dishonour** I try to hide my dishonour from your sight by brooding
   here over what I lost in the disgrace
   of my defeat
56 **strings** heart-strings; Bevington suggests a play on 'rigging'
59 **beck** nod or gesture of silent command

To the young man send humble treaties, dodge
And palter in the shifts of lowness, who
With half the bulk o'th' world played as I pleased,
Making and marring fortunes. You did know
How much you were my conqueror, and that   65
My sword, made weak by my affection, would
Obey it on all cause.

CLEOPATRA   Pardon, pardon!

ANTHONY
Fall not a tear, I say: one of them rates
All that is won and lost. Give me a kiss—
        (*He kisses Cleopatra*)
Even this repays me.   70
(*To an Attendant*) We sent our schoolmaster, is a come
        back?
Love, I am full of lead. (*Calling*) Some wine,
Within there, and our viands! Fortune knows
We scorn her most when most she offers blows.

                                              Exeunt

3.12 *Enter Caesar, Agrippa, Dolabella, ⌈and Thidias⌉,*
         with others.

CAESAR
Let him appear that's come from Anthony.

69.1 *He . . . Cleopatra*] OXFORD; *not in* F   72 *Calling*] OXFORD; *not in* F
3.12.0.1 *Dolabella, and Thidias*] ROWE; *and Dollabello* F

61 **treaties** entreaties; terms for negotia-
tion
    dodge shift ground, act evasively;
    haggle
62 **palter** equivocate, prevaricate, deal
    crookedly
    shifts of lowness desperate recourses to
    which the humiliated are driven
66–7 **My sword . . . cause** This figure of
    the hero's metonymic sword enfeebled
    and transformed into the mere instru-
    ment of sexual passion again recalls the
    traditional imagery of Mars and Venus.
67 **on all cause** on any pretext
68 **rates** is worth
70–3 **Even . . . knows** Most editors reline
    in order to remove the two incomplete
    lines, usually at the cost of creating a
    hypermetrical line in the closing
    couplet. But a pause at l. 70 is neces-

sary to accommodate the kiss; and a
second, shorter pause at l. 72, after
'lead', effectively underscores a sudden
shift of direction characteristic of Anthony's emotional turmoil; the senten-
tious couplet then registers as an
attempt to pull himself together rhe-
torically.
70 **even this repays** this one kiss alone is
    enough to repay
72 **lead** i.e. the heaviness of grief
73 **viands** food
3.12 This scene again owes much to
    Plutarch (see Appendix A).
0.1 **Agrippa . . . Thidias** Agrippa has no
    speaking part in the scene, unlike Thi-
    dias who is absent from the F s.d.
    Perhaps this anomaly reflects a change
    of authorial intention, and Thidias
    should simply replace Agrippa.

Know you him?

DOLABELLA   Caesar, 'tis his schoolmaster—
An argument that he is plucked, when hither
He sends so poor a pinion of his wing,
Which had superfluous kings for messengers   5
Not many moons gone by.

Enter Ambassador from Anthony

CAESAR Approach, and speak.

AMBASSADOR
Such as I am, I come from Anthony.
I was of late as petty to his ends
As is the morn-dew on the myrtle leaf   10
To his grand sea.

CAESAR   Be't so. Declare thine office.

AMBASSADOR
Lord of his fortunes he salutes thee, and
Requires to live in Egypt—which not granted
He lessens his requests, and to thee sues
To let him breathe between the heavens and earth   15
A private man in Athens. This for him.
Next, Cleopatra does confess thy greatness,
Submits her to thy might, and of thee craves
The circle of the Ptolemies for her heirs,
Now hazarded to thy grace.

CAESAR   For Anthony,   20
I have no ears to his request. The Queen
Of audience nor desire shall fail, so she
From Egypt drive her all-disgracèd friend,
Or take his life there. This if she perform,

---

14 lessens] F2; lessons F1

3 **plucked** i.e. stripped of all the signs of authority (like the 'plume-plucked' King in *Richard II* 4.1.99)
11 **his grand sea** the mighty ocean from which it originated
  Declare thine office get down to the business you are entrusted with. Caesar exhibits some impatience with the ambassador's flowery rhetoric.
13 **Requires** requests
14 **lessens** A number of editors (most recently Jones) defend F's 'lessons' as both more vivid and more appropriate

to the schoolmaster who speaks it, while admitting that the distinction would be virtually impossible to convey to an audience.
19 **circle** crown
20 **hazarded ... grace** helplessly at the disposal of your favour
21–2 **The Queen ... shall fail** the Queen shall lack neither a hearing nor the gratification of her wishes
23 **friend** lover; in this public context the term is deliberately insulting

She shall not sue unheard. So to them both.   25
AMBASSADOR Fortune pursue thee!
CAESAR   Bring him through the bands.
                                    Exit Ambassador, attended
(*To Thidias*) To try thy eloquence now 'tis time—
     dispatch:
From Anthony win Cleopatra; promise,
And in our name, what she requires; add more
From thine invention—offers. Women are not   30
In their best fortunes strong; but want will perjure
The ne'er-touched vestal. Try thy cunning, Thidias,
Make thine own edict for thy pains, which we
Will answer as a law.
THIDIAS   Caesar, I go.
CAESAR
Observe how Anthony becomes his flaw,   35
And what thou think'st his very action speaks
In every power that moves.
THIDIAS   Caesar, I shall.
                                              Exeunt.

3.13 *Enter Cleopatra, Enobarbus, Charmian, and Iras.*
CLEOPATRA
What shall we do, Enobarbus?
ENOBARBUS   Think, and die.
CLEOPATRA
Is Anthony or we in fault for this?

26.1 *Exit Ambassador, attended*] OXFORD *after* ROWE ('*Exit Ambassador*'); *not in* F
30 From ... offers] F (invention, offers); As thine invention offers HANMER   32 Thidias]
F *and throughout* (*except* 'Thidius', 3.13.104.1); Thyreus THEOBALD (*following* North)

26 **Bring...bands** escort him through
   the troops
28-30 **From...offers** Hanmer's emendation supposes that 'From' has been
   accidentally repeated from l. 28. But
   the F reading makes perfectly good
   sense: it emphasizes that Thidias is
   empowered not merely to respond to
   Cleopatra's requests, but to make offers
   of his own.
31 **in...fortunes** in the most fortunate
   circumstances
31-2 **perjure...vestal** The six Vestal Vir-
   gins, priestesses of Vesta in Rome,
   were supposed to be of such irre-

proachable character that they were
allowed to give evidence without the
customary oath; the penalty for breach
of their vows was to be immured alive.
33 **Make...pains** name your own reward
34 **answer** honour
35 **becomes his flaw** behaves in the face
   of his collapse
36-7 **And...moves** and see what you
   can deduce from every detail of his
   behaviour
37 **power that moves** 'faculty of mind and
   body that is put in action' (Case)

ENOBARBUS

  Anthony only, that would make his will
  Lord of his reason. What though you fled
  From that great face of war, whose several ranges   5
  Frighted each other? Why should he follow?
  The itch of his affection should not then
  Have nicked his captainship—at such a point,
  When half to half the world opposed—he being
  The mooted question? 'Twas a shame no less   10
  Than was his loss to course your flying flags,
  And leave his navy gazing.

CLEOPATRA Prithee, peace.

    Enter the Ambassador with Anthony

ANTHONY

  Is that his answer?

AMBASSADOR   Ay, my lord.

ANTHONY

  The Queen shall then have courtesy,   15
  So she will yield us up.

AMBASSADOR   He says so.

ANTHONY   Let her know't.

  (*To Cleopatra*) To the boy Caesar send this grizzled
    head,
  And he will fill thy wishes to the brim

3.13.10 mooted] OXFORD (*conj.* Johnson); meered, F

3.13.3–4 **Anthony . . . reason** This scene
is framed by Enobarbus's commentary
on Anthony, a perspectival device very
like that created by Philo's commentary in 1.1. Enobarbus ascribes Anthony's defeat to the subjugation of his
reason by sexual desire ('will'), just as
at the end of the scene he sees Anthony's recovery as exemplifying the
overthrow of reason by blind courage
('valour preys on reason'). Both passages invite us to read Anthony's behaviour as illustrating the central
tenet of classical and Renaissance
moral philosophy—that all true virtue
depends upon reason's retaining strict
government of the passions.
3 **will** (sexual) desire
5 **ranges** battle lines (cf. 'ranged empire',
1.1.36)
7 **affection** desire

8 **nicked** Various senses of the verb are
possible: (1) cut, damage, cut short;
(2) catch, take unawares; (3) to win
against a competitor (as in the game
of hazard); (4) cheat, defraud.
10 **mooted question** the occasion of dispute. Most editors retain F's 'meered'
as 'mered', supposing a coinage from
'mere'; Johnson, on the other hand,
suggested it might derive from 'mere'
= boundary, citing Spenser's *Ruins of
Rome*, 22 ('When that brave honour
of the Latin name, | Which mear'd
her rule with Africa and Byze').
But Johnson's alternative conjecture,
'mooted' gives better sense and could
plausibly be misread as 'meered'.
11 **course** pursue
16 **So** provided that
   us (royal plural)

With principalities.

CLEOPATRA   That head, my lord?

ANTHONY (*to the Ambassador*)

To him again, tell him he wears the rose   20
Of youth upon him, from which the world should note
Some thing particular: his coin, ships, legions,
May be a coward's, whose ministers would prevail
Under the service of a child as soon
As i'th'command of Caesar; I dare him therefore   25
To lay his gay caparisons apart
And answer me, declined sword against sword,
Ourselves alone. I'll write it. Follow me.

                         Exeunt Anthony and Ambassador

ENOBARBUS (*aside*)

Yes, like enough, high-battled Caesar will
Unstate his happiness, and be staged to th'show   30
Against a sworder! I see men's judgements are

22 Some thing] This edition; Something F   26 caparisons] POPE; comparisons F
27 me, declined] This edition; me declined F; me, sword against sword declined DEIGHTON
28.1 *Exeunt . . . Ambassador*] ROWE (*subs.*); *not in* F

20-2 **tell . . . particular** since he is in the bloom of youth, the world has a right to expect some distinguished action. Jones comments: 'the oddly slack rhythm may indicate that the text is defective; perhaps some words have dropped out'; but the rhythm may seem less obviously slack and the sense less vague if F's 'something' is broken up. The 'thing particular' which Anthony has in mind is single combat; 'thing' = *deed* (*OED thing*, sb. 4) or *attribute* (*OED thing*, sb. 7b).

23 **ministers** agents

26 **gay** showy
    caparisons trappings; most editors prefer to keep F's 'comparisons', for which Johnson's explanation ('comparative superiority in fortune') has been widely accepted, though it seems a little strained. Pope's conjecture seems even stronger in light of the fact that 'comparisons' sometimes appears as a corrupt form of 'caparisons', *OED* citing two examples from 1540. Significantly the two words are punned on in Chapman's *Sir Giles Goosecap* (4.2).

27 **declined sword** The pointing adopted here makes the line easier to deliver

than the awkward Latinism 'me declined'; the sword stands metonymically for the diminished Anthony himself (cf. 3.11.66, 'My sword, made weak by my affection'), but there is also a play on the semi-technical use of *decline* = bring (a sword) down upon (one's enemy).

29 **high-battled** defended with mighty armies

30 **Unstate his happiness** abandon the lofty position which his good fortune has given him

30-1 **staged . . . sworder** Sword-and-buckler fights were a regular entertainment in Elizabethan and Jacobean theatres; but Shakespeare probably also had Roman gladiatorial displays in mind.

31-4 **I see . . . alike** A variation on Enobarbus's theme of reason overcome by passion. Stoic philosophy, in particular, insisted that outward events were indifferent and could not affect the inward condition of the virtuous man, governed as it was by reason to the exclusion of all passion. Renaissance moralists insisted that to allow oneself to be affected by the vicissitudes of fortune was, *ipso facto*, to surrender

A parcel of their fortunes, and things outward
Do draw the inward quality after them
To suffer all alike. That he should dream,
Knowing all measures, the full Caesar will   35
Answer his emptiness! Caesar, thou hast subdued
His judgement too.

   Enter a Servant

SERVANT   A messenger from Caesar.

CLEOPATRA

What, no more ceremony? See, my women,
Against the blown rose may they stop their nose
That kneeled unto the buds. Admit him, sir.   40

        Exit Servant

ENOBARBUS *(aside)*

Mine honesty and I begin to square:
The loyalty well held to fools does make
Our faith mere folly; yet he that can endure
To follow with allegiance a fall'n lord
Does conquer him that did his master conquer,   45
And earns a place i'th'story.

   Enter Thidias

CLEOPATRA   Caesar's will?

THIDIAS

Hear it apart.

40.1 *Exit Servant*] CAPELL; *not in* F

the government of one's inner world
to the passions, whose erratic motions
corresponded to the whimsical activity
of fortune in the outer world.

32 **parcel of** inseparably connected to (cf.
 'part and parcel')
34 **To . . . alike** so that the inner self is
 made to share in the (otherwise indifferent) suffering of the physical self
35 **Knowing all measures** knowing all
 that he does about how power is
 measured
 full at the peak of his power
36 **Answer his emptiness** (1) agree to fight
 with someone as powerless as he; (2)
 match his impotence
39 **blown** overblown, decaying
41 **honesty** honour, truth
 square disagree, fall out, quarrel
42–6 **The loyalty . . . story** Enobarbus's re-

flections echo the Fool's ironic advice
to Kent: 'Let go thy hold when a great
wheel runs down a hill, lest it break
thy neck with following . . . I would
have none but knaves follow [this ad-
vice], since a fool gives it . . . But I will
tarry, the fool will stay, | And let the
wise man fly. | The knave turns fool
that runs away, | The fool no knave,
pardie' (*Lear* 2.2.245–58). Enobarbus's role corresponds in important
ways to that of the fool; but his desire
to earn a place in the story is quite
uncharacteristic of the world of foolery
and associates him with the heroic
aspiration of Anthony (cf. l. 176: 'I
and my sword will earn our
chronicle').
46–194 *Enter Thidias . . .* **pestilent scythe**
The episode is closely based on Plutarch (see Appendix A).

CLEOPATRA   None but friends—say boldly.
THIDIAS
So haply are they friends to Anthony.
ENOBARBUS
He needs as many, sir, as Caesar has,
Or needs not us. If Caesar please, our master   50
Will leap to be his friend; for us, you know,
Whose he is we are—and that is Caesar's.
THIDIAS   So.
Thus then, thou most renowned: Caesar entreats
Not to consider in what case thou stand'st
Further than he is Caesar.
CLEOPATRA   Go on: right royal!   55
THIDIAS
He knows that you embraced not Anthony
As you did love, but as you feared him.
CLEOPATRA   O.
THIDIAS
The scars upon your honour, therefore, he
Does pity as constrainèd blemishes,
Not as deserved.
CLEOPATRA   He is a god, and knows   60
What is most right. Mine honour was not yielded,
But conquered merely.
ENOBARBUS *(aside)*   To be sure of that,
I will ask Anthony! Sir, sir, thou art so leaky
That we must leave thee to thy sinking, for
Thy dearest quit thee.   *Exit Enobarbus*
THIDIAS   Shall I say to Caesar   65
What you require of him?—for he partly begs
To be desired to give. It much would please him
That of his fortunes you should make a staff

51 us, you know] STEEVENS; vs you know F   55 Caesar] F2; CAESARS FI
56 embraced] HUDSON (*conj.* Thirlby); embrace F

50 Or...us or else his position is so
   hopeless that even we are superfluous
54–5 Not...Caesar A somewhat devious
   tautology: 'don't be any more anxious
   about your predicament than your
   awareness of Caesar's natural magnanimity should allow'.
55 right royal thoroughly generous; but

there is probably an anachronistic
quibble on 'Caesar' as a royal name.
61 right true
62 merely Probably has the sense of
   'utterly' as well as 'only'.
63–5 leaky...quit thee (like rats deserting a sinking ship (Dent M 1243))

To lean upon. But it would warm his spirits
To hear from me you had left Anthony,   70
And put yourself under his shroud, who is
The universal landlord.

CLEOPATRA   What's your name?

THIDIAS My name is Thidias.

CLEOPATRA   Most kind messenger,
Say to great Caesar this in deputation:
I kiss his conqu'ring hand. Tell him I am prompt   75
To lay my crown at's feet, and there to kneel
Till from his all-obeying breath I hear
The doom of Egypt.

THIDIAS   'Tis your noblest course:
Wisdom and Fortune combating together,
If that the former dare but what it can,   80
No chance may shake it. Give me grace to lay
My duty on your hand.

    He kisses her hand

CLEOPATRA   Your Caesar's father oft,
When he hath mused of taking kingdoms in,
Bestowed his lips on that unworthy place,
As it rained kisses.

    Enter Anthony and Enobarbus

ANTHONY   Favours, by Jove that thunders!   85
What art thou, fellow?

THIDIAS   One that but performs
The bidding of the fullest man, and worthiest

71 who is] COLLIER 1853; *not in* F   74 deputation] THEOBALD (*conj.* Warburton); disputation F   77 Till from] JONES (*conj.* Muir); Tell him, from F   82 *He . . . hand*] ROWE (*subs.*); *not in* F

71 **And . . . is** Not only is the F line two syllables short for no apparent dramatic reason, it also suffers from a slightly awkward syntactical compression. Jones suggests that 'a word has dropped out before *shroud*', but it seems more probable that something has gone from the end of the line, 'who is', 'who's now', 'who stands'— or 'the great' (Hanmer).
   his shroud, who is the shelter of him who is (with a possible ironic play on *shroud* = 'winding-sheet')
74 **in deputation** as my representative
77 **all-obeying** obeyed by all

78 **doom** judgement, sentence; fate
   your noblest course the course that best accords with your nobility
80 **If . . . can** if wisdom only has the courage to act on its potential
82 **Caesar's father** Julius Caesar (see 3.6.6)
83 **taking . . . in** conquering
85 **As** as if
86 **fellow** Used contemptuously—'a person of no esteem or worth'; *thou* is also contemptuous here, and throughout Anthony's exchange with Thidias.
87 **fullest** 'best and most fortunate' (Jones); but cf. also l. 35

To have command obeyed.

ENOBARBUS   You will be whipped.

ANTHONY (*calling for Servants*)

Approach there!—Ah, you kite! Now, gods and devils,
Authority melts from me. Of late, when I cried 'Ho!',   90
Like boys unto a muss, kings would start forth
And cry, 'Your will?' Have you no ears? I am
Anthony yet.

    Enter Servants

           Take hence this jack and whip him!

ENOBARBUS (*aside*)

'Tis better playing with a lion's whelp
Than with an old one dying.

ANTHONY   Moon and stars!   95

Whip him! Were't twenty of the greatest tributaries
That do acknowledge Caesar, should I find them
So saucy with the hand of she here—what's her name
Since she was Cleopatra? Whip him, fellows,
Till like a boy you see him cringe his face   100
And whine aloud for mercy. Take him hence.

THIDIAS Mark Anthony—

ANTHONY   Tug him away! Being whipped,
Bring him again. The jack of Caesar's shall
Bear us an errand to him.

           Exeunt Servants with Thidias

89 *calling . . . servants*] WILSON (*subs.*); *not in* F   90 from me. Of late, when] JOHNSON
(*subs.*; *conj.* Thirlby 3); from me of late. When F   93 *Servants*] DYCE; *a Servant.* F (*after*
'whip him')   103 The] F; this POPE   104.1 *Servants*] CAPELL (*subs.*); *not in* F

88 **You . . . whipped** Capell gave this
   speech, as well ll. 94–5, as an aside.
   Both or neither may have been intended as asides; F does not help, since
   it fails to mark even the obvious aside
   at ll. 41–6. In the end the decision
   must lie with the actor playing Enobarbus: this line, for example, might
   be played as a mocking aside, as de-
   risive mockery, or as a more-or-less
   friendly warning.
89 **kite** metaphorically 'one who preys on
   others; a whore'
91 **muss** scramble
93 **jack** knave, underling
94–5 **'Tis . . . dying** The sentence has a
   proverbial ring to it; cf. Dent L321.1
   'It is dangerous to play with lions'.

The Oxford . . . Proverbs cites 'Destroy
the lion while he is yet but a whelp'
but gives 1762 as its earliest occurrence.
98–9 **what's . . . Cleopatra** The paradoxical dissociation of name and identity recalls Philo's 'sometimes when he
   is not Anthony . . .' (1.1.59).
98 **she** The pronoun is used dismissively.
100 **like a boy** What is at stake in Anthony's vindictive cruelty is suggested
   by his contemptuous 'the boy Caesar'
   (l. 17) and his recollection of the tribu-
   tary kings starting 'like boys unto a
   muss' (l. 91); in this scene 'boy' carries much the same psychological
   charge that it has in the last scene of
   Coriolanus.

You were half blasted ere I knew you. Ha!   105
Have I my pillow left unpressed in Rome,
Forborne the getting of a lawful race,
And by a gem of women, to be abused
By one that looks on feeders?
CLEOPATRA Good my lord—   110
ANTHONY
You have been a boggler ever.
But when we in our viciousness grow hard—
O misery on't!—the wise gods seel our eyes,
In our own filth drop our clear judgements, make us
Adore our errors, laugh at's while we strut   115
To our confusion.
CLEOPATRA   O, is't come to this?
ANTHONY
I found you as a morsel, cold upon
Dead Caesar's trencher—nay, you were a fragment
Of Gneius Pompey's—besides what hotter hours,
Unregistered in vulgar fame, you have   120
Luxuriously picked out. For I am sure,
Though you can guess what temperance should be,
You know not what it is.
CLEOPATRA   Wherefore is this?
ANTHONY
To let a fellow that will take rewards

113–14 eyes, | In our own filth drop] WARBURTON; eyes | In our owne filth, drop F

105 **blasted** withered
107 **Forborne . . . race** In fact Antonius had several children by Octavia, something out of which Dryden made extensive capital in his reworking of Shakespeare, *All for Love*; but given the apparent time-scheme of *Anthony and Cleopatra*, it seems unlikely that any irony is intended.
109 **feeders** servants, retainers, or clients who were fed at a great man's table
111 **boggler** waverer, equivocator; the *OED*'s first recorded use of the noun
113 **seel** stitch up. When training hawks, falconers temporarily *seeled* the eyes of hawks to prepare them for the hood. Bevington finds an allusion to 'the Greek doctrine of *Ate*, according to

which the Gods allow anyone who hubristically believes in his own self-sufficiency to persevere in his delusion until he brings about his own fall'. But the idea is also proverbial: 'When God will punish he will first take away the understanding' (Dent G257)
116 **confusion** destruction
118 **trencher** wooden platter
   fragment leftover, scrap
119 **Gneius Pompey** Presumably Cneius Pompeius Magnus, son of Pompey the Great whose name he inherited; but Shakespeare sometimes seems to confuse the two (see note to 1.5.31.).
   hotter more lustful
120 **vulgar fame** common gossip
121 **Luxuriously** lasciviously

And say 'God quit you' be familiar with   125
My playfellow, your hand, this kingly seal,
And plighter of high hearts! O that I were
Upon the hill of Basan, to outroar
The hornèd herd, for I have savage cause,
And to proclaim it civilly were like   130
A haltered neck which does the hangman thank
For being yare about him.

    Enter a Servant with Thidias

                Is he whipped?

SERVANT Soundly, my lord.

ANTHONY   Cried he, and begged a pardon?

SERVANT He did ask favour.

ANTHONY (*to Thidias*)

If that thy father live, let him repent   135
Thou wast not made his daughter, and be thou sorry
To follow Caesar in his triumph, since
Thou hast been whipped for following him. Henceforth
The white hand of a lady fever thee,
Shake thou to look on't! Get thee back to Caesar,   140
Tell him thy entertainment. Look thou say
He makes me angry with him, for he seems
Proud and disdainful, harping on what I am,
Not what he knew I was. He makes me angry,
And at this time most easy 'tis to do't,   145
When my good stars, that were my former guides,
Have empty left their orbs, and shot their fires

---

132 *Enter . . . Thidias*] F (*after* 'whipt')   138 whipped for . . . him. Henceforth] ROWE
(*subs.*); whipt. For . . . him, henceforth F

125 **'God quit you'** A beggar's phrase, the
Jacobean equivalent of 'God bless you,
guv.'
126 **seal** token, pledge
128 **hill of Basan . . . herd** For Basan (or
Bashan), a large fertile region east of
the sea of Galilee, see Ps. 68:15 and
22:12: 'As the hill of *Basan*, so is God's
hill: even an high hill'; 'Many oxen
are come about me; fat bulls of *Basan*
close me in on every side'; Anthony
imagines the 'horned herd' as emblems
of cuckoldry.
131 **haltered neck** i.e. a man about to be
hanged
132 **yare** quick and deft

136 **his daughter** (in whom crying would
not be shameful—or who might have
escaped whipping)
137 **follow . . . triumph** (1) to count yourself among the triumphant Caesar's
followers; (2) to walk behind Caesar in
his triumphal procession
139 **fever thee** make you shake as if with
fever
141 **entertainment** reception
147 **orbs** spheres (in which the 'stars',
including the 'fixed stars' or planets,
were thought to move (cf. note to
2.7.14–16). Bevington finds an echo
of the apocalyptic imagery in Rev.
9:1–2.

Into th'abysm of hell. If he mislike
My speech and what is done, tell him he has
Hipparchus, my enfranchèd bondman, whom   150
He may at pleasure whip, or hang, or torture,
As he shall like, to quit me. Urge it thou.
Hence with thy stripes, be gone!   *Exit Thidias*
CLEOPATRA Have you done yet?
ANTHONY   Alack, our terrene moon
Is now eclipsed, and it portends alone   155
The fall of Anthony.
CLEOPATRA   I must stay his time.
ANTHONY
To flatter Caesar, would you mingle eyes
With one that ties his points?
CLEOPATRA   Not know me yet?
ANTHONY
Cold-hearted toward me?
CLEOPATRA   Ah, dear, if I be so,
From my cold heart let heaven engender hail,   160
And poison it in the source, and the first stone
Drop in my neck: as it determines, so
Dissolve my life; the next Caesarion smite,
Till by degrees the memory of my womb,
Together with my brave Egyptians all,   165

---

163 smite] ROWE; smile F

150-2 **Hipparchus...me** Plutarch records that this man, one of Antonius's
  favourites, was among the first to desert to Caesar (see Appendix A). If
  Shakespeare was remembering this detail, then Anthony's suggestion is a
  stinging irony; but if not, it suggests a
  petulant callousness about an insignificant follower that contrasts strikingly
  with his magnanimous display of
  cameraderie in 4.2.
  enfranchèd enfranchised
152 **quit** requite
154 **terrene moon** i.e. Cleopatra as the
  earthly incarnation of the moon-goddess, Isis
156 **stay his time** wait until he is finished
157-8 **mingle eyes | With** make eyes at
158 **one...points** one that fastens his
  clothes, a valet. In place of a fly, seven-

teenth-century hose had a codpiece
  tied with metal-tagged laces called
  points.
159 **Cold-hearted** The first use of this
  compound adjective recorded in *OED*.
160-8 **From...prey** Bevington notes the
  apocalyptic strain in Cleopatra's language here, citing parallels in Exod.
  8:24, 9:23–5, Rev. 16:21, and Acts
  4, 5.
162 **neck** throat
  determines comes to an end (i.e. melts)
163 **Caesarion** an ironically exact prophecy: after her fall Cleopatra's son
  was put to death by Octavius who
  feared him as a possible rival to the
  mantle of Julius Caesar; Daniel's
  Cleopatra makes considerable pathetic
  capital out of this story (see note to
  5.2.130–3)

By the discandying of this pelleted storm,
Lie graveless, till the flies and gnats of Nile
Have buried them for prey.

ANTHONY   I am satisfied.
Caesar sits down in Alexandria, where
I will oppose his fate. Our force by land   170
Hath nobly held, our severed navy too
Have knit again, and fleet, threat'ning most sea-like.
Where hast thou been, my heart? Dost thou hear,
    lady?
If from the field I shall return once more
To kiss these lips, I will appear in blood;   175
I and my sword will earn our chronicle—
There's hope in't yet.

CLEOPATRA   That's my brave lord!

ANTHONY
I will be treble-sinewed, -hearted, -breathed,
And fight maliciously; for when mine hours
Were nice and lucky, men did ransom lives   180
Of me for jests; but now I'll set my teeth,
And send to darkness all that stop me. Come,
Let's have one other gaudy night. Call to me
All my sad captains, fill our bowls once more—
Let's mock the midnight bell.

---

166 discandying] THEOBALD (*conj.* Thirlby); discandering F

166 **discandying** melting; a Shakespearian coinage found only in this play where it occurs again at 4.13.22 (*OED*).
pelleted storm hail-storm
169 **sits down in** encamps before, lays siege to
172 **fleet** float
sea-like in a fashion like the sea itself; or perhaps, seamanlike, shipshape
173 **thou** The change of pronoun helps to register Anthony's sudden tenderness here. Cf. Appendix C.
my heart Either 'my courage'; or 'my love' (addressed to Cleopatra).
175 **in blood** (1) drenched in blood; (2) in full vigour
176 **chronicle** the heroic history in which Enobarbus too hopes to make a place for himself (see 3.13.42–6)
177, 192 **There's hope ... sap in't yet**

Variants of the proverbial formulation 'There is life in it' (Dent L265)
179 **maliciously** violently, fiercely (*OED maliciously* adv. 2)
180 **nice** pampered
181 **Of** from
for jests for derisory sums (or 'for the price of a joke', Jones)
183–94 **Let's have ... pestilent scythe** Anthony's bravado echoes Plutarch's description of the lovers' defiant revels after their return to Alexandria (see Appendix A).
183 **gaudy** luxurious; brilliantly gay; cf. also *gaudy-day* = festival or gala day
184 **sad** both 'melancholy' and 'sober'
185 **mock ... bell** i.e. burn the midnight oil; but, given the play's powerful imaginative emphasis on the traditional association of darkness and death, the

CLEOPATRA   It is my birthday—   185
  I had thought to've held it poor; but since my lord
  Is Anthony again, I will be Cleopatra.
ANTHONY We will yet do well.
CLEOPATRA
  Call all his noble captains to my lord!
ANTHONY Do so, we'll speak to them; and tonight I'll
     force   190
  The wine peep through their scars. Come on, my
     queen,
  There's sap in't yet. The next time I do fight
  I'll make Death love me, for I will contend
  Even with his pestilent scythe.
                       Exeunt all but Enobarbus

ENOBARBUS
  Now he'll outstare the lightning. To be furious   195
  Is to be frighted out of fear, and in that mood
  The dove will peck the estridge; and I see still
  A diminution in our captain's brain
  Restores his heart. When valour preys on reason,
  It eats the sword it fights with. I will seek   200
  Some way to leave him.   *Exit*

194.1 *all ... Enobarbus*] CAPELL (*subs.*); *not in* F   199 on] ROWE; *in* F   201 *Exit*]
ROWE; *Exeunt.* F

metaphor has deeper resonances—defiance of time becomes defiance of death, the midnight bell a passing bell.

185 **birthday** The detail is from Plutarch; but, as Bevington notes, the motivation is apparently changed—for where Plutarch's Cleopatra chooses to celebrate her birthday with exceptional 'sumptuousness and magnificence' in order to 'clear herself of the suspicion he had of her' (see Appendix A), Shakespeare is simply responding to Anthony's gesture of defiance.

192 **sap** life

194 **contend ... scythe** Usually interpreted as 'rival Death's slaughters in the plague' (in the Triumphs of Death, symbolizing the swathes of mortality cut by the pestilence, Death is depicted standing on his chariot with a scythe, mowing down all before). But perhaps Anthony imagines a more active contention, his sword against Death's scythe, in which he and Death become sweet enemies, linked by the murderous intimacy of combat, like Coriolanus and Aufidius.

195 **furious** frenzied, mad with rage

197 **estridge** goshawk. *OED* gives it only as a variant of 'ostrich'; but Arden makes it plain that 'estridge' (med. L. *estricium*) was a common term for goshawk, and cites several semi-proverbial references to doves attacking hawks.
    still always

198–9 **A diminution ... with** Cf. note to ll. 3–4.

199 **heart** courage

4.1   *Enter Caesar, Agrippa and Mecenas, with his*
     army; Caesar reading a letter; ⌈ *a Messenger in*
     attendance ⌉

CAESAR

He calls me boy, and chides as he had power
To beat me out of Egypt. My messenger
He hath whipped with rods, dares me to personal
     combat.
Caesar to Anthony: let the old ruffian know
I have many other ways to die—meantime   5
Laugh at his challenge.   ·⌈ *Exit Messenger* ⌉

MECENAS   Caesar must think,
When one so great begins to rage, he's hunted
Even to falling. Give him no breath, but now
Make boot of his distraction. Never anger
Made good guard for itself.

CAESAR   Let our best heads   10
Know that tomorrow the last of many battles
We mean to fight. Within our files there are,
Of those that served Mark Anthony but late,
Enough to fetch him in. See it done,
And feast the army—we have store to do't,   15
And they have earned the waste. Poor Anthony!

                              Exeunt

4.1.0.2–3 *a Messenger in attendance*] This edition; *not in* F   3–4 combat. | Caesar to
Anthony: let] F; combat, | Caesar to Anthony. Let ROWE   6 *Exit Messenger*] This
edition; *not in* F

4.1.1 **boy** Anthony's calculated insult
rankles with Caesar as Aufidius's gibe
will do with Coriolanus (*Coriolanus*
5.6.102 ff.). Shakespeare probably
derived the detail from Suetonius's *Life
of Augustus*, which records that his
enemies frequently referred contemptuously to Octavius Caesar as 'the
boy'.

3–5 **dares me . . . die** The passage is closely based on Plutarch, who places this
episode after the first battle of Alexandria (see Appendix A). In Plutarch
Caesar scornfully suggests that *Antonius* must have 'many other ways to
die', but Shakespeare evidently mis-
understood the ambiguous syntax of
North's translation.

4 **Caesar . . . let** Although a majority of
editors prefer Rowe's emendation, the

F punctuation (as Ridley notes) is
defensible, since it assumes that
'Caesar to Anthony' is the formulaic
opening of a message to be delivered
to his rival. It thus implies the stage
direction inserted at this point.
ruffian In addition to its usual meaning, the word may be coloured by two
obsolete senses current at the time: (1)
a swaggering bully; (2) a protector or
confederate of courtesans.

8 **Give . . . breath** allow him no time to
recover his breath

9 **Make . . . distraction** take advantage of
his madness

10 **best heads** principal commanders

12 **files** ranks

14 **fetch him in** capture him

15 **store** adequate supplies

16 **waste** extravagance

4.2   *Enter Anthony, Cleopatra, Enobarbus, Charmian,*
        Iras, Alexas, with others

ANTHONY
  He will not fight with me, Domitius?

ENOBARBUS   No.

ANTHONY Why should he not?

ENOBARBUS
  He thinks, being twenty times of better fortune,
  He is twenty men to one.

ANTHONY   Tomorrow, soldier,
  By sea and land I'll fight. Or I will live,   5
  Or bathe my dying honour in the blood
  Shall make it live again. Woot thou fight well?

ENOBARBUS
  I'll strike, and cry 'Take all!'

ANTHONY   Well said, come on!
  Call forth my household servants. Let's tonight
  Be bounteous at our meal.

        Enter Servitors

                              Give me thy hand,   10
  Thou hast been rightly honest—so hast thou—
  Thou—and thou—and thou. You have served me
        well,
  And kings have been your fellows.

CLEOPATRA (*aside to Enobarbus*)   What means this?

ENOBARBUS (*aside to Cleopatra*)
  'Tis one of those odd tricks which sorrow shoots

4.2.1 Domitius] ROWE; *Domitian* F   10 *Enter Servitors*] OXFORD; *Enter* 3 *or* 4 *Seruitors.*
F (*after* 'lets to night')

Out of the mind.

ANTHONY   And thou art honest too.   15
I wish I could be made so many men,
And all of you clapped up together in
An Anthony, that I might do you service
So good as you have done.

SERVITORS   The gods forbid.

ANTHONY
Well, my good fellows, wait on me tonight;   20
Scant not my cups, and make as much of me
As when mine empire was your fellow too,
And suffered my command.

CLEOPATRA *(aside to Enobarbus)* What does he mean?

ENOBARBUS *(aside to Cleopatra)*
To make his followers weep.

ANTHONY   Tend me tonight:
Maybe it is the period of your duty—   25
Haply you shall not see me more; or if,
A mangled shadow. Perchance tomorrow
You'll serve another master. I look on you
As one that takes his leave. Mine honest friends,
I turn you not away, but, like a master   30
Married to your good service, stay till death:
Tend me tonight two hours, I ask no more;
And the gods yield you for't!

ENOBARBUS   What mean you, sir,
To give them this discomfort? Look, they weep,
And I, an ass, am onion-eyed—for shame,   35
Transform us not to women!

ANTHONY   Ho, ho, ho!

---

19 SERVITORS] OXFORD; *Omnes.* F

20-2 **fellows...fellow** There is an interesting modulation between the two
  uses of the noun: 'my good fellows'
  might be addressed either to servants
  or to companions and equals; clearly
  'wait on me tonight' tilts it towards
  the first meaning, but the hyperbolic
  'mine empire was your fellow too' re-
  instates the other meaning—only for
  'suffered my command' to reassert the
  master-servant relationship.

21 **Scant...cups** don't stint my wine
25 **period** end
26-7 **or...shadow** or if you do, it will
  be as a mutilated ghost
31 **Married to** bound forever to; the metaphor is continued in 'stay till death'
  with its echo of the marriage service's
  'till death us depart' (thus in all editions prior to 1662).
33 **yield** repay
35 **onion-eyed** Cf. note to 1.2.168.

Now the witch take me if I meant it thus!
Grace grow where those drops fall! My hearty friends,
You take me in too dolorous a sense;
For I spake to you for your comfort, did desire you   40
To burn this night with torches. Know, my hearts,
I hope well of tomorrow, and will lead you
Where rather I'll expect victorious life
Than death and honour. Let's to supper, come,
And drown consideration.   *Exeunt*   45

4.3   *Enter a company of Soldiers*
FIRST SOLDIER
Brother, good night—tomorrow is the day.
SECOND SOLDIER
It will determine one way. Fare you well.
Heard you of nothing strange about the streets?
FIRST SOLDIER Nothing. What news?
SECOND SOLDIER
Belike 'tis but a rumour, good night to you.   5

---

38 fall! My . . . friends,] THEOBALD; fall (my hearty Friends) F
   4.3.1, FIRST SOLDIER] F ('1. *Sol.*')   2 SECOND SOLDIER] F ('2. *Sol.*')   4 ff. FIRST, SECOND,
THIRD, FOURTH SOLDIER] F ('1, 2, 3, 4')

37 take bewitch
38 Grace herb of grace; here punning on
   divine grace—Anthony means something like 'God bless you for those
   tears'.
   hearty Plays on several senses of the
   word: (1) noble, courageous, zealous
   in support; (2) full of warm affection;
   (3) sincere (*OED hearty* adj. 1, 3, 4)
41 burn . . . torches i.e. light up the darkness with burning torches at the
   'gaudy night' Anthony has announced
   (3.13.183); but the metaphor suggests
   flamboyant extravagance, the con-
   spicuous consumption of time itself.
4.3. This scene is closely modelled on an
   episode in Plutarch, where, however,
   it is the god Bacchus whose departure
   is marked by mysterious music (see
   Appendix A).
   Lineation. This is one of several scenes
   in the play where the verse arrangement is particularly uncertain (see Appendix D).

0–6 *Enter a company . . . meeting them* The
   stage directions here are vague: '*a company*' may be simply equivalent to an
   authorial 'as many as can be'; but a
   minimum of four soldiers, two in each
   party, are required, and if '*every corner
   of the stage*' is to be taken literally,
   then four may be exactly the number
   intended. On 'Walk' (l. 15) Soldiers 1
   and 2 appear to cross the stage to
   converse more intimately with the
   others. F's 'They meet' (l. 6) leaves it
   uncertain whether the two groups
   should enter severally at the beginning
   of the scene, or whether the second
   group should enter here; perhaps Shakespeare had not made up his own mind,
   or simply left it to the company to
   work out the best arrangement.
2 determine one way produce a result
   one way or the other; but the remark
   is given a pessimistic tinge by another
   sense of *determine* = come to an end.

FIRST SOLDIER
  Well sir, good night.
    Enter other Soldiers, meeting them
SECOND SOLDIER   Soldiers, have careful watch.
THIRD SOLDIER
  And you—good night, good night.
    They place themselves in every corner of the stage
SECOND SOLDIER   Here we. An if tomorrow
  Our navy thrive, I have an absolute hope
  Our landmen will stand up.
FIRST SOLDIER   'Tis a brave army,
  And full of purpose.
    Music of the hautboys is under the stage
SECOND SOLDIER   Peace, what noise?
FIRST SOLDIER   List, list!   10
SECOND SOLDIER
  Hark!
FIRST SOLDIER Music i'th'air.
THIRD SOLDIER   Under the earth.
FOURTH SOLDIER
  It signs well, does it not?
THIRD SOLDIER   No.
FIRST SOLDIER   Peace, I say!
  What should this mean?
SECOND SOLDIER
  'Tis the god Hercules, whom Anthony loved, |
  Now leaves him.
FIRST SOLDIER   Walk—let's see if other watchmen   15
  Do hear what we do.
SECOND SOLDIER   How now, masters?

6 *Enter . . . them*] OXFORD (*after* F '*They meete other Soldiers*')   7 THIRD SOLDIER] CAPELL;
1 F   an if] OXFORD; and if F

7 **An if** This double conditional is common in Elizabethan English; but F's 'and if' could equally represent the modern colloquial form.
8 **absolute** positive
10 **hautboys** woodwind instruments, ancestral to the oboe
12 **signs well** is a good omen. Shakespeare's audience would normally

have associated sounds coming from under the stage with hell and evil spirits.
14 **Hercules** Shakespeare substitutes Hercules, Anthony's supposed ancestor and patron of heroic virtue, for Plutarch's Bacchus.
15 **Walk** See note to ll. 0–6.

ALL (*speaking together*)   How now?
   How now? Do you hear this?
FIRST SOLDIER   Ay, is't not strange?
THIRD SOLDIER
   Do you hear, masters? Do you hear?
FIRST SOLDIER
   Follow the noise so far as we have quarter.
   Let's see how it will give off.
ALL   Content. 'Tis strange!   20

                   Exeunt

4.4   *Enter Anthony and Cleopatra, with Charmian and*
         others
ANTHONY (*calling*)
   Eros! Mine armour, Eros!
CLEOPATRA   Sleep a little.
ANTHONY
   No, my chuck. Eros, come—mine armour, Eros!
     Enter Eros with armour
   Come, good fellow, put thine iron on.
   If Fortune be not ours today, it is
   Because we brave her. Come.
     Eros begins to arm Anthony
CLEOPATRA   Nay, I'll help too.   5

---

16 ALL . . . *together*] F ('Speake together. | Omnes.')   20 ALL] *Omnes.* F
   4.4.0 *Charmian and*] JOHNSON; *not in* F   1 *calling*] OXFORD; *not in* F   2.1 *with armour*]
CAPELL; *not in* F   3 thine] F; mine HANMER (*conj.* Thirlby)   5 *Eros . . . Anthony*] This
edition; *not in* F   5–6 too. | What's this for? ANTHONY Ah] MALONE (*conj.* Capell); too,
Anthony. | What's this for? Ah

16 *speaking together* i.e. the different
   questions are distributed among several soldiers who all speak at once
19 so . . . **quarter** within the limits (spatial
   and temporal) of the watch assigned
   to us
20 **give off** cease
4.4.0.1–2 *and others* The F direction is
   vague, the sort of thing a dramatist
   might jot down in the course of composition before the requirements of the
   scene were fully clear in his own mind:
   perhaps, since the opening of the scene
   has an uncharacteristically private and
   domestic feel, it should be interpreted
   as referring only to Charmian and Iras.

2 **chuck** chick (familiar term of endear-
   ment)
3 **thine iron** the armour you are holding
5 **brave** defy
5–15 **Nay . . . dispatch** The sequence in-
   corporates an unusually elaborate series
   of dramatized stage directions as Cleopatra assists Eros to put on Anthony's
   armour. Shakespeare found the name of
   Anthony's servant, Eros, in Plutarch,
   but makes metaphoric capital of it: here
   the spectacle of the hero armed by Eros
   and a mortal Venus recalls and reverses the iconography of Mars and
   Venus, in which the love-goddess and
   her cupids strip Mars of his armour.

What's this for?
          She attempts to assist Eros
ANTHONY   Ah, let be, let be! Thou art
The armourer of my heart. False, false! This, this!
CLEOPATRA
Sooth-la, I'll help! Thus it must be.
ANTHONY   Well, well,
We shall thrive now. Seest thou, my good fellow?
Go, put on thy defences.
EROS   Briefly, sir.   10
CLEOPATRA
Is not this buckled well?
ANTHONY   Rarely, rarely:
He that unbuckles this, till we do please
To doff't for our repose, shall hear a storm.
Thou fumblest, Eros, and my queen's a squire
More tight at this than thou—dispatch. O love,   15
That thou couldst see my wars today and knew'st
The royal occupation, thou shouldst see
A workman in't.
          Enter an armed Soldier
                    Good morrow to thee, welcome!
Thou look'st like him that knows a warlike charge.
To business that we love we rise betime,   20
And go to't with delight.
SOLDIER   A thousand, sir,
Early though't be, have on their riveted trim,

6 *She . . . Eros*] This edition; *not in* F   8 CLEOPATRA] MALONE (*conj.* Capell)   13 doff't]
F (daft)

7 **armourer of my heart** 'your work is to steel my *heart* with courage, not ...' (Deighton)
False, false not like that, you've got it wrong
10 **Briefly** in a moment
11 **Rarely** wonderfully well
14 **Thou fumblest** The playful rebuke may be an indication that Eros is overcome with emotion at this point and that Anthony is trying to joke him out of it.
squire Arming his knight was one of the duties of a squire. Anachronisms

of this sort ought to serve as warnings against inappropriate attempts to 'Romanize' the play.
15 **tight** capable, deft
dispatch be quick
17 **royal occupation** i.e. warfare
18 **workman** master craftsman (for *work* = masterpiece, see 1.2.153)
19 **charge** either 'command' or 'attack'
22 **riveted trim** armour (*trim* = gear); *OED*'s earliest instance of ppl. a. 'riveted'. Some pieces of sixteenth-century armour had to be riveted into place.

And at the port expect you.
                              Shout within. Trumpets flourish.
              Enter ⌈ Scarrus with other⌉ Captains, and
              Soldiers
⌈SCARRUS⌉   The morn is fair. Good morrow, general!
SOLDIERS Good morrow, general!
ANTHONY   'Tis well blown, lads!   25
   This morning, like the spirit of a youth
   That means to be of note, begins betimes.
   So, so—come give me that—this way—well said.
              Cleopatra and Eros finish arming Anthony, who
              embraces the Queen
   Fare thee well, dame. Whate'er becomes of me,
   This is a soldier's kiss—rebukable   30
   And worthy shameful check it were to stand
   On more mechanic compliment—I'll leave thee
   Now like a man of steel. You that will fight,
   Follow me close, I'll bring you to't. Adieu.
                      Exeunt all but Cleopatra and Charmian
CHARMIAN Please you retire to your chamber?
CLEOPATRA   Lead me.   35
   He goes forth gallantly. That he and Caesar might
   Determine this great war in single fight,
   Then Anthony . . . but now—well, on.   *Exeunt*

23.1 *Shout within*] OXFORD; *Showt.* F   23.2 *Scarrus with other*] This edition; *not in* F   24 SCARRUS] This edition; *Alex.* F; *Captain* ROWE   25 SOLDIERS] OXFORD; *All.* F   28.1–2 *Cleopatra . . . Queen*] This edition; *not in* F   34.1 *all . . . Charmian*] CAPELL (subs.); *not in* F

23 **port** Probably 'gate', though the location of the battle makes the meaning uncertain.
24 SCARRUS F's *Alex.* presumably marks a change of authorial intention, since at 4.6.11–15 we learn that Alexas has already deserted to Caesar. Capell suggested that the lines belonged to a Captain whose part was doubled with that of Alexas. But Scarrus seems a logical substitute, since Shakespeare seems to have designed him for the role of Anthony's principal commander in the final phase of the play. See note to 3.7.60.
25 **well blown** Almost certainly referring to the flourish of trumpets; but some editors take 'blown' to mean 'blossomed', metaphorically describing a dawn that has fully broken.
27 **of note** famous
31 **check** rebuke
32 **mechanic compliment** conventional displays of courtly manners
37 **Determine** decide, finish

4.5 *Trumpets sound. Enter Anthony,* ⌈ *Scarrus* ⌉ *and*
Eros

⌈ SCARRUS ⌉
  The gods make this a happy day to Anthony!
ANTHONY
  Would thou and those thy scars had once prevailed
  To make me fight at land.
⌈ SCARRUS ⌉   Hadst thou done so,
  The kings that have revolted, and the soldier
  That has this morning left thee, would have still   5
  Followed thy heels.
ANTHONY   Who's gone this morning?
⌈ SCARRUS ⌉   Who?
  One ever near thee—call for Enobarbus,
  He shall not hear thee; or from Caesar's camp,
  Say 'I am none of thine.'
ANTHONY   What sayst thou?
⌈ SCARRUS ⌉   Sir,
  He is with Caesar.
EROS   Sir, his chests and treasure   10
  He has not with him.
ANTHONY   Is he gone?

4.5.0 *Scarrus*] This edition; *not in* F; *Eros; a Soldier meeting them* THEOBALD   1 SCARRUS]
This edition; *Eros.* F; *Soldier* THEOBALD (*conj.* Thirlby)   3, 6 SCARRUS] This edition; *Eros.*
F; *Soldier* CAPELL   9, 11 SCARRUS] This edition; *Sold., Sol.* F

4.5.1, 3, 6 SCARRUS Thirlby and Capell between them rightly saw that these
  speeches can hardly belong to Eros, to
  whom they are assigned by F, since
  'those thy scars' is evidently addressed
  to the same scarred veteran whose advice Anthony ignored at Actium. But
  there is no easy explanation for the
  compositor's having misread 'Sold.' as
  'Eros'. However, if Barroll is right that
  in the copy-text the scarred Soldier
  was in the process of metamorphosis
  into Scarrus (see note to 3.7.60), the
  s.p. for these speeches may have been
  'Scar.', which a compositor, not recognizing the Soldier's *alter ego*, might
  plausibly have interpreted as 'Eros'.
1 happy fortunate
4 kings . . . revolted See Appendix A.
7 Enobarbus The desertion of Domitius
  Ahenobarbus (a very minor character

  in Plutarch), Anthony's generosity in
  sending his treasure after him, and
  Domitius's death all occur in Plutarch
  just before Actium (see Appendix A).
  In the *Lives* it is the unnamed soldier
  corresponding to Scarrus who deserts
  in Egypt, after winning glory in the
  first battle of Alexandria (see Appendix
  A). The theatrical prominence given to
  Enobarbus's desertion and remorse here
  and in 4.9 may have been partly suggested by the remorse of Seleucus and
  Rodon for their betrayal of 'the bounteous Queen' at the equivalent point
  in Daniel's tragedy (4.805–1069).
10–11 Sir . . . him Eros means to reassure
  Anthony—since Enobarbus has not
  taken his belongings he cannot have
  deserted; but the information provides
  Anthony with the cue for a characteristic exhibition of magnanimity.

⌈SCARRUS⌉   Most certain.
ANTHONY Go, Eros, send his treasure after—do it,
  Detain no jot, I charge thee. Write to him—
  I will subscribe—gentle adieus and greetings;
  Say that I wish he never find more cause   15
  To change a master. O, my fortunes have
  Corrupted honest men! Dispatch.—Enobarbus!

                                              Exeunt

4.6   *Flourish. Enter Caesar and Agrippa, with*
        Enobarbus, and Dolabella

CAESAR
  Go forth, Agrippa, and begin the fight.
  Our will is Anthony be took alive—
  Make it so known.
AGRIPPA   Caesar, I shall.   *Exit*
CAESAR
  The time of universal peace is near.
  Prove this a prosperous day, the three-nooked world   5

17 Dispatch.—Enobarbus!] STEEVENS (*subs.*); Dispatch *Enobarbus.* F1; Dispatch *Eros* F2
exeunt] ROWE; *Exit* F
  4.6.0 *Enter . . . Agrippa*] This edition; *Enter Agrippa, Cæsar* F   3 *Exit*] CAPELL (*subs.*);
not in F

14 subscribe sign
4.6.0 *Enter . . . Agrippa* F reverses the
  normal order of precedence for no apparent reason. Ridley conjectures that
  entry by different doors is indicated,
  but this seems unlikely. Perhaps one
  of the names was left out and inserted
  later in the manuscript, resulting in an
  accidental ordering by the compositor.
4 time of universal peace Christian commentary habitually associated the *Pax
  Romana* established under Octavius
  (the Emperor Augustus) with the *Pax
  Christiana* ushered in by the beginning
  of the Christian era, with which it
  roughly coincided; the *loci classici* for
  such interpretation were Virgil's *Aeneid*
  6.791–5 and especially his *Fourth
  Eclogue*, which prophesied the advent
  of a new Golden Age following the
  birth of Augustus's son in terms that
  were readily transferable to Christ. In
  the final chorus of Garnier's *Tragedy of
  Antony*, loosely modelled on Virgil's
  poem, a group of Roman soldiers pro-

claim that, following their defeat of
Antony, war and discord will end and
'our banks shall cherish now | the
branchy pale-hued bow | of Olive'
(4.1758–60 ; Bullough, p. 400). See
also note to 1.1.17. For a discussion
of this passage that relates it to the
play's pattern of Christian allusions,
see Andrew Fichter, '*Antony and Cleopatra*: the Time of Universal Peace',
SSu 33 (1980), pp. 99–111. The
Fourth Eclogue had developed a particular currency in England because of
its association of the new Golden Age
with the return of the virgin goddess
Astraea—one of the cult names appro-
priated to Queen Elizabeth; but here
the prophecy is probably meant to flatter James I's notion of himself as the
peacemaker of Europe.
5 three-nooked three-cornered. Various
explanations have been offered: it refers to the political division of the
world between the triumvirs; or to its
racial division amongst the offspring of

Shall bear the olive freely.
Enter a Messenger

MESSENGER   Anthony
Is come into the field.

CAESAR   Go charge Agrippa
Plant those that have revolted in the van,
That Anthony may seem to spend his fury
Upon himself.   10
Exeunt all but Enobarbus

ENOBARBUS
Alexas did revolt, and went to Jewry on
Affairs of Anthony; there did dissuade
Great Herod to incline himself to Caesar,
And leave his master, Anthony. For this pains,
Caesar hath hanged him. Camidius and the rest   15
That fell away have entertainment, but
No honourable trust. I have done ill,
Of which I do accuse myself so sorely
That I will joy no more.
Enter a Soldier of Caesar's

SOLDIER   Enobarbus, Anthony
Hath after thee sent all thy treasure, with   20
His bounty overplus. The messenger
Came on my guard, and at thy tent is now
Unloading of his mules.

ENOBARBUS   I give it you.

SOLDIER
Mock not, Enobarbus,
I tell you true. Best you safed the bringer   25

---

8 van] F (vant)   10.1 *all but Enobarbus*] CAPELL *(subs.)*; *not in* F   15 Camidius] F
(Camindius)   19 more] F2; mote F1

the three sons of Noah (Shem, Ham, and Japhet); or to its geographical division into the three continents of Europe, Asia, and Africa; or to its elemental division into earth, sea, and sky (Ovid's *triplex mundus*).

6 **olive** (emblem of peace)
9–10 **Anthony ... himself** Caesar's order turns the battle into an enactment of Anthony's self-division.
11–15 **Alexas ... hanged him** For Plu-

tarch's description of this episode, in which it is Herod who executes Alexas (albeit at Caesar's behest) see Appendix A.

12 **dissuade** Sometimes emended to 'persuade'; but Johnson originally justified 'dissuade' as meaning 'persuade away from his allegiance'.
16 **entertainment** maintenance, pay
22 **on my guard** during my watch
25 **safed** gave safe-conduct to

Out of the host—I must attend mine office,
Or would have done't myself. Your Emperor
Continues still a Jove.   *Exit*

ENOBARBUS

I am alone the villain of the earth,
And feel I am so most. O Anthony,   30
Thou mine of bounty, how wouldst thou have paid
My better service, when my turpitude
Thou dost so crown with gold! This blows my heart—
If swift thought break it not, a swifter mean
Shall outstrike thought; but thought will do't, I feel.   35
I fight against thee? No, I will go seek
Some ditch wherein to die—the foul'st best fits
My latter part of life.   *Exit*

4.7   *Alarum. Enter Agrippa* ⌈ *with drummers and*
         trumpeters ⌉

AGRIPPA

Retire! We have engaged ourselves too far—
Caesar himself has work, and our oppression
Exceeds what we expected.   *Exeunt*

33–6 heart— | If . . . not, a . . . thought; but . . . do't, I feel. | I . . . thee?] ROWE (*subs*);
hart, | If . . . not: a . . . thought, but . . . doo't. I feele | I . . . thee: F
  4.7.0.1–2 *Alarum . . . trumpeters*] OXFORD, *after* F ('*Alarum, Drummes and Trumpets.* |
Enter Agrippa')   3 *Exeunt*] CAPELL; *Exit.* F

26 **office** duties
28 **a Jove** i.e. godlike in his generosity
29 **alone the villain** the single most vil-
    lainous person
31 **mine of bounty** cf. *1 Henry IV* 3.1.
    164–5 'as bountiful | As mines of
    India' (Case). Antony's liberality and
    bounty, stressed in this scene, as well
    as in Cleopatra's great aria of lament
    (5.5.77–93), is one of the themes
    of Plutarch's characterization.
33 **blows** Usually glossed as 'swells', but
    'break' and 'outstrike' suggest that
    'beats upon' may be the more appro-
    priate sense. Perhaps a quibble on the
    two is intended.
34, 35 **thought** Usually glossed as
    'melancholy', but this seems not quite
    appropriate to 'swift thought'; perhaps
    as Enobarbus reiterates the word its
    sense slides between 'grief' and 'think-
    ing'. Compare his earlier 'Think, and

die' (3.13.1). For the proverbial swiftness of thought see Dent T240.
4.7–9 For Plutarch's description of this
    skirmish, significantly expanded by
    Shakespeare, so that in theatrical
    terms it seems to bulk as large as
    Actium itself, see Appendix A.
4.7.0.1–2 *Alarum . . . drummers and trum-*
    peters The Oxford editors point out
    that F's *Drummes and Trumpets* seems
    redundant as a gloss on '*Flourish*' (a
    call normally sounded by drums and
    trumpets), and plausibly suggest that
    it refers to musicians who accompany
    Agrippa on stage. This removes the
    necessity to add '*and others*' to the
    stage direction as most editors do. Ag-
    rippa's 'Retire' now becomes an order
    to sound the retreat.
  2 **has work** is in difficulties
    our oppression the pressure upon us

4.8   *Alarums. Enter Anthony, and Scarrus wounded*

SCARRUS

O my brave emperor, this is fought indeed!
Had we done so at first, we had droven them home
With clouts about their heads.

ANTHONY   Thou bleed'st apace.

SCARRUS

I had a wound here that was like a T,
But now 'tis made an H.

    Retreat sounded far off

ANTHONY   They do retire.   5

SCARRUS

We'll beat 'em into bench-holes. I have yet
Room for six scotches more.

    Enter Eros

EROS

They are beaten, sir, and our advantage serves
For a fair victory.

SCARRUS   Let us score their backs,
And snatch 'em up as we take hares, behind.   10
'Tis sport to maul a runner.

ANTHONY   I will reward thee—
Once for thy sprightly comfort, and tenfold
For thy good valour. Come thee on.

SCARRUS   I'll halt after.   *Exeunt*

4.9   *Alarum. Enter Anthony again in a march;*
    ⌈*drummers and trumpeters;*⌉ *Scarrus, with others.*

ANTHONY

We have beat him to his camp. Run one before,

4.8] OXFORD; *Eds. mark no division here*   5 Retreat . . . off] Capell (*subs.*); 'Far off.' (*after* 'heads', l. 3) F
   4.9.0.2 *drummers and trumpeters*] OXFORD (*after* Wilson); *not in* F

4.8. The traditional scene division treats this scene as a continuation of 4.7; the point is a purely technical one, given the practice of continuous staging in the Shakespearian theatre, but since the stage is cleared after Agrippa's speech it is inconsistent not to mark these as separate scenes.

2 **droven** (old form of 'driven')

3 **clouts** (1) blows; (2) cloths, bandages
5 **an H** Punning on 'an ache' (often sounded 'aitch' in Shakespeare's time).
6 **bench-holes** latrine holes
7 **scotches** wounds
9 **score** cut; whip
11 **runner** coward (one who runs away)
12 **sprightly** cheerful, spirited
13 **halt after** limp behind

And let the Queen know of our gests.   ⌈*Exit a Soldier*⌉
                                Tomorrow,
Before the sun shall see's, we'll spill the blood
That has today escaped. I thank you all,
For doughty-handed are you, and have fought   5
Not as you served the cause, but as't had been
Each man's like mine. You have shown all Hectors.
Enter the city, clip your wives, your friends,
Tell them your feats, whilst they with joyful tears
Wash the congealment from your wounds, and kiss   10
The honoured gashes whole.
    Enter Cleopatra
(*To Scarrus*)   .   Give me thy hand—
To this great fairy I'll commend thy acts,
Make her thanks bless thee. (*To Cleopatra*) O thou day
    o'th'world,
Chain mine armed neck; leap thou, attire and all,
Through proof of harness to my heart, and there   15
Ride on the pants triumphing!
CLEOPATRA   Lord of lords!
O infinite virtue, com'st thou smiling from
The world's great snare uncaught?
ANTHONY   My nightingale,
We have beat them to their beds. What girl! Though grey
Do something mingle with our younger brown,   20

---

2 gests] THEOBALD (*conj.* Warburton); guests F   *Exit a Soldier*] OXFORD; *not in* F
18 My] F2; Mine FI

4.9.2 **gests** deeds; even in 1606 the word
    had a slightly archaic, chivalric ring
    to it
6–7 **Not ... mine** not as if you were mere-
    ly obeying orders, but as if each one
    of you had as much at stake as I
7 **You ... Hectors** you have all behaved
    as gallantly as Hector. The allusion to
    the legendary Trojan hero is semi-
    proverbial, but may have larger reson-
    ances in a play which, like the *Iliad*,
    involves the overthrow of an oriental
    empire by an ascendant occidental
    power. The death of Hector at the
    hands of Achilles, a turning point in
    the Greek siege of Troy, provides the
    tragic catastrophe of Shakespeare's
    own earlier play, *Troilus and Cressida*.
8 **clip** embrace

12 **fairy** enchantress; the word has power-
    ful associations with the world of chival-
    ric romance (compare Spenser's incar-
    nation of Queen Elizabeth as *The Faerie
    Queene*; and see note to 1.2.128).
13 **day light.** Cf. Cleopatra's descriptions of
    Anthony, 4.16.86, 5.2.80–1.
15 **proof of harness** impenetrable armour
    (more usually 'proof' or 'proof armour')
16 **Ride ... triumphing** ride in triumph
    on my beating heart; Anthony ima-
    gines his heart as a triumphal cha-
    riot bearing Cleopatra as Queen of
    Love or mortal Venus. The image
    derives ultimately from the Triumph of
    Love in Petrarch's *Trionfi*. Accent on
    the second syllable of 'triumphing'.
17 **virtue** valour (Latin *virtus*)
20 **something** somewhat

274

Yet ha' we a brain that nourishes our nerves,
And can get goal for goal of youth. Behold this man,
Commend unto his lips thy favouring hand—
Kiss it, my warrior.
           Scarrus kisses Cleopatra's hand
                         He hath fought today,
As if a god, in hate of mankind, had   25
Destroyed in such a shape.
CLEOPATRA   I'll give thee, friend,
An armour all of gold—it was a king's.
ANTHONY
He has deserved it, were it carbuncled
Like holy Phoebus' car. Give me thy hand.
Through Alexandria make a jolly march;   30
Bear our hacked targets, like the men that owe them.
Had our great palace the capacity
To camp this host, we all would sup together
And drink carouses to the next day's fate,
Which promises royal peril. Trumpeters,   35
With brazen din blast you the city's ear,
Make mingle with our rattling taborins,
That heaven and earth may strike their sounds
           together,

---

23 favouring] THEOBALD (*conj.* Thirlby); savouring F   24.1 *Scarrus ... hand*] OXFORD;
not in F

21 **nerves** sinews
22 **get goal ... youth** give youth as good
   as it gets (Anthony is once again
   thinking of the 'boy' Caesar)
24 **Kiss it, my warrior** Peter Hall's production stressed the ironic visual echo
   here of Thidias's handkissing in 3.13.
25 **mankind** (accent on first syllable)
28 **carbuncled** jewel-encrusted
29 **holy Phoebus' car** the chariot of the
   sun
31 **targets** shields
   like ... owe them Either 'in the spirited
   fashion proper to men who own such
   honourable weapons' (Johnson *subs*);
   or 'hack'd as much as the men to
   whom they belong' (Warburton).
33 **camp** accommodate
34 **carouses** toasts
35 **royal peril** great or extreme peril; but
   the oxymoronic sense of 'magnificent
   peril' fits Anthony's exalted mood of

chivalric self-display (cf. 'royal occupation' 4.4.17). Perhaps a quibble on the
literal sense of 'danger to the queen
and kingdom' is also involved.
36 **brazen** (1) brass; (2) bold
37 **taborins** OED describes the *taborin* as
   a small drum played in combination
   with a flute, a type of tabor; but its
   own examples suggest that the word
   was also applied to the larger military
   drums used with trumpets. Naylor, citing this passage and another from *Troilus*, concludes that the term was used
   for 'the full-sized military drum' (p.
   157).
38 **That heaven ... together** so that their
   mingled sounds echo back and forth
   from earth to heaven (cf. *Hamlet*
   5.2.222–4 : 'And let the kettle to the
   trumpet speak, | The trumpet to the
   cannoneer without, | The cannons to
   the heavens, the heaven to earth').

Applauding our approach!

Sound drums and trumpets. Exeunt

4.10   *Enter a Sentry, and his company of the watch;*
       Enobarbus follows apart

SENTRY
   If we be not relieved within this hour,
   We must return to th'court of guard. The night
   Is shiny, and they say we shall embattle
 ˙ By th'second hour i'th'morn.

FIRST WATCH   This last day was
   A shrewd one to's.

ENOBARBUS   O bear me witness, night—   5

SECOND WATCH
   What man is this?

FIRST WATCH   Stand close, and list him.

ENOBARBUS
   Be witness to me, O thou blessèd moon,
   When men revolted shall upon record
   Bear hateful memory, poor Enobarbus did
   Before thy face repent.

SENTRY   Enobarbus?

SECOND WATCH   Peace—   10

39.1 *Sound . . . trumpets*] This edition (*after* OXFORD); *not in* F
   4.10.0.1 *Sentry*] F1 (*Centerie*); *Centery* F2; *Century* F3   *of the watch*] BEVINGTON
(*subs.*); *not in* F   0.2 *apart*] This edition; *not in* F   4 FIRST WATCH] F ('1 *Watch.*')
6 ff. SECOND WATCH] F ('2')   FIRST WATCH] F ('1')

4.10 The contrast between the nervous
   quiet of this night-scene and the noise
   and colour of what has gone before
   creates a powerful theatrical effect,
   somewhat resembling the celebrated
   juxtaposition of the gloomy battle-
   ments and brilliantly illuminated court
   in the opening of *Hamlet*.
0.1 *Sentry* The textual history of this
   word is slightly peculiar. F2's modernization of *-ie* to *-y* is comprehensible,
   but F3's alteration of *-e-* to *-u-* is less
   easy to account for. *Century* was certainly a viable mid-century spelling for
   Sentry, but there seems no obvious
   reason why it should have been preferred to *Centery*. Spevack asserts that
   Centerie may mean centurion, but *OED*
   provides no authority for this. Given,

however, that the Sentry seems to be
distinguished from the rest of the Watch
as some sort of subordinate officer ('his
company'), I have wondered whether
the original copy may not indeed have
read '*Cent.*' for Centurion.
2   **court of guard** guard room, or muster
    place
3   **embattle** prepare for battle; take up
    battle stations
5   **shrewd** difficult, bad
6   **close** hidden
    list listen
8–9 **Men   revolted . . . memory** deserters
    shall be remembered with hatred in
    the annals. Compare Enobarbus's ear-
    lier desire to 'earn a place in the story'
    (3.13.46). *record* is accented on the
    second syllable.

Hark further.

ENOBARBUS

 O sovereign mistress of true melancholy,
 The poisonous damp of night disponge upon me,
 That life, a very rebel to my will,
 May hang no longer on me. Throw my heart   15
 Against the flint and hardness of my fault,
 Which being dried with grief, will break to powder,
 And finish all foul thoughts. O Anthony,
 Nobler than my revolt is infamous,
 Forgive me in thine own particular,   20
 But let the world rank me in register
 A master-leaver, and a fugitive.
 O Anthony! O Anthony!   *He dies*

FIRST WATCH   Let's speak to him.

SENTRY

 Let's hear him, for the things he speaks
 May concern Caesar.

SECOND WATCH   Let's do so—but he sleeps.   25

SENTRY

 Swoons rather, for so bad a prayer as his

---

23 *He dies*] ROWE ('*Dies*'); *not in* F

12 **O . . . melancholy** the moon (supposed to have a governing influence on all forms of madness and instability, including melancholia)

13 **poisonous damp** night dew was supposed to be full of unhealthy exhalations. In *News from Graves-end* (1604), for example, Thomas Dekker describes the causes of the great plague of 1603 'From standing pools . . . From bogs; from rank and dampish fens, | From moorish breaths, and nasty dens, | The sun draws up contagious fumes, | Which falling down burst into rheums, | And thousand maladies beside, | By which our blood grows putrified . . . which, sucked in by our spirits, there flies | Swift poison through our arteries, | And (not resisted) straight it choaks | The heart with those pestiferous smoaks' (C3ᵛ–C4).
 disponge squeeze as from a sponge

17 **dried with grief** Such a condition in seventeenth-century physiology would be a sign of the extreme form of melancholy illness known as 'melancholy adust'. J. B. Bamborough, *The Little World of Man* (1952), p. 121, cites contemporary anatomical evidence of the parched hearts of those who supposedly died of melancholy.

20 **in . . . particular** for your own part
21 **rank . . . register** assess me in its records as
22 **fugitive** deserter
23 *He dies* Death from a broken heart was considered to be a matter of physiological fact in the seventeenth century. In 1600, for example, the autopsy of Margaret Ratcliffe, one of Queen Elizabeth's Maids of Honour, who expired from 'extreme grief' at the death of her brother, revealed 'certaine strings striped all over her heart'—evidently the broken heart strings whose 'crack' Princess Calantha announces in John Ford's *The Broken Heart*, ed. Brian Morris (1965), 5.3.77.

Was never yet for sleep.

FIRST WATCH   Go we to him.

SECOND WATCH

Awake, sir, awake; speak to us.

FIRST WATCH   Hear you, sir?

SENTRY

The hand of death hath raught him.

    Drums afar off

                       Hark, the drums

Demurely wake the sleepers. Let us bear him   30

To th'court of guard—he is of note. Our hour

Is fully out.

SECOND WATCH

Come on then, he may recover yet.

                      Exeunt with the body

4.11   *Enter Anthony and Scarrus, with their army*

ANTHONY

Their preparation is today by sea—

We please them not by land.

SCARRUS   For both, my lord.

ANTHONY

I would they'd fight i'th'fire, or i'th'air;

We'd fight there too. But this it is: our foot

Upon the hills adjoining to the city   5

Shall stay with us—order for sea is given,

They have put forth the haven—

33.1 *with the body*] CAPELL; *not in* F
   4.11.6–7 us—order . . . haven—] KNIGHT (*subs.*); vs, Order   Hauen. F

---

27 **for sleep** a prelude to sleep
29 **raught** Obsolete past participle of
  reach; here = 'grasped'.
  Drums The drums should probably
  continue as the watch leave the stage,
  turning their exeunt into the sem-
  blance of a funeral march for Enobarbus.
30 **Demurely** soberly, solemnly; in a subdued manner
31–2 **hour . . . out** time is up
4.11.3 **fire . . . Because** the contest is already being fought on land and sea (representing the elements of earth and

water) Anthony imagines extending it
to the regions of fire and air as well.
4–9 **But . . . endeavour** The detail is Plutarch's (see Appendix A).
4 **this** thus. For the use of 'this' see
  Schmidt, p. 1213.
  foot infantry
6–7 **order . . . haven** Metrically l. 7 is sus-
piciously incomplete, and many editors
assume that something is missing, but
if, as Knight suggested, Anthony's
naval orders are treated parenthetic-
ally, there are no difficulties with the
sense.

Where their appointment we may best discover,
And look on their endeavour.   *Exeunt*

4.12 *Enter Caesar, and his army*
CAESAR
But being charged, we will be still by land—
Which, as I take't, we shall, for his best force
Is forth to man his galleys. To the vales,
And hold our best advantage!   *Exeunt*

4.13 *Alarum afar off, as at a sea-fight. Enter Anthony*
        and Scarrus.
ANTHONY
Yet they are not joined. Where yon pine does stand
I shall discover all. I'll bring thee word
Straight how 'tis like to go.   *Exit*
SCARRUS   Swallows have built
In Cleopatra's sails their nests. The augurers
Say they know not, they cannot tell, look grimly,   5
And dare not speak their knowledge. Anthony
Is valiant, and dejected; and by starts
His fretted fortunes give him hope and fear

4.13.0.1 *Alarum . . . sea-fight*] F; *at l. 9* CAPELL   4 augurers] CAPELL (*conj.* Thirlby);
Auguries F; augures SINGER (*and conj.* Ridley *as Latin plural*); augurs POPE

8 **appointment** resolution, purpose. Ironically, in view of the imminent surrender of Anthony's fleet, the word
could also mean 'coming to terms of
capitulation'.
4.12.1 **But being charged** unless we are
attacked
    be still remain in a defensive posture
4 **hold . . . advantage** occupy the most
advantageous position
4.13.0.1 *Alarum . . . sea fight* Many editors transpose this direction to l. 3,
after Anthony's exit, or even to l. 9,
at the end of Scarrus's speech, on the
ground that it otherwise makes nonsense of his opening line; but F's typo-
graphy leaves the s.d. ambiguously
poised between the two scenes; perhaps, as Ridley suggests, the noise of
the sea-fight should fade out before
Anthony's entry, thus leaving the
audience better informed than he.
However, since Plutarch makes it plain

that no sea-battle was ever joined at
Alexandria, the direction probably signifies only a distant naval alarum, prelude to a fight that never actually
begins.
1 **Yet . . . joined** the battle has not yet
begun
3 **Swallows** Plutarch records this omen
as occurring before Actium (see Appendix A).
4 **sails** ships
    augurers augurs, soothsayers. This
seems to have been Shakespeare's preferred version of the term (see e.g.
Julius Caesar 2.1.200, *Coriolanus* 2.1.1,
Anthony 5.2.332), and would plausibly
account for F's misreading, 'auguries';
'*augures*' (plural of Latin '*augur*'), as
adopted by Singer and independently
conjectured by Ridley remains an outside possibility.
8 **fretted** (1) chequered; (2) wasted, decayed

Of what he has, and has not.
>   *Enter Anthony*
ANTHONY   All is lost!
This foul Egyptian hath betrayèd me.   10
My fleet hath yielded to the foe, and yonder
They cast their caps up, and carouse together
Like friends long lost. Triple-turned whore! 'Tis thou
Hast sold me to this novice, and my heart
Makes only wars on thee. Bid them all fly—   15
For when I am revenged upon my charm,
I have done all. Bid them all fly, be gone!
>   *Exit Scarrus*
O sun, thy uprise shall I see no more;
Fortune and Anthony part here, even here
Do we shake hands. All come to this? The hearts   20
That spanieled me at heels, to whom I gave
Their wishes, do discandy, melt their sweets
On blossoming Caesar; and this pine is barked,
That overtopped them all. Betrayed I am.
O this false soul of Egypt! this grave charm,   25
Whose eye becked forth my wars and called them
>   home,
Whose bosom was my crownet, my chief end,

17.1 *Exit Scarrus*] CAPELL; *not in* F   21 spanieled] HANMER; pannelled F

9–49 **All is lost ... she dies for't** For Plutarch's description of the abortive battle, see Appendix A.
13 **Triple-turned** Anthony probably has two things in mind: after her marriage to Ptolemy, Cleopatra had 'turned whore' three times in her adulterous liaisons with Julius Caesar, Gnaeus Pompey, and Anthony himself; but 'turned' also carries the sense of 'change sides, betray' and refers to the successive switches in political allegiance that accompanied her sexual alliances.
16, 25 **charm** enchantress
21 **spanieled ... heels** followed me like fawning spaniels. F's 'pannelled' may reflect the dialect spelling 'spannel' for 'spaniel'.
22 **discandy** dissolve
23 **barked** stripped bare (and therefore destroyed)
24–5 **Betrayed ... Egypt** While the F

punctuation of this passage makes perfect sense, 'Betrayed I am' seems a little weak on its own, and I am inclined to think that what Shakespeare may have written was 'Betrayed I am | O' this false soul of Egypt!' If, as John Jowett and Gary Taylor have argued (see Editorial Procedures, p. 133 n. 1), 'O' was Shakespeare's preferred form of the exclamation, it might easily be confused with an abbreviated 'of'. Although Shakespeare seems normally to have used 'by' rather than 'of' with *betrayed*, the number of instances is less than decisive, and the prepositional 'of' with passive verbs was a standard form up to *c.*1600 (see *OED of* prep. V. 15, and Schmidt, p. 795).
25 **grave** (1) serious, sincere seeming; (2) mortally dangerous
27 **crownet** coronet; i.e. the supreme object of all my actions. The language

Like a right gypsy hath at fast and loose
Beguiled me to the very heart of loss.
What Eros, Eros!

Enter Cleopatra

Ah, thou spell! Avaunt!   30

CLEOPATRA

Why is my lord enraged against his love?

ANTHONY

Vanish, or I shall give thee thy deserving,
And blemish Caesar's triumph. Let him take thee,
And hoist thee up to the shouting plebeians—
Follow his chariot, like the greatest spot   35
Of all thy sex; most monster-like be shown
For poor'st diminutives, for dolts; and let
Patient Octavia plough thy visage up
With her preparèd nails.   *Exit Cleopatra*
                     'Tis well thou'rt gone,
If it be well to live; but better 'twere   40
Thou fell'st into my fury, for one death
Might have prevented many. Eros, ho!
The shirt of Nessus is upon me—teach me

here plays with one of the most popular of Latin tags, *Finis coronat opus*
('the end crowns all'), to which Cleopatra's coronation-in-death will give a
literalizing enactment.

28 **gypsy** See note to 1.1.10.
    fast and loose a cheating game at
    which gypsies were especially adept, in
    which a carefully coiled belt or cord
    appeared to be skewered to a table
    ('made fast'), but would prove to be
    loose as soon as it was pulled away.
    Gulls were duped into betting on the
    seemingly fast attachment of the cord.
    Another variant which involved trick
    knots may be the appropriate one here
    since it would pick up the familiar
    metaphor of the love-knot which also
    lies behind Anthony's conceit at
    3.11.56.
29 **Beguiled** charmed; cheated
    heart of loss utmost possible loss; but
    the unusually strong stress that falls
    on 'heart' after five very lightly stressed
    syllables is likely to bring out other
    resonances in the word, suggesting at

once a loss felt in the very heart, and
the loss of Anthony's own heart (both
as the source of courage and the symbol of his love).

30 **Avaunt** begone
33 **Caesar's triumph** See note to 3.1.0.2;
    Anthony's is the first of a series of
    speeches in which the protagonists'
    imagination focuses more and more
    desperately on the humiliating theatre
    of being led captive in Rome.
34 **plebeians** (accent on first syllable)
35 **spot** blemish, defilement
36 **monster-like be shown** be displayed
    like a creature in a freak-show; pun-
    ning on the folk-etymology which
    derived *monster* from Latin *monstrare* =
    show, rather than *monere* = warn.
37 **diminutives** stunted weaklings
38 **Patient** long-suffering. Anthony's bru-
    tal reminder of Octavia's rivalry is
    enough to drive Cleopatra from the
    stage.
39 **preparèd** specially grown, or sharp-
    ened for the purpose
43 **shirt of Nessus** One of a series of allu-
    sions associating Anthony with the

Alcides, thou mine ancestor, thy rage:
Let me lodge Lichas on the horns o'th'moon,   45
And with those hands that grasped the heaviest club,
Subdue my worthiest self. The witch shall die!
To the young Roman boy she hath sold me, and I fall
Under this plot—she dies for't. Eros, ho!   *Exit*

4.14 *Enter Cleopatra, Charmian, Iras, Mardian*
CLEOPATRA
Help me, my women! O, he's more mad
Than Telamon for his shield, the boar of Thessaly
Was never so embossed.
CHARMIAN   To th'monument,
There lock yourself, and send him word you are dead.
The soul and body rive not more in parting   5

mythology of his supposed ancestor,
Hercules. In revenge for the attempted
rape of his wife, Deianira, Hercules
slew the centaur, Nessus, with poisoned arrows. In revenge, Nessus
presented Deianira with some of his
poisoned blood in the guise of a love-
charm, to use if her husband were ever
unfaithful. Jealous of the Oechalian
princess, Iolé, Deianira sent Hercules a
garment soaked in Nessus's charm.
When he donned it, the poison began
to devour him; but his attempts to
remove it resulted only in his tearing
away pieces of his own flesh. In his
dying rage Hercules flung his servant
Lichas, who had brought the garment,
into the sea. Although Deianira was
the largely innocent agent of the centaur's malice, Anthony seems to imagine this as a kind of Delilah story,
illustrative of woman's proverbial treachery. In his version the motif of self-
destruction, implicit in the garment
that tears away the wearer's flesh, is
made explicit by Anthony's imagining
himself simultaneously in the Hercules
and Lichas roles ('subdue my worthiest
self'). Anthony's sword is his equivalent for the club which traditionally
emblematized Hercules' heroic manhood.
  Peter Hall saw Anthony in this scene
as 'going to pieces physically', telling
Hopkins 'I believe he gets the shakes

on "The shirt of Nessus is upon me." '
(Lowen, p. 87.)

47 **worthiest** noblest, most heroic
48 **young Roman boy** Editors worry about
    the hypermetricality of the line and,
    finding 'young . . . boy' tautologous,
    suggest that Shakespeare probably in-
    tended 'Roman' to substitute for
    'young', but forgot to cancel the latter.
    But the alleged tautology is only an
    over-emphatic expression of contempt;
    if the unstressed syllables 'To the', 'she
    hath', and 'and I' are slurred in a way
    that Anthony's rage makes natural,
    the result is a perfectly manageable
    five-stress line, with a striking dra-
    matic emphasis on 'young Roman boy'.
4.14 The story of Cleopatra's panic is once
    again Plutarch's (see Appendix A).
2 **Telamon** Telamonian Ajax ran mad
    and killed himself when defeated by
    Ulysses in a contest for the armour and
    celebrated shield of Achilles. Cleopatra
    is made to echo Anthony's own theme
    of heroic frenzy.
    boar of Thessaly better known as the
    Calydonian boar; sent by Diana to
    ravage the kingdom of Calydon, it was
    finally slaughtered by Meleager, but
    not before it had killed many heroes.
3 **embossed** driven to extremity; foaming
    at the mouth with distress (like a
    hunted animal)
5 **rive** split, tear asunder

Than greatness going off.

CLEOPATRA   To th'monument!
Mardian, go tell him I have slain myself;
Say that the last I spoke was 'Anthony',
And word it, prithee, piteously. Hence, Mardian,
And bring me how he takes my death. To th'monument!   10
                                                    Exeunt

4.15 *Enter Anthony and Eros*

ANTHONY
Eros, thou yet behold'st me?

EROS   Ay, noble lord.

ANTHONY
Sometime we see a cloud that's dragonish,
A vapour sometime like a bear or lion,
A towered citadel, a pendant rock,
A forkèd mountain, or blue promontory   5
With trees upon't that nod unto the world
And mock our eyes with air. Thou hast seen these
    signs—
They are black vesper's pageants.

EROS   Ay, my lord.

ANTHONY
That which is now a horse, even with a thought
The rack dislimns, and makes it indistinct   10

4.14.10 death. To] POPE; death to F
4.15.4 towered] ROWE; toward F   10 dislimns] THEOBALD; dislimes F; distains OXFORD

6 **greatness going off** greatness when it
   deserts its owner
8 **'Anthony'** Ironically this was actually
   the last word spoken by Enobarbus.
4.15 Anthony's suicide follows closely
   Plutarch's account (see Appendix A);
   but Shakespeare gives particular dramatic stress to Anthony's botching of
   his heroic suicide—an effect which can
   help to overcome the problem of potential anticlimax created by the hero's
   dying in Act 4.
2–14 **Sometime we see . . . this visible
   shape** Anthony's discovery of himself
   as a creature of mutable 'becoming'
   rather than absolute 'being' depends
   on a sceptical understanding of human

subjectivity of the kind widely popu-
larized by the *Essays* of Montaigne at
the beginning of the seventeenth century. See Introduction pp. 82–5.
7 **signs** images; portents
8 **black vesper's pageants** the spectacular
   displays of evening, as night begins to
   fall; but 'black . . . pageants' are also
   bound to suggest funeral rites and the
   Triumph of Death.
10 **The rack dislimns** the drifting cloud
   obliterates (*limn* = paint); but Jones
   detects word-play 'involving the idea
   of a *body* . . . being "dislimbed"—torn
   limb from limb—upon a rack'. Theobald's emendation of F's 'dislimes'
   makes good sense and 'dislimn' seems

As water is in water.

EROS   It does, my lord.

ANTHONY

My good knave Eros, now thy captain is
Even such a body: here I am Anthony,
Yet cannot hold this visible shape, my knave.
I made these wars for Egypt, and the Queen—   15
Whose heart I thought I had, for she had mine,
Which, whilst it was mine, had annexed unto't
A million more, now lost—she, Eros, has
Packed cards with Caesar, and false played my glory
Unto an enemy's triumph.   20
Nay, weep not, gentle Eros, there is left us
Ourselves to end ourselves.

　　Enter Mardian

　　　　　　　　　　　O, thy vile lady,
She has robbed me of my sword!　eliminated
　　　　　　　　　　　　　　　　masculinity

14–15 shape, my knave. | I] ROWE 1714 (*subs.*); shape (my Knave) | I F   19 Caesar]
ROWE; *Cæsars* F

a plausible reversal of *limn* = paint. A
case might be made, however, for F's
'dislimes' as a coinage meaning 'paints
out with lime whitewash'—the fate of
many church paintings in the 16th
cent. Since no other instance of 'dislimn' is recorded in *OED* before De
Quincey's citation of it as 'a Shakespearian word' (1826), this word too
must (if correct) be a Shakespearian
coinage—but one which is arguably
warranted by a contextual echo of the
proverbial 'to limn in water' (Dent
W114; and cf. *OED limn* 4); see also
Bacon *Poems* (1620), cited in *OED*:
'Who then to frail Mortality shall trust
| But limns the water'). This is per-
haps sufficient to discount Oxford's
'distains' (= deprive of its colour,
brightness, or splendour), an ingenious
alternative which has the advantage
of being a well-established term.

11 **as water is in water** In 'Of Isis and
Osiris' Plutarch explains the dissolution of the Nile into the sea as an
enactment of Osiris's death at the
hands of Typhon: 'Typhon is the sea
(into which Nilus falling loseth himself, and is dispatched here and there),

unless it be that portion which the
earth receiveth and whereby it is made
fertile' (*Morals*, p. 1300).

19 **Packed cards** stacked the deck
20 **Unto ... triumph** Anthony's speech
breaks off, either because he chokes on
his mounting rage or because he suddenly notices that Eros has broken
down. The melancholy resignation to
which he returns in the following two
lines is broken in turn by a fresh erup-
tion of rage provoked by Mardian's
entry. The violent shifts of mood characteristic of Anthony after Actium, as
well as enacting the transformations of
his cloud conceit, match Cleopatra's
mercurial 'becomings' in the first half
of the play.
　triumph Punning on the 'triumph' or
(in the modern abbreviation) 'trump'
card. The figure here seems to require
that 'glory' also play on the terminology of gaming; perhaps it stands for
king or *court card*, but *OED* records no
such meaning.

23 **robbed ... sword** Strikingly echoes
several versions of the Mars and Venus
motif, notably the painting by Veronese
(see Fig. 11), in which one of Venus's
putti holds up the god's sword, emble-

MARDIAN   No, Anthony,
My mistress loved thee, and her fortunes mingled
With thine entirely.
ANTHONY   Hence, saucy eunuch, peace!   25
She hath betrayed me, and shall die the death.
MARDIAN
Death of one person can be paid but once;
And that she has discharged. What thou wouldst do
Is done unto thy hand. The last she spake
Was 'Anthony, most noble Anthony!'   30
Then in the midst a tearing groan did break
The name of Anthony—it was divided
Between her heart and lips; she rendered life
Thy name so buried in her.
ANTHONY   Dead then?
MARDIAN   Dead.
ANTHONY
Unarm, Eros, the long day's task is done,   35
And we must sleep. (*To Mardian*) That thou depart'st
    hence safe
Does pay thy labour richly. Go.   *Exit Mardian*
                         Off! Pluck off!
    Eros helps Anthony to unarm

37.1 *Eros . . . unarm*] WILSON (*subs.*); *not in* F

matic of his aggressive masculinity, as
if to hold at bay the warrior's horse
which stands for uncurbed passion.

26 **die the death** be put to death—as
Johnson pointed out the phrase has a
solemn legal ring (notes to *Measure*
2.4.165).
27 **Death . . . once** Dent M219: 'A man
can die but once'.
29 **done . . . hand** already done without
exertion on your part (*OED hand* sb.
34*c*)
29–34 **The last . . . her** Ironically Mardian's fiction gives a fairly true account
of *Enobarbus's* death.
31 **tearing** harrowing, causing a sensation as of rending (*OED*—which cites
this as the earliest recorded occurrence
of this participial adjective)
33–4 **she rendered . . . her** Most editors insert a comma after 'life' and interpret
Mardian to mean: 'She surrendered

life, and thus your name was buried
in her', or 'her name being thus buried
in her, she surrendered life'. But F's
punctuation makes perfectly good, if
conceited, sense: Anthony's name, according to a familiar erotic trope, has
been 'buried' in Cleopatra's heart; as
she dies the name escapes her lips, so
that she yields it up, as it were, to life
again. Mardian's conceit contrives to
imply, among other things, that Cleopatra has sacrificed herself in order to
preserve Anthony's life.
35 **Unarm, Eros** Shakespeare's stress on
the name of Anthony's servant, which
is only passingly mentioned in Plutarch, repeatedly emphasizes the emblematic possibilities of the scene, with its
rhetorical conflation of love and death.
36 **thou** Takes a strong stress here, emphasizing the contemptuous use of the
intimate singular form of the pronoun.
Cf. Appendix C.

The sevenfold shield of Ajax cannot keep
The battery from my heart. O, cleave my sides!
Heart, once be stronger than thy continent,   40
Crack thy frail case! Apace, Eros, apace!
No more a soldier. Bruisèd pieces, go,
You have been nobly borne.—From me awhile.

Exit Eros

I will o'ertake thee, Cleopatra, and
Weep for my pardon. So it must be, for now   45
All length is torture. Since the torch is out,
Lie down and stray no farther. Now all labour
Mars what it does; yea, very force entangles
Itself with strength. Seal then, and all is done.
Eros!—I come, my queen.—Eros!—Stay for me.   50
Where souls do couch on flowers we'll hand in hand,
And with our sprightly port make the ghosts gaze.
Dido and her Aeneas shall want troops,

Classical allusion

38 **sevenfold shield of Ajax** Cf. Ovid, *Metamorphoses* (trans. Arthur Golding, 1593), 13.2, 'The owner of the sevenfold shield, to these did Ajax rise'. Ajax's shield was of brass, backed with six layers of oxhide.
39 **battery** violent assault (as with a battering ram)
39–41 **cleave … case** The image echoes Philo's description of the heroic Anthony (1.1.6–8), confirming its implication of something self-destructive in the Herculean ideal itself.
40 **thy continent** what contains you
42 **Bruisèd pieces** dented armour
46 **length** extension of my life
   torch i.e. Cleopatra, the light of his life, is dead. The torch was a classical symbol of life, and an extinguished or inverted brand was often used in memorial sculpture to signify death. There is also a melancholy echo of Anthony's earlier defiant desire 'to burn this night with torches' (4.3.41).
47–9 **Now … strength** These paradoxes of self-confounding power may have been suggested by the concluding lines of Daniel's final chorus 'Is greatness of this sort, | That greatness greatness mars, | And wracks itself, self driven, | On rocks of her own might' (Bullough, p. 449).

48–9 **force … strength** i.e. as a powerful animal entangles itself in a net by the force of its exertion to escape
49 **Seal** finish
51–4 **Where … ours** An imitation, in the emulatory Renaissance tradition of *paragone*, of Virgil's description of that part of the Elysian fields given over to lovers. Cf. e.g. the speech by the Ghost of Andrea which opens Kyd's *The Spanish Tragedy*.
   couch lie
52 **sprightly** (1) spirited, lively; (2) ghostly
   port bearing; style of behaviour; dignified conduct
53 **Dido … Aeneas** Chosen as types of tragic lovers; but ironically Aeneas, upon whose destiny depended the future foundation of Rome, chose to place his public duty before his passion for the African queen. He sailed for Italy, leaving the distraught Dido to kill herself. Virgil's *Aeneid* implicitly presents the hero as a type of Augustus (Octavius Caesar), the founder of imperial Rome. This celebrated epic is among several classical analogues which supply a kind of unspoken commentary on the action of *Anthony*—see Introduction pp. 5–9.
   want troops lack followers

And all the haunt be ours. Come, Eros, Eros!
   Enter Eros
EROS
What would my lord?
ANTHONY   Since Cleopatra died,   55
I have lived in such dishonour that the gods
Detest my baseness. I, that with my sword
Quartered the world, and o'er green Neptune's back
With ships made cities, condemn myself to lack
The courage of a woman, less noble mind   60
Than she which by her death our Caesar tells
'I am conqueror of myself.' Thou art sworn, Eros,
That when the exigent should come—which now
Is come indeed—when I should see behind me
Th'inevitable prosecution of   65
Disgrace and horror, that on my command,
Thou then wouldst kill me. Do't—the time is come.
Thou strik'st not me; 'tis Caesar thou defeat'st.
Put colour in thy cheek.
EROS   The gods withhold me!
Shall I do that which all the Parthian darts,   70
Though enemy, lost aim and could not?
ANTHONY   Eros,
Wouldst thou be windowed in great Rome, and see
Thy master thus with pleached arms, bending down
His corrigible neck, his face subdued
To penetrative shame, whilst the wheeled seat   75

---

54 **all the haunt be ours** everyone will attend on us (with an obvious pun on 'haunt')

59 **ships . . . cities** Shakespeare may be remembering Lucius Florus's description of Anthony's fleet at Actium: 'their fights were raised so high with decks, and turrets, as they resembled castles, and cities, making the very sea groan under' (Bullough, p. 337).

59–60 **condemn . . . less noble mind** i.e. 'condemn myself for lacking even the courage of a woman, [and for having] a less noble mind'; the awkwardness of the condensed expression might suggest corruption, but the reading is confirmed by the corresponding passage in North: 'I am indeed condemned to be

judged of less courage and noble mind than a woman' (see Appendix A).

63 **exigent** moment of extreme need

65 **inevitable prosecution** pursuit from which there is no escape

69 **Put . . . cheek** i.e. pluck up courage

72 **windowed** placed in a window (to watch Caesar's triumph—or perhaps placed there on display). Apparently a Shakespearian coinage: the earliest citation of the verb 'window', and the only example of this particular usage.

73 **pleached** bound, or folded (as in the conventional posture of a melancholic)

74 **corrigible** submissive, prepared for correction or punishment

75 **penetrative** piercing
    wheeled seat triumphal chariot. The

Of fortunate Caesar, drawn before him, branded
His baseness that ensued?

EROS   I would not see't.

ANTHONY

Come then—for with a wound I must be cured.
Draw that thy honest sword, which thou hast worn
Most useful for thy country.

EROS   O sir, pardon me.   80

ANTHONY

When I did make thee free, swor'st thou not then
To do this when I bade thee? Do it at once,
Or thy precedent services are all
But accidents unpurposed. Draw, and come.

EROS

Turn from me then that noble countenance,   85
Wherein the worship of the whole world lies.

ANTHONY *(turning from him)* Lo thee!

EROS

My sword is drawn.

ANTHONY   Then let it do at once
The thing why thou hast drawn it.

EROS   My dear master,

My captain, and my emperor, let me say   90
Before I strike this bloody stroke, farewell.

ANTHONY 'Tis said man, and farewell.

EROS

Farewell, great chief. Shall I strike now?

ANTHONY   Now, Eros.

EROS Why, there then!
      Eros stabs himself
                        Thus I do escape the sorrow

---

87 *turning from him*] ROWE; *not in* F   94 *Eros stabs himself*] OXFORD; *Kills himselfe.* F
(*after 'Eros', l. 93*)

image of formal triumph will recall the
processional entry of Ventidius in 3.1.
OED's earliest example of the adjective
'wheeled'.

76 **fortunate** The sense of the word is
  stronger than for us: 'blessed by the
  goddess Fortune'.
76–7 **branded . . . ensued** marked, like a

brand on a criminal, the abject state
of the man following him

79 **honest** honourable
83 **precedent** previous (accent on second
  syllable)
86 **worship** honour, worthiness, worth. Perhaps also suggesting the idea of Anthony
  as an object of universal adulation.

288

Of Anthony's death.   *He dies*

ANTHONY   Thrice nobler than myself,   95
Thou teachest me, O valiant Eros, what
I should, and thou couldst not. My queen and Eros
Have by their brave instruction got upon me
A nobleness in record. But I will be
A bridegroom in my death, and run into't   100
As to a lover's bed. Come then—and Eros,
Thy master dies thy scholar: to do thus
I learned of thee.
     He falls on his sword
              How? Not dead? Not dead?
The guard, ho! O, dispatch me!
     Enter a Guard ⌈ Dercetus following⌉
FIRST GUARD   What's the noise?
ANTHONY I have done my work ill, friends.   105
O make an end of what I have begun.
SECOND GUARD
The star is fall'n.
FIRST GUARD   And time is at his period.
ALL THE GUARDS Alas, and woe!

95 *He dies*] OXFORD; *not in* F   103 *He falls on his sword*] ROWE ('*Falling on his sword*' *after* '*thus*', *l*. 102); *not in* F   104 *Dercetus following*] ARDEN (*after* Rowe); *not in* F
104–12 FIRST, SECOND, THIRD GUARD] F ('1, 2, 3')   108, 135 ALL THE GUARDS] OXFORD;
All. F

97–8 **Have . . . record** have, through the
   lesson in courage and nobility which
   they have taught me, won from me
   the honourable mention in history
   [which rightly belongs to the hero].
   This is Enobarbus's 'place in the story'
   again.
100–1 **bridegroom . . . bed** The idea of
   death as a species of erotic consummation (playing on the familiar use of *die*
   = experience orgasm) is a commonplace of Renaissance poetry, lovingly
   elaborated at the end of *Romeo*, as in
   the death scenes of both Anthony and
   Cleopatra. Dent lists the proverbial 'To
   go to one's grave (death) like a bed'
   (B192.1).
102 **master** Picking up 'instruction' and
   playing on the two senses of 'lord' and
   'schoolmaster'.
   to do thus The phrase deliberately
   echoes the grand erotic gesture of
   1.1.38–9.

103 **How, not dead** The anticlimax can
   often seem unfortunately comic in the
   theatre; the intended effect is perhaps
   closer to embarrassment. Shakespeare
   registers the ambivalence of Plutarch's judgement in 'The Comparison':
   'Antonius . . . slew himself (to confess
   a truth) cowardly and miserably, to his
   great pain and grief; and yet it was
   before his body came into his enemies'
   hands' (Bullough, p. 321).
104.1 *Dercetus* On the spelling of this
   name see Editorial Procedures, p. 132.
107 **star** i.e. the guiding star of their des-
   tinies (cf. 4.16.67). Falling stars reputedly often accompanied the fall of
   great men. Since the Second Guard
   hyperbolically sees Anthony's death as
   a sign of the end of time, Bevington is
   probably right to detect an echo of the
   apocalyptic imagery of Rev. 8:10–13.
   his period its appointed end; death

ANTHONY Let him that loves me strike me dead.

FIRST GUARD Not I.   110

SECOND GUARD Nor I.

THIRD GUARD Nor any one.   *Exeunt Guard*

DERCETUS

    Thy death and fortunes bid thy followers fly.

       He takes Anthony's sword

    This sword, but shown to Caesar with this tidings,

    Shall enter me with him.

       Enter Diomedes

DIOMEDES   Where's Anthony?   115

DERCETUS

    There, Diomed, there.

DIOMEDES   Lives he? Wilt thou not answer, man?

      Exit Dercetus

ANTHONY

    Art thou there, Diomed? Draw thy sword, and give me

    Sufficing strokes for death.

DIOMEDES   Most absolute lord,

    My mistress Cleopatra sent me to thee.

ANTHONY

    When did she send thee?

DIOMEDES   Now, my lord.

ANTHONY   Where is she?   120

DIOMEDES

    Locked in her monument. She had a prophesying fear

    Of what hath come to pass; for when she saw—

    Which never shall be found—you did suspect

    She had disposed with Caesar, and that your rage

    Would not be purged, she sent you word she was dead.   125

    But, fearing since how it might work, hath sent

---

112 *Guard*] POPE; *not in* F   113 DERCETUS] F; *Decre.* F2; *Decretas* ROWE; *Dercetas* POPE
113.1 *He...sword*] WILSON (subs.); *not in* F   116 DERCETUS] WILSON; *Decre.* F; *Der.* POPE
116.1 *Exit Dercetus*] CAPELL (subs.); *not in* F   125 sent you word] F; sent word POPE

113–15 **thy death...with him** Dercetus's
    betrayal is recorded in Plutarch,
    though a little more casually (see Ap-
    pendix A).
114 **this sword** Dercetus's theft of An-
    thony's sword is the final betrayal and
    amounts to a symbolic emasculation of
    the hero.

115 **enter...him** get me into his favour
118 **Sufficing** The first occurrence of this
    adjective recorded in *OED*.
123 **Which...found** something that will
    never prove true of her
124 **disposed with** come to terms with
126 **how...work** what effect it might
    have

Me to proclaim the truth; and I am come,
I dread, too late.

ANTHONY

Too late, good Diomed. Call my guard, I prithee.

DIOMEDES

What ho, the Emperor's guard! The guard, what ho!   130
Come, your lord calls.

Enter four or five of the Guard of Anthony.

ANTHONY

Bear me, good friends, where Cleopatra bides—
'Tis the last service that I shall command you.

FIRST GUARD

Woe, woe are we, sir, you may not live to wear
All your true followers out.

ALL THE GUARDS   Most heavy day!   135

ANTHONY

Nay, good my fellows, do not please sharp fate
To grace it with your sorrows. Bid that welcome
Which comes to punish us, and we punish it
Seeming to bear it lightly. Take me up.
I have led you oft; carry me now, good friends,   140
And have my thanks for all.

Exeunt bearing Anthony ⌈ and the body of Eros⌉

4.16 *Enter Cleopatra and her maids aloft, with*
    Charmian and Iras

CLEOPATRA

O Charmian, I will never go from hence.

141.1 *and ... Eros*] OXFORD; *not in* F
4.16.0.1 *and her Maids*] F; *omitted* ROWE

134–5 **wear ... out** outlive
136–9 **do not ... lightly** The Stoics, attempting to reconcile their apparently
conflicting doctrines of free will and
fate, taught that the wise man could
triumph over Fate by freely accepting
his destiny and thus making it truly
his own.
137 **grace** favour, honour, adorn
4.16.0.1 *and her maids* Many editors follow Rowe in supposing this to be redundant; Shakespeare may originally
have written 'her maids' and failed to

cancel it clearly after adding the cla-
rification 'with Charmian and Iras'.
The anonymous maids may of course
belong to the 'train' which follows the
Queen in 1.1, for example; but it is
difficult to imagine any solution to the
problems of staging this scene (see
below) which would allow for much
more than four characters to be
presented 'aloft'.
aloft See Appendix B for a note on the
staging of this scene.

CHARMIAN

Be comforted, dear madam.

CLEOPATRA   No, I will not.

All strange and terrible events are welcome,
But comforts we despise. Our size of sorrow,
Proportioned to our cause, must be as great   5
As that which makes it.

     Enter ⌈below⌉ Diomedes

                  How now? Is he dead?

DIOMEDES

His death's upon him, but not dead.
Look out o'th'other side your monument:
His guard have brought him thither.

     Enter below Anthony, borne by the Guard

CLEOPATRA   O sun,   10

Burn the great sphere thou mov'st in; darkling stand
The varying shore o'th'world! O Anthony,

---

6 *below*] COLLIER; *not in* F   9 *Enter . . . Guard*] COLLIER (*subs.*); *Enter Anthony, and the Guard.* F

6 Most editors follow Collier in having Diomedes enter below, but as the Oxford editor notes: 'Collier's direction is not as certain as subsequent acceptance of it suggests. Realistically Diomed is unlikely to gain admission to the monument; yet his subsequent instruction to Cleopatra "Look out o'th other side your monument" may suggest that he enters behind her, "*aloft*".' On the other hand, if Diomedes were in the monument he might be more likely to say 'the' rather than '*your* monument'.

8 Look . . . monument Perhaps a reminder to the audience as to how they are to 'read' the stage. See below, Appendix B.

10 ff. This account of Anthony's death is closely modelled on Plutarch, even down to the details of hauling the dying man up into the monument (see Appendix A).

10 O sun These words, set separately in F, are usually treated as part of l. 9, and this may well have been Shakespeare's intention (though they leave the line still one syllable short). Alternatively (as Bevington assumes) they may be meant to stand alone, in which

case the metrical gap probably signals that they are to be treated as a long drawn-out cry. A more remote possibility is that they are meant to form a hexameter with l. 11.

11–12 **Burn the . . . world** In the Ptolemaic system, the sun, like the other planets, was imagined to revolve around the earth within its own sphere; should its great heat succeed in burning the crystalline walls of the sphere, it would presumably whirl away from its appointed orbit, leaving the earth without light. Bevington suggests an apocalyptic echo of Rev. 8;12.

12 **varying shore** The earth is imagined as a coastline (cf. Hamlet's description of the earth as 'a sterile *promontory*', *Hamlet* 2.2.300), and the alternation of light and dark as the tides which lap upon it.

Anthony For the only time in the entire text, F spells the name 'Antony' here—presumably an expedient adopted by the compositor in order to fit the thrice-repeated name into the line (see Editorial Procedures, p. 134)—though Greg took the anomalous spelling as evidence of textual disturbance (see note to ll. 13–33).

Anthony, Anthony! Help, Charmian!
Help, Iras, help! Help, friends below!
Let's draw him hither.

ANTHONY   Peace!   15
Not Caesar's valour hath o'erthrown Anthony,
But Anthony's hath triumphed on itself.

CLEOPATRA
So it should be, that none but Anthony
Should conquer Anthony, but woe 'tis so.

ANTHONY
I am dying, Egypt, dying—only   20
I here importune death awhile, until
Of many thousand kisses the poor last
I lay upon thy lips.

CLEOPATRA   I dare not, dear—
Dear my lord, pardon—I dare not,
Lest I be taken. Not th'imperious show   25
Of the full-fortuned Caesar ever shall
Be brooched with me, if knife, drugs, serpents have

12–20 The F versification is extremely erratic at this point, and various rearrangements have been proposed; this one assumes a pause after Anthony's cry of 'Peace!', registering the painful effort it costs the dying man.

13–33 Much debated since Bernard Jenkin first drew attention to the odd duplication of Cleopatra's instruction to draw Anthony up (*RES* 21 (1945), pp. 1–14). The argument, supported and refined by Wilson (p. 128–30), Greg (p. 403), and Ridley, was that two versions of this part of the scene had been conflated, presumably by the compositor's including cancelled material (ll. 13–31, 'Anthony, Anthony . . . upon me') which had not been adequately marked; the repetition of 'I am dying, Egypt, dying' at l. 43 would then have resulted from an attempt to preserve a powerful line that would otherwise have been lost. While it is true that the cut would make the scene more economical and coherent, David Galloway has argued (*N&Q* 203 (1958), pp. 330–5) that the scene's repetitions, confusions, and contradictions are entirely appropriate to the mood of the scene. His judgement is borne out by the weight of twentieth-century theatrical experience.

15, 32 **draw him hither . . . draw thee up** Leslie Thomson, *SSu* 41 (1989), pp. 82–3 elaborates Malone's observations on this strange echo of Cleopatra's fishing-sport in 2.5.11–15: 'I will betray | Tawny-fine fishes . . . and as I *draw them up*, | I'll think them every one an Anthony, | And say "Ah, ha! you're caught." '

18–19 **none . . . Anthony** As Arden notes, evidently modelled on Ovid, *Metamorphoses* 13. 472: 'That none may Ajax overcome save Ajax' (Golding's translation).

21 **importune death** beg death's indulgence

25 **imperious show** triumph; literally a show exhibiting the power and authority (*imperium*) of an emperor or general (*imperator*)

27 **brooched** ornamented, adorned; the first recorded usage of the verb, according to *OED* which erroneously cites this passage as from '*Troilus and Cressida*, 1606'

Edge, sting, or operation. I am safe.
Your wife, Octavia, with her modest eyes,
And still conclusion, shall acquire no honour   30
Demuring upon me. But come, come, Anthony—
Help me, my women—we must draw thee up.
Assist, good friends.

ANTHONY   O, quick, or I am gone!

CLEOPATRA

Here's sport indeed! How heavy weighs my lord!
Our strength is all gone into heaviness—   35
That makes the weight. Had I great Juno's power,
The strong-winged Mercury should fetch thee up
And set thee by Jove's side. Yet come a little—
Wishers were ever fools—O come, come, come,

          They heave Anthony aloft to Cleopatra

And welcome, welcome! Die when thou hast lived!   40
Quicken with kissing! Had my lips that power,
Thus would I wear them out.

ALL THE LOOKERS ON   A heavy sight!

ANTHONY I am dying, Egypt, dying.

40 when] F; where POPE   42 ALL THE LOOKERS ON] OXFORD *(after* F *All.)*

28 **operation** efficacy
30 **still conclusion** silent censoriousness
31 **Demuring upon me** by turning her demure gaze on me; the first use of the verb *demure* recorded in *OED*
34 **sport** There is an echo, at once wry and plangent, of 1.1.49, 'What sport tonight?'. Here, as elsewhere, the word *sport* has erotic connotations.
   heavy There is a further ironic echo here of Cleopatra's rapturous contemplation of the absent Anthony in 1.5: 'O happy horse, to bear the weight of Anthony!' (l. 21).
35 **heaviness** (1) grief (2) weight. Cf. also l. 42.
36 **Juno** queen of heaven, Jove's wife
37 **Mercury** messenger of the gods, proverbial for swiftness
39 **Wishers . . . fools** proverbial (Tilley W539)
39.1 *They . . . aloft* The staging is controversial: in Plutarch Cleopatra 'cast out certain chains and ropes in which Antonius was trussed; and Cleopatra her own self, with two women only . . . trised Antonius up', but it is not easy

to see how three boy actors would accomplish this feat; see Appendix B for discussion of the problems involved and some possible solutions.
40 **Die . . . lived** it will be time enough to die when you have lived out your full life; or, don't die until you have really lived (i.e. until after I have restored you to life with a kiss). The sexual sense of 'die' is present just below the surface here. John Bayley (*Shakespeare and Tragedy* (1981), p. 126) cites A. E. Housman 'he that drinks in season | Shall live before he dies' and interprets 'Antony has drunk; he has lived; and it is now time for him to die.' Some editors adopt Pope's plausible emendation of 'when' to 'where' (i.e. 'here, in my arms').
41 **Quicken** come alive. In conjunction with 'die' it is difficult to exclude the bawdy sense ('to be impregnated'): it is as if the onset of death, by rendering Anthony the passive object of Cleopatra's ministrations, had actually produced the reversal of gender roles with which the lovers formerly played.

Give me some wine, and let me speak a little.

CLEOPATRA

No, let me speak, and let me rail so high   45
That the false huswife Fortune break her wheel,
Provoked by my offence.

ANTHONY   One word, sweet queen:
Of Caesar seek your honour with your safety—O!

CLEOPATRA They do not go together.

ANTHONY   Gentle, hear me:
None about Caesar trust but Proculeius.   50

CLEOPATRA

My resolution and my hands I'll trust—
None about Caesar.

ANTHONY

The miserable change now at my end
Lament nor sorrow at, but please your thoughts
In feeding them with those my former fortunes,   55
Wherein I lived the greatest prince o'th'world,
The noblest; and do now not basely die,

56 lived the] THEOBALD; liued. The F

46 **huswife** archaic form of *housewife*; pronounced 'huzzif' and by the early seventeenth century normally derogatory in meaning, like its corrupt form *hussy*. Editors frequently substitute either 'hussy' or 'housewife', but neither seems fully satisfactory: the latter misses the derogatory sense which Cleopatra intends (Fortune in her familiar guise as faithless whore; see Dent F603.1 'Fortune is a Strumpet (whore, huswife)', while the former excludes the domestic connotations which the word still had (even *hussy* could still be used as a neutral equivalent for *housewife*); to brand Fortune as a huswife is to associate the goddess with domestic drudges like 'the married woman,' Fulvia (1.3.20) and 'your wife Octavia' (4.16.29).
Fortune ... wheel The goddess Fortuna was conventionally pictured turning a wheel whose arbitrary motion, raising some to the height of prosperity as it cast others to the depths of wretchedness, symbolized the whimsicality of chance.

47 **offence** i.e. Cleopatra's railing against her

48, 54 **your** It is worth noting that after the intense erotic yearning of ll. 20–3 Anthony's speech becomes more formal and controlled, the formality being marked partly by his shift to the plural pronoun (cf. Appendix C). Though it is partly right to speak of this scene as a *Liebestod*, the emotional rapture is almost entirely supplied by Cleopatra. In his last speech Anthony, in contrast with Romeo (or even, despite his reputation for theatrical self-display, Othello) is almost entirely preoccupied with re-composing his former heroic self.

49 **They ... together** Bevington suggests that Cleopatra is thinking of the proverbial 'The more danger the more honour' (Dent D35).

50 **None ... Proculeius** This detail is from Plutarch (Appendix A); but the staging of 5.2 underscores the irony he found there—that it was Proculeius who trapped Cleopatra into Caesar's hands.

51 **My ... trust** possibly echoing Daniel, 1.54: 'I have both hands, and will, and I can die' (Bullough, p. 409)

Not cowardly put off my helmet to
My countryman—a Roman, by a Roman
Valiantly vanquished. Now my spirit is going,   60
I can no more.
CLEOPATRA   Noblest of men, woot dye?
Hast thou no care of me—shall I abide
In this dull world, which in thy absence is
No better than a sty? O, see, my women,
The crown o'th'earth doth melt.
> *Anthony dies*

                                        My lord?   65
O, withered is the garland of the war,
The soldiers' pole is fall'n—young boys and girls
Are level now with men, the odds is gone,
And there is nothing left remarkable
Beneath the visiting moon.
CHARMIAN   O, quietness, lady!   70
> *Cleopatra faints* ← genuine
IRAS She's dead too, our sovereign.
CHARMIAN Lady!
IRAS   Madam!
CHARMIAN   O madam, madam, madam!
IRAS Royal Egypt! Empress!
CHARMIAN   Peace, peace, Iras!
CLEOPATRA
No more but e'en a woman, and commanded

---

65 *Anthony dies*] ARDEN (*after Rowe who prints it after* 'no more', *l. 61*)); *not in* F   70.1
Cleopatra faints] WILSON (*after Rowe who prints it after* 'moon', *l. 70*); *not in* F

66 **withered . . . garland** Evergreen bays
   crowned a victorious hero; withered
   bays were a token of death (*Richard II*,
   2.4.8).
67 **pole** Much disputed: the apparent echo
   of the Second Guard's 'The star is fallen' suggests that the primary sense is
   'polestar', but 'standard' also seems
   appropriate; and the link with 'garland' on the one hand, and 'young boys
   and girls' on the other, is bound to
   suggest 'maypole'. The image probably
   plays across all three meanings, and
   may even (more remotely) include the
   bawdy sense, 'phallus'.
68 **odds** measure of distinction or difference

69 **remarkable** extraordinary, wonderful.
   A new word, not recorded before 1604
   in *OED*, its sense was much stronger
   than in modern English; Cleopatra's
   hyperbolic vision is of a featureless
   world in which all marks of distinction
   have been levelled.
70 **visiting** So called because, unlike the
   sun, it appears only intermittently;
   but, since the moon is sometimes associated with sickness, as well as with
   the vicissitudes of fortune and mutability, the sense of 'bringing punishment' may also be intended. The
   earliest recorded example of this participial adjective in *OED*.

By such poor passion as the maid that milks   75
And does the meanest chores. It were for me
To throw my sceptre at the injurious gods,
To tell them that this world did equal theirs,
Till they had stol'n our jewel. All's but naught;
Patience is sottish, and impatience does   80
Become a dog that's mad—then is it sin
To rush into the secret house of death
Ere death dare come to us? How do you, women?
What, what, good cheer! Why, how now, Charmian?
My noble girls? Ah, women, women, look,   85
Our lamp is spent, it's out. Good sirs, take heart;
We'll bury him; and then, what's brave, what's noble,
Let's do't after the high Roman fashion,
And make death proud to take us. Come, away.
This case of that huge spirit now is cold.   90
Ah, women, women! Come, we have no friend
But resolution, and the briefest end.
            Exeunt; those aloft bearing off Anthony's body

5.1   *Enter Caesar with his council of war, Agrippa,*
            Dolabella, ⌜Mecenas, Gallus, Proculeius⌝
CAESAR ⌜*aside to Dolabella*⌝
Go to him, Dolabella, bid him yield.

---

74 e'en] CAPELL (*conj.* Thirlby); in F   76 chores] OXFORD *after* F ('chares')   88 do't]
F; do it POPE   92.1 *those aloft*] CAPELL (*subs.*); *not in* F
   5.1.0.1–2 *Enter . . . Proculeius*] RIVERSIDE (*after* Hanmer); *Enter Cæsar, Agrippa, Dolla-
bella, Menas, with his Counsell of Warre.* F

75 **poor passion** J. H. Walter, *N&Q* 214
(1969), p. 139, cites Edward Jorden's
description of *hysterica passio* or 'the
mother' in *A Brief Discourse of a Disease
called the Suffocation of the Mother*
(1603): this sudden affliction, to which
women exposed to strong emotion
were supposedly prone, manifested
itself in 'swounding, the very image of
death'. Cleopatra's fainting is thus a
symptom of her mere womanhood.
79 **naught** (1) worth nothing; (2) lost,
ruined
80 **sottish** foolish
86 **Our lamp is spent** cf. 4.15.46
   Good sirs In Elizabethan usage 'sir'
could be used playfully or affectionate-

ly between women.
87 **brave** both 'splendid' and 'courageous'
88 **Roman fashion** Cleopatra invokes a
Roman idea of heroism; but suicide
was also thought of as an especially
'Roman' remedy for affliction—as, for
example, by Horatio when he declares
himself 'more an antique Roman than
a Dane' (*Hamlet* 5.2.292).
92 **briefest end** quickest death. The
couplet, with its stressed rhyme-word
'end', produces an unusually powerful sense of closure; with the solemn
funeral exeunt it creates the false
ending whose effect Anne Barton describes (see Introduction, p. 70 n. 3).
   5.1 Much of the detail of this scene

Being so frustrate, tell him he but mocks
The pauses that he makes.

DOLABELLA   Caesar, I shall.   *Exit*

Enter Dercetus with the sword of Anthony

CAESAR

Wherefore is that? And what art thou that dar'st
Appear thus to us?

DERCETUS   I am called Dercetus—   5

Mark Anthony I served, who best was worthy
Best to be served; whilst he stood up and spoke
He was my master, and I wore my life
To spend upon his haters. If thou please
To take me to thee, as I was to him   10
I'll be to Caesar; if thou pleasest not,
I yield thee up my life.

CAESAR   What is't thou sayst?

DERCETUS

I say, O Caesar, Anthony is dead.

CAESAR

The breaking of so great a thing should make
A greater crack. The round world   15

2 he but mocks] HANMER; he mockes F   3 *Exit*] THEOBALD; *not in* F   3.1 *Dercetus*]
WILSON; *Decretas* F   5, 13, 19 DERCETUS] WILSON; *Dec.* F   15 round] F; ruin'd STEEVENS
1793 (*conj.*); rivèd OXFORD

derives from Plutarch, where however
Caesar's lament is a much more private affair, and its sincerity therefore
less open to question.

1 *aside to Dolabella* This instruction must
be an aside since it is clear from ll.
70–2 below that the others are una-
ware of Dolabella's mission. The effect,
when juxtaposed with the rhetorical
sense of occasion apparent in Dercetus's entry, is to emphasize the conniving politician in Caesar.

2 **Being so frustrate** since his efforts have
proved so fruitless
he but mocks F's 'he mocks' leaves the
line one syllable short. A case might
be made for it, however, on the
grounds that it sharpens Caesar's
ironic edge by allowing a slight mock-
ing pause before 'he mocks | The
pauses.'

2–3 **mocks . . . makes** his delays are
pointless and absurd

4–5 **Wherefore . . . thus** Together with
the stage direction, Caesar's reaction
draws attention to the powerfully gestural nature of Dercetus's entry as he
displays the sign of Anthony's vanquished manhood, the naked blood-
stained sword. Bevington notes that in
Medieval and Renaissance England it
was a treasonable offence to appear
before the monarch with an un-
sheathed weapon.

11 **thou** Since Dercetus plays a somewhat
ignoble role, it is perhaps surprising to
sense a certain stubborn independence
in his insistence on *thou*ing a man who
has just rebuffed him with a royal
plural (ll. 4–5).

14 **breaking** (1) destruction, end; (2) dis-
closure, telling (Jones)

15 **crack** (1) loud noise, thunder-clap (cf.

Should have shook lions into civil streets,
And citizens to their dens. The death of Anthony
Is not a single doom, in the name lay
A moiety of the world.

DERCETUS   He is dead, Caesar,
Not by a public minister of justice,   20
Nor by a hirèd knife, but that self hand
Which writ his honour in the acts it did
Hath, with the courage which the heart did lend it,
Splitted the heart. This is his sword;
I robbed his wound of it—behold it stained   25
With his most noble blood.

CAESAR   Look you sad, friends?
The gods rebuke me, but it is tidings
To wash the eyes of kings.

AGRIPPA   And strange it is
That nature must compel us to lament
Our most persisted deeds.

MECENAS   His taints and honours 30
Waged equal with him.

AGRIPPA   A rarer spirit never
Did steer humanity; but you gods will give us
Some faults to make us men. Caesar is touched.

MECENAS
When such a spacious mirror's set before him,
He needs must see himself.

18 the] F; that POPE 26 Look you sad, friends?] CAPELL (*after* Theobald); Looke you
sad Friends, F1; Look you, sad friends, F3 28, 31 AGRIPPA] THEOBALD; *Dol., Dola.* F

'crack of doom' and below, l. 18);
(2) fissure, fracture
round world The line is three syllables
short and this, together with the allegedly weak sense of 'round' has led
editors to suspect corruption. But
'round world' is quite satisfactory if
one takes it to mean 'the whole world,
every part of the world'; and in any
case it is not obvious that making a
tetrameter of the line much improves
matters. If anything, as various editors
have suggested, some words may have
dropped off the end of the line: e.g. 'the
round world *at his fall*'. But, as Ridley
points out, a pause after 'crack' would

be dramatically effective here.
16 **civil** urban; perhaps also 'orderly,
well-governed'
18 **doom** (1) ruin; (2) fate, nemesis; (3)
day of judgement
19 **moiety** half, half-share
21 **self** same
31 **Waged . . . him** fought an evenly
matched battle in his nature
31–2 **A rarer . . . humanity** no human
being was ever governed by a more
splendid spirit
32 **steer humanity** either 'guide any person' (Bevington), or 'govern human-
kind'
34 **spacious** great and comprehensive

CAESAR   O Anthony,   35
  I have followed thee to this; but we do lance
  Diseases in our bodies. I must perforce
  Have shown to thee such a declining day,
  Or look on thine: we could not stall together
  In the whole world. But yet let me lament   40
  With tears as sovereign as the blood of hearts
  That thou, my brother, my competitor
  In top of all design, my mate in empire,
  Friend and companion in the front of war,
  The arm of mine own body, and the heart   45
  Where mine his thoughts did kindle—that our stars
  Unreconciliable should divide
  Our equalness to this. Hear me, good friends—
    Enter an Egyptian
  But I will tell you at some meeter season:
  The business of this man looks out of him;   50
  We'll hear him what he says.—Whence are you?
EGYPTIAN
  A poor Egyptian yet, the Queen my mistress,
  Confined in all she has—her monument—

---

36 lance] F (launch)   48.1 *Enter an Egyptian*] CAPELL (*after* F—*prints after* 'what he sayes', *l. 51*)   52 Egyptian yet, the] F; Egyptian yet; the ROWE 1709 (2); Egyptian, yet the WILSON (*conj.* Tyrwhitt; *and* Lloyd *cited in Cambridge*)

36 **lance** This word and F's 'launch' (though now differentiated) were simply variant spellings in Shakespeare's time.
39 **stall** dwell
41 **sovereign** potent, efficacious; Case suggests Caesar has in mind the medicinable properties of blood (cf. note to 4.2.6–7).
42 **competitor** colleague (and rival)
43 **In top . . . design** in the boldest enterprises
44 **front of war** forefront of the battle
45 **arm . . . body** Jonathan Dollimore notices a 'carefully placed suggestion of Antony's inferiority' in this figure (*Radical Tragedy*, p. 212).
45–6 **heart . . . kindle** Caesar's heart took fire (courage) from Anthony's; the suggestion—contrary to all that we have seen of their relationship in the play—is that their hearts (like those of friends and lovers) were bonded as one.
47–8 **divide . . . this** should drive such a

wedge between the two of us who were linked in such perfect and peaceful equality ('equalness' may carry the sense of *equanimity* as well as *equality*)
50 **looks out of him** is written on his face
52 **A . . . mistress** I see no particular reason to alter F's punctuation, though, unlike Johnson, I take the opening phrase to refer to Cleopatra rather than the Egyptian himself: he means '[I come from] the queen who is still a humble Egyptian [rather than a Roman subject]—despite your conquest which has reduced her to all that she now rules, her own monument.'
53 **Confined . . . monument** Given the lack of specificity in the stage directions for 5.2, the Egyptian's line may be intended as a reminder to the audience that they are to read the action of the following scene as taking place within the monument. See notes to 5.2.0, 8.1, 354–64 and Appendix C.

Of thy intents desires instruction,
That she preparèdly may frame herself   55
To th'way she's forced to.
CAESAR   Bid her have good heart:
She soon shall know of us, by some of ours,
How honourable and how kindly we
Determine for her. For Caesar cannot live
To be ungentle.
EGYPTIAN   So, the gods preserve thee!   *Exit*   60
CAESAR
Come hither, Proculeius. Go and say
We purpose her no shame; give her what comforts
The quality of her passion shall require,
Lest in her greatness by some mortal stroke
She do defeat us—for her life in Rome   65
Would be eternal in our triumph. Go,
And with your speediest bring us what she says,
And how you find of her.
PROCULEIUS   Caesar, I shall.   *Exit*
CAESAR
Gallus, go you along.   *Exit Gallus*
                    Where's Dolabella
To second Proculeius?
ALL BUT CAESAR   Dolabella!   70
CAESAR
Let him alone, for I remember now
How he's employed—he shall in time be ready.
Go with me to my tent, where you shall see
How hardly I was drawn into this war,
How calm and gentle I proceeded still   75

---

59 live] ROWE 1714 (*conj.* Southern); leaue F; learn DYCE (*conj.* Tyrwhitt)   So, the]
OXFORD (*subs.*); So the F   68 *Exit*] F ('*Exit Proculeius.*')   69 *Exit Gallus*] THEOBALD; *not
in* F   70 ALL BUT CAESAR] OXFORD; *All.* F

---

55 **preparèdly** The earliest instance of this
   adverb cited in *OED*
63 **quality of her passion** intensity of her
   grief
65–6 **her life … triumph** her live presence in Rome as a prisoner in my
   triumph would render it immortal
73–7 **Go … see … Go … see … show**

Caesar's reiterated insistence on dem-
onstrating what the audience are never
allowed to see, seems calculated to
produce a sceptical response. In Plutarch the letters are read and displayed.
74 **How hardly** with what reluctance

301

In all my writings. Go with me, and see
What I can show in this.   *Exeunt*

5.2   *Enter Cleopatra, Charmian, Iras*
CLEOPATRA
My desolation does begin to make
A better life. 'Tis paltry to be Caesar—
Not being Fortune, he's but Fortune's knave,
A minister of her will—and it is great
To do that thing that ends all other deeds,   5
Which shackles accidents and bolts up change,
Which sleeps, and never palates more the dung,

5.2.0 *Enter . . . Iras*] CAPELL; F *adds and Mardian*   7 dung] F; dug THEOBALD (dugg)

5.2.0 *Enter Cleopatra . . . Iras* As Ridley
  pointed out, the inclusion of Mardian
  in the F stage direction seems to represent a changed authorial intention:
  not only is Mardian given nothing to
  do or say in the scene, he is never even
  addressed by the Queen, who frequently speaks to Charmian and Iras as if
  they alone (as at the beginning of
  4.16) accompany her; Shakespeare
  presumably intended to make use of
  him, but having changed his mind
  forgot to cancel the entry (cf. the inclusion of Agrippa at the opening of
  3.12).
    F gives no indication that any part
  of this scene is to be played 'above',
  and the probability is that the main
  stage was now intended to represent
  the monument—see Appendix B.
 1 **desolation** Not merely 'ruin', but also
  conveying its original Latin sense 'the
  condition of having been left alone or
  abandoned'—as Cleopatra is after Anthony's death.
 2 **better life** i.e. a good life in the terms of
  Renaissance moral philosophy with its
  strong stoical colouring, according to
  which suffering was to be welcomed as
  an occasion for the exhibition of virtue
  in extremes. Above all, a life was to be
  judged by one's ability to make a good
  end; and this last scene, with its con-
  cluding ritual of coronation-in-death,
  might be read as an elaborate enactment of the favourite tag *finis coronat*

opus ('the end crowns all').
 3 **knave** servant, underling. A variant of
  the proverbial 'fortune's fool' (Dent
  F617.1). J. P. Brockbank has suggested
  a possible pun on 'nave' (i.e. the hub
  of Fortune's wheel) in 'Shakespeare
  and the Fashion of these Times', *SSu*
  16 (1963), pp. 30–41 (p. 31).
 5 **do . . . deeds** i.e. commit suicide. For
  comment on the resonances of 'do' in
  the play, see notes to 1.5.15–16 and
  5.2.324.
 6 **bolts up** fetters
 7–8 **never   palates . . . Caesar's**   never
  again tastes (the produce of) the
  earth, which gives life to beggar and
  emperor alike. Theobald's emendation
  of 'dung' to 'dug' has won some support, but it renders the sense more
  commonplace and eliminates the suggestive echo of Anthony's first big
  speech: 'our dungy earth alike | Feeds
  beast as man' (1.1.37–8). Behind this
  image of the nurturing earth may lie
  a recollection of the Egyptian dung-
  beetle which, like serpents and crocodiles, was supposed to be spontaneously generated in the mud of
  Egypt. In *Death's Duel*, John Donne
  writes of serpents as being born 'out
  of dung'. Perhaps the compression of
  the eating figure will also suggest
  earth in the mouths of the dead; certainly 'dung' here is a leveller, like the
  'dust' and 'clay' which link beggar
  and king in Hamlet's graveyard. F's

The beggar's nurse, and Caesar's.
Enter Proculeius

PROCULEIUS

Caesar sends greeting to the Queen of Egypt,
And bids thee study on what fair demands   10
Thou mean'st to have him grant thee.

CLEOPATRA   What's thy name?

PROCULEIUS

My name is Proculeius.

CLEOPATRA   Anthony
Did tell me of you, bade me trust you, but
I do not greatly care to be deceived
That have no use for trusting. If your master   15
Would have a queen his beggar, you must tell him
That majesty, to keep decorum, must
No less beg than a kingdom. If he please
To give me conquered Egypt for my son,
He gives me so much of mine own as I   20
Will kneel to him with thanks.

PROCULEIUS   Be of good cheer—

8.1 *Enter Proculeius*] F; *Enter Proculeius, and Gallus, below* HANMER; *Enter* PROCULEIUS *and* GALLUS *with Soldiers, to the Door of the Monument* CAPELL

comma after 'nurse' creates the pause necessary to emphasize the satiric particularity of 'Caesar's' here. The name chimes mockingly with the opening of Proculeius's official announcement.

8.1, 34 *Enter Proculeius ... Enter Gallus ... at another door.* See Appendix B for a discussion of the staging problems here. The account of Cleopatra's capture is closely modelled on Plutarch (see Appendix A).

10 **study on** consider, ponder
    fair liberal

14 **I ... deceived** Usually explained 'it is a matter of indifference to me whether I am deceived or not'; but there seems no good reason against taking 'I do not ... care' in its modern sense ('I have no wish to ...'), which better fits the context.

16 **a queen his beggar** Cleopatra continues to play on the familiar trope of the beggar and the king, glanced at in 'the beggar's nurse and Caesar's' (l. 8)

which may give an ironic inflection to her display of humility here. Deriving from the old ballad of 'King Cophetua and the Beggar Maid', the trope is several times invoked by Shakespeare, notably in *Richard II* 5.3.77–8 where Aumerle begs for mercy from the newly crowned Bolingbroke.

17 **keep decorum** behave in accordance with its lofty rank. Here (as at 1.2.73) F italicizes *decorum*, presumably to indicate the use of a foreign or technical term—the earliest substantial use of *decorum* cited by *OED* is in Foxe's *Acts and Monuments* (1576), where it is italicized and apparently regarded as a Latin word. For whatever reason, Compositor D did not follow the same practice in *Measure for Measure* (4.1.321), the only other occurrence of the word in Shakespeare. But the effect here is to highlight the metatheatrical aesthetic of Cleopatra's death scene.

You're fall'n into a princely hand, fear nothing.
Make your full reference freely to my lord,
Who is so full of grace that it flows over
On all that need. Let me report to him   25
Your sweet dependency, and you shall find
A conqueror that will pray in aid for kindness
Where he for grace is kneeled to.

CLEOPATRA   Pray you, tell him
I am his fortune's vassal, and I send him
The greatness he has got. I hourly learn   30
A doctrine of obedience, and would gladly
Look him i'th'face.

PROCULEIUS   This I'll report, dear lady.
Have comfort, for I know your plight is pitied
Of him that caused it.

⌈ *Enter Gallus and Soldiers breaking in at*
another door ⌉

GALLUS   Proculeius,

---

34 *Enter . . . door*] This edition, *after* ARDEN ('*Enter* GALLUS *and soldiers behind*'); *not in* F
GALLUS] MALONE; *Pro.*, F   Proculeius] ARDEN; *as s.p.* ('*Pro.*') F

23 **Make . . . lord** put yourself absolutely
  and unquestioningly in Caesar's hands
24–5 **full of grace . . . need** Proculeius's
  language, as well as transferring to
  Caesar the imagery of overflowing
  bounty previously associated with
  Cleopatra and Egypt, is tinged with religious suggestion; by recalling descriptions of the overflowing grace of God,
  it implicitly identifies Caesar as a god
  on earth. The exaggerated alliteration
  of ll. 22–4, with the repetition of 'full',
  emphasizes Proculeius's ingratiating
  tone.
26 **sweet dependency** docile submissive-
  ness
27 **pray . . . kindness** beg for your assistance in showing him how to express
  his generosity. 'Pray in aid' is legal
  terminology, but Proculeius's elegant
  courtly figure quibblingly associates it
  with the religious suggestions of kneel-
  ing for grace.
29–30 **send . . . got** acknowledge the majesty and authority that his conquest
  has won for him
31 **doctrine of obedience** Cleopatra is announcing her formal submission to the

imperial authority of Caesar. The Anglican 'doctrine of obedience', set out in
the three parts of 'An Exhortation to
Obedience' and the six parts of 'An
Homily against Disobedience and wil-
ful Rebellion' in the 1562 book of
Sermons or Homilies, required subjects
to obey their monarch as part of their
religious duty: 'In God's Word subjects
must learn obedience both to God and
their princes', as the sixth part of the
'Homily against Disobedience' put it.
The topic had particular currency in
1606 because the Convocation of
Bishops, in a mistaken effort to please
the king, had produced a version of
the doctrine so extreme that it required
absolute obedience even to a ruler
whose sole claim to authority was that
of immediate conquest.
34 **Of** by
  Enter . . . door Hinman (ii. 508–9)
  shows that the stage direction was almost certainly dropped when the compositor ran seriously short of space.
  Gallus has been ordered by Caesar to
  follow Proculeius (5.1.69); and while in
  Plutarch it is Proculeius who carries

You see how easily she may be surprised.   35
Guard her till Caesar come.   *Exit Gallus*
IRAS Royal queen!
CHARMIAN
O Cleopatra, thou art taken, queen!
CLEOPATRA (*drawing a dagger*)
Quick, quick, good hands!
PROCULEIUS (*disarming her*) Hold, worthy lady, hold!
Do not yourself such wrong, who are in this   40
Relieved but not betrayed.
CLEOPATRA   What—of death too,
That rids our dogs of languish?
PROCULEIUS   Cleopatra,
Do not abuse my master's bounty by
Th'undoing of yourself. Let the world see
His nobleness well acted, which your death   45
Will never let come forth.
CLEOPATRA   Where art thou, Death?
Come hither, come! Come, come, and take a queen
Worth many babes and beggars!
PROCULEIUS   O, temperance, lady!
CLEOPATRA
Sir, I will eat no meat; I'll not drink, sir;

---

36 *Exit Gallus*] MALONE; *not in* F   39 *drawing a dagger*] THEOBALD (*subs.*); *not in* F
disarming her] THEOBALD; *not in* F

out the surprise attack whilst Gallus
holds the queen in conversation, Shakespeare, having collapsed together the
separate embassages of Proculeius and
Gallus, changes over their roles at this
point.

35–6 **You ... come** F gives a second
speech-prefix for Proculeius before
these lines. Although Hinman is able
to cite several instances in the Folio
where the breaking of a speech by a
stage direction justified the repetition
of a speech-prefix, I believe that the
editors who have given the lines to
Gallus are right. It is, after all, Proculeius who stays to guard Cleopatra, so
it seems natural that Gallus should act
as Caesar's proxy in ordering him to
remain—especially since F has Gallus

(re-) enter with Caesar at l. 111.1.
41 **Relieved** rescued
42 **languish** wasting grief or sickness
44 **undoing of yourself** Proculeius's
phrase plays ironically against Cleopatra's notion of suicide as the final deed
of self-fashioning (l. 5).
44–5 **Let ... acted** let him demonstrate
his real nobility to the world; but the
emphasis on display makes the theatrical connotations of 'acted' inescapable.
45–6 **which ... forth** which if you die he
will have no opportunity of doing
48 **O, temperance** Proculeius's invocation
of this Roman value, asserted so
strongly in Act 1, here seems almost
comically inept.
49 **meat** food

If idle talk will once be necessary,   50
I'll not sleep neither! This mortal house I'll ruin,
Do Caesar what he can. Know, sir, that I
Will not wait piniond at your master's court,
Nor once be chastised with the sober eye
Of dull Octavia. Shall they hoist me up   55
And show me to the shouting varletry
Of censuring Rome? Rather a ditch in Egypt
Be gentle grave unto me! Rather on Nilus' mud
Lay me stark naked, and let the water-flies
Blow me into abhorring! Rather make   60
My country's high pyramides my gibbet,
And hang me up in chains!
PROCULEIUS   You do extend
These thoughts of horror further than you shall
Find cause in Caesar.
            Enter Dolabella
DOLABELLA   Proculeius,

50 **If idle . . . necessary** If I really must
waste time in useless talking. Johnson's
interpretation of this rather awkward
passage, especially when allied with
Case's decision to treat it as a paren-
thesis, is the most plausible so far
offered; but Malone may well have
been correct in supposing that a line
had dropped out—such as 'I'll not so
much as syllable a word'. Doubting
that anything could 'be gained by
trying to extract meaning from the . . .
line', Granville-Barker concluded that
'as a setting of hysterical gibbering to
verbal music it is perfect' (p. 58).
51 **this mortal house** my body; perhaps
also the royal house of Ptolemy
53–5 **wait piniond . . . Octavia** Shakespeare may be remembering Daniel's
Cleopatra: 'That Rome should see my
sceptre-bearing hands | Behind me
bound, and glory in my tears, | That I
should pass whereas Octavia stands, |
To view my misery that purchased
hers' (1. 67–70; Bullough, p. 409).
54 **chastised** (accent on the first syllable)
56 **varletry** rabble; the earliest occurrence
of this noun recorded in *OED*
57 **censuring** censorious; the earliest use
of this participle recorded in *OED*
58 **gentle grave** Cleopatra's irony depends
on the assumption that gentle birth

entitles one to a noble monument; the
sarcasm is intensified by the pun on
gentle = 'maggot, the larva of the flesh-
fly or bluebottle' (*OED gentle* sb. 3)
suggested by the juxtaposition of
'grave' and 'blow'.
59 **water-flies** *OED*'s earliest citation; but,
as Schäfer points out, water-flies also
appear in *Hamlet* 5.2.84 and *Troilus*
5.1.30.
60 **blow** lay maggots upon. Bevington
adds 'Following "Lay me stark nak'd",
the image takes on an erotic suggestion, one that couples sex and death'.
Certainly by the later seventeenth century 'to blow upon' had become a
bawdy term for copulation
61 **pyramides** (four syllables, accent on
the second)
gibbet Here, as elsewhere, Shakespeare, like most Elizabethans, imagines the pyramids as tall and slender
obelisks (see note to 2.7.16–23).
64–6 **Proculeius . . . thee** Dolabella was to
be sent to 'second' Proculeius; but
there is something a touch peremptory
about his tone, not least in his emphatic use of the singular pronoun.
Perhaps he is merely exercising the
familiar policeman's technique for
winning the confidence of a prisoner.
Cf. Appendix C.

What thou hast done thy master Caesar knows,   65
And he hath sent for thee. For the Queen,
I'll take her to my guard.
PROCULEIUS   So, Dolabella,
It shall content me best. Be gentle to her.
(*To Cleopatra*) To Caesar I will speak what you shall
    please,
If you'll employ me to him.
CLEOPATRA   Say, I would die.   70
                                                  Exit Proculeius

DOLABELLA
Most noble empress, you have heard of me?
CLEOPATRA
I cannot tell.
DOLABELLA   Assurèdly you know me.
CLEOPATRA
No matter, sir, what I have heard or known.
You laugh when boys or women tell their dreams,
Is't not your trick?
DOLABELLA   I understand not, madam.   75
CLEOPATRA
I dreamt there was an Emperor Anthony—
O, such another sleep, that I might see

70.1 *Exit Proculeius*] F (*after* 'him')

73 **empress** Jones notes the deliberate flattery involved in a Roman's according
   this title (which implicitly identifies her
   as the consort of the emperor, Anthony) to the defeated Cleopatra.
73–100 **No matter ... hear me** Cleopatra's rhetorical dominance of this
   exchange with Dolabella, once she
   rouses herself at l. 74, is nicely emphasized by the verse lineation: where
   each of her speeches begins with a full
   line of verse, Dolabella's replies and
   interjections invariably pick up un-
   completed lines of the Queen's. Only
   after l. 101 does Dolabella successfully
   regain the dominant position acknowledged in Cleopatra's submissive half-
   line, 'I thank you, sir' (1.106).
75 **trick** way, habit
76–92 **I dreamt ... pocket** The nearest
   equivalent for this speech in Plutarch
   is the lament which Cleopatra makes

at Antonius's tomb after Dolabella informs her of Caesar's plan to send her
to Rome (see Appendix A). Despite its
great difference in both tone and content, the Plutarch model, with its fu-
nereal context, serves as a reminder
that this is Cleopatra's version of the
funeral orations with which tragic
heroes are conventionally farewelled:
part of its emotional power depends on
the transposition of this high public
rhetoric into a curiously private reverie, so that the hyperbolic imagery
seems to well up from the depths of
Cleopatra's being. Even here, however,
it would be unwise to discount the
possibility that this is only another
magnificent performance, designed to
manipulate Dolabella's sympathy. In
Peter Hall's National Theatre production, Judi Dench delivered it directly to
the audience.

But such another man!

DOLABELLA   If it might please ye—

CLEOPATRA

His face was as the heavens, and therein stuck
A sun and moon, which kept their course and lighted   80
The little O o'th'earth.

DOLABELLA   Most sovereign creature—

CLEOPATRA

His legs bestrid the ocean; his reared arm
Crested the world; his voice was propertied
As all the tunèd spheres—and that to friends—
But when he meant to quail and shake the orb,   85
He was as rattling thunder. For his bounty,
There was no winter in't—an autumn 'twas
That grew the more by reaping. His delights

---

81 O o'th'earth] THEOBALD; o'th'earth F; O, the earth STEEVENS   87 autumn 'twas]
THEOBALD (Theobald *and* Thirlby); *Anthony* it was F

---

79 **stuck** were placed
80 **sun and moon** The comparison of eyes
to heavenly bodies (especially the sun)
was routine in Renaissance love-
poetry; it depended partly on a theory
of eyesight as produced by beams
emitted from the eye. Compare also the
elaborate astronomical blazon of the
hero in Marlowe's *Tamburlaine* 2.1.14–
16.
81 **little O o'th'earth** F's 'little o'th'earth'
makes no sense as it stands. Either the
compositor mistook an original 'O' for
an abbreviated 'of' or a single-syllable
noun was dropped—understandable if
that noun was itself 'O', which is used
elsewhere in Shakespeare to refer to
the heavenly bodies (*Dream* 3.2.189),
and even to the circular form of the
theatre itself (*Henry V*, Prologue 13).
Either correction is metrically possible,
depending on whether 'sovereign' is
treated as two or three syllables.
82 **His legs ... ocean** Like Julius Caesar
(*Caesar* 1.2.136–8) Anthony is compared to the Colossus, the gigantic
statue spanning the entrance to
Rhodes harbour, that ranked as one of
the Seven Wonders of the ancient
world.
83 **Crested** A raised arm, normally flour-
ishing a sword, was a common motif
in heraldic crests.

83–4 **propertied ... tunèd spheres** was as
musical as the spheres themselves; alluding to the widely accepted Pytha-
gorean doctrine that the harmonious
organization of the universe was expressed in a music, inaudible to human
ears, created by the movement of the
planetary spheres. The earliest recorded instance of adj. 'propertied' in
OED.
85 **quail** terrify
   orb globe; but, in accordance with
Cleopatra's colossic image of Anthony,
also playing on the item of regalia
which symbolized a monarch's power
over the world.
87 **autumn** As Dover Wilson demonstrated, an MS reading 'Automne'
could easily be mistaken for 'Antonie'
in Elizabethan handwriting. Ridley's
half-hearted objection that Shakespeare seems normally to have spelt
the name with an *h*, carries no particular weight, since the compositor's
own practice at 4.16.11 shows that he
saw 'Anthonie' and 'Anthony' merely
as preferred alternatives. While Thirlby's emendation is very persuasive, the
F reading is nevertheless not wholly
impossible in this compressed speech,
as Jones argues.
88–90 **His delights ... lived in** Usually
glossed 'he rose above the pleasures

Were dolphin-like; they showed his back above
The element they lived in. In his livery   90
Walked crowns and crownets; realms and islands
          were
As plates dropped from his pocket.
DOLABELLA   Cleopatra—
CLEOPATRA
Think you there was, or might be such a man
As this I dreamt of?
DOLABELLA   Gentle madam, no.
CLEOPATRA
You lie up to the hearing of the gods!   95
But if there be, or ever were one such,
It's past the size of dreaming. Nature wants stuff
To vie strange forms with Fancy, yet t'imagine
An Anthony were nature's piece 'gainst Fancy,
Condemning shadows quite.
DOLABELLA   Hear me, good madam.   100
Your loss is as your self, great, and you bear it
As answering to the weight. Would I might never
O'ertake pursued success, but I do feel,
By the rebound of yours, a grief that smites
My very heart at root!
CLEOPATRA   I thank you, sir.   105
Know you what Caesar means to do with me?

96 or] F3; nor FI   104 smites] CAPELL; suites F

that he lived in as a dolphin rises above
the surface of the sea' (Mack). But this
is surely wrong; the 'delight' anthro-
pomorphically attributed to dolphins has
always been discovered in their leaping
play; and since for Shakespeare's contemporaries the dolphin was a fish, its
leaps must have seemed to express a
delight so intense that they enabled the
creature to transcend its natural element,
water. Anthony's delights seem like
those of dolphins to Cleopatra because
they had the same transcendent intensity; the element in which they lived may
be understood as the world of politics,
the sphere of his greatness, or perhaps
as his merely human condition.

90–1 **In his livery . . . crownets** kings and
    princes were his liveried servants
92 **plates** silver coins
97 **past . . . dreaming** beyond the capacity
    of any mere dream
97–100 **Nature . . . quite** Even though
    Nature seems to lack the material
    needed to match the strange creatures
    which fancy can create, yet for Nature
    to imagine (and so bring into being)
    an Anthony would be a triumphant
    masterpiece sufficient to discredit
    Fancy's wildest fictions.
102–3 **Would . . . do feel** may I never
    achieve the success I seek, if I do not
    feel

DOLABELLA
I am loath to tell you what I would you knew.
CLEOPATRA
Nay, pray you, sir.
DOLABELLA   Though he be honourable—
CLEOPATRA He'll lead me then in triumph?
DOLABELLA Madam, he will: I know't.   110

Flourish. Enter Caesar, Proculeius, Gallus, Mecenas,
and others of his train

ALL Make way there! Caesar!
CAESAR Which is the Queen of Egypt?
DOLABELLA
It is the Emperor, madam.   *Cleopatra kneels*
CAESAR Arise! You shall not kneel—
I pray you rise, rise Egypt.
CLEOPATRA   Sir, the gods   115
Will have it thus: my master and my lord
I must obey.
CAESAR   Take to you no hard thoughts.
The record of what injuries you did us,
Though written in our flesh, we shall remember
As things but done by chance.
CLEOPATRA   Sole sir o'th'world,   120
I cannot project mine own cause so well
To make it clear, but do confess I have
Been laden with like frailties which before
Have often shamed our sex.
CAESAR   Cleopatra, know
We will extenuate rather than enforce.   125
If you apply yourself to our intents,

110.1 *Caesar, Proculeius*] F (*Proculeius, Cæsar*)   113 *Cleopatra*] F ('*Cleo.*')

110.1–190 *Enter Caesar . . . Adieu* The
detail of Cleopatra's encounter with
Octavius Caesar is substantially Plutarch's. Plutarch makes it appear that
the entire episode was a feint designed
to persuade Caesar that she intended
to survive Anthony's disaster—a point
stressed by North's marginal gloss:
'Cleopatra finely deceiveth Octavius
Caesar, as though she desired to live'
(see Appendix A).

115–17 *the gods . . . obey* Another reference to the Doctrine of Obedience. See
l. 31.
116 *my master and my lord* i.e. Caesar
120 *sir* lord
121 *project* lay out, present (accent on
first syllable)
122 *clear* blameless
125 *enforce* press home, emphasize (your
faults)
126 *apply* accommodate

Which towards you are most gentle, you shall find
A benefit in this change; but if you seek
To lay on me a cruelty by taking
Anthony's course, you shall bereave yourself   130
Of my good purposes, and put your children
To that destruction which I'll guard them from,
If thereon you rely. I'll take my leave.

CLEOPATRA

And may through all the world—'tis yours, and we
Your scutcheons and your signs of conquest shall   135
Hang in what place you please. Here, my good lord.
            She proffers a paper

CAESAR You shall advise me in all for Cleopatra.

CLEOPATRA

This is the brief of money, plate, and jewels
I am possessed of—'tis exactly valued,
Not petty things admitted. Where's Seleucus?   140
            Enter Seleucus

SELEUCUS Here, madam.

CLEOPATRA

This is my treasurer. Let him speak, my lord,
Upon his peril, that I have reserved

136.1 *She proffers a paper*] CRAIG (*subs., after* Collier MS); *not in* F   138 brief of] POPE;
breefe: of F   140.1 *Enter Seleucus*] ARDEN; *not in* F

129-30 **seek . . . cruelty** try to make me
  seem cruel
130-3 **you . . . rely** Caesar's circumlocu-
  tory language and serpentine syntax
  only thinly conceal a familiar kind of
  protection racket: 'your children are
  likely to be murdered, but I am luckily
  in a position to protect them from that
  fate, if you co-operate with me'. Plutarch recorded Caesar's suspicion that
  Cleopatra might attempt suicide (Appendix A); a little earlier he had described the actual fate of Cleopatra's
  children by Marcus Antonius and
  Julius Caesar, including the treacher-
  ous murder of Caesarion. Both Garnier
  and Daniel had extensively exploited
  the pathos inherent in Cleopatra's
  duties as mother, Garnier introducing
  a group of anonymous children to
  make their farewell in Act 5, and Daniel giving a whole scene at the beginning of Act 4 to recount the death of

Caesario[n]. Shakespeare, perhaps anxious not to confuse the emotional
  focus of his catastrophe, gives the
  children a purely nominal existence.
134 **And . . . world** *you* may leave and go
  anywhere you please in the whole
  world
135 **scutcheons** shields displaying heraldic coats-of-arms; often the wooden
  hatchments with armorial bearings
  displayed at funerals and hung up on
  monuments as badges of honour
138 **brief** schedule, catalogue
140 **Not . . . admitted** with the exception
  of trivial items
  Where's Seleucus F gives no entry for
  Seleucus, but Cleopatra's line sounds
  like a cue; on the other hand—as
  North's 'by chance there stood Seleucus by' might suggest—he may be
  present throughout the scene, or even
  enter in Caesar's train, as Capell proposed.

To myself nothing. Speak the truth, Seleucus.

SELEUCUS

Madam, I had rather seel my lips   145
Than to my peril speak that which is not.

CLEOPATRA What have I kept back?

SELEUCUS

Enough to purchase what you have made known.

CAESAR

Nay, blush not, Cleopatra, I approve
Your wisdom in the deed.

CLEOPATRA   See, Caesar! O, behold   150
How pomp is followed! Mine will now be yours,
And should we shift estates, yours would be mine.
The ingratitude of this Seleucus does
Even make me wild.—O slave, of no more trust
Than love that's hired! What, goest thou back? Thou
    shalt   155
Go back, I warrant thee, but I'll catch thine eyes
Though they had wings! Slave, soulless villain, dog!
O rarely base!

CAESAR   Good Queen, let us entreat you.

CLEOPATRA

O Caesar, what a wounding shame is this,
That—thou vouchsafing here to visit me,   160
Doing the honour of thy lordliness
To one so meek—that mine own servant should
Parcel the sum of my disgraces by

160–2 That—thou . . . meek—that] This edition; that thou . . . meek, that F

145 **seel** stitch up (cf. note to 3.3.113)
151 **pomp is followed** majesty is served
    Mine my servants
153–4 **ingratitude . . . wild** Although Plutarch and North (in his marginal note) imply that Cleopatra's rage at Seleucus's betrayal was at least partly a theatrical imposition, Shakespeare appears to leave open the possibility that even at this stage the Queen may still be hoping to preserve her throne. However, it should be noted that Daniel's *Cleopatra*, whose action seems to allow for a similar ambiguity, is prefaced by an argument explaining the Queen's behaviour as designed to de-

ceive Caesar as to her real intentions. For a detailed treatment of the scene's ambiguity, see Brents Stirling, 'Cleopatra's Scene with Seleucus: Plutarch, Daniel, and Shakespeare', *SQ* 15 (1964), pp. 299–311.
163 **Parcel** *OED* cites this passage as a usage that has not been satisfactorily explained. Johnson interpreted it as 'make up into a mass', a sense that otherwise does not seem to be found before the last quarter of the eighteenth century; from the usual sense, 'divide into small portions', Schmidt derived 'enumerate by items, specify', but this is not what Seleucus has done;

Addition of his envy. Say, good Caesar,
That I some lady trifles have reserved,   165
Immoment toys, things of such dignity
As we greet modern friends withal; and say
Some nobler token I have kept apart
For Livia and Octavia, to induce
Their mediation—must I be unfolded   170
With one that I have bred? The gods! It smites me
Beneath the fall I have. (*To Seleucus*) Prithee go hence,
Or I shall show the cinders of my spirits
Through th'ashes of my chance. Wert thou a man,
Thou wouldst have mercy on me.
CAESAR   Forbear, Seleucus.   175

Exit Seleucus

CLEOPATRA
Be it known that we, the greatest, are misthought
For things that others do; and when we fall,
We answer others' merits in our name—
Are therefore to be pitied.
CAESAR   Cleopatra,
Not what you have reserved, nor what acknowledged   180
Put we i'th'roll of conquest—still be't yours,
Bestow it at your pleasure, and believe
Caesar's no merchant to make prize with you

175.1 *Exit Seleucus*] CAPELL; *not in* F   178–9 merits in our name— | Are] This edition
(*after* JOHNSON); merits, in our name | Are F

as Malone saw, the required meaning
is something like 'add to, extend', but
there is no other warrant for it.

164–170 **Say . . . mediation** Although these
lines, like the rest of the episode, are
closely modelled on North, some details of the wording suggest the additional influence of Daniel: 'If I reserved
some certain *women's toys . . .* what I
kept, I kept to make my way, | Unto
thy Livia's and Octavia's grace, | That
thereby in compassion moved, they |
Might *mediate* thy favour in my case'
(3.679–86; Bullough, p. 424).
166 **Immoment** of no moment or significance. Apparently a Shakespearian
coinage, since *OED* cites no other use
of the word.

167 **modern** ordinary, everyday
169 **Livia** Caesar's wife
170–1 **unfolded | With** exposed by
171 **bred** given his breeding, brought up
as a member of my household
173 **cinders** live coals
174 **chance** fortunes
a man a real man, and not a eunuch
175 **Forbear** withdraw
176 **we** The heavy stress draws attention
to Cleopatra's shift from the submissive
singular she has used throughout her
scene with Caesar to a reassertion of
her royal plural.
misthought misjudged
178 **answer . . . merits** are brought to
book for the deserts of others
183 **make prize** haggle

Of things that merchants sold. Therefore be cheered,
Make not your thoughts your prisons—no, dear
    Queen,   185
For we intend so to dispose you as
Yourself shall give us counsel. Feed and sleep:
Our care and pity is so much upon you
That we remain your friend; and so adieu.

CLEOPATRA
My master and my lord!

CAESAR   Not so. Adieu.   190
    Flourish. Exeunt Caesar and his train

CLEOPATRA
He words me, girls, he words me, that I should not
Be noble to my self. But hark thee, Charmian.
    Cleopatra whispers to Charmian

IRAS
Finish, good lady, the bright day is done,
And we are for the dark.

CLEOPATRA (*to Charmian*) Hie thee again.
I have spoke already, and it is provided—   195
Go put it to the haste.

CHARMIAN   Madam, I will.
    Enter Dolabella

DOLABELLA
Where's the Queen?

CHARMIAN   Behold, sir.

CLEOPATRA   Dolabella!

DOLABELLA
Madam, as thereto sworn by your command
(Which my love makes religion to obey)

192.1 *Cleopatra . . . Charmian*] THEOBALD (*subs.*); *not in* F

185 **Make . . . prisons** don't imagine your-
    self a prisoner (when you are really
    free)
191 **words me** is trying to fob me off with
    mere words
192 **Be noble to my self** take the noble
    course of action appropriate to my
    royal identity. The heavy stress falling
    on *self* after three unstressed syllables
    indicates a stronger meaning than that
    normally conveyed by the reflexive
    pronoun *myself.*

197–207 *Enter Dolabella . . .* **thanks** Do-
    labella's warning derives from Plu-
    tarch, but his interview with the
    Queen is of Shakespeare's invention
    (see Appendix A).
199 **my love . . . obey** Dolabella addresses
    Cleopatra in the language of religious
    devotion and unswerving obedience
    characteristic of the Renaissance
    courtly lover (cf. 'servant', l. 205); the
    idea of Dolabella as being 'far forsooth
    in love' with Cleopatra derives not from

I tell you this: Caesar through Syria   200
Intends his journey, and within three days
You with your children will he send before.
Make your best use of this. I have performed
Your pleasure and my promise.
CLEOPATRA   Dolabella,
I shall remain your debtor.
DOLABELLA   I, your servant.   205
Adieu, good Queen, I must attend on Caesar.
CLEOPATRA
Farewell, and thanks.   *Exit Dolabella*
                    Now Iras, what think'st thou?
Thou, an Egyptian puppet shall be shown
In Rome as well as I. Mechanic slaves
With greasy aprons, rules, and hammers shall   210
Uplift us to the view. In their thick breaths,
Rank of gross diet, shall we be enclouded,
And forced to drink their vapour.
IRAS   The gods forbid!
CLEOPATRA
Nay, 'tis most certain, Iras. Saucy lictors
Will catch at us like strumpets, and scald rhymers   215
Ballad us out o'tune. The quick comedians
Extemporally will stage us, and present
Our Alexandrian revels—Anthony
Shall be brought drunken forth, and I shall see
Some squeaking Cleopatra boy my greatness   220

207 *Exit Dolabella*] CAPELL; *Exit* F (*after 'Cæsar'*)   216 Ballad] F2; Ballads F1

Plutarch, but from Daniel (5.1078; Bullough, p. 433).

205 **I...debtor** Cf. Daniel's Cleopatra, who says of Dolabella and his love, 'I must die his debtor' (5. 1084; Bullough, p. 433).

208 **an Egyptian puppet** Probably 'as if you were some exotic puppet or doll'; but *puppet* could also be used to mean 'pantomime actor', appropriate to the prisoners' roles in Caesar's triumphal pageant.

209 **Mechanic slaves** base labourers

211 **thick** foul

214 **lictors** officers who accompanied

Roman magistrates and were responsible for carrying out punishments; as Dover Wilson suggested, Shakespeare seems to have equated them with English beadles whose job included the disciplining of prostitutes.

215 **scald rhymers** scurvy hack poets

216 **quick** lively, quick-witted
comedians In Elizabethan usage, *actors* of any sort; but in this case Shakespeare seems to have in mind the improvisational *commedia dell'arte* troupes who flourished in the Rome of his own day.

220 **squeaking...greatness** A daring piece of self-referentiality, since Cleopatra's

I'th'posture of a whore.

IRAS   O the good gods!

CLEOPATRA Nay, that's certain.

IRAS

I'll never see't! For I am sure my nails
Are stronger than mine eyes.

CLEOPATRA   Why, that's the way
To fool their preparation and to conquer   225
Their most absurd intents.

    Enter Charmian

                Now, Charmian!
Show me, my women, like a queen. Go fetch
My best attires. I am again for Cydnus,
To meet Mark Anthony. Sirrah Iras, go—
Now, noble Charmian, we'll dispatch indeed!—   230
And when thou hast done this chore, I'll give thee
    leave
To play till doomsday; bring our crown and all.

                    Exit Iras. A noise within

---

223 my] F2; mine F1   232.1 *Exit Iras*] CAPELL; *not in* F

part, like all female roles in Shakespeare's theatre, was written for a boy-actor.

221 **posture of a whore** posing in the attitude of a whore (the earliest recorded usage of *posture* in OED). Partridge, noting that '*posture* is, ostensibly, a theatrical term', finds a bawdy play on 'sexual posture—a *figura Veneris*' (p. 165). Perhaps Cleopatra imagines the boy mimicking scenes out of Pietro Aretino's notorious sonnets, *I Modi*, written to accompany a series of pornographic engravings of courtesans by Giulio Romano, and vulgarly known in the seventeenth century as *Aretine's Postures*.

228 **Cydnus** Cleopatra presents her carefully staged death as a re-enactment of the great water-pageant evoked by Enobarbus in 2.2, deliberately pre-empting the humiliating public pageantry of Caesar's triumph. This touch may have been suggested by Daniel whose Nuntius describes the dead Cleopatra 'Glittering in all her pompous rich array ... Even as she was when on thy crystal streams, | Clear Cydnus she did show what earth could show.... Even as she went at first to meet her love, | So goes she now at last again to find him' (5.1457–65; Bullough, pp. 442–3).

229 **Sirrah** form of address used to inferiors, usually male, but sometimes playfully to children of either sex; hence here affectionately to Iras

230 **dispatch** (1) hurry; (2) make an end

231–2 **And ... doomsday** Most editors assume these words are directed to Charmian, and punctuate accordingly; but F prints l. 230 ('Now ... indeed') in parentheses, suggesting that the following lines continue Cleopatra's instructions to Iras, and that 'this chore' refers to her fetching of the royal robes.

232 **play** In the context of Cleopatra's self-conscious regal 'show' the innocent childlike connotations of the word are not entirely separable from its theatrical meaning.

Wherefore's this noise?
> *Enter a Guard*

GUARD   Here is a rural fellow
That will not be denied your highness' presence.
He brings you figs.   235
CLEOPATRA
Let him come in.   *Exit Guard*
                    What poor an instrument
May do a noble deed! He brings me liberty.
My resolution's placed, and I have nothing
Of woman in me—now from head to foot
I am marble constant; now the fleeting moon   240
No planet is of mine.
> *Enter Guard and Clown with a basket*

GUARD   This is the man.
CLEOPATRA
Avoid, and leave him.   *Exit Guard*
                Hast thou the pretty worm

233, 236, 241, 242 *Guard*] F (*Guardsman*)   233, 241 GUARD] F (*Guards.*)   240 marble constant] F (Marble constant); marble-constant CAPELL *and most eds.*   241 *with a basket*] ROWE; *not in* F

233–278 **a rural fellow . . . joy o'th'worm** The scene with the clown is an imaginative expansion of a small detail in Plutarch whose 'countryman' also has a line in gallows humour (see Appendix A).

235 **figs** The basket of figs derives from Plutarch; but it is also likely to recall Charmian's 'I love long life better than figs', with its bawdy suggestiveness (see note to 1.2.32).

236 **What** how

237 **liberty** drawing on the Stoic doctrine that suicide is the pathway to freedom; see for example Lodge's Seneca, 'Of Anger', p. 565: 'Enquirest thou which is the way to liberty? Every vein in thy body.'

240 **marble constant** Most editors follow Capell in assuming this means 'constant as marble', and so hyphenate; but Cleopatra may be imagining her woman's flesh as metamorphosed into marble, and the phrase could equally well be a poetic inversion of 'constant marble'—a supposition which is given some support by F's capitalization of

'Marble', since nouns are far more commonly capitalized in F than other parts of speech. For the classical trope of marble as a symbol of monumental endurance, see e.g. Sonnet 55: 'Not marble nor the gilded monuments of princes | Shall outlive this powerful rhyme' (ll. 1–2).
fleeting moon In Renaissance cosmology, the changing moon presided over that part of creation which was subject to mutability and inconstancy. The fickle nature of all women was supposedly evidenced by the moon's government of their biological cycles (just as it governed the changeable element of water, see note to 5.2.288); but Cleopatra is specifically associated with the moon through her assumption of the attributes of Isis, the Egyptian moon-goddess (see 3.6.17, 3.13.154).

241 *Clown* rustic

242 **Avoid** withdraw
worm serpent; cf. the description of Cleopatra herself as 'serpent of old Nile' 1.5.25)

Of Nilus there, that kills and pains not?

CLOWN Truly I have him, but I would not be the party
    that should desire you to touch him, for his biting is   245
    immortal—those that do die of it do seldom or never
    recover.

CLEOPATRA Remember'st thou any that have died on't?

CLOWN Very many, men and women too. I heard of one
    of them no longer than yesterday—a very honest   250
    woman, but something given to lie, as a woman
    should not do, but in the way of honesty—how she
    died of the biting of it, what pain she felt. Truly, she
    makes a very good report o'th'worm. But he that will
    believe all that they say, shall never be saved by half   255
    that they do. But this is most falliable: the worm's an
    odd worm.

CLEOPATRA Get thee hence, farewell.

CLOWN I wish you all joy of the worm.

CLEOPATRA Farewell.   260

CLOWN You must think this, look you, that the worm
    will do his kind.

CLEOPATRA Ay, ay, farewell.

CLOWN Look you, the worm is not to be trusted but in
    the keeping of wise people—for indeed there is no   265
    goodness in the worm.

CLEOPATRA Take thou no care, it shall be heeded.

CLOWN Very good. Give it nothing I pray you, for it is not
    worth the feeding.

CLEOPATRA Will it eat me?   270

CLOWN You must not think I am so simple but I know
    the devil himself will not eat a woman. I know that a
    woman is a dish for the gods, if the devil dress her not.

---

246 **immortal** The clown means 'mortal';
  but Cleopatra intends that it shall satisfy 'immortal longings' (l. 280).
250 **honest** (1) truthful; (2) chaste
251 **lie** (1) tell lies; (2) fornicate
252–4 **she died ... o'th'worm** In the
  Clown's bawdy play on the sexual
  sense of *die*, the worm (as Jones points
  out) becomes a phallic creature.
256 **falliable** The clown means 'infallible';
  perhaps, amid all this talk of women
  and serpents, his malapropism should

involve a clumsy pun on 'Fall'.
262 **do his kind** act according to its nature
270 **Will it eat me** In Cleopatra's mind the
  worm is now associated with the
  worms of the grave.
273 **dish for the gods** A curious echo of
  Enobarbus's description of Cleopatra
  (2.6.125; and cf. 3.13.118–9).
  dress (1) prepare for the table; (2)
  attire

But truly these same whoreson devils do the gods
great harm in their women: for in every ten that they   275
make, the devils mar five.

CLEOPATRA Well, get thee gone, farewell.

CLOWN Yes, forsooth—I wish you joy o'th'worm.

Exit ⌈ leaving the basket ⌉
Enter Iras with a robe, crown and other regalia

CLEOPATRA

Give me my robe, put on my crown—I have
Immortal longings in me. Now no more   280
The juice of Egypt's grape shall moist this lip.
Yare, yare, good Iras, quick—methinks I hear
Anthony call; I see him rouse himself
To praise my noble act; I hear him mock
The luck of Caesar, which the gods give men   285
To excuse their after wrath. Husband, I come!
Now to that name my courage prove my title!
I am fire and air—my other elements

278.1 *leaving the basket*] OXFORD; *not in* F   278.2 *Enter . . . regalia*] CAPELL. (*subs.*); *not*
in F

274 **whoreson** bastard; Elizabethan slang,
a mild oath, roughly equivalent to
modern 'bloody' or 'damned'

278.1 *leaving the basket* Most editors follow Capell and insert a direction for
the Clown to set down the basket at
l. 259 (after 'all joy of the worm'); but
the scene clearly invites a lot of comic
business with the basket and its con-
tents, which will vary from production
to production. The only certain thing
is that the Clown must leave the basket behind when he exits.

278.2–end The account of Cleopatra's
death is closely modelled on Plutarch,
who, however, also reported rival versions of the event (see Appendix A).

282 **Yare** quickly, deftly

284 **To . . . act** Once again the context
makes the theatrical sense of 'act'
difficult to avoid; Cleopatra imagines
Anthony as the admiring audience of
her last performance. Cf. l. 329. Shakespeare's sense of the theatricality of
Cleopatra's death was perhaps influenced by Daniel: 'she performs that
part | That hath so great a part of
glory won. . . . Well, now this work is
done (said she) here ends | This act of

life, that part the Fates assigned.
. . . And now, O earth, the theatre
where I | Have acted this, witness I
die unforced' (5.1592–607; Bullough,
p. 446).

285–6 **which . . . wrath** which the gods
give men only so that they can afterwards punish them for the hubris it
induces

286 **Husband** Cf. Cleopatra's earlier contempt for such domestic terms; Daniel's Cleopatra, as she prepares to
'come unto' Antony, similarly identifies herself as his 'woeful wife'
(5.1167, 1133; Bullough, p. 435).

288–9 **fire . . . life** A metaphor for the
separation of soul and body; living
creatures were thought to be compounded of two higher elements (air and
fire) and two lower ones (earth and
water). While the hot and dry elements
of air and fire were supposed to pre-
dominate in men, the cold and moist
elements of earth and water predomi-
nated in women and this accounted for
their supposedly changeable and deceptive natures. In the symbology of the
play Cleopatra is typically associated
with the earth and water that make up

I give to baser life. So, have you done?
Come then, and take the last warmth of my lips.   290
Farewell, kind Charmian, Iras, long farewell.
She kisses them. Iras falls and dies
Have I the aspic in my lips? Dost fall?
If thou and nature can so gently part,
The stroke of death is as a lover's pinch
Which hurts, and is desired. Dost thou lie still?   295
If thus thou vanishest, thou tell'st the world
It is not worth leave-taking.

CHARMIAN

Dissolve, thick cloud, and rain, that I may say
The gods themselves do weep.

CLEOPATRA   This proves me base—
If she first meet the curlèd Anthony,   300
He'll make demand of her, and spend that kiss
Which is my heaven to have.
She applies an aspic to her breast
                        Come, thou mortal wretch,

291.1 *She . . . dies*] HANMER (*subs.*); *not in* F   302 *She . . . breast*] HANMER (*subs.*); *not in* F

the fertile mud of Egypt. Dent (A94.1) cites 'To be air and fire' as proverbial—but since his earliest example is from 1607 the phrase may very well derive from Shakespeare's play.

292 **aspic** asp (the form of the name in North). The 'asp' is usually taken to be the Egyptian sacred cobra (*Naja haje*), often associated with the goddess Isis—though the name is also used of a number of vipers, including *Vipera aspis* and *Cerastes vipera* (the so called Cleopatra's asp). The cobra's bite apparently produces a sensation of drowsy intoxication followed by slow paralysis, and this snake is appropriate to Cleopatra's role as an avatar of Isis.

294 **stroke** blow; but the context creates a delicate ambivalence in which the sense of 'amorous stroking' is also suggested (cf. above, 2.2.204). The eroticization of Cleopatra's death, though absent from Plutarch's account, is not necessarily Shakespeare's invention: Garnier's Cleopatra addressing the dead Antony is 'most happy . . . To die with thee, and dying thee embrace; |

My body joined with thine, my mouth with thine. . . . And wrapped with thee in one self sheet to rest. . . . A thousand kisses, thousand thousand more | Let you my mouth for honour's farewell give; | That in this office weak my limbs may grow, | Fainting in you, and forth my soul may flow' (5.1964–8, 1997–2000; Bullough, pp. 405–6); more severely, Daniel's Cleopatra offers to 'sacrifice these arms to Death, | That Lust late dedicated to Delights', but later her smile seems to tell Death 'how much her death did please her' (5.1534–5, 1629; Bullough, pp. 444, 446).

300 **curlèd Anthony** Cf. Enobarbus's description of Anthony on the Cydnus 'barbered ten times o'er' (2.2.231).

301 **spend** There is probably a shading of the bawdy sense ('to discharge seminally') here; cf. Garnier, 5.1990–1, 'I spent in tears, not able more to spend, | But kiss him now, what rests me more to do?' (Bullough, p. 406).

302 **wretch** little creature (used as a term of humorous depreciation or affectionate mockery, like 'fool', l. 304)

With thy sharp teeth this knot intrinsicate
Of life at once untie. Poor venomous fool,
Be angry, and dispatch. O, couldst thou speak,   305
That I might hear thee call great Caesar 'Ass
Unpolicied!'
CHARMIAN   O eastern star!
CLEOPATRA   Peace, peace!
Dost thou not see my baby at my breast,
That sucks the nurse asleep?
CHARMIAN   O, break! O, break!
CLEOPATRA
As sweet as balm, as soft as air, as gentle.   310
O Anthony! Nay, I will take thee too.
        She applies another aspic to her arm
What should I stay—   *She dies*
CHARMIAN   In this vile world? So fare thee well.

311.1 *She applies . . . arm*] THEOBALD (*subs.*); *not in* F   312 *She dies*] *Dyes.* F   vile]
CAPELL (*conj.* Thirlby); wilde F

303 **intrinsicate** intricately tangled
307 **Unpolicied** whose political strata-
    gems have been brought to nothing;
    stripped of all his pretensions to
    political cunning. The first example of
    this participial adjective recorded in
    OED.
    eastern star i.e. Venus (Jones)
308 **breast** Although Plutarch has Cleo-
    patra bitten only 'in the arm', she is
    more usually shown in medieval and
    Renaissance iconography with asps at
    her breast, and this version of her
    death was sufficiently widespread for
    Sir Thomas Browne to seek to refute it
    in *Pseudodoxia Epidemica . . . Vulgar and
    Common Errors*, 'Of the Picture De-
    scribing the Death of Cleopatra'. Bev-
    ington cites Thomas Nashe's *Christ's
    Tears over Jerusalem* (1593): 'At thy
    breasts (as at Cleopatra's) asps shall be
    put out to nurse' (*Works*, ii. 140); and
    Shakespeare may also have known
    Peele's *Edward I*, where the murderous
    Queen Elinor, having applied a serpent
    to the Mayoress's breast, mocks the
    Mayoress as 'nurse' to the serpent
    which is killing her: 'Suck on, sweet
    babe' (Scene 15, ll. 2095–6; in *Works*,
    ed. C. T. Prouty, ii. 148).

309–10 **asleep . . . gentle** Cf. Daniel's de-
    scription of the aspic: 'Better than
    Death, Death's office thou dischargest,
    | That with one gentle touch canst
    free our breath: | And in a pleasing
    sleep our soul enlargest' (5.1500–2;
    Bullough, pp. 443–4).
310 **As sweet . . . gentle** proverbial (Dent
    B63.1, A91.1, A88.1)
    gentle When applied to a 'worm'
    which is both serpent and prover-
    bial worm of death, the pun on *gentle*
    = maggot (see l. 58) seems inescap-
    able.
312 **vile** Capell's emendation depends on
    the easy misreading of the obsolete
    form *vilde* as *wilde*. Some editors retain
    F's perfectly tenable 'wild' (laid waste,
    desert—i.e. by Anthony's defeat and
    death), but the double alliteration jan-
    gles here, and 'vile' makes a proper
    antithesis with Cleopatra's 'gentle'
    (l. 310); Daniel's Cleopatra similarly
    declares her repugnance for 'base
    life' (5.1583; Bullough, p. 445). Cf.
    also Sonnet 71, 'Give warning to
    the world that I am fled | From *this
    vile world* with vilest worms to dwell'
    ll. 3–4).

Now boast thee, Death, in thy possession lies
A lass unparalleled. Downy windows, close;
And golden Phoebus never be beheld   315
Of eyes again so royal. Your crown's awry,
I'll mend it, and then play—
  Enter the Guard rustling in
FIRST GUARD
  Where's the Queen?
CHARMIAN   Speak softly, wake her not.
FIRST GUARD
  Caesar hath sent—
CHARMIAN   Too slow a messenger.
  She applies an aspic
O, come apace, dispatch, I partly feel thee.   320
FIRST GUARD
  Approach, ho! All's not well. Caesar's beguiled.
SECOND GUARD
  There's Dolabella sent from Caesar—call him!
                                          ⌜ *Exit a Guard* ⌝
FIRST GUARD
  What work is here, Charmian? Is this well done?
CHARMIAN
  It is well done, and fitting for a princess

---

316 awry] ROWE 1714; away F   317.1 in] ROWE; in, and Dolabella. F   318, 337, 338,
349 FIRST GUARD] F ('I. Guard.')   319, 321, 323 FIRST GUARD] F ('I')   319 She...
aspic] POPE (subs.); not in F   322 SECOND GUARD] F ('2')   322.1 Exit a Guard] OXFORD
(subs.); not in F

313 **possession** Includes 'sexual possession', since behind the figure lies the
  familiar trope of Death as bridegroom.
313–14 **lies | A lass unparalleled** Given the
  theatricality of the occasion, the audience may well hear a punning echo of
  Act I's 'Excellent falsehood!' (1.42)
  and 'excellent dissembling' (3.79)—
  'lies, alas, unparalleled'.
314 **Downy windows** eyelids
315 **Phoebus** i.e. the sun
316 **play** Charmian tenderly recalls Cleopatra's affectionate irony at ll. 231–2.
317.1 **rustling** The required meaning
  seems to be something like 'bustling',
  which *OED* records only as an American colloquial usage from the late

19th cent. Conceivably, as some editors assume, Shakespeare may have
  written 'rushing', easily misread as
  'rustling'—but the misreading seems
  unlikely unless something like the still
  current meaning of 'rustling' was then
  available. However the word is read,
  the stage direction is of the sort which
  belongs more with the imaginative excitement of an authorial manuscript
  than with the practicalities of a theatrical prompt-book.
324 **well done, and fitting** The phrase
  derives directly from North (see Appendix A), but is transformed by its delicate and poignant echo of Anthony's
  'the nobleness of life | Is to do thus'

Descended of so many royal kings. 325
Ah, soldier! *Charmian dies*
   Enter Dolabella
DOLABELLA
How goes it here?
SECOND GUARD   All dead.
DOLABELLA   Caesar, thy thoughts
Touch their effects in this. Thyself art coming
To see performed the dreaded act which thou
So sought'st to hinder. 330
   Enter Caesar and all his train, marching
ALL   A way there, a way for Caesar.
DOLABELLA
O sir, you are too sure an augurer—
That you did fear is done.
CAESAR   Bravest at the last,
She levelled at our purposes, and, being royal,
Took her own way. The manner of their deaths? 335
I do not see them bleed.
DOLABELLA   Who was last with them?
FIRST GUARD
A simple countryman that brought her figs.
This was his basket.
CAESAR   Poisoned, then.
FIRST GUARD   O Caesar,
This Charmian lived but now, she stood and spake—
I found her trimming up the diadem 340
On her dead mistress—tremblingly she stood,
And on the sudden dropped.
CAESAR   O noble weakness!
If they had swallowed poison, 'twould appear
By external swelling; but she looks like sleep,

---

327 SECOND GUARD] F ('2. *Guard*')   340-1 diadem | On . . . mistress—tremblingly] ROWE (*subs.*); Diadem; | On . . . Mistris tremblingly F

(1.1.38–9). Cf. also above 5.2.5, and Enobarbus's despairing 'I have done ill' (4.6.17).

327–8 thy thoughts . . . this your fears

334 **levelled at** anticipated and aimed to overlap with their own realization frustrate (literally 'took aim at')
337 **simple** humble; harmless

As she would catch another Anthony   345
In her strong toil of grace.
DOLABELLA   Here on her breast
There is a vent of blood, and something blown—
The like is on her arm.
FIRST GUARD
This is an aspic's trail; and these fig-leaves
Have slime upon them, such as th'aspic leaves   350
Upon the caves of Nile.
CAESAR   Most probable
That so she died, for her physician tells me
She hath pursued conclusions infinite
Of easy ways to die. Take up her bed,
And bear her women from the monument;   355
She shall be buried by her Anthony—
No grave upon the earth shall clip in it
A pair so famous. High events as these
Strike those that make them; and their story is
No less in pity than his glory which   360
Brought them to be lamented. Our army shall

---

346 **strong toil of grace** strong net or
snare of beauty. The oxymoronic language (cf. 'noble weakness') registers
an uncharacteristic ambivalence in
Caesar's response to Cleopatra. Cf. Daniel, 5.1622–3: 'Yet lo that face the
wonder of her life, | Retains in death,
a grace that graceth death' (Bullough,
p. 446).
347 **vent** discharge
   blown 'swollen' (Johnson), 'deposited'
(Jones, who compares l. 60); 'I think
... that *blown* must refer to something
like the track of a snail' (Ridley).
352–4 **her physician ... die** Plutarch records in rather unpleasant detail Cleopatra's experiments with poison after
the débâcle of Actium (see Appendix
A).
353 **conclusions** experiments
354–64 **Take up ... solemnity** Caesar's
gestures of magnanimity, like much
else in this scene, derive from Plutarch, where he expressly orders that
'she should be nobly buried and laid
by Antonius' (see Appendix A). Although Plutarch is not clear about

this, the natural assumption must be
that Cleopatra was buried in her
monument; in Shakespeare the gesture
is more ambiguous: Caesar's instruction may only provide a convenient
way of clearing the stage and initiating
the solemn funeral procession which
was the conventional sign of tragic
ending; or it may imply that the
Queen is to be buried more obscurely,
away from the regal spendours of
her monument. Nevertheless this last
incantatory reminder of the scene's
nominal setting serves to highlight
once again the ritual of self-monu-
mentalization which supplies the emotional and metaphoric climax of the
play.
357 **clip** embrace
359 **Strike** shock, afflict, overwhelm
359–61 **their story ... lamented** the story
of this pair is not less pitiable than the
glory of their conqueror is splendid;
but perhaps 'no less in pity' also carries the sense 'none the less lofty for
being pitiable'.

In solemn show attend this funeral—
And then to Rome. Come, Dolabella, see
High order in this great solemnity.

> *Exeunt, ⌈ soldiers carrying the bodies of Cleopatra (upon*
> *her bed), Charmian and Iras⌉*

FINIS

364.1–2 *Exeunt . . . Iras*] F ('*Exeunt omnes*')   364.1ᵛ *upon her bed*] OXFORD; *not in* F

364.2 *upon her bed* Indicated, as the Oxford editor points out, by Caesar's command at l. 354. Modern productions often use a throne to emphasize the ritual of re-coronation incorporated in Cleopatra's suicide; but a seventeenth-century day-bed of the kind shown in the earliest illustration of the play (Rowe 1709) could be used to suggest regal enthronement without effacing the erotic associations of the bed (see Fig. 2).

Excerpts from
THE LIFE OF MARCUS ANTONIUS
in Sir Thomas North's translation of Plutarch's
The Lives of the Noble Grecians and Romans (1579).

(Passages on which Shakespeare seems especially dependent are
followed by relevant citations; significant omissions are paraphrased
in italics between square brackets)

[Account of Antonius's family, upbringing, and education]

. . . Now Antonius being a fair young man and in the prime of his
youth, he fell acquainted with Curio, whose friendship and acquaintance (as it is reported) was a plague unto him. For he was a dissolute
man, given over to all lust and insolency, who, to have Antonius
the better at his commandment, trained him on into great follies
and vain expenses upon women, in rioting and banqueting. So that
in short time he brought Antonius into a marvellous great debt, and
too great for one of his years—to wit, of two hundred and fifty
talents. . . . [Clodius] he followed for a time in his desperate attempts,
who bred great stir and mischief in Rome. But at length he forsook him, being weary of his rashness and folly. . . . Thereupon he
left Italy and went into Greece; and there bestowed the most part
of his time, sometime in wars and otherwhile in the study of
eloquence.
  He used a manner of phrase in his speech called Asiatic, which
carried the best grace and estimation at that time, and was much
like to his manners and life—for it was full of ostentation, foolish
bravery, and vain ambition.

*[Account of Antonius's early military career in Syria, Judaea, and
Egypt]*

. . . Antonius did many noble acts of a valiant and wise captain. . . .
So was his great courtesy also much commended of all . . . and he
was also thought a worthy man of all the soldiers in the Roman's
camp. But, besides all this, he had a noble presence and showed a
countenance of one of a noble house. He had a goodly thick beard,
a broad forehead, crook-nosed; and there appeared such a manly
look in his countenance as is commonly seen in Hercules' pictures,
stamped or graven in metal. Now it had been a speech of old time

that the family of the Antonii were descended from one Anton, the son of Hercules, whereof the family took name. This opinion did Antonius seek to confirm in all his doings, not only resembling him in the likeness of his body, as we have said before, but also in the wearing of his garments. For when he would openly show himself abroad before many people, he would always wear his cassock girt down low upon his hips, with a great sword hanging by his side, and upon that some ill-favoured cloak. [1.3.84] Furthermore, things that seem intolerable in other men, as to boast commonly, to jest with one or other, to drink like a good fellow with everybody, to sit with the soldiers when they dine, and to eat and drink with them soldierlike—it is incredible what wonderful love it won him amongst them. And furthermore, being given to love, that made him the more desired; and by that means he brought many to love him. For he would further every man's love, and also would not be angry that men should merrily tell him of those he loved.

But besides all this, that which most procured his rising and advancement was his liberality, who gave all to the soldiers and kept nothing for himself. And when he was grown to great credit, then was his authority and power also very great, the which notwithstanding himself did overthrow by a thousand other faults he had. [1.4.12–13]

[*Account of Antonius's part in the factional struggles of Roman politics and the resulting civil war between Julius Caesar and Gnaeus Pompey; his role in Caesar's victory at Pharsalia; and his quarrel with the popular tribune, Dolabella*]

. . . by this means he got the ill will of the common people; and, on the other side, the noblemen (as Cicero saith) did not only mislike him, but also hate him for his naughty life; for they did abhor his banquets and drunken feasts he made at unseasonable times, and his extreme wasteful expenses upon vain light huswives; and then in the day time he would sleep or walk out his drunkenness, thinking to wear away the fume of the abundance of wine which he had taken overnight. In his house they did nothing but feast, dance, and mask. And himself passed away the time in hearing of foolish plays, or in marrying these players, tumblers, jesters, and such sort of people. . . . and besides also, in honest men's houses in the cities where he came he would have common harlots, courtesans, and these tumbling gillots lodged.

[*Julius Caesar alienated by Antonius's behaviour*]

. . . And therefore Caesar . . . being created Consul the third time, he took not Antonius, but chose Lepidus his colleague and fellow-Consul. Afterwards, when Pompey's house was put to open sale,

Antonius bought it; but when they asked him money for it, he made it very strange and was offended with them; [2.6.27] and writeth himself that he would not go with Caesar into the wars of Afric, because he was not well recompensed for the service he had done him before.

Yet Caesar did somewhat bridle his madness and insolency, not suffering him to pass his fault so lightly away, making as though he saw them not. And therefore he left his dissolute manner of life, and married Fulvia, that was Clodius' widow, a woman not so basely minded to spend her time in spinning and housewifery, and was not contented to master her husband at home, but would also rule him in his office abroad, and command him that commanded legions and great armies; so that Cleopatra was to give Fulvia thanks for that she had taught Antonius this obedience to women, that learned so well to be at their commandment. Now, because Fulvia was somewhat sour and crooked of condition, [1.1.21] Antonius devised to make her pleasanter and somewhat better disposed; and therefore he would play her many pretty youthful parts to make her merry.

[*Events leading up to the assassination of Julius Caesar; power struggle after Caesar's death; quarrel with Octavius Caesar*]

. . . Cicero on the other side being at that time the chiefest man of authority and estimation in the city, he stirred up all men against Antonius . . . and moreover sent Hircius and Pansa, then Consuls, to drive Antonius out of Italy. These two Consuls, together with Caesar who also had an army, went against Antonius that besieged the city of Modena, and there overthrew him in battle. But both the Consuls were slain there.

Antonius, flying upon this overthrow, fell into great misery all at once; but the chiefest want of all other, and that pinched him most, was famine. Howbeit he was of such a strong nature that by patience he would overcome any adversity; and the heavier fortune lay upon him, the more constant showed he himself. Every man that feeleth want or adversity knoweth by virtue and discretion what he should do. But when indeed they are overlaid with extremity and be sore oppressed, few have the hearts to follow that which they praise and commend, and much less to avoid that they reprove and mislike. But rather to the contrary, they yield to their accustomed easy life, and through faint heart and lack of courage do change their first mind and purpose. And therefore it was a wonderful example to the soldiers to see Antonius, that was brought up in all fineness and superfluity, so easily to drink puddle water and to eat wild fruits and roots. And moreover it is reported that, even as they passed the Alps, they did eat the barks of trees and such beasts as never man tasted of their flesh before. [1.4.56-68]

[Antonius's cause rescued by Lepidus; reconciliation with Octavius]

... all three met together (to wit, Caesar, Antonius, and Lepidus) in an island environed round about with a little river; and there remained three days together. Now, as touching all other matters, they were easily agreed and did divide all the Empire of Rome between them, as if it had been their own inheritance. But yet they could hardly agree whom they would put to death; for every one of them would kill their enemies, and save their kinsmen and friends. Yet at length, giving place to their greedy desire to be revenged of their enemies, they spurned all reverence of blood and holiness of friendship at their feet. For Caesar left Cicero to Antonius' will; Antonius also forsook Lucius Caesar, who was his uncle by his mother; and both of them together suffered Lepidus to kill his own brother Paulus. Yet some writers affirm that Caesar and Antonius requested Paulus might be slain, and that Lepidus was contented with it.

In my opinion there was never a more horrible, unnatural, and crueller change than this was. For, thus changing murder for murder, they did as well kill those whom they did forsake and leave unto others, as those also which others left unto them to kill; but so much more was their wickedness and cruelty great unto their friends, for that they put them to death being innocents and having no cause to hate them. [3.6.32] ...

Now the government of these Triumviri grew odious and hateful to the Romans, for divers respects. But they most blamed Antonius, because he, being elder than Caesar and of more power and force than Lepidus, gave himself again to his former riot and excess when he left to deal in the affairs of the commonwealth. But, setting aside the ill name he had for his insolency, he was yet much more hated in respect of the house he dwelt in, the which was the house of Pompey the Great, a man as famous for his temperance, modesty, and civil life, as for his three triumphs. For it grieved them to see the gates commonly shut against the captains, magistrates of the city, and also ambassadors of strange nations, which were sometimes thrust from the gate with violence; and that the house within was full of tumblers, antic dancers, jugglers, players, jesters, and drunkards, quaffing and guzzling, and that on them he spent and bestowed the most part of his money he got by all kind of possible extortions, bribery, and policy [2.6.27] ...

Octavius Caesar perceiving that no money would serve Antonius' turn, he prayed that they might divide the money between them; and so did they also divide the army, for them both to go into Macedon to make war against Brutus and Cassius; and in the meantime they left the government of the city of Rome unto Lepidus. When they had passed over the seas, and that they began to make war, they being both camped by their enemies, to wit, Antonius against Cassius, and Caesar against Brutus, Caesar did no great matter, but Antonius had alway the upper hand and did all. For at the first battle Caesar was overthrown by Brutus and lost his camp, and very hardly saved himself by flying from them that followed him. Howbeit he writeth himself in his Commentaries that he fled before the charge was given, because of a dream one of his friends had. Antonius on the other side overthrew Cassius in battle, though some write that he was not there himself at the battle, but that he came after the overthrow whilst his men had the enemies in chase. So Cassius at his earnest request was slain by a faithful servant of his own called Pindarus, whom he had enfranchised, because he knew not in time that Brutus had overcome Caesar. Shortly after they fought another battle again, in the which Brutus was overthrown, who afterwards also slew himself.

Thus Antonius had the chiefest glory of all this victory, specially because Caesar was sick at that time. [3.11.35–40] Antonius having found Brutus' body after this battle ... he cast his coat armour (which was wonderful rich and sumptuous) upon Brutus' body and gave commandment to one of his slaves enfranchised to defray the charge of his burial.

[*Octavius returns to Rome, while Antonius takes his army east, through Greece into Asia; his fondness for the Greeks and especially the Athenians; his relapse into riot and excess; corruption of his subordinates and Antonius's excessive trust*]

... [Antonius] had a noble mind, as well to punish offenders as to reward well-doers; and yet he did exceed more in giving than in punishing. Now for his outrageous manner of railing he commonly used, mocking and flouting of every man, that was remedied by itself. For a man might as boldly exchange a mock with him, and he was as well contented to be mocked as to mock others. But yet it oftentimes marred all. For he thought that those which told him so plainly and truly in mirth would never flatter him in good earnest in any matter of weight. But thus he was easily abused by the praises they gave him, not finding how these flatter[er]s mingled their flattery, under this familiar and plain manner of speech unto him, as a fine device to make difference of meats with sharp and tart sauce, and also to keep him, by this frank jesting and bourding with him at the table, that their common flattery should not be troublesome unto him, as men do easily mislike to have too much of one thing; and that they handled him finely thereby, when they would give him place in any matter of weight and follow his counsel, that it might not appear to him they did it so much to please him, but because they were ignorant and understood not so much as he did. [1.2.132–74 ff.]

Antonius being thus inclined, the last and extremest mischief of all other (to wit, the love of Cleopatra) lighted on him, who did waken and stir up many vices yet hidden in him, and were never seen to any; and, if any spark of goodness or hope of rising were left him, Cleopatra quenched it straight and made it worse than before. [1.1.1–13]

The manner how he fell in love with her was this. Antonius, going to make war with the Parthians, sent to command Cleopatra to appear personally before him when he came into Cilicia, to answer unto such accusations as were laid against her—being this, that she had aided Cassius and Brutus in their war against him. . . . [Cleopatra,] guessing by the former access and credit she had with Julius Caesar and Gnaeus Pompey (the son of Pompey the Great) only for her beauty, [1.5.29–34] she began to have good hope that she might more easily win Antonius. For Caesar and Pompey knew her when she was but a young thing, and knew not then what the world meant; but now she went to Antonius at the age when a woman's beauty is at the prime, and she also of best judgement. [1.5.73–4] So she furnished herself with a world of gifts, store of gold and silver, and of riches and other sumptuous ornaments, as is credible enough she might bring from so great a house and from so wealthy and rich a realm as Egypt was. But yet she carried nothing with her wherein she trusted more than in herself and in the charms and enchantment of her passing beauty and grace.

Therefore when she was sent unto by divers letters, both from Antonius himself and also from his friends, she made so light of it and mocked Antonius so much that she disdained to set forward otherwise but to take her barge in the river of Cydnus, the poop whereof was of gold, the sails of purple, and the oars of silver, which kept stroke in rowing after the sound of the music of flutes, hautboys, citherns, viols, and such other instruments as they played upon in the barge. And now for the person of herself: she was laid under a pavilion of cloth-of-gold of tissue, apparelled and attired like the goddess Venus commonly drawn in picture; and hard by her, on either hand of her, pretty fair boys apparelled as painters do set forth god Cupid, with little fans in their hands, with the which they fanned wind upon her. Her ladies and gentlewomen also, the fairest of them were apparelled like the nymphs Nereides (which are the mermaids of the waters) and like the Graces, some steering the helm, others tending the tackle and ropes of the barge, out of the which there came a wonderful passing sweet savour of perfumes that perfumed the wharf's side, pestered with innumerable multitudes of people. Some of them followed the barge all alongst the river's side; others also ran out of the city to see her coming in; so that in the end there ran such multitudes of people one after another to see her that Antonius was left post-alone in the market-place in his imperial seat to give audience. And there went a rumour in the people's mouths that the goddess Venus was come to play with the god Bacchus for the general good of all Asia.

When Cleopatra landed, Antonius sent to invite her to supper to him. But she sent him word again, he should do better rather to come and sup with her. Antonius therefore, to show himself courteous unto her at her arrival, was contented to obey her, and went to supper to her, where he found such passing sumptuous fare, that no tongue can express it. [2.2.198–233] But amongst all other things he most wondered at the infinite number of lights and torches hanged on the top of the house, giving light in every place, so artificially set and ordered by devices, some round, some square, that it was the rarest thing to behold that eye could discern, or that ever books could mention. The next night, Antonius feasting her contended to pass her in magnificence and fineness; but she overcame him in both. So that he himself began to scorn the gross service of his house, in respect of Cleopatra's sumptuousness and fineness. And, when Cleopatra found Antonius' jests and slents to be but gross and soldierlike in plain manner, she gave it him finely and without fear taunted him thoroughly.

Now her beauty, as it is reported, was not so passing as unmatchable of other women, nor yet such as upon present view did enamour men with her; but so sweet was her company and conversation that a man could not possibly but be taken. And, besides her beauty, the good grace she had to talk and discourse, her courteous nature that tempered her words and deeds was a spur that pricked to the quick. Furthermore, besides all these, her voice and words were marvellous pleasant; for her tongue was an instrument of music to divers sports and pastimes, the which she easily turned to any language that pleased her. She spake unto few barbarous people by interpreter, but made them answer herself, or at the least the most part of them—as, the Ethiopians, the Arabians, the Troglodytes, the Hebrews, the Syrians, the Medes, and the Parthians, and to many others also, whose languages she had learned. Whereas divers of her progenitors, the Kings of Egypt, could scarce learn the Egyptian tongue only, and many of them forgot to speak to Macedonian.

Now Antonius was so ravished with the love of Cleopatra that, though his wife Fulvia had great wars and much ado with Caesar for his affairs, and that the army of the Parthians (the which the king's lieutenants had given to the only leading of Labienus) was now assembled in Mesopotamia ready to invade Syria; yet, as though all this had nothing touched him, he yielded himself to go with Cleopatra into Alexandria, where he spent and lost in childish sports (as a man might say) and idle pastimes the most precious thing a man can spend, as Antiphon saith: and that is, time. [1.1.47–9; 1.4.3–33] For they made an order between them which they called *Amimetobion* (as much to say, 'no life comparable and matchable with it'), one feasting each other by turns, and in cost exceeding all measure and reason. And, for proof hereof, I have heard my grandfather Lampryas [1.2.0.1–4] report that one Philotas a physician, born in the city of Amphissa, told him that he was at that present time in Alexandria and studied physic; and that, having acquaintance with one of Antonius' cooks, he took him with him to Antonius' house (being a young man desirous to see things), to show him the wonderful sumptuous charge and preparation of one only supper. When he was in the kitchen and saw a world of diversities of meats, and, amongst others, eight wild boars roasted whole, he began to wonder at it and said: 'Sure you have a great number of guests to supper.' The cook fell a- laughing, and answered him: 'No,' quoth he, 'not many guests, nor above twelve in all. But yet all that is boiled or roasted must be served in whole, or else it would be marred straight. For Antonius peradventure will sup presently; or it may be a pretty while hence; or likely enough he will defer it longer, for that he hath drunk well today or else hath had some other great matters in hand; and therefore we do not dress one supper only, but many suppers, because we are uncertain of the hour he will sup in.' [2.2.186–7] Philotas the physician told my grandfather this tale. . . .

But now again to Cleopatra. Plato writeth that there are four kinds of flattery; but Cleopatra divided it into many kinds. For she, were it in sport or in matter of earnest, still devised sundry new delights to have Antonius at commandment, never leaving him night nor day, nor once letting him go out of her sight. For she would play at dice with him, drink with him, and hunt commonly with him, and also be with him when he went to any exercise or activity of body. And sometime also when he would go up and down the city disguised like a slave in the night, and would peer into poor men's windows and their shops, and scold and brawl with them within the house, Cleopatra would be also in a chambermaid's array, and amble up and down the streets with him, so that oftentimes Antonius bare away both mocks and blows. [1.1.55–6] Now, though most men misliked this manner, yet the Alexandrians were commonly glad of this jollity and liked it well, saying very gallantly and widely that Antonius showed them a comical face—to wit, a merry countenance; and the Romans a tragical face—to say, a grim look. [1.2.82]

But to reckon up all the foolish sports they made, revelling in this sort, it were too fond a part of me; and therefore I will only tell you one among the rest. On a time he went to angle for fish; and when he could take none he was as angry as could be, because Cleopatra stood by. Wherefore he secretly commanded the fishermen that when he cast in his line they should straight dive under the water and put a fish on his hook which they had taken before; and so snatched up his angling rod and brought up fish twice or thrice. Cleopatra found it straight; yet she seemed not to see it, but wondered at his excellent fishing. But when she was alone by herself among her own people, she told them how it was and bade them the next morning to be on the water to see the fishing. A number of people came to the haven and got into the fisher-boats to see this fishing. Antonius then threw in his line; and Cleopatra straight commanded one of her men to dive under water before Antonius' men and to put some old salt fish upon his bait, like unto those that are brought out of the country of Pont. When he had hung the fish on his hook, Antonius, thinking he had taken a fish indeed, snatched up his line presently. Then they all fell a-laughing. Cleopatra, laughing also, said unto him: 'Leave us, my lord, Egyptians, which dwell in the country of Pharus and Canobus, your angling rod. This is not thy profession: thou must hunt after conquering of realms and countries.' [1.4.3–4; 2.5.15–18]

Now Antonius delighting in these fond and childish pastimes, very ill news were brought him from two places. The first from Rome, that his brother Lucius and Fulvia his wife fell out first between themselves, and afterwards fell to open war with Caesar, and had brought all to nought, that they were both driven to fly out of Italy. The second news, as bad as the first, that Labienus conquered all Asia with the army of the Parthians, from the river of Euphrates and from Syria unto the countries of Lydia and Ionia. Then began Antonius, with much ado, a little to rouse himself, as if he had been wakened out of a deep sleep and, as a man may say, coming out of a great drunkenness. So first of all he bent himself against the Parthians, and went as far as the country of Phoenicia. But there he received lamentable letters from his wife Fulvia. Whereupon he straight returned towards Italy with two hundred sail; and, as he went, took up his friends by the way that fled out of Italy to come to him. By them he was informed that his wife Fulvia was the only cause of this war; who, being of a peevish, crooked, and troublesome nature, had purposely raised this uproar in Italy, in hope thereby to withdraw him from Cleopatra. [1.2.88–111; 2.2.99–100]

But, by good fortune, his wife Fulvia, going to meet with Antonius, sickened by the way, and died in the city of Sicyon. And therefore Octavius Caesar and he were the easilier made friends together. For when Antonius landed in Italy, and that men saw Caesar asked nothing of him, and that Antonius on the other side laid all the fault and burden on his wife Fulvia, the friends of both parties would not suffer them to unrip any old matters, and to prove or defend who had the wrong or right, and who was the first procurer of this war, fearing to make matters worse between them; but they made them friends together, and divided the Empire of Rome between them, making the sea Ionium the bounds of their division. For they gave all the provinces eastward unto Antonius, and the countries westward unto Caesar, and left Afric unto Lepidus; and made a law that they three one after another should make their friends Consuls, when they would not be themselves.

This seemed to be a sound counsel, but yet it was to be confirmed with a straiter bond, which fortune offered thus: there was Octavia, the eldest sister of Caesar (not by one mother, for she came of Ancharia, and Caesar himself afterwards of Accia). It is reported that he dearly loved his sister Octavia, for indeed she was a noble lady, and left the widow of her first husband Caius Marcellus, who had died not long before; and it seemed also that Antonius had been widower ever since the death of his wife Fulvia. For he denied not that he kept Cleopatra; but so did he not confess that he had her as his wife; and so with reason he did defend the love he bare unto this Egyptian Cleopatra. Thereupon every man did set forward this marriage, hoping thereby that this lady Octavia, having an excellent grace, wisdom, and honesty, joined unto so rare a beauty, that when she were with Antonius (he loving her as so worthy a lady deserveth) she should be a good mean to keep good love and amity betwixt her brother and him. [2.2.65–160] . . .

Sextus Pompeius at that time kept in Sicilia, and so made many an inroad into Italy with a great number of pinnaces and other pirates' ships, of the which were captains two notable pirates, Menas and Menecrates, who so scoured all the sea thereabouts that none durst peep out with a sail. [1.4.48–54] Furthermore, Sextus Pompeius had dealt very friendly with Antonius, for he had courteously received his mother when she fled out of Italy with Fulvia; and therefore they thought good to make peace with him. So they met all three together by the mount of Misena, [2.2.161–8] upon a hill that runneth far into the sea, Pompey having his ships riding hard by at anchor, and Antonius and Caesar their armies upon the shore side, directly over against him.

Now after they had agreed that Sextus Pompeius should have Sicilia and Sardinia, with this condition, that he should rid the sea of all thieves and pirates and make it safe for passengers, and withal that he should send a certain [sic] of wheat to Rome, one of them did feast another, and drew cuts who should begin. It was Pompeius' chance to invite them first; whereupon Antonius asked him: 'And where shall we sup?' 'There', said Pompey, and showed him his admiral galley which had six banks of oars. 'That', said he, 'is my father's house they have left me.' He spake it to taunt Antonius, because he had his father's house, that was Pompey the Great. So he cast anchors enow into the sea to make his galley fast, and then built a bridge of wood to convey them to his galley from the head of Mount Misena; and there he welcomed them, and made them great cheer. [2.6.1–82]

Now in the midst of the feast, when they fell to be merry with Antonius' love unto Cleopatra, Menas the pirate came to Pompey and, whispering in his ear, said unto him:
'Shall I cut the cables of the anchors, and make thee lord not only of Sicilia and Sardinia, but of the whole Empire of Rome besides?' Pompey, having paused awhile upon it, at length answered him: 'Thou shouldst have done it, and never have told it me; but now we must content us with that we have. As for myself, I was never taught to break my faith nor to be counted as a traitor.' [2.7.36–81] . . .

Antonius, after this agreement made, sent Ventidius before into Asia to stay the Parthians and to keep them they should come no further; [2.3.38–40; 3.1] and he himself in the meantime, to gratify

Caesar, was contented to be chosen Julius Caesar's priest and sacrificer; and so they jointly together dispatched all great matters concerning the state of the Empire. But in all other manner of sports and exercises wherein they passed the time away the one with the other, Antonius was ever inferior unto Caesar, and alway lost, which grieved him much. With Antonius there was a soothsayer or astronomer of Egypt that could cast a figure and judge of men's nativities to tell them what should happen to them. He, either to please Cleopatra or else for that he found it so by his art, told Antonius plainly that his fortune, which of itself was excellent good and very great, was altogether blemished and obscured by Caesar's fortune; and therefore he counselled him utterly to leave his company and to get him as far from him as he could. 'For thy Demon,' said he, '(that is to say, the good angel and spirit that keepeth thee) is afraid of his; and, being courageous and high when he is alone, becometh fearful and timorous when he cometh near unto the other.' Howsoever it was, the events ensuing proved the Egyptian's words true. For it is said that as often as they two drew cuts for pastime who should have anything, or whether they played at dice, Antonius alway lost. Oftentimes when they were disposed to see cock-fight, or quails that were taught to fight one with another, Caesar's cocks or quails did ever overcome. The which spited Antonius in his mind—although he made no outward show of it; and therefore he believed the Egyptian the better. [2.3.9–36.]

In fine, he recommended the affairs of his house unto Caesar, and went out of Italy with Octavia his wife, whom he carried into Greece, after he had a daughter by her. So Antonius lying all the winter at Athens, news came unto him of the victories of Ventidius, who had overcome the Parthians in battle, in the which also were slain Labienus and Pharnabates, the chiefest captain King Orodes had. [3.1] For these good news he feasted all Athens, and kept open house for all the Grecians; and many games of price were played at Athens, of the which he himself would be judge. . . . In the meantime, Ventidius once again overcame Pacorus (Orodes' son, King of Parthia) in a battle fought in the country of Cyrrestica, he being come again with a great army to invade Syria; at which battle was slain a great number of the Parthians, and among them Pacorus the King's own son slain. This noble exploit, as famous as ever any was, was a full revenge to the Romans of the shame and loss they had received before by the death of Marcus Crassus. And he made the Parthians fly, and glad to keep themselves within the confines and territories of Mesopotamia and Media, after they had thrice together been overcome in several battles. Howbeit Ventidius durst not undertake to follow them any further, fearing lest he should have gotten Antonius' displeasure by it. [3.1]

. . . . after [Antonius] had set order for the state and affairs of Syria, he returned again to Athens; and, having given Ventidius such honours as he deserved, he sent him to Rome, to triumph for the

Parthians. Ventidius was the only man that ever triumphed of the Parthians until this present day[1]—a mean man born, and of no noble house nor family, who only came to that he attained unto through Antonius' friendship, the which delivered him happy occasion to achieve to great matters. And yet, to say truly, he did so well quit himself in all his enterprises that he confirmed that which was spoken of Antonius and Caesar: to wit, that they were alway more fortunate when they made war by their lieutenants than by themselves. For Sossius, one of Antonius' lieutenants in Syria, did notable good service; and Canidius, whom he had also left his lieutenant in the borders of Armenia, did conquer it all. [3.1]

... But Antonius, notwithstanding, grew to be marvellously offended with Caesar, upon certain reports that had been brought unto him, and so took sea to go towards Italy with three hundred sail. And, because those of Brundusium would not receive his army into their haven, he went farther unto Tarentum. There his wife Octavia, that came out of Greece with him, besought him to send her unto her brother; the which he did. Octavia at that time was great with child, and moreover had a second daughter by him; and yet she put herself in journey, and met with her brother Octavius Caesar by the way, who brought his two chief friends, Maecenas and Agrippa, with him. She took them aside and, with all the instance she could possible, entreated them they would not suffer her, that was the happiest woman of the world, to become now the most wretched and unfortunatest creature of all other. 'For now', said she, 'every man's eyes do gaze on me, that am the sister of one of the Emperors and wife of the other. And if the worst counsel take place (which the gods forbid!) and that they grow to wars, for yourselves, it is uncertain to which of them two the gods have assigned the victory or overthrow; but for me, on which side soever victory fall, my state can be but most miserable still'. (3.4)

These words of Octavia so softened Caesar's heart that he went quickly unto Tarentum. But it was a noble sight for them that were present, to see so great an army by land not to stir, and so many ships afloat in the road, quietly and safe; and, furthermore, the meeting and kindness of friends, lovingly embracing one another. First, Antonius feasted Caesar, which he granted unto for his sister's sake. Afterwards they agreed together that Caesar should give Antonius two legions to go against the Parthians, and that Antonius should let Caesar have a hundred galleys armed with brazen spurs at the prows. Besides all this, Octavia obtained of her husband twenty brigantines for her brother, and of her brother for her husband a thousand armed men. After they had taken leave of each other, Caesar went immediately to make war with Sextus Pompeius,

---

[1] North's text draws attention to Ventidius's triumph with a marginal annotation: '*Ventidius, the only man of the Romans that triumphed for the Parthians.*'

to get Sicilia into his hands (3.4.4). Antonius also, leaving his wife Octavia and little children begotten of her with Caesar, and his other children which he had by Fulvia, he went directly into Asia.

Then began this pestilent plague and mischief of Cleopatra's love—which had slept a long time, and seemed to have been utterly forgotten, and that Antonius had given place to better counsel—again to kindle and to be in force, so soon as Antonius came near unto Syria. And in the end, 'the horse of the mind', as Plato termeth it, that is so hard of rein (I mean the unreined lust of concupiscence), did put out of Antonius' head all honest and commendable thoughts. For he sent Fonteius Capito to bring Cleopatra into Syria—unto whom, to welcome her, he gave no trifling things, but unto that she had already he added the provinces of Phoenicia, those of the nethermost Syria, the isle of Cyprus, and a great part of Cilicia, and that country of Jewry where the true balm is, and that part of Arabia where the Nabatheians do dwell, which stretcheth out towards the Ocean.

These great gifts much misliked the Romans. But now, though Antonius did easily give away great signiories, realms, and mighty nations unto some private men . . . yet all this did not so much offend the Romans as the unmeasurable honours which he did unto Cleopatra. But yet he did much more aggravate their malice and ill will towards him, because that, Cleopatra having brought him two twins, a son and a daughter, he named his son Alexander and his daughter Cleopatra, and gave them to their surnames, 'the Sun' to the one and 'the Moon' to the other. This notwithstanding, he that could finely cloak his shameful deeds with fine words said that the greatness and magnificence of the Empire of Rome appeared most not where the Romans took, but where they gave much; and nobility was multiplied amongst men by the posterity of kings when they left of their seed in divers places; and that by this means his first ancestor was begotten of Hercules, who had not left the hope and continuance of his line and posterity in the womb of one only woman, fearing Solon's laws or regarding the ordinances of men touching the procreation of children; but that he gave it unto nature, and established the foundation of many noble races and families in divers places. [1.3.84]

[Antonius's disastrous campaigns against the Parthians; destruction of a large part of his army. The love and loyalty of his followers unaffected by his reverses]

. . . Howbeit then the great haste he made to return unto Cleopatra caused him to put his men to so great pains, forcing them to lie in the field all winter long when it snew unreasonably, that by the way he lost eight thousand of his men; and so came down to the sea side with a small company, unto a certain place called Blancbourg, which standeth betwixt the cities of Berytus and Sidon; and there tarried for Cleopatra. And, because she tarried longer than he would have had her, he pined away for love and sorrow; so that he was at such a strait that he wist not what to do, and therefore, to wear it out, he gave himself to quaffing and feasting. But he was so drowned with the love of her that he could not abide to sit at the table till the feast were ended; but many times, while others banqueted, he ran to the sea side to see if she were coming. At length she came, and brought with her a world of apparel and money to give unto the soldiers. But some say, notwithstanding, that she brought apparel but no money, and that she took of Antonius' money and caused it to be given amongst the soldiers in her own name, as if she had given it them. . . . Hereupon . . . he prepared himself once more to go through Armenia and to make more cruel war with the Parthians than he had done before.

Now, whilst Antonius was busy in this preparation, Octavia his wife, whom he had left at Rome, would needs take sea to come unto him. Her brother Octavius Caesar was willing unto it, not for his respect at all (as most authors do report), as for that he might have an honest colour to make war with Antonius if he did misuse her and not esteem of her as she ought to be. But, when she was come to Athens, she received letters from Antonius willing her to stay there until his coming, and did advertise her of his journey and determination; the which though it grieved her much and that she knew it was but an excuse, yet by her letters to him of answer she asked him whether he would have those things sent unto him which she had brought him, being great store of apparel for soldiers, a great number of horse, sum of money and gifts to bestow on his friends and captains he had about him; and, besides all those, she had two thousand soldiers, chosen men, all well armed like unto the Praetors' bands.

When Niger, one of Antonius' friends whom he had sent unto Athens, had brought these news from his wife Octavia, and withal did greatly praise her, as she was worthy and well deserved, Cleopatra, knowing that Octavia would have Antonius from her and fearing also that, if with her virtue and honest behaviour (besides the great power of her brother Caesar) she did add thereunto her modest kind love to please her husband, that she would then be too strong for her and in the end win him away, she subtly seemed to languish for the love of Antonius, pining her body for lack of meat. Furthermore, she every way so framed her countenance that, when Antonius came to see her, she cast her eyes upon him like a woman ravished for joy. Straight again, when he went from her, she fell a weeping and blubbering, looked ruefully of the matter, and still found the means that Antonius should oftentimes find her weeping; and then, when he came suddenly upon her, she made as though she dried her eyes, and turned her face away, as if she were unwilling that he should see her weep.[2] All these tricks she used. . . .

Then the flatters that furthered Cleopatra's mind blamed Antonius and told him that he was a hard-natured man and that he had small love in him that would see a poor lady in such torment for his sake, whose life depended only upon him alone. For Octavia, said they, that was married unto him as it were of necessity, because her brother Caesar's affairs so required it, hath the honour to be called Antonius' lawful spouse and wife; and Cleopatra, being born a queen of so many thousands of men, is only named Antonius' leman; and yet that she disdained not so to be called, if it might please him she might enjoy his company and live with him; but, if he once leave her, that then it is unpossible she should live. To be short, by these their flatteries and enticements they so wrought Antonius' effeminate mind that, fearing lest she would make herself away, he returned again unto Alexandria . . . although he received news that the Parthians at that time were at civil wars among themselves . . . being fully bent to make war with Caesar.

When Octavia was returned to Rome from Athens, Caesar commanded her to go out of Antonius' house and to dwell by herself, because he had abused her. Octavia answered him again that she would not forsake her husband's house and that, if he had no other occasion to make war with him, she prayed him then to take no thought for her.[3] 'For,' said she, 'it were too shameful a thing that two so famous captains should bring in civil wars among the Romans, the one for the love of a woman and the other for the jealousy betwixt one another.' Now, as she spake the word, so did she also perform the deed. For she kept still in Antonius' house, as if he had been there, and very honestly and honorably kept his children, not those only she had by him, but the other which her husband had by Fulvia. Furthermore, when Antonius sent any of his men to Rome to sue for any office in the commonwealth, she received him very courteously, and so used herself unto her brother that she obtained the thing she requested. Howbeit thereby, thinking no hurt, she did Antonius great hurt. For her honest love and regard to her husband made every man hate him when they saw he did so unkindly use so noble a lady.

But yet the greatest cause of their malice unto him was for the division of lands he made amongst his children in the city of Alexandria. And, to confess a troth, it was too arrogant and insolent a part, and done (as a man would say) in derision and contempt of the Romans. For he assembled all the people in the show-place where young men do exercise themselves; and there, upon a high tribunal

---

[2] North's marginal note emphasizes '*The flickering enticements of Cleopatra unto Antonius.*'

[3] The marginal gloss advertises '*The love of Octavia to Antonius her husband, and her wise and womanly behaviour.*'

silvered, he set two chairs of gold, the one for himself and the other for Cleopatra, and lower chairs for his children. Then he openly published before the assembly that first of all he did establish Cleopatra Queen of Egypt, of Cyprus, of Lydia, and of the lower Syria, and at that time also Caesarion King of the same realms. (This Caesarion was supposed to be the son of Julius Caesar, who had left Cleopatra great with child.) Secondly he called the sons he had by her 'the Kings of Kings'; and gave Alexander for his portion, Armenia, Media, and Parthia (when he had conquered the country); and unto Ptolemy for his portion, Phoenicia, Syria, and Cilicia. And therewithal he brought out Alexander in a long gown after the fashion of the Medes, with a high copped-tank hat on his head, narrow in the top, as the Kings of the Medes and Armenians do use to wear them; and Ptolemy apparelled in a cloak after the Macedonian manner, with slippers on his feet, and a broad hat with a royal band or diadem—such was the apparel and old attire of the ancient kings and successors of Alexander the Great. So, after his sons had done their humble duties and kissed their father and mother, presently a company of Armenian soldiers, set there of purpose, compassed the one about, and a like company of the Macedonians the other. Now, for Cleopatra, she did not only wear at that time, but at all other times else when she came abroad, the apparel of the goddess Isis—and so gave audience unto all her subjects as a new Isis. [3.6.1–19]

Octavius Caesar reporting all these things unto the Senate, and oftentimes accusing him to the whole people and assembly in Rome, he thereby stirred up all the Romans against him. Antonius on the other side sent to Rome likewise to accuse him; and the chiefest points of his accusations he charged him with were these: first that, having spoiled Sextus Pompeius in Sicilia, he did not give him his part of the isle; secondly that he did detain in his hands the ships he lent him to make that war; thirdly that, having put Lepidus, their companion and triumvirate, out of his part of the Empire and having deprived him of all honours, he retained for himself the lands and revenues thereof, which had been assigned unto him for his part; and last of all, that he had in manner divided all Italy amongst his own soldiers and had left no part of it for his soldiers. Octavius Caesar answered him again that, for Lepidus, he had indeed deposed him and taken his part of the Empire from him, because he did over-cruelly use his authority; and secondly, for the conquests he had made by force of arms, he was contented Antonius should have his part of them, so that he would likewise let him have his part of Armenia; and thirdly, that, for his soldiers, they should seek for nothing in Italy, because they possessed Media and Parthia, the which provinces they had added to the Empire of Rome, valiantly fighting with their emperor and captain. [3.6.22–38]

Antonius hearing these news, being yet in Armenia, commanded Canidius to go presently to the sea side with his sixteen legions he had; and he himself with Cleopatra went unto the city of Ephesus, and there gathered together his galleys and ships out of all parts, which came to the number of eight hundred, reckoning the great ships of burden; and of those Cleopatra furnished him with two hundred, and twenty thousand talents besides, and provision of victuals also to maintain all the whole army in this war. So Antonius, through the persuasions of Domitius, commanded Cleopatra to return again into Egypt, and there to understand the success of this war. But Cleopatra fearing lest Antonius should again be made friends with Octavius Caesar by the means of his wife Octavia, she so plied Canidius with money and filled his purse that he became her spokesman unto Antonius, and told him there was no reason to send her from this war, who defrayed so great a charge; neither that it was for his profit, because that thereby the Egyptians would, then be utterly discouraged, which were the chiefest strength of the army by sea; considering that he could see no king of all the kings their confederates that Cleopatra was inferior unto either for wisdom or judgement, seeing that long before she had wisely governed so great a realm as Egypt, and besides that she had been so long acquainted with him, by whom she had learned to manage great affairs. These fair persuasions won him; for it was predestined that the government of all the world should fall into Octavius Caesar's hands. [3.7.1–19]

Thus, all their forces being joined together, they hoisted sail towards the isle of Samos, and there gave themselves to feasts and solace. . . . all players, minstrels, tumblers, fools and jesters were commanded to assemble in the isle of Samos; so that, where in manner all the world in every place was full of lamentations, sighs and tears, only in this isle of Samos there was nothing for many days' space but singing and piping, and all the theatre full of these common players, minstrels, and singing men. Besides all this, every city sent an ox thither to sacrifice; and kings did strive one with another who should make the noblest feasts and give the richest gifts; so that every man said: 'What can they do more for joy of victory if they win the battle, when they make already such sumptuous feasts at the beginning of the war?' . . .

Afterwards Antonius sent to Rome to put his wife Octavia out of his house, who, as it was reported, went out of his house with all Antonius' children (saving the eldest of them he had by Fulvia, who was with his father), bewailing and lamenting her cursed hap that had brought her to this, that she was accompted one of the chiefest causes of this civil war. The Romans did pity her, but much more Antonius, and those specially that had seen Cleopatra, who neither excelled Octavia in beauty, nor yet in young years.

Octavius Caesar understanding the sudden and wonderful preparation of Antonius, he was not a little astonied at it (fearing he should be driven to fight that summer), because he wanted many things, and the great and grievous exactions of money did sorely oppress the people ... so that, among the greatest faults that ever Antonius committed, they blamed him most for that he delayed to give Caesar battle. For he gave Caesar leisure to make his preparations and also to appease the complaints of the people. When such a great sum of money was demanded of them, they grudged at it and grew to mutiny upon it; but, when they had once paid it, they remembered it no more.

Furthermore, Titius and Plancus (two of Antonius' chiefest friends and that had been both of them Consuls), for the great injuries Cleopatra did them because they hindered all they could that she should not come to this war, they went and yielded themselves unto Caesar, and told him where the testament was that Antonius had made, knowing perfectly what was in it. The will was in the custody of the Vestal nuns, of whom Caesar demanded for it. They answered him that they would not give it him; but if he would go and take it, they would not hinder him. Thereupon Caesar went thither; and having read it first to himself he noted certain places worthy of reproach. So, assembling all the Senate, he read it before them all. Whereupon divers were marvellously offended, and thought it a strange matter that he, being alive, should be punished for that he had appointed by his will to be done after his death. Caesar chiefly took hold of this that he ordained touching his burial; for he willed that his body, though he died at Rome, should be brought in funeral pomp through the midst of the market-place and that it should be sent in Alexandria unto Cleopatra. [3.4.4] ...

Now after Caesar had made sufficient preparation, he proclaimed open war against Cleopatra, and made the people to abolish the power and empire of Antonius because he had before given it up unto a woman. And Caesar said furthermore that Antonius was not master of himself, but that Cleopatra had brought him beside himself by her charms and amorous poisons, and that they that should make war with them should be Mardian the eunuch, Photinus, and Iras, a woman of Cleopatra's bed-chamber, that frizzled her hair and dressed her head, and Charmion, the which were those that ruled all the affairs of Antonius' empire. [3.7.13–15]

Before this war, as it is reported, many signs and wonders fell out. First of all, the city of Pisaurum, which was made a colony to Rome and replenished with people by Antonius, standing upon the shore side of the sea Adriatic, was by a terrible earthquake sunk into the ground. One of the images of stone which was set up in the honour of Antonius in the city of Alba did sweat many days together, and, though some wiped it away, yet it left not sweating still. In the city of Patras, whilst Antonius was there, the Temple of Hercules was burnt with lightning. And at the city of Athens also, in a place where the war of the giants against the gods is set out in imagery, the statue of Bacchus with a terrible wind was thrown down in the theatre. (It was said that Antonius came of the race of Hercules, as you have heard before, and in the manner of his life he followed

Bacchus; and therefore he was called the new Bacchus.) Further-more, the same blustering storm of wind overthrew the great mon-strous images at Athens, that were made in the honour of Eumenes and Attalus, the which men had named and entitled 'the Antonians'; and yet they did hurt none of the other images which were many besides. The admiral galley of Cleopatra was called Antoniad, in the which there chanced a marvellous ill sign. Swallows had bred under the poop of her ship; and there came others after them that drave away the first and plucked down their nests. [4.13.3]

Now when all things were ready and that they drew near to fight, it was found that Antonius had no less than five hundred good ships of war, among which there were many galleys that had eight and ten banks of oars, the which were sumptuously furnished, not so meet for fight as for triumph, a hundred thousand footmen and twelve thousand horsemen; and had with him to aid him these kings and subjects following: Bocchus, King of Libya; Tarcondemus, King of High Cilicia; Archelaus, King of Cappadocia; Philadelphus, King of Paphlagonia; Mithridates, King of Comagena; and Adallas, King of Thracia; all the which were there every man in person. The residue that were absent sent their armies: as Polemon, King of Pont; Manchus, King of Arabia; Herodes, King of Jewry; and furthermore, Amyntas, King of Lycaonia and of the Galatians; and, besides all these, he had all the aid the King of Medes sent unto him. [3.6.68–76] Now for Caesar, he had two hundred and fifty ships of war, fourscore thousand footmen, and well near as many horsemen as his enemy Antonius. Antonius for his part had all under his dominion from Armenia and the river of Euphrates unto the sea Ionium and Illyricum. Octavius Caesar had also for his part all that which was in our hemisphere, or half part of the world, from Illyria unto the Ocean sea upon the west; then all from the Ocean unto Mare Siculum; and from Afric all that which is against Italy, as Gaul and Spain. Furthermore, all from the province of Cyrenia to Ethiopia was subject unto Antonius.

Now Antonius was made so subject to a woman's will that, though he was a great deal the stronger by land, yet for Cleopatra's sake he would needs have this battle tried by sea; though he saw before his eyes that, for lack of watermen, his captains did press by force all sorts of men out of Greece that they could take up in the field, as travellers, muleteers, reapers, harvest men, and young boys, and yet could they not sufficiently furnish his galleys; so that the most part of them were empty, and could scant row, because they lacked watermen enow. But on the contrary side Caesar's ships were not built for pomp, high and great, only for a sight and bravery; but they were light of yarage, armed and furnished with watermen as many as they needed, and had them all in readiness in the havens of Tarentum and Brundusium. [3.7.34–40]

So Octavius Caesar sent unto Antonius to will him to delay no more time, but to come on with his army into Italy; and that for his own part he would give him safe harbour, to land without any trouble and that he would withdraw his army from the sea as far as one horse could run, until he had put his army ashore and lodged his men. Antonius on the other side bravely sent him word again, and challenged the combat of him man to man, though he were the elder; and that, if he refused him so, he would then fight a battle with him in the fields of Pharsalia, as Julius Caesar and Pompey had done before. [3.7.30–4]

Now, whilst Antonius rode at anchor, lying idly in harbour at the head of Actium, in the place where the city of Nicopolis standeth at this present, Caesar had quickly passed the sea Ionium and taken a place called Toryne, before Antonius understood that he had taken ship. Then began his men to be afraid, because his army by land was left behind. But Cleopatra making light of it: 'And what danger, I pray you,' said she, 'if Caesar keep at Toryne?'[4] The next morning by break of day, his enemies coming with full force of oars in battle against him, Antonius was afraid that if they came to join they would take and carry away his ships that had no men of war in them. So he armed all his watermen, and set them in order of battle upon the fore-castle of their ships, and then lift up all his ranks of oars towards the element, as well of the one side as on the other, with the prows against the enemies, at the entry and mouth of the gulf which beginneth at the point of Actium; and so kept them in order of battle, as if they had been armed and furnished with watermen and soldiers. Thus Octavius Caesar, being finely deceived by this stratagem, retired presently and therewithal Antonius very wisely and suddenly did cut him off from fresh water. [3.7.20–56] . . .

Furthermore, he dealt very friendly and courteously with Domitius, and against Cleopatra's mind. For he, being sick of an ague, when he went and took a little boat to go unto Caesar's camp, Antonius was very sorry for it, but yet he sent after him all his carriage, train, and men; and the same Domitius, as though he gave him to understand that he repented his open treason, he died immediately after. [4.5.7–17; 4.6; 4.10] There were certain kings also that forsook him, and turned on Caesar's side; as Amyntas and Deiotarus.

Furthermore his fleet and navy, that was unfortunate in all things and unready for service, compelled him to change his mind and to hazard battle by land. And Canidius also, who had charge of his army by land, when time came to follow Antonius' determination, he turned him clean contrary, and counselled him to send Cleopatra back again, and himself to retire into Macedon, to fight there on the mainland. And furthermore told him that Dicomes, King of the Getes,

---

[4] The marginal note reads '*The grace of this taunt cannot properly be expressed in any other tongue because of the equivocation of this word Toryne, which signifieth a city of Albania, and also a ladle to skim the pot with—as if she meant, Caesar sat by the fire side, scumming of the pot.*'

promised him to aid him with a great power; and that it should be no shame nor dishonour to him to let Caesar have the sea, because himself and his men both had been well practised and exercised in battles by sea, in the war of Sicilia against Sextus Pompeius; but rather that he should do against all reason, he having so great skill and experience of battles by land as he had, if he should not employ the force and valiantness of so many lusty armed footmen as he had ready, but would weaken his army by dividing them into ships. But now, notwithstanding all these good persuasions, Cleopatra forced him to put all to the hazard of battle by sea; considering with herself how she might fly and provide for her safety, not to help him win the victory, but to fly more easily after the battle lost. [3.7.30–70]

Betwixt Antonius' camp and his fleet of ships there was a great high point of firm land that ran a good way into the sea, the which Antonius used often for a walk, without mistrust of fear or danger. One of Caesar's men perceived it, and told his master that he would laugh and they could take up Antonius in the midst of his walk. Thereupon Caesar sent some of his men to lie in ambush for him, and they missed not much of taking of him; for they took him that came before him, because they discovered too soon; and so Antonius scaped very hardly.

So, when Antonius had determined to fight by sea, he set all the other ships a fire but three-score ships of Egypt, and reserved only but the best and greatest galleys, from three banks unto ten banks of oars. [3.7.50] Into them he put two-and-twenty thousand fighting men, with two thousand darters and slingers. Now, as he was setting his men in order of battle, there was a captain (and a valiant man) that had served Antonius in many battles and conflicts and had all his body hacked and cut, who, as Antonius passed by him, cried out unto him and said: 'O noble Emperor, how cometh it to pass that you trust to these vile brittle ships? What, do you mistrust these wounds of mine and this sword? Let the Egyptians and Phoenicians fight by sea, and set us on the mainland, where we use to conquer, or to be slain on our feet.' Antonius passed by him and said never a word, but only beckoned to him with his hand and head, as though he willed him to be of good courage, although indeed he had no great courage himself. [3.7.60–6] . . .

All that day, and the three days following, the sea rose so high and was so boisterous that the battle was put off. The fifth day the storm ceased and the sea calmed again; and then they rowed with force of oars in battle one against the other, Antonius leading the right wing with Publicola, and Caelius the left, and Marcus Octavius and Marcus Justeius the midst. Octavius Caesar, on the other side, had placed Agrippa in the left wing of his army, and had kept the right wing for himself. For the armies by land Canidius was general of Antonius' side, and Taurus of Caesar's side; who kept their men in battle ray the one before the other, upon the sea side, without stirring one against the other. [3.7.70–8] . . .

About noon there rose a little gale of wind from the sea; and then Antonius' men waxing angry with tarrying so long, and trusting to the greatness and height of their ships, as if they had been invincible, they began to march forward with their left wing. Caesar seeing that was a glad man, and began a little to give back from the right wing, to allure them to come farther out of the strait and gulf, to the end that he might with his light ships well manned with watermen turn and environ the galleys of the enemies, the which were heavy of yarage, both for their bigness as also for lack of watermen to row them. When the skirmish began and that they came to join, there was no great hurt at the first meeting, neither did the ships vehemently hit one against the other, as they do commonly in fight by sea. For, on the one side, Antonius' ships for their heaviness could not have the strength and swiftness to make their blows of any force; and Caesar's ships, on the other side, took great heed not to rush and shock with the forecastles of Antonius' ships, whose prows were armed with great brazen spurs. Furthermore they durst not flank them, because their points were easily broken, which way so ever they came to set upon his ships, that were made of great main square pieces of timber bound together with great iron pins. So that the battle was much like to a battle by land, or, to speak more properly, to the assault of a city. For there were always three or four of Caesar's ships about one of Antonius' ships, and the soldiers fought with their pikes, halberds, and darts, and threw pots and darts with fire. Antonius' ships on the other side bestowed among them, with their cross-bows and engines of battery, great store of shot from their high towers of wood that were upon their ships.

Now Publicola, seeing Agrippa put forth his left wing of Caesar's army to compass in Antonius' ships that fought, he was driven also to loof off to have more room, and, going a little at one side, to put those farther off that were afraid and in the midst of the battle—for they were sore distressed by Antonius.

Howbeit the battle was yet of even hand, and the victory doubtful, being indifferent to both, when suddenly they saw the three-score ships of Cleopatra busy about their yard-masts, and hoisting sail to fly. So they fled through the midst of them that were in fight, for they had been placed behind the great ships, and did marvellously disorder the other ships. For the enemies themselves wondered much to see them sail in that sort with full sail towards Peloponnesus. There Antonius showed plainly that he had not only lost the courage and heart of an Emperor but also of a valiant man, and that he was not his own man—proving that true which an old man spake in mirth, that the soul of a lover lived in another body, and not in his own. He was so carried away with the vain love of this woman as if he had been glued unto her and that she could not have removed without moving of him also. For when he saw Cleopatra's ship under sail he forgot, forsook, and betrayed them that fought for him, and embarked upon a galley with five banks of oars, to follow her that had already begun to overthrow him, and would in the end be his utter destruction. [3.10] When she knew this galley afar off, she lift up a sign in the poop of her ship, and so Antonius coming to it was plucked up where Cleopatra was; howbeit he saw her not at his first coming, nor she him, but went and sat down alone in the prow of his ship, and said never a word, clapping his head between both his hands. [3.11.1–24] ...

[*Antonius fights off Caesar's pursuit ships*]

After [this] he returned again to his place and sat down, speaking never a word as he did before; and so lived three days alone, without speaking to any man. But when he arrived at the head of Taenarus, there Cleopatra's women first brought Antonius and Cleopatra to speak together and afterwards to sup and lie together. [3.11.25–74]

Then began there again a great number of merchants' ships to gather about them, and some of their friends that had escaped from this overthrow, who brought news that his army by sea was overthrown, but that they thought the army by land was yet whole. Then Antonius sent unto Canidius to return with his army into Asia by Macedon. Now for himself, he determined to cross over into Afric; and took one of his carects or hulks loaden with gold and silver and other rich carriage, and gave it unto his friends, commanding them to depart and to seek to save themselves. They answered him weeping that they would neither do it nor yet forsake him. Then Antonius very courteously and lovingly did comfort them, and prayed them to depart; and wrote unto Theophilus, governor of Corinth, that he would see them safe and help to hide them in some secret place until they had made their way and peace with Caesar. [3.11.8–24] This Theophilus was the father of Hipparchus, who was had in great estimation about Antonius. He was the first of all his enfranchised bondmen that revolted from him and yielded unto Caesar, [3.13.149–52] and afterwards went and dwelt at Corinth. And thus it stood with Antonius.

Now, for his army by sea, that fought before the head or foreland of Actium, they held out a long time; and nothing troubled them more than a great boisterous wind that rose full in the prows of their ships; and yet with much ado his navy was at length overthrown, five hours within night. There were not slain above five thousand men; but yet there were three hundred ships taken, as Octavius Caesar writeth himself in his commentaries. Many plainly saw Antonius fly, and yet could very hardly believe it that he, that had nineteen legions whole by land and twelve thousand horsemen upon the sea side, would so have forsaken them, and have fled so cowardly; as if he had not oftentimes proved both the one and the other fortune, and that he had not been throughly acquainted with the diverse changes and fortunes of battles. And yet his soldiers still wished for him, and ever hoped that he would come by some means or other unto them. Furthermore they showed themselves so valiant and faithful unto him that, after they certainly knew he was fled, they kept themselves whole together seven days. In the end Canidius, Antonius' lieutenant, flying by night and forsaking his camp, when they saw themselves thus destitute of their heads and leaders, they yielded themselves unto the stronger. [3.10] ...

Antonius being arrived in Libya, he sent Cleopatra before into Egypt from the city of Paraetonium; and he himself remained very solitary, having only two of his friends with him. . . . But when Antonius heard that he whom he had trusted with the government of Libya, and unto whom he had given the charge of his army there, had yielded unto Caesar, he was so mad withal, that he would have slain himself for anger, had not his friends about him withstood him, and kept him from it.

So he went unto Alexandria, and there found Cleopatra about a wonderful enterprise and of great attempt. Betwixt the Red Sea and the sea between the lands that point upon the coast of Egypt there is a little piece of land that divideth both the seas and separateth Afric from Asia; the which strait is so narrow at the end where the two seas are narrowest that it is not above three hundred furlongs over. Cleopatra went about to lift her ships out of the one sea, and to hale them over the strait into the other sea; that, when her ships were come into this Gulf of Arabia, she might then carry all her gold and silver away, and so with a great company of men go and dwell in some place about the Ocean sea far from the sea Mediterranean, to scape the danger and bondage of this war. But now, because the Arabians dwelling about the city of Petra did burn the first ships that were brought to land, and that Antonius thought that his army by land, which he left at Actium, was yet whole, she left off her enterprise and determined to keep all the ports and passages of her realm.

Antonius, he forsook the city and company of his friends, and built him a house in the sea, by the isle of Pharos, upon certain forced mounts which he caused to be cast into the sea, and dwelt there, as a man that banished himself from all men's company, saying that he would lead Timon's life, because he had the like wrong offered him that was before offered unto Timon; and that, for the unthankfulness of those he had done good unto and whom he took to be his friends, he was angry with all men and would trust no man. [3.11.]

[The story of Timon of Athens, the misanthrope]

But now to return to Antonius again. Canidius himself came to bring him news that he had lost all his army by land at Actium. On the other side he was advertised also that Herodes, King of Jewry, who had also certain legions and bands with him, was revolted unto

Caesar, and all the other kings in like manner; so that, saving those that were about him, he had none left him. [3.10–11]

All this notwithstanding did nothing trouble him; and it seemed that he was contented to forgo all his hope, and so to be rid of all his care and troubles. Thereupon he left his solitary house he had built by the sea, which he called 'Timoneon'; and Cleopatra received him into her royal palace. He was no sooner comen thither, but he straight set all the city of rioting and banqueting again, and himself to liberality and gifts. He caused the son of Julius Caesar and Cleopatra to be enrolled, according to the manner of the Romans, amongst the number of young men; and gave Antyllus, his eldest son he had by Fulvia, the man's gown (the which was a plain gown without guard or embroidery of purple). For these things there was kept great feasting, banqueting, and dancing in Alexandria many days together.

Indeed, they did break their first order they had set down, which they call '*Amimetobion*' (as much to say 'no life comparable'), and did set up another, which they called '*Synapothanumenon*' (signifying 'the order and agreement of those that will die together'), the which in exceeding sumptuousness and cost was not inferior to the first. For their friends made themselves to be enrolled in this order of those that would die together, and so made great feasts one to another; for every man, when it came to his turn, feasted their whole company and fraternity. [3.13.183–94]

Cleopatra in the meantime was very careful in gathering all sorts of poisons together, to destroy men. Now, to make proof of those poisons which made men die with least pain, she tried it upon condemned men in prison. For, when she saw the poisons that were sudden and vehement and brought speedy death with grievous torments, and, in contrary manner, that such as were more mild and gentle had not that quick speed and force to make one die suddenly, she afterwards went about to prove the stinging of snakes and adders, and made some to be applied unto men in her sight, some in one sort and some in another. So, when she had daily made divers and sundry proofs, she found none of them all she had proved so fit as the biting of an aspic, the which only causeth a heaviness of the head, without swounding or complaining, and bringeth a great desire also to sleep, with a little sweat in the face, and so by little and little taketh away the senses and vital powers, no living creature perceiving that the patients feel any pain. For they are so sorry when anybody awaketh them, and taketh them up, as those that being taken out of a sound sleep are very heavy and desirous to sleep. [5.2.308–9, 352–4]

This notwithstanding, they sent ambassadors unto Octavius Caesar in Asia, Cleopatra requesting the realm of Egypt for their children, and Antonius praying that he might be suffered to live at Athens like a private man, if Caesar would not let him remain in Egypt. And because they had no other men of estimation about them (for that some were fled, and those that remained they did not greatly trust them), they were enforced to send Euphronius the schoolmaster of their children. [3.12] For Alexas Laodician, who was brought into Antonius' house and favour by means of Timagenes and afterwards was in greater credit with him than any other Grecian (for that he had alway been one of Cleopatra's ministers to win Antonius and to overthrow all his good determinations to use his wife Octavia well), him Antonius had sent unto Herodes King of Jewry, hoping still to keep him his friend, that he should not revolt from him. But he remained there, and betrayed Antonius. For, where he should have kept Herodes from revolting from him, he persuaded him to turn to Caesar; and, trusting King Herodes, he presumed to come in Caesar's presence. Howbeit Herodes did him no pleasure; for he was presently taken prisoner, and sent in chains to his own country; and there by Caesar's commandment put to death. Thus was Alexas in Antonius' lifetime put to death for betraying of him. [4.6.11–15]

Furthermore, Caesar would not grant unto Antonius' requests. But, for Cleopatra, he made her answer that he would deny her nothing reasonable, so that she would either put Antonius to death or drive him out of her country. Therewithal he sent Thyreus, one of his men, unto her, a very wise and discreet man, who, bringing letters of credit from a young lord unto a noble lady, and that besides greatly liked her beauty, might easily by his eloquence have persuaded her. [3.12.27–37] He was longer in talk with her than any man else was, and the Queen herself also did him great honour; insomuch as he made Antonius jealous of him. Whereupon Antonius caused him to be taken and well-favouredly whipped, and so sent him unto Caesar; and bade him tell him that he made him angry with him, because he showed himself proud and disdainful towards him, and now specially when he was easy to be angered, by reason of his present misery. 'To be short, if this mislike thee,' said he, 'thou hast Hipparchus, one of my enfranchised bondmen, with thee. Hang him if thou wilt, or whip him at thy pleasure, that we may cry quittance.'

From thenceforth Cleopatra, to clear herself of the suspicion he had of her, she made more of him than ever she did. For first of all, where she did solemnize the day of her birth very meanly and sparingly, fit for her present misfortune, she now in contrary manner did keep it with such solemnity, that she exceeded all measure of sumptuousness and magnificence, so that the guests that were bidden to the feasts and came poor, went away rich. [3.13.46–194] . . .

[Caesar, distracted by problems at home,] did defer the war till the next year following. But, when winter was done, he returned again through Syria by the coast of Afric, to make wars against Antonius and his other captains. When the city of Pelusium was taken, there ran a rumour in the city that Seleucus, by Cleopatra's consent, had surrendered the same. But, to clear herself that she did not, Cleopatra brought Seleucus' wife and children unto Antonius, to be revenged of them at his pleasure. Furthermore Cleopatra had long before made many sumptuous tombs and monuments, as well for excellency of workmanship as for height and greatness of building, joining hard to the Temple of Isis. Thither she caused to be brought all the treasure and precious things she had of the ancient Kings her predecessors—as gold, silver, emeralds, pearls, ebony, ivory, and cinnamon—and besides all that, a marvellous number of torches, faggots, and flax. So Octavius Caesar being afraid to lose such a treasure and mass of riches, and that this woman for spite would set it afire, and burn it every whit, he always sent some one or other unto her from him, to put her in good comfort, whilst he in the meantime drew near the city with his army.

So Caesar came, and pitched his camp hard by the city, in the place where they run and manage their horses. Antonius made a sally upon him, and fought very valiantly, so he drave Caesar's horsemen back, fighting with his men even into their camp. Then he came again to the palace greatly boasting of this victory, and sweetly kissed Cleopatra, armed as he was when he came from the fight, recommending one of his men-of-arms unto her, that had valiantly fought in this skirmish. Cleopatra, to reward his manliness, gave him an armour and head-piece of clean gold; [4.7–9] howbeit the man-at-arms, when he had received this rich gift, stole away by night and went to Caesar. [4.5.7]

Antonius sent again to challenge Caesar to fight with him hand to hand. Caesar answered him that he had many other ways to die than so. [4.1.4–5] Then Antonius, seeing there was no way more honourable for him to die than fighting valiantly, he determined to set up his rest, both by sea and land. So, being at supper, as it is reported, he commanded his officers and household servants, that waited on him at his board, that they should fill his cups full, and make as much of him as they could. 'For,' said he, 'you know not whether you shall do so much for me tomorrow or not, or whether you shall serve another master; and it may be you shall see me no more, but a dead body.' This notwithstanding, perceiving that his friends and men fell a-weeping to hear him say so, to salve that he had spoken he added this more unto it: that he would not lead them to battle where he thought not rather safely to return with victory than valiantly to die with honour. [4.2.]

Furthermore, the selfsame night within little of midnight, when all the city was quiet, full of fear and sorrow, thinking what would be the issue and end of this war, it is said that suddenly they heard a marvellous sweet harmony of sundry sorts of instruments of music, with the cry of a multitude of people, as they had been dancing and had sung as they use in Bacchus' feasts, with movings and turnings after the manner of the satyrs. And it seemed that this dance went through the city unto the gate that opened to the enemies, and that all the troop that made this noise they heard went out of the city at that gate. Now such as in reason sought the depth of the interpretation of this wonder thought that it was the god, unto whom Antonius bare singular devotion to counterfeit and resemble him, that did forsake them. [4.3]

The next morning by break of day he went to set those few footmen he had in order upon the hills adjoining unto the city; and there he stood to behold his galleys which departed from the haven and rowed against the galleys of his enemies; and so stood still, looking what exploit his soldiers in them would do. But when by force of rowing they were come near unto them, they first saluted Caesar's men, and then Caesar's men re-saluted them also, and of two armies made but one, and then did all together row toward the city. [4.11; 4.13.1–13]

When Antonius saw that his men did forsake him and yielded unto Caesar, and that his footmen were broken and overthrown he then fled into the city, crying out that Cleopatra had betrayed him unto them with whom he had made war for her sake. [4.13.13–39] Then she, being afraid of his fury, fled into the tomb which she had caused to be made; and there locked the doors unto her, and shut all the springs of the locks with great bolts; and in the meantime sent unto Antonius to tell him that she was dead. [4.14] Antonius, believing it, said unto himself: 'What dost thou look for further, Antonius, sith spiteful fortune hath taken from thee the only joy thou hadst, for whom thou yet reservedst thy life?' When he had said these words, he went into a chamber and unarmed himself; and being naked said thus: 'O Cleopatra, it grieveth me not that I have lost thy company, for I will not be long from thee. But I am sorry that, having been so great a captain and Emperor, I am indeed condemned to be judged of less courage and noble mind than a woman.' [4.15.55–62]

Now he had a man of his called Eros, whom he loved and trusted much and whom he had long before caused to swear unto him that he should kill him when he did command him; and then he willed him to keep his promise. His man drawing his sword lift it up as though he had meant to have stricken his master. But, turning his head at one side, he thrust his sword into himself and fell down dead at his master's foot. Then said Antonius: 'O noble Eros, I thank thee for this; and it is valiantly done of thee, to show men what I should do to myself, which thou couldst not do for me.' Therewithal he took his sword and thrust it into his belly; and so fell down upon a little bed.

The wound he had killed him not presently, for the blood stinted a little when he was laid; and when he came somewhat to himself again, he prayed them that were about him to dispatch him. But they all fled out of the chamber, and left him crying out and tormenting himself; until at last there came a secretary unto him called Diomedes, who was commanded to bring him into the tomb or monument where Cleopatra was. When he heard that she was alive, he very earnestly prayed his men to carry his body thither;

[4.15] and so he was carried in his men's arms into the entry of the monument.

Notwithstanding, Cleopatra would not open the gates, but came to the high windows, and cast out certain chains and ropes, in the which Antonius was trussed; and Cleopatra her own self, with two women only which she had suffered to come with her into these monuments, triced Antonius up.

They that were present to behold it said they never saw so pitiful a sight. For they plucked up poor Antonius, all bloody as he was and drawing on with pangs of death, who, holding up his hands to Cleopatra, raised up himself as well as he could. It was a hard thing for these women to do, to lift him up. But Cleopatra, stooping down with her head, putting to all her strength to her uttermost power, did lift him up with much ado and never let go her hold, with the help of the women beneath that bade her be of good courage, and were as sorry to see her labour so, as she herself. So when she had gotten him in after that sort and laid him on a bed, she rent her garments upon him, clapping her breast and scratching her face and stomach. Then she dried up his blood that had berayed his face, and called him her lord, her husband, and Emperor, forgetting her own misery and calamity for the pity and compassion she took of him.

Antonius made her cease her lamenting, and called for wine— either because he was athirst, or else for that he thought thereby to hasten his death. When he had drunk, he earnestly prayed her and persuaded her that she would seek to save her life, if she could possible without reproach and dishonour; and that chiefly she should trust Proculeius above any man else about Caesar; and, as for himself, that she should not lament nor sorrow for the miserable change of his fortune at the end of his days; but rather that she should think him the more fortunate for the former triumphs and honours he had received, considering that while he lived he was the noblest and greatest prince of the world, and that now he was overcome not cowardly, but valiantly, a Roman by another Roman. [4.16.10 ff.]

As Antonius gave the last gasp, Proculeius came that was sent from Caesar. For, after Antonius had thrust his sword in himself, as they carried him into the tombs and monuments of Cleopatra, one of his guard, called Dercetaeus, took his sword with the which he had stricken himself and hid it; then he secretly stale away, and brought Octavius Caesar the first news of his death, and showed him his sword that was bloodied. [4.15.113–15; 5.1.3.1–26.] Caesar hearing these news straight withdrew himself into a secret place of his tent, and there burst out with tears, lamenting his hard and miserable fortune that had been his friend and brother-in-law, his equal in the Empire, and companion with him in sundry great exploits and battles. Then he called for all his friends, and showed them the letters Antonius had written to him, and his answers also sent him again, during their quarrel and strife; and how fiercely and proudly the other answered him to all just and reasonable matters he wrote unto him. After this he sent Proculeius, and commanded him to do what he could possible to get Cleopatra alive, fearing lest otherwise all the treasure would be lost; and furthermore, he thought that if he could take Cleopatra and bring her alive to Rome, she would marvellously beautify and set out his triumph. [5.1.35–77.]

But Cleopatra would never put herself into Proculeius' hands, although they spake together. For Proculeius came to the gates that were very thick and strong, and surely barred, but yet there were some cranews through the which her voice might be heard. And so they without understood that Cleopatra demanded the kingdom of Egypt for her sons, and that Proculeius answered her that she should be of good cheer and not be afraid to refer all unto Caesar. After he had viewed the place very well, he came and reported her answer unto Caesar; who immediately sent Gallus to speak once again with her, and bade him purposely hold her with talk whilst Proculeius did set up a ladder against that high window by the which Antonius was triced up, and came down into the monument with two of his men, hard by the gate where Cleopatra stood to hear what Gallus said unto her. One of her women which was shut in her monuments with her saw Proculeius by chance as he came down, and shrieked out: 'O poor Cleopatra, thou art taken.' Then, when she saw Proculeius behind her as she came from the gate, she thought to have stabbed herself in with a short dagger she wore of purpose by her side. But Proculeius came suddenly upon her, and taking her both by the hands said unto her: 'Cleopatra, first thou shalt do thyself great wrong, and secondly unto Caesar, to deprive him of the occasion and opportunity openly to show his bounty and mercy, and to give his enemies cause to accuse the most courteous and noble prince that ever was, and to appeach him, as though he were a cruel and merciless man that were not to be trusted.' So even as he spake the word he took her dagger from her, and shook her clothes for fear of any poison hidden about her. Afterwards Caesar sent one of his enfranchised men called Epaphroditus, whom he straitly charged to look well unto her, and to beware in any case that she made not herself away; and, for the rest, to use her with all the courtesy possible. [5.2.8.1–70] . . .

[*Caesar woos the good opinion of the Alexandrians*]

Now, touching Antonius' sons, Antyllus his eldest son by Fulvia was slain, because his schoolmaster Theodorus did betray him unto the soldiers, who strake off his head. And the villain took a precious stone of great value from his neck, the which he did sew in his girdle, and afterwards denied that he had it. But it was found about him; and so Caesar trussed him up for it. For Cleopatra's children, they were very honourably kept, with their governors and train that waited on them. But for Caesarion, who was said to be Julius

Caesar's son, his mother Cleopatra had sent him unto the Indians through Ethiopia, with a great sum of money. But one of his governors also called Rhodon, even such another as Theodorus, persuaded him to return into his country, and told him that Caesar sent for him to give him his mother's kingdom. So, as Caesar was determining with himself what he should do, Arrius said unto him:

Too many Caesars is not good,

alluding unto a certain verse of Homer that saith:

Too many lords doth not well.

Therefore Caesar did put Caesarion to death, after the death of his mother Cleopatra.

Many princes, great kings, and captains did crave Antonius' body of Octavius Caesar, to give him honourable burial. But Caesar would never take it from Cleopatra, who did sumptuously and royally bury him with her own hands, whom Caesar suffered to take as much as she would to bestow upon his funerals.

Now was she altogether overcome with sorrow and passion of mind, for she had knocked her breast so pitifully that she had martyred it and in divers places had raised ulcers and inflammations, so that she fell into a fever withal; whereof she was very glad, hoping thereby to have good colour to abstain from meat, and that so she might have died easily without any trouble. She had a physician called Olympus, whom she made privy of her intent, to the end he should help her to rid her out of her life, as Olympus writeth himself, who wrote a book of all these things. But Caesar mistrusted the matter by many conjectures he had, and therefore did put her in fear, and threatened her to put her children to shameful death. [5.2.130–3] With these threats Cleopatra for fear yielded straight as she would have yielded unto strokes; and afterwards suffered herself to be cured and dieted as they listed.

Shortly after, Caesar came himself in person to see her and to comfort her. Cleopatra being laid upon a little low bed in poor estate, when she saw Caesar come into her chamber, she suddenly rose up, naked in her smock, and fell down at his feet marvellously disfigured—both for that she had plucked her hair from her head, as also for that she had martyred all her face with her nails; and besides, her voice was small and trembling, her eyes sunk into her head with continual blubbering, and moreover they might see the most part of her stomach torn in sunder. To be short, her body was not much better than her mind. Yet her good grace and comeliness and the force of her beauty was not altogether defaced. But notwithstanding this ugly and pitiful state of hers, yet she showed herself within by her outward looks and countenance. When Caesar had made her lie down again, and sat by her bed's side, Cleopatra began to clear and excuse herself for that she had done, laying all to the fear she had of Antonius. Caesar, in contrary manner, reproved her in every point. Then she suddenly altered her speech, and prayed him to pardon her, as though she were afraid to die and desirous to live. At length, she gave him a brief and memorial of all the ready money and treasure she had. But by chance there stood Seleucus by, one of her treasurers, who, to seem a good servant, came straight to Caesar to disprove Cleopatra, that she had not set in all but kept many things back of purpose. Cleopatra was in such a rage with him that she flew upon him, and took him by the hair of the head, and boxed him well-favouredly. Caesar fell a-laughing and parted the fray.

'Alas,' said she, 'O Caesar, is not this a great shame and reproach, that thou having vouchsafed to take the pains to come unto me, and hast done me this honour, poor wretch and caitiff creature brought into this pitiful and miserable estate, and that mine own servants should come now to accuse me; though it may be I have reserved some jewels and trifles meet for women (but not for me, poor soul) to set out myself withal, but meaning to give some pretty presents and gifts unto Octavia and Livia, that, they making means and intercession for me to thee, thou mightest yet extend thy favour and mercy upon me?'

Caesar was glad to hear her say so, persuading himself thereby that she had yet a desire to save her life. So he made her answer that he did not only give her that to dispose of at her pleasure which she had kept back, but further promised to use her more honourably and bountifully than she would think for. And so he took his leave of her, supposing he had deceived her; but indeed he was deceived himself. [5.2.136–90.]

There was a young gentleman, Cornelius Dolabella, that was one of Caesar's very great familiars, and besides did bear no evil will unto Cleopatra. He sent her word secretly, as she had requested him, that Caesar determined to take his journey through Syria, and that within three days he would send her away before with her children. [5.2.106–10, 197–207.] When this was told Cleopatra, she requested Caesar that it would please him to suffer her to offer the last oblations of the dead unto the soul of Antonius.[5] This being granted her, she was carried to the place where his tomb was; and there, falling down on her knees, embracing the tomb with her women, the tears running down her cheeks, she began to speak in this sort: 'O my dear lord Antonius, not long sithence I buried thee here, being a free woman; and now I offer unto thee the funeral sprinklings and oblations, being a captive and prisoner; and yet I am forbidden and kept from tearing and murdering this captive body of mine with blows, which they carefully guard and keep, only to triumph of thee. Look therefore henceforth for no other honours, offerings, nor sacrifices from me, for these are the last which Cleopatra can give thee,

[5] The marginal note comments: '*Cleopatra finely deceiveth Octavius Caesar, as though she desired to live.*'

sith now they carry her away. Whilst we lived together, nothing could sever our companies. But now at our death I fear me they will make us change our countries. For as thou being a Roman hast been buried in Egypt, even so wretched creature, I an Egyptian shall be buried in Italy, which shall be all the good that I have received by thy country. If therefore the gods where thou art now have any power and authority, sith our gods here have forsaken us, suffer not thy true friend and lover to be carried away alive, that in me they triumph of thee. But receive me with thee, and let me be buried in one self tomb with thee. For though my griefs and miseries be infinite, yet none hath grieved me more, nor that I could less bear withal than this small time which I have been driven to live alone without thee'. [5.2.76–92]

Then, having ended these doleful plaints, and crowned the tomb with garlands and sundry nosegays, and marvellous lovingly embraced the same, she commanded they should prepare her bath; and when she had bathed and washed herself she fell to her meat, and was sumptuously served. Now whilst she was at dinner there came a countryman, and brought her a basket. The soldiers that warded at the gates asked him straight what he had in his basket. He opened the basket and took out the leaves that covered the figs, and showed them that they were figs he brought. They all of them marvelled to see so goodly figs. The countrymen laughed to hear them, and bade them take some if they would. They believed he told them truly, and so bade him carry them in. [5.2.233–78] After Cleopatra had dined, she sent a certain table written and sealed unto Caesar, and commanded them all to go out of the tombs where she was, but the two women. Then she shut the doors to her. Caesar, when she received this table and began to read her lamentation and petition, requesting him that he would let her be buried with Antonius, found straight what she meant, and thought to have gone thither himself. Howbeit, he sent one before, in all haste that might be, to see what it was.

Her death was very sudden. For those whom Caesar sent unto her ran thither in all haste possible, and found the soldiers standing at the gate, mistrusting nothing, nor understanding of her death. But when they had opened the doors they found Cleopatra stark dead, laid upon a bed of gold, attired and arrayed in her royal robes, and one of her two women, which was called Iras, dead at her feet; and her other woman called Charmion half dead and trembling, trimming the diadem which Cleopatra ware upon her head. One of the soldiers, seeing her, angrily said unto her: 'Is that well done, Charmion?' 'Very well,' said she again, 'and meet for a princess descended from the race of so many noble kings.' She said no more, but fell down dead hard by the bed.

Some report that this aspic was brought unto her in the basket with figs, and that she had commanded them to hide it under the fig leaves, that, when she should think to take out the figs, the aspic should bite her before she should see her. Howbeit that, when she would have taken away the leaves for the figs, she perceived it, and said: 'Art thou here then?' And so, her arm being naked, she put it to the aspic to be bitten. Others say again she kept it in a box; and that she did prick and thrust it with a spindle of gold, so that the aspic, being angered withal, leapt out with great fury, and bit her in the arm. Howbeit few can tell the truth; for they report also that she had hidden poison in a hollow razor which she carried in the hair of her head. And yet was there no mark seen of her body, or any sign discerned that she was poisoned; neither also did they find this serpent in her tomb. But it was reported only that there were seen certain fresh steps or tracks where it had gone, on the tomb side toward the sea and specially by the door side. Some say also that they found two little pretty bitings on her arm, scant to be discerned; the which it seemeth Caesar himself gave credit unto, because in his triumph he carried Cleopatra's image, with an aspic biting of her arm. And thus goeth the report of her death. [5.2.289–352]

Now Caesar, though he was marvellous sorry for the death of Cleopatra, yet he wondered at her noble mind and courage; and therefore commanded she should be nobly buried and laid by Antonius; and willed also that her two women should have honourable burial. [5.2.327–35, 356–64]

Cleopatra died, being eight-and-thirty year old, after she had reigned two-and-twenty years and governed above fourteen of them with Antonius. And for Antonius, some say that he lived three-and-fifty years, and others say, six-and-fifty. All his statues, images, and metals were plucked down and overthrown, saving those of Cleopatra which stood still in their places, by means of Archibius, one of her friends, who gave Caesar a thousand talents that they should not be handled as those of Antonius were.

Antonius left seven children by three wives; of the which Caesar did put Antyllus, the eldest son he had by Fulvia, to death. Octavia his wife took all the rest, and brought them up with hers, and married Cleopatra, Antonius' daughter, unto King Juba, a marvellous courteous and goodly prince. And Antonius the son of Fulvia came to be so great that, next to Agrippa, who was in greatest estimation about Caesar, and next unto the children of Livia, which were the second in estimation, he had the third place. . . .

The Comparison of Demetrius with Antonius.

Now, sithence it falleth out that Demetrius and Antonius were one of them much like to the other, having fortune alike divers and variable unto them, let us therefore come to consider their power and authority, and how they came to be so great.

First of all it is certain that Demetrius' power and greatness fell unto him by inheritance from his father. . . . Antonius, in contrary manner, born of an honest man who otherwise was no man of war and had not left him any mean to arise to such greatness, durst take upon him to contend for the empire with Caesar, that had no right unto it by inheritance, but yet made himself successor of the power the which the other by great pain and travail had obtained, and by his own industry became so great, without the help of any other, that, the empire of the whole world being divided into two parts, he had the one half, and took that of the greatest countenance and power. Antonius, being absent, oftentimes overcame the Parthians in battle by his lieutenants [3.1.16–17] . . . Demetrius' father made him gladly marry Phila, Antipater's daughter, although she was too old for him, because she was of a nobler house than himself. Antonius, on th'other side, was blamed for marrying of Cleopatra, a queen that for power and nobility of blood excelled all other kings in her time but Arsaces; and moreover made himself so great that others thought him worthy of greater things than he himself required.

Now for the desire that moved the one and the other to conquer realms: the desire of Demetrius was unblameable and just, desiring to reign over people which had been governed at all times (and desired to be governed) by kings. But Antonius' desire was altogether wicked and tyrannical, who sought to keep the people of Rome in bondage and subjection, but lately before rid of Caesar's reign and government. For the greatest and most famous exploit Antonius ever did in wars (to wit, the war in which he overthrew Cassius and Brutus) was begun to no other end but to deprive his countrymen of their liberty and freedom. Demetrius in contrary manner, before fortune had overthrown him, never left to set Greece at liberty, and to drive the garrisons away which kept the cities in bondage; and not like Antonius that boasted he had slain them that set Rome at liberty. The chiefest thing they commended in Antonius was his liberality and bounty, in the which Demetrius excelled him so far that he gave more to his enemies than Antonius did to his friends, although he was marvellously well thought of for the honourable and sumptuous funeral he gave unto Brutus' body. . . .

They were both in their prosperity very riotously and licentiously given; but yet no man can ever say that Demetrius did at any time let slip any opportunity to follow great matters, but only gave himself indeed to pleasure when he had nothing else to do. . . . But indeed when he was to make any preparation for war, he had not then ivy at his dart's end, nor had his helmet perfumed, nor he came not out of ladies' closets picked and prinked to go to battle, but he let all dancing and sporting alone, and became, as the poet Euripides saith, 'the soldier of Mars, cruel and bloody'. But, to conclude, he never had overthrow or misfortune through negligence, nor by delaying time to follow his own pleasure. As we see in painted tables where Omphale secretly stealeth away Hercules' club and took his lion's skin from him, even so Cleopatra oftentimes unarmed Antonius and enticed him to her, making him lose matters of great importance and very needful journeys to come and be dandled with her [2.5.21–3]. . . . In the end, as Paris fled from the battle and went to hide himself in Helen's arms, even so did he in Cleopatra's arms; or, to speak more properly, Paris hid himself in Helen's closet, but Antonius, to follow Cleopatra, fled and lost the victory.

Furthermore, Demetrius had many wives that he had married, and all at one time (the which was not disallowable or not forbidden by the kings of Macedon . . .) and did honour all them that he married. But Antonius first of all married two wives together, the which never Roman durst do before but himself. Secondly, he put away his first Roman wife which he had lawfully married, for the love of a strange woman he fondly fell in fancy withal, and contrary to the laws of Rome. And therefore Demetrius' marriages never hurt him for any wrong he had done to his wives; but Antonius contrarily was undone by his wives. . . . Antonius by his incontinency did no hurt but to himself; and Demetrius did hurt unto all others.

Demetrius never hurt any of his friends; and Antonius suffered his uncle by his mother's side to be slain, that he might have his will of Cicero to kill him—a thing so damnable, wicked, and cruel of itself that he hardly deserved to have been pardoned, though he had killed Cicero to have saved his uncle's life.

Now where they falsified and brake their oaths . . . Antonius, out of doubt, had best cause and justest colour . . . Demetrius himself did many noble feats in war, as we have recited of him before; and, contrarily, Antonius, when he was not there in person, won many famous and great victories by his lieutenants [3.1.16–17]. And they were both overthrown being personally in battle, but yet not after one sort. For the one was forsaken of his men, being Macedonians; and the other contrarily forsook his that were Romans—for he fled and left them that ventured their lives for his honour. So that the fault the one did was that he made them his enemies that fought for him; and the fault in the other that he so beastly left them that loved him best and were most faithful to him.

And for their deaths, a man can not praise the one nor the other, but yet Demetrius' death the more reproachful. For he suffered himself to be taken prisoner; and when he was sent away to be kept in a strange place, he had the heart to live yet three year longer, to serve his mouth and belly as brute beasts do. Antonius, on the other side, slew himself (to confess a truth) cowardly and miserably, to his great pain and grief; and yet was it before his body came into his enemies' hands.

A NOTE ON THE STAGING OF 4.16 AND 5.2[1]

These scenes have given trouble to directors ever since the play began to be regularly revived in the nineteenth century, Anthony's death scene proving especially awkward. Although Garrick had had Anthony hauled up to Cleopatra in 'certain Tackle' let down by the women, Kemble evidently decided that this was either unmanageable or too undignified, and initiated a long tradition, followed by Samuel Phelps and others, of having Anthony carried offstage and then reintroduced to the monument above.[2] The intended staging of this scene has occasioned a great deal of debate. Opinion is sharply divided between those who believe that Cleopatra and her maids were to be placed in the gallery above the entrances on the tiring house facade, and those who adhere to Dover Wilson's proposal that they occupied the upper level of a specially built structure representing the monument. Useful summaries of the debate can be found in Ridley (Appendix IV), Lamb (Appendix A, 'Heaving Antony Aloft'), and Leslie Thomson, '*Antony and Cleopatra*, 4.16: "A Heavy Sight" ', *SSu* 41 (1989), pp. 77–89. The arguments are especially difficult to resolve because each provokes major objections. On the one hand the word 'aloft' seems to be used in stage directions only to refer to action in the gallery; on the other hand if the acting space 'above' at the Globe was anything like the gallery illustrated in the Swan drawing, which shows a high railing and dividing pillars between each pair of occupants, the scene (as Granville-Barker pointed out)[3] would have been very difficult to play there—and indeed there are no scenes of comparable length and importance which were certainly designed to be performed in such a space. Nevertheless a majority of editors and theatre historians tend to the view that the gallery (or 'tarras') was intended. It is possible to overcome the technical difficulties involved in heaving Anthony's body 10–12 feet to the level of the gallery by supposing that ropes and pulleys were installed in the tiring house above the 'heavens'; it is even possible to remove some of the problems of visibility by supposing that part of the balustrade at the front of the gallery could be opened or removed. But the F stage direction *Exeunt, bearing of*

---

[1] For an extensive summary of the literature which has accumulated around the controversial staging of these two scenes, see Spevack's New Variorum edition, pp. 777–93, 'Staging the Monument Scenes at the Globe'.

[2] Lamb, pp. 50, 58; the Folger Library's prompt-book for Phelps's influential 1849 production begins the scene with '*Cleopatra and Charmian discovered leading forward Antony*'.

[3] *Preface*, p. 44.

12. The monument scene (4.16), Shakespeare Memorial Theatre, 1951.

Anthonies body, indicating as it does a relatively formal processional exit modelled on funeral custom, is difficult to reconcile with what we can piece together about staging possibilities in the gallery. Moreover, there remain formidable visual and acoustic obstacles in the way of staging an emotional climax of this sort at the very back of the stage—so that Peter Thomson, in one of the most recent studies of the Shakespearian stage, dismisses the proposal as 'lunacy', and insists that 'the preference must be for some structure erected on the platform proper'.[4]

[4] Peter Thomson, *Shakespeare's Theatre* (London, 1983), p. 52. Thomson himself was particularly enthusiastic about Trevor Nunn's 1973 staging in which the monument became 'a fortress, so visibly impregnable that its capture by Roman soldiers achieved the status of a major event' (*SSu* 26 (1973), p. 148). By contrast Peter Brook in 1978 (Fig. 13) triumphantly showed how the entire scene could be managed as a stylized mime, in which the monument was suggested by a square of red cloth onto which Cleopatra and her maids dragged the wounded Anthony (see Roger Warren in *SSu* 33 (1980), p. 177).

13. The monument scene, Royal Shakespeare Theatre, 1978. In Peter Brook's highly stylized production the monument was represented by a carpet, and Anthony was hauled 'aloft' along the floor.

However, while tombs and monuments were common enough stage-properties, they were not normally large enough to accommodate a scene as elaborate as this one, and a structure big enough to accommodate a minimum of four actors 'aloft' would clearly interfere with the sightlines of a significant part of the audience. Furthermore, a structure on this scale would be exceedingly difficult to bring onto the stage in the course of the action, yet it seems highly improbable that Shakespeare would have wished to clutter the stage with it for the whole action—especially since (as Ridley argued) there are good reasons for thinking that 5.2, while imagined as taking place in the monument, was meant to be played on the main platform in the usual way. On balance the argument is probably narrowly in favour of the gallery solution—Diomedes' line 'Look out o'th'other side your monument' looks as though it were there to inform the audience's imagination that the tiring house façade has, for the purposes of this scene, *become* the monument; but the whole debate is an uncomfortable illustration of how little, despite the most ingenious efforts of theatre historians, we still know about playing conditions at the Globe. Had the Folio text derived from a prompt-book we might have a better idea of what was done; as it is, we must conclude either that the technical solutions were so self-evident that Shakespeare did not bother to elaborate his stage direction, or that he relied on the ingenuity of his colleagues to realize a scene he had conceived in largely symbolic terms. What is important about the imaginative design of the scene, as Leslie Thomson has reminded us, is the way it makes use of a hierarchy of theatrical levels to act out 'the related ideas of weight, bearing, drawing, rising and falling that fill the play'.[5] Any clumsiness involved in resolving the scene's technical problems, she argues, is appropriate to the ambiguous and unstable mood of the scene, and indeed of the whole play, with its tense contradictions of matter and manner, action and rhetoric: so that, for example, the raising of Anthony stages a symbolism of tragic transcendence, yet ironically offers itself at the same time as black-comic re-enactment of Cleopatra's fishing sport described in 2.5. A rather different approach to the problems of the scene is represented by Toby Robertson's striking, but arguably gratuitous, *coup de théâtre* in the 1986 Theatre Clwyd production: here, in a shocking parody-crucifixion that variously recalled Caravaggio, El Greco, and Francis Bacon, the dying hero was hauled up by his wrist on a winch, 'three-quarters naked, one quarter disembowelled', 'his greatness reduced to a bleeding piece of meat'— an effect more tactfully echoed in Peter Hall's 1987 *Anthony* at the National, where Anthony was winched into the monument in a fashion recalling 'a Renaissance image of the crucifixion of Christ'.[6]

The intended staging of the second monument scene (5.2) is also debatable, but the problems are rather more easily resolved. Although Hanmer and others assumed that this scene should, like 4.16, make use of the gallery 'aloft', there are no indications in the text of stage directions of F to suggest that two-level staging is intended. Ridley (Appendix IV) convincingly disposes of Malone's alternative suggestion that Shakespeare meant to copy Plutarch's description of events by representing the monument in the 'inner stage' with a barred gate across its opening. Ridley's arguments are reinforced by the view of recent stage historians that the small 'discovery space' between the two stage doors was suited to little more than brief tableau scenes. The easiest solution is to suppose that, in the interests of theatrical clarity and economy, Shakespeare decided to dispense with the vivid physical detail of Plutarch's account, which has Cleopatra speaking to Proculeius through 'some

[5] Leslie Thomson, 'A Heavy Sight', p. 81. John Bayley (*Shakespeare and Tragedy*, pp. 125–7 sees the 'slow-motion clumsiness' of the scene as a touching parallel to the débâcle of Anthony's suicide. See also Richard Hosley, 'The Staging of the Monument Scenes in *Antony and Cleopatra*', *Library Chronicle*, 300 (1964), pp. 62–71.

[6] Benedict Nightingale, *New Statesman*, 30 May 1986; John Barber, *Daily Telegraph*, 24 May 1986; Michael Billington, *Guardian*, 28 May 1986; Alison Chitty (Hall's designer) cited in Lowen, p. 10. The odd religious overtones were evidently deliberate in both cases and part of a wider pattern of sober-faced parody: Robertson costumed Cleopatra like the Virgin Mary for her final scene, while Chitty's design for Pompey's galley was borrowed from da Vinci's *Last Supper*.

cranews' in the heavy gates of the monument; and that the scene was simply played on the open stage, with Proculeius entering from one door and holding the Queen in conversation whilst Gallus's soldiers broke in through the other to take her by surprise.[7] There is nothing in Proculeius's speeches to suggest any difficulty in gaining access to the Queen, and since he has apparently come on his own to treat with her, there is nothing fundamentally improbable about his having been admitted to the Queen's presence as an emissary.

[7] Samuel Phelps contrived to preserve Plutarch's version of events by having Gallus and his men lower a ladder at the rear 'by which they stealthily descend onto the stage, throw back bar of grated door and let in Proculeius and 2 guards'.

A NOTE ON PRONOUN USAGE

It is sometimes difficult for modern readers to sense the important nuances involved in seventeenth-century pronoun usage. While most readers are accustomed to the shift in register conveyed by movements between the singular and plural first persons, involving use of the so-called 'royal *we*', the distinctions between 'thou' and 'you' are less well appreciated, the former being thought of simply as an archaic alternative to the modern 'you'. The difficulty is compounded by the fact that the process which was to lead to the abandonment of the singular pronoun had already begun in late sixteenth-century English. Thus while the choice of the plural form, *you*, can sometimes seem quite neutral, at other times it involves the exercise of social discriminations as critical as those that can still be registered by *tu* and *vous* in modern French. In general, *thou* is preferred in contexts of intimacy (as between lovers) or when addressing children or social inferiors; it can thus be used to convey degrees of condescension or presumption which, depending on the exact relationship between the speakers, can range from the mildly irksome to the extremely insulting. *You* is used to register formality, a respectful distance between speakers, or sometimes (in the case of family and intimates) a degree of hauteur or coldness. At 1.1.17–34, for example, Cleopatra's shift from the intimate *thou* to the formal *you* at l. 23 shows her discarding the role of mistress in favour of a more public persona. Her mimicry of Caesar's voice, on the other hand, returns to the singular form, so that Caesar will sound like an authoritarian schoolmaster addressing a disobedient child; this is doubly insulting in view of Anthony's much-emphasized disdain for his opponent as 'the boy Caesar'. Similarly, when Cleopatra returns to *thou* in her own voice at l. 32, it is meant less as a return to her former teasing intimacy than as a way of marking the distinction between 'Egypt's queen' and a mere 'homager'. By contrast the Messengers' use of the singular pronoun in addressing Caesar at 1.4.34–47 may seem to be an example of a purely neutral usage. But perhaps it is not quite so; it is notable that while Caesar's inferiors often *thou* him, only three characters (apart from Anthony) dare use the form with Cleopatra—the presumptuous Thidias (3.13.53–4), the insolent Proculeius (5.2.10–11), and Charmian in a rare moment of intense feeling after the Queen's death (5.2.312). A difference is surely being registered between the protocols of the two worlds, the royal court of Egypt, and a Rome which, publicly at least, still preserves republican institutions, forms, and manners.

The modulation between *I* and *we* by speakers of royal rank is clearly less problematic, being analogous to the well-known distinction between the king's two bodies, or his public and private selves. But in a play like *Anthony and Cleopatra*, whose principal characters include a queen whose monarchy is under threat from an expanding imperial power, and at least two soldier-politicians who aspire to royal rank and who already enjoy a position corresponding to *de facto* kingship, the decision to use one or other pronoun often carries an intense political charge. When, for example, in the last speech of the play Caesar reassumes the royal pronoun *our* as he announces his imminent return to Rome he is, in effect, looking forward to his elevation as Augustus, the first Roman emperor.

It would clearly be impossible to comment on every significant pronoun usage, but readers (and actors) need to be constantly alert to the social and emotional shadings involved.

A NOTE ON LINEATION

Among the more difficult decisions facing any editor of *Anthony and Cleopatra* are those which involve the proper setting of the verse.[1] Mislineation is common in F, some of it the product of mere compositorial carelessness; some occurring when a compositor, faced with a line too long for his column, cut it into two, producing two anomalous short lines; some apparently resulting from confusion when the compositor was faced with lines that the copy-text must have run together in order to save space. In the worst cases such mislineation might have the effect of reducing to prose what was clearly intended as verse. On other occasions quite extensive passages of verse seem to have been deliberately rendered as prose in order to correct for faulty casting off of copy which had left a compositor with too many verse lines to fit onto a given page.

A fairly straightforward example of verse reduced to prose occurs at the end of 1.1, where the Folio version of Demetrius's closing speech seems an odd inconsistency in a scene that is otherwise printed entirely as verse:

I am full sorry, that he approves the common
Lyar, who thus speakes of him at Rome; but I will hope
of better deeds to morrow. Rest you happy. (1.1.61–4)

Here the anomaly is easily removed. If 'I am full sorry' is treated as a half-line, completing Philo's 'Which still should go with Anthony' in a loose hexameter, the remainder of the speech easily resolves itself into three pentameters:

> I am full sorry,
> That he approves the common liar who
> Thus speaks of him at Rome; but I will hope
> Of better deeds tomorrow. Rest you happy.

By contrast there seems to be little point in struggling to reset Enobarbus's speech at 2.2.108–11 ('Or if you borrow . . . else to do') as verse, though it contains two and a half lines of regular iambic pentameter ('Or if . . . love . . . You shall . . . when you | Have . . . do'); for the sardonically common-sensical tone of Enobarbus's interjections is frequently marked by a switch to prose, and the

---

[1] The most comprehensive recent treatment of Shakespeare's versification is Wright, *Shakespeare's Metrical Art*; but the topic of lineation is perhaps best treated in Paul Werstine's 'Line Division in Shakespeare's Verse: An Editorial Problem', *Analytical and Enumerative Bibliography* 8 (1984), pp. 73–125.

presence of such fossil pentameters merely shows how a dramatist accustomed to writing in blank verse may reproduce its cadences in his prose from time to time.

The problems presented by the first soothsayer scene (1.2.1–77) are less tractable. Since it immediately follows Demetrius's speech at the end of 1.1, there are reasons for suspecting misaligned verse in its opening speeches; but much of the dialogue, up to Cleopatra's entry, seems to have been written as prose, especially the longer speeches. Once again, however, several speeches have pentameter lines embedded in them, and some of the dialogue can fairly readily be rearranged as verse. As often, F's own intentions are difficult to discern with complete certainty—except that the compositor appears to treat all the longer speeches as prose, and nowhere does he unambiguously signal verse lineation. In printing most of the scene, except for the Soothsayer's speeches, as cadenced prose, this edition follows the judgement of Granville-Barker, whose *Preface* contains a particularly sensitive account of how the play's verse works theatrically (pp. 51–66). In general the keynote of this scene is one of relaxed conversational informality to which prose is appropriate; but the Soothsayer affects a solemn incantatory style, sometimes echoed or parodied by those around him, which is partly registered in his formal iambic rhythms. As the repartee develops the women's lively prose progressively overwhelms the Soothsayer's pentameters, emphasizing the change of mood when Cleopatra's entry restores the formality of blank verse.

At other points F's lineation is simply ambiguous: the lack of any established printing-house convention for signalling shared lines meant that F printed each new speech without indentation, regardless of whether it completed an existing line. Rapid dialogue often involves a series of such incomplete lines, whose regularization is sometimes made even more difficult by the doubly ambiguous status of lines which can be quite satisfactorily combined with the part lines on *either* side of them. Past editors, struggling to fit as many lines as possible to the pentameter pattern, were often happy to settle for somewhat arbitrary solutions to this kind of uncertainty. But recent editorial practice, alert to the increasing permissiveness of late Shakespearian verse, has been rather more cautious about regularization, preferring to regard some half-lines as 'amphibiously' linked to lines on *both* sides—a licence which Shakespeare often seems to have allowed himself in the latter part of his career. Thus, for example, at 1.4.72 Lepidus's deprecatory ' 'Tis pity of him' can be read either as completing the final line of Caesar's expostulation, or as belonging with the opening half-line of his following speech:

> [CAESAR]   And all this—
> It wounds thine honour that I speak it now—
> Was borne so like a soldier that thy cheek
> So much as lanked not.

LEPIDUS 'Tis pity of him.
CAESAR Let his shames quickly
  Drive him to Rome.

1.4.68–74

Editors usually opt for the first alternative. But, as Fredson Bowers has shown, unattached half-lines are on balance more likely to occur at the end than at the beginning of speeches.[2] Moreover it arguably makes better dramatic sense to allow for an embarrassed pause before Lepidus's rather lame endorsement of Caesar's views, and to give Caesar a quick cue at l. 73 which reinforces his rhetorical dominance of the scene. But, given the frequency with which such problems arise, especially in Shakespeare's later verse, it may very well be that the ambiguity is his own, and that he expected the listener's ear to respond to Lepidus's half-line as amphibiously attached to the metre of either (or both) adjacent lines.

A more complex example, involving both verse printed as prose and what may be amphibious half-lines occurs at 2.6.62–70:

[*Pom.*] Draw lots who shall begin.
Ant. That will I *Pompey.*
Pompey. No *Anthony* take the lot: but first or last, your fine Egyptian cookerie shall haue the fame, I haue heard that *Iulius Caesar*, grew fat with feasting there.
Anth. You haue heard much.
Pom. I haue faire meaning Sir.
Ant. And faire words to them.
Pom. Then so much haue I heard,
And I haue heard *Appolodorus* carried—
Eno. No more that: he did so.
Pom. What I pray you?

Various attempts have been made to rearrange Pompey's clearly anomalous prose as verse and to determine the proper relationship of the half-lines. Oxford adopts a fairly conservative solution, based on Rowe's original rearrangement of the prose:

Draw lots who shall begin.
ANTHONY That will I, Pompey.
POMPEY No, Anthony take the lot.
  But first or last, your fine Egyptian cookery
  Shall have the fame, I have heard that Julius Caesar
  Grew fat with feasting there.
ANTHONY   You have heard much.
POMPEY I have fair meanings, sir.
ANTHONY And fair words to them.
POMPEY Then so much have I heard.

---

[2] Fredson Bowers, 'Establishing Shakespeare's Text: Notes on Short Lines and the Problem of Verse Division', *SB* 33 (1980), pp. 74–130.

And I have heard Apollodorus carried—
ENOBARBUS
No more o' that. He did so.
POMPEY   What I pray you?

Here Anthony's first line becomes amphibious, forming a hexameter
with 'No . . . lot' whilst still notionally completing Pompey's previous
line. Similarly, in the cluster of half-lines that follow the rearranged
prose, Anthony's 'And fair words to them' is assumed to be amphibious. The advantage of such an indeterminate arrangement is that
it allows the actors a number of alternative ways to handle a
particularly tense passage of dialogue. For example, if Anthony's
'That will I, Pompey' is taken as a quick cue, taking up Pompey's
incomplete 'Draw . . . begin', and leaving l. 64 as an unattached
half-line, the effect will be to emphasize how Anthony's eagerness
to host the first banquet has provoked another of this scene's edgy
disputes over precedence: Pompey abruptly insists that Anthony
draw lots with the rest; and then, after an uneasy pause, tries to
smooth matters over with flattery—only to mar the effect with the
tactless allusion to Cleopatra's previous affair with Julius Caesar that
provokes Anthony's irritable, 'You have heard much' (l. 66). Alternatively, if Anthony's offer to begin the feasting is treated as beginning a new line, then it may seem to fill a slightly embarrassed
silence after Caesar's suggestion of drawing lots; and Pompey's quick
response will seem much more conciliatory. Similarly, the three
half-lines that follow Anthony's interruption at l. 66 can be treated
either as a series of rapid and aggressive cues (taking advantage of
their amphibious linkage), or as incomplete lines punctuated by tense
pausing.

On balance, however, the Oxford solution, for all its dramatic
flexibility, seems to me less elegant than Ridley's, which depends on
a slightly different rearrangement of F's prose:

[*Pom.*] Draw lots who shall begin.
Ant.   That will I, Pompey.
Pom. No, Antony, take the lot: but, first or last,
   Your fine Egyptian cookery shall have
   The fame. I have heard that Julius Caesar
   Grew fat with feasting there.
Ant.   You have heard much.
Pom. I have fair meanings, sir.
Ant.   And fair words to them.
Pom. Then so much have I heard,
   And I have heard Apollodorus carried—
Eno. No more of that: he did so.
Pom.   What, I pray you?

Apart from a slight metrical awkwardness at l. 65 ('The . . .
Caesar'), the only disadvantage of this is that it leaves Pompey's

penultimate speech beginning with an unattached half-line ('Then so much have I heard') that is difficult to justify in theatrical terms. This, however, is easily remedied by adopting Capell's line division after 'And I have heard', which has the additional advantage of providing a metrical equivalent for Pompey's aposiopesis at l. 69.

In some cases apparent anomalies can be solved by linkages that combine intractable fragments into hexameters or other irregularly formed lines. However, while such solutions are consistent with late Shakespearian practice, the results are often metrically ungainly, and I follow Bevington's example in treating them with caution.[3] In any case it is important to recognize the possibility that individual half-lines are sometimes meant to stand alone, signalling (as they often do within a longer speech) a significant pause, or (more rarely) the need to stretch out the words into the imaginary space of a complete line—in a cry of anguish, for example. Thus in 4.16, while Case and others treat Cleopatra's 'O sun' as completing Diomedes' line ('His guard have brought him thither', l. 9), there seems little point in a rearrangement which only serves to create a line that is still one syllable short—especially since the dramatic context surely calls for a pause followed by an extended cry of pain as Cleopatra takes in the spectacle of the dying Anthony.

In some cases I have found satisfactory decisions more than usually difficult to arrive at. In 4.3, for example, I have substantially rearranged the sentries' dialogue into complete verse lines in the fashion favoured by most modern editors, whilst remaining uneasily aware that the sequence of very short speeches may be intended to represent nervous, halting exchanges, full of tense pauses and hesitations.[4] In such a scene, while there are a great many possible solutions, there is much to be said for Bevington's conservative approach, which treats much of the dialogue as either broken verse or prose.

The following list records all changes in lineation, as well as changes from prose to verse. In a few cases, where correct relineation is especially problematic and where several solutions seem equally possible, I have collated alternatives not adopted here. The format of the list follows that used in Gary Taylor's *Henry V*, and differs from the textual collation in that spelling is modernized and end-of-line punctuation ignored. Attribution of an emendation indicates only a given edition's *arrangement of the lines*, and has no necessary implications for its *wording* of a particular passage.

---

[3] See Bevington's 'Textual Analysis', p. 267.

[4] John Barton's *Playing Shakespeare* (1984) contains some useful discussion of these problems from the perspective of directors and actors, graphically illustrating the different theatrical effects that various solutions can produce (see esp. ch. 2, 'Using the Verse'). For a more technical analysis see Wright, ch. 8, 'Short and Shared Lines'.

1.1.5 Have ... turn] *one line* ROWE; F *divides after* 'Mars'
44–5 I'll ... himself] POPE; *as one line* F
54–5 No ... note] ROWE; F *divides after* 'tonight'
61–4 I ... happy] JOHNSON (*after* POPE); *as prose* F
1.2.10–11 In ... read] THEOBALD; *as prose* F
33–4 You ... approach] CAPELL; *as prose* F
37–8 If ... million] ROWE; *as prose* F
82 A ... Enobarbus] ROWE; F *divides after* 'him'
85 Here ... approaches] ROWE; F *divides after* 'service'
86–7 We ... field] ROWE; F *divides after* 'him ... wife'
88–90 Against ... state] STAUNTON; F *divides after* 'Lucius ... end ... state'
99–104 Labienus ... say] STEEVENS 1793; F *divides after* 'news ... force ... conquering ... Lydia ... Whilst'
105–6 Speak ... Rome] ROWE; F *divides after* 'home ... name'
119–20 In ... serious] POPE; F *divides after* 'sickness ... serious'
175 No ... officers] ROWE; F *divides after* 'answers'
1.3.2 See ... does] ROWE; F *divides after* 'is'
29 Who ... madness] ROWE; F *divides after* 'Fulvia'
33 But ... staying] ROWE; F *divides after* 'go'
102–3 Let ... flies] POPE; F *divides after* 'go'
1.4.7–9 More ... faults] CAPELL; F *divides after* 'audience ... You
10–11 I ... goodness] RIDLEY; F *divides after* 'think'
43 And ... love] ROWE; F *divides after* 'man'
80–1 Till ... farewell] STEEVENS 1778; *as one line* F
84–5 Doubt ... bond] This edition; *as one line* F
1.5.63–7 Who's ... brave Caesar] ROWE; *as prose* F
77–8 He ... Egypt] JOHNSON; *as prose* F
2.1.2–5 Know ... sue for] ROWE; *as prose* F
16–17 Caesar ... carry] HANMER (*conj.* Thirlby); F *divides after* 'field'
2.2.8–10 I ... in't] This edition; F *divides after* 'to day ... stomaching'
12–14 Your ... Caesar] POPE; F *divides after* 'stir ... Anthony'
16–17 Hark ... friends] CAPELL; F *divides after* 'Ventidius ... Agrippa'
34–5 I ... little, I] ROWE; *as one line* F
58–60 You ... excuses] POPE; *as prose* F
75–6 I ... Alexandria you] ROWE; *as one line* F
78–9 Sir ... then] CAPELL; *as one line* F
85–7 You ... with] ROWE; *as prose* F
93–4 To lend ... denied] F4; *as prose* F
124–6 Thou ... widower] ROWE; *as prose* F
126–8 Say ... rashness] THEOBALD (*after* POPE); *as prose* F
129–30 I am ... speak] ROWE; *as prose* F
135–6 No ... speak] F2; F *divides after* 'whose'
150–1 The ... never] THEOBALD; F *divides after* 'Caesar'
168–70 About ... sea] HANMER (*conj.* Thirlby); F *divides after* 'increasing'

175–7 Let . . . me] HANMER (*conj.* Thirlby); F *divides after* 'company'
201 The . . . silver] POPE; F *divides after* 'love-sick'
250–2 Let . . . here] ROWE; *as prose* F
2.3.1–2 The . . . bosom] ROWE; F *divides after* 'will'
2–4 All . . . you] ROWE; *as prose* F
10–11 Would . . . thither] OXFORD; *as one line* F
13–16 Say . . . side] CAPELL; F *divides after* 'higher . . . mine'
2.4.1–2 Trouble . . . after] ROWE; *as prose* F
2–3 Sir . . . follow] THEOBALD (*conj.* Thirlby); *as prose* F
5–9 We . . . me] POPE; *as prose* F
2.5.1–2 Give . . . love] ROWE; *as prose* F
5–6 As . . . sir] ROWE; *as prose* F
8 And . . . short] ROWE; F *divides at* 'showed'
15–18 'Twas . . . up] POPE; *as prose* F
26–8 Antonio's . . . here] SINGER 1856; F *divides after* 'dead . . . mistress . . . him'
32 Why . . . use] ROWE; F *divides after* 'gold'
63–4 Good . . . eyes] CAPELL (*conj.* Tyrwhitt); F *divides after* 'you'
93 The gods . . . still] ROWE; F *divides after* 'thee'
106–7 Are . . . 'em!] CAPELL (*conj.* Thirlby); F *divides after* 'me'
2.6.2–3 And we . . . have we] ROWE; F *divides after* 'fight . . . words'
32–4 Which . . . offer] ROWE; F *divides after* 'to . . . embraced . . . Fortune'
40–1 Our targes . . . prepared] POPE; F *divides after* 'offer . . . here'
53–4 Since . . . you] ROWE; *as one line* F
63–6 No . . . there] RIDLEY; *as prose* F
68–9 Then . . . carried] CAPELL; F *divides after* 'I heard'
76–7 Sir . . . ye] POPE; *as one line* F
2.7.29–30 I am . . . out] CAPELL; *as verse* F (*divides after* 'be:')
58–9 Thou . . . lords] HANMER; *as prose* F
63 Wilt . . . twice] ROWE; F *divides after* 'world'
64–6 But . . . world] POPE; *as prose* F
82 For . . . more] OXFORD; F *divides after* 'follow'; POPE *divides after* 'this'
85 Bear . . . Pompey] POPE; F *divides after* 'ashore'
88–9 A bears . . . not] CAPELL; *as one line* F
90–1 The third . . . wheels] KEIGHTLEY; *as prose* F
95–7 I . . . fouler] POPE; *as prose* F
99–103 Possess . . . drink] KNIGHT (*conj.* Thirlby); *as prose* F
118 What . . . brother] ROWE; F *divides after* 'more'
126–30 And shall . . . what] STEEVENS 1793; F *divides after* 'hand . . . house . . . friends . . . boat . . . shore . . . drums'
3.1.27–9 Thou . . . Anthony] CAPELL; *as prose* F
3.2.16 Hoo . . . cannot] ROWE; F *divides after* 'Figure'
33–4 Make . . . distrust] ROWE; *as one line* F
48 Her heart . . . feather] ROWE; F *divides after* 'tongue'
53–4 He . . . man] POPE; *as prose* F
3.3.2–6 Good . . . near] POPE; *as prose* F

8–10 Madam ... Anthony] STAUNTON; *as prose* F
12 Didst ... low] ROWE; F *divides after* 'speak'
18–19 She ... one] ROWE; *as one line* F
22–4 Or ... perceive't] THEOBALD; F *divides after* 'observance ... note ... perceive't'
26–7 Guess ... widow] CAPELL; F *divides after* 'prithee'
31–2 For ... colour] F3; *as prose* F
42–6 Hath ... enough] ROWE; *as prose* F
3.4.5–6 To public ... not] This edition; F *divides at* 'me'
3.5.12–14 Then ... Anthony] HANMER; *as prose* F
21–2 'Twill ... Anthony] HANMER (*conj.* Thirlby); *as one line* F
3.6.10–11 Of ... queen] ROWE; *as one line* F
22–3 The ... accusations] POPE; F *divides after* 'knows it'
28–30 That ... revenue] ROWE; F *divides after* 'deposed'
34–7 And ... like] ROWE; *as one line* F
63–4 And ... now] ROWE; *as one line* F
79–80 Welcome ... forth] F4; *as one line* F
3.7.5–9 Is't ... horse] HANMER (*conj.* Thirlby); *as prose* F
19–20 Nay ... Emperor] HANMER; *as one line* F
70–1 You ... not] ROWE; *as prose* F
80–1 With ... some] ROWE; F *divides after* 'labour'
3.8.1–4 Strike ... jump] Steevens 1793; F *divides after* 'land ... battle ... exceed ... lies'
3.10.4–5 Gods ... them] THEOBALD; *as one line* F
31–2 'Tis ... comes] HANMER; F *divides after* 'to't'
3.11.70–3 Even ... knows] F; HANMER *divides after* 'schoolmaster ... lead'
3.13.16–18 Let ... brim] ROWE; *as prose* F
52–3 So ... entreats] POPE; *as one line* F
60–3 He ... leaky] POPE; F *divides after* 'god ... honour ... merely ... Anthony'
71–2 And ... landlord] This edition (*after* HANMER); *as one line* F
85–6 Favours ... fellow] F4; *as one line* F
92–3 And ... him] CAPELL (*conj.* Tyrwhitt); F *divides after* 'ears'
154–6 Alack ... Anthony] CAPELL; F *divides after* 'eclipsed'
190–1 Do ... queen] ROWE; F *divides after* 'them ... force ... scars'
4.1.10–11 Let ... battles] F *divides after* 'know'
4.3.9–10 'Tis ... purpose] STEEVENS 1793; *as one line* F
12–13 Peace ... mean] OXFORD; *as one line* F
16–17 How now? ... this] CAPELL; *as one line* F
4.4.8–10 Well ... defences] HANMER; F *divides after* 'now ... defences'
21–3 And go ... expect you] ROWE; F *divides after* 'delight ... their'
4.5.6–7 Who ... Enobarbus] POPE; *as one line* F
9–11 Sir ... certain] THEOBALD; F *divides after* 'Caesar ... him'
4.6.6–7 Anthony ... field] CAPELL; *as one line* F
4.9.1 We ... before] ROWE; F *divides after* 'one'
19 We ... grey] ROWE; F *divides after* 'beds'

20–2 Do . . . man] JOHNSON; F *divides after* 'we . . . can'
4.10.4–5 This . . . to's] HANMER; *as one line* F
10–11 Peace . . . further] HANMER; *as one line* F
29–32 The hand . . . out] OXFORD; F *divides after* 'him . . . sleepers
. . . note'
4.13.1–3 Yet . . . go] CAPELL F *divides after* 'joined . . . all'
4.14.3–4 To . . . dead] POPE; F *divides after* 'self'
4.15.7 And . . . signs] ROWE F *divides after* 'air'
22–3 O . . . sword] ROWE; *as one line* F
25–6 Hence . . . death] HANMER; F *divides after* 'me'
37 Does . . . off] ROWE; F *divides after* 'Go'
65–9 Th'inevitable . . . cheek] OXFORD; F *divides after* 'horror . . . kill
me . . . not me'; ROWE *divides after* 'disgrace . . . then . . . come . . .
defeat'st'
94–5 Why . . . death] POPE; F *divides after* 'then . . . death'
117 Art . . . give me] F *divides after* 'Diomed'
130–1 What . . . calls] POPE; F *divides after* 'Emperor's guard'
4.16.12–15 The varying . . . hither] OXFORD; F *divides after* 'Anthony, Anthony, Anthony . . . friends'
18–19 So . . . 'tis so] ROWE; F *divides after* 'be . . . conquer Anthony'
34 Here's . . . Lord!] F *divides after* 'indeed'
5.1.2–3 Being . . . makes] HANMER; F *divides after* 'him'
11–12 I'll . . . life] F4; *as one line* F
30–1 His . . . him] POPE; *as one line* F
47–8 Unreconciliable . . . friends] POPE; F *divides after* 'this'
59–60 Determine . . . ungentle] POPE; *as one line* F
69–70 Gallus . . . Proculeius] ALEXANDER; *as prose* F
5.2.41–2 What . . . languish] CAPELL; *as one line* F
42–3 Cleopatra . . . by] OXFORD; *as one line* F
115–7 Sir . . . obey] POPE; F *divides after* 'thus . . . obey'
191–2 He words . . . Charmian] HANMER; F *divides after* 'me . . . self'
204–5 Dolabella . . . debtor] POPE; *as one line* F
207 Farewell . . . thou] ROWE; F *divides after* 'thanks'
224–6 Why . . . intents] ROWE; F *divides after* 'preparation'
242–3 Hast . . . not?] OXFORD; F *divides after* 'there'
306–7 That . . . unpolicied] POPE; *as one line* F
321 Approach . . . beguiled] THEOBALD; F *divides after* 'ho'
323 What . . . done] ROWE; F *divides after* 'Charmian'
349–51 This . . . Nile] JOHNSON; F *divides after* 'trail . . . such . . . Nile'

INDEX

This is a guide to words and phrases glossed in the Commentary and to a selection of names and topics in the Introduction and Commentary, excluding the Appendices. Citations of first recorded use are indicated by asterisks, while biblical and proverbial allusions are grouped together.

A, 2.7.88
abode, 1.2.174
absolute, 4.3.8
abstract, 1.4.9
abused, 3.6.87
act, 5.2.284
act of grace, 2.2.154
acted, 5.2.44–5
action, 3.7.68–69
actor, 2.5.8–9
Adelman, Janet, pp. 68, 70, 72, 88, 89, 95, 96, 101, 102, 103, 111, 119, 122
admiral, 3.10.2
adornings, 2.2.215
a-ducking, 3.7.64
Aeneas, 4.15.53
affection, 3.13.7
affections, 1.5.12
affects, 1.3.71
Ajax, 4.15.38
*Alexandrian, 2.7.93
Alexas, 4.6.11–15
All's Well that Ends Well, p. 127
allay, 2.5.51
all-obeying, 3.13.77
alms-drink, 2.7.5
angle, 2.5.10
Annaeus Florus, Lucius, p. 10
answer, 3.12.34; 3.13.36; 5.2.178
Anthony (spelling), 4.16.12
anticked, 2.7.124
anticlimax, pp. 67–77, 99
Apollodorus, 2.6.69
appeal, 3.5.10
Appian, p. 10
apply, 5.2.126
appointment, 4.11.8
approof, 3.2.26–7
as, 1.2.99; 2.2.57
Arabian bird, 3.2.12
Aristotle, pp. 104–5
arm-gaunt, 1.5.48

aspect, 1.5.33
aspic, 5.2.292
Atlas, 1.5.23
atone, 2.2.107
attend, 2.2.64
augurers, 4.13.4
avaunt, 4.13.30
avoid, 5.2.242

bacchanals, 2.7.102
Bacchus, pp. 4, 5
Bacon, Francis, pp. 67–8
bands, 3.12.26
banquet, 1.2.12; 2.7.0.2
*barbered, 2.2.231
Barkan, Leonard, p. 128
barked, 4.13.23
Barroll, J. Leeds, pp. 125, 129
Barton, Anne, p. 70
Basan, 3.13.128
battery, 4.15.39
battle, 3.9.2
Bayley, John, pp. 13, 73–4, 118
be in, 2.7.31
be noble to, 5.2.192
beck, 3.11.59
become, 1.3.84–5; 1.5.60; 2.2.246; 3.6.17; 3.12.35
becoming(s), p. 85; 1.3.97
beguiled, 4.13.29
bench-holes, 4.8.6
bends, 2.2.215
best heads, 4.1.10
biblical (and liturgical) allusions, 1.1.17, 1.2.69–70; 1.4.59; 2.2.153; 3.13.128, 160–8; 4.2.31; 4.15.107; 4.16.11–12; 4.16.51
blasted, 3.10.4; 3.13.105
blood, 1.5.74; 3.13.175
blood and life, 1.2.189
blow, 5.2.60
'blown, 3.13.39; 4.4.25; 5.2.347

379

Index

crested, 5.2.83
cropped, 2.2.235
crownet, 4.13.27; 5.2.90-1
cunning, 2.3.32
cup, 2.7.116
curious, 3.2.35
cut, 1.2.165
Cydnus, 2.2.194; 5.2.228

daemon, 2.3.17
danger, *vb.*, 1.2.190-1
Daniel, Samuel, pp. 17-20, 21-2
Dante, p. 11
darken, 3.1.23-4
deared, 1.4.44
death, pp. 123-4
declined, 3.13.27
decorum, 5.2.17
deign, 1.4.63
Demetrius, p. 89; 1.1.0
demurely, 4.10.30
*demuring, 4.16.31
denounce, 3.7.5
dependency, 5.2.26
deputation, 3.13.74
Dercetus, pp. 107, 120; 4.15.104
derogately, 2.2.38
design, 5.1.43
desolation, 5.2.1
determine, 4.3.2; 4.4.37
determined, 3.6.85-6
determines, 3.13.162
devised, 2.2.196
Dido, p. 5; 4.15.53
die, 1.2.140; 1.5.33; 4.16.40
die the death, 4.15.26
difference, 2.1.49
digested, 2.2.182-3
diminutives, 4.13.37
Dio Cassius, p. 10
*discandying, 3.13.166
discontents, 1.4.39
dislimns, 4.15.10
dismission, 1.1.28
dispatch, 4.4.15; 5.2.230
disponge, 4.10.13
disposed, 4.15.124
disposition, 2.7.6
distract, 3.7.43
distraction, 4.1.9
distractions, 3.7.76
dissuade, 4.6.12
divide, 5.1.47-8

divine of, 2.6.115
do, done, pp. 104-7, 123-30;
  1.1.39; 1.5.15-16; 2.2.27.1;
  2.7.80; 4.15.102; 5.2.5, 324
do his kind, 5.2.262
doctrine of obedience, 5.2.31
dodge, 3.11.61
Dolabella, 5.2.64-6, 197-207, 199
Dollimore, Jonathan, pp. 79, 97-8
dolphin-like, 5.2.88-90
doom, 3.13.78; 5.1.18
dotage, 1.1.1
draw, 3.4.21
drench, 2.6.18
dress, 5.2.273
droven, 4.8.2
Dryden, John (*All for Love*),
  pp. 25-9
dumbed, 1.5.50
dungy, 1.1.37

ear, 1.4.49
earing, 1.2.111
*ebbed, 1.4.43-4
Egyptian, pp. 81, 102-3, 106-7,
  120-1; 2.2.225 (*see also*
  Orientalism)
elements, 2.7.44
embattle, 4.10.3
embossed, 4.14.3
empress, 5.2.73
emptiness, 3.13.36
enforce, 2.2.104-5; 5.2.125
enfranched, 3.13.150-2
engrossed, 3.7.36
enjoy, 2.6.79
enlarge, 3.5.11
Enobarbus, pp. 2, 13, 90-4, 97,
  99-100, 103-4, 121; 2.2.197;
  3.13.42-6; 4.5.7
ensued, 4.15.76-7
enter, 4.15.115
entertainment, 3.13.141; 4.6.16
*enthroned, 3.6.5
epicure, 2.7.5
equalness, 5.1.47-8
Eros, p. 122; 4.15.35
estridge, 3.13.197
even, 3.11.70
excess, 1.1.7-8
exigent, 4.15.63
expedience, 1.2.177
extended, 1.2.101